The Monetary Imagination
of Edgar Allan Poe

The Monetary Imagination of Edgar Allan Poe

Banking, Currency and Politics in the Writings

HEINZ TSCHACHLER

McFarland & Company, Inc., Publishers

Jefferson, North Carolina, and London

LIBRARY OF CONGRESS CATALOGUING-IN-PUBLICATION DATA

Tschachler, Heinz.
The monetary imagination of Edgar Allan Poe : banking,
currency, and politics in the writings / Heinz Tschachler.
p. cm.
Includes bibliographical references and index.

ISBN 978-0-7864-7583-4

softcover : acid free paper ∞

1. Poe, Edgar Allan, 1809–1849—Knowledge—Economics.
2. Money in literature. 3. Gold in literature. 4. Finance in literature.
5. Money—Political aspects—United States. 6. Currency question—
United States. 7. Banks and banking—Social aspects—
United states. I. Title.
PS2642.E25M66 2013   813'.3—dc23   2013016862

BRITISH LIBRARY CATALOGUING DATA ARE AVAILABLE

Front cover images: young crow
and cash bag (iStockphoto/Thinkstock)

Manufactured in the United States of America

*McFarland & Company, Inc., Publishers
Box 611, Jefferson, North Carolina 28640
www.mcfarlandpub.com*

For Gerhild, my wife,
for Katrin, Max, Moritz and Ulle,
for Hilde,
and to the memory of my father and mother

Table of Contents

Acknowledgments

The idea of writing this book began to germinate while I was at work on *The Greenback: Paper Money and American Culture* (Jefferson, NC: McFarland, 2010), in which I analyze the currency as a proxy for the nation's power and its citizens' social identities. I then took some preliminary thoughts about the project to the "International Edgar Allan Poe Bicentennial Conference: The Long Shadow of a Tormented Genius," held at the University of Extremadura, Cáceres, Spain, November 19–21, 2009. An early version of "Green and Red Tints" was presented to the 34th International AEDEAN (Spanish Association for English and American Studies) Conference, Almería, Spain, November 11–13, 2010. A version of Chapter 2 was presented at "The Backyard of the U.S. Mansion," X Congreso SAAS (Spanish Association for American Studies), Alcalá de Henares, Madrid, Spain, April 14–16, 2011.

This book is all about money, banking, and the literary imagination, though the obligations I have accumulated are personal rather than financial. Without naming particular names, I wish to thank the friendly and efficient staff of the library and interlibrary loan desks at Alpen-Adria-Universität Klagenfurt. I am also grateful for a special grant from the Dean of the School of Humanities and Culture Studies at Alpen-Adria-Universität Klagenfurt to help cover the costs of reproductions and rights. A leave of absence award from the university in support of this project helped me to bring it to a conclusion. Finally, I would like to thank by name several friends and scholars who shared their time, knowledge, and advice: Richard G. Doty, Director, and Karen Lee, Curator, National Numismatic Collection, Smithsonian Institution; Douglas A. Mudd, Curator, American Numismatic Association; Jeffrey A. Savoye, the Edgar Allan Poe Society of Baltimore; Bob Brugger, the Johns Hopkins University Press, Baltimore; Elizabeth Watts Pope, Andrew Bourque, and Jaclyn Penny, American Antiquarian Society, Worcester, Massachusetts; Ruth Bowler, the Walters Art Museum, Baltimore; Sue Bell, Museum of Fine Arts, Boston; Winfried Fluck, John-F.-Kennedy-Institut, Freie Universität, Berlin; Eva Muhm, American Reference Center, United States Embassy, Vienna; Eugen Banauch, American Studies, University of Vienna; Herbert Emmerig, Numismatics, University of Vienna; and Gerwin Gallob, University of California at Santa Cruz.

A particular thank you goes to colleagues and friends who took time from impossible schedules to read the manuscript, in whole or in part, and otherwise offered useful criticism and valuable suggestions: Stephen Mihm, Department of History, University of Georgia; Richard Kopley, Department of English, Penn State University at Dubois; Walter Grünzweig, Universität Dortmund; Daniel Shanahan, Faculty of Humanities, Charles University,

Prague; Nadja Gernalzick, International Cultural Studies, Universität Mannheim; Stephen Berry, Department of History, University of Georgia; Paul Lauter, Department of English, Trinity College; and Eleonore Wildburger, Simone Puff, and Gerda Elisabeth Moser of Alpen-Adria-Universität Klagenfurt. I owe an intellectual debt of gratitude also to Isabell Koinig, Martina Maierbrugger, Manuela Pischelmayer, and students of my graduate research seminar in culture studies for suggestions given to me directly.

Certain personal obligations were accumulated in a more distant past. I was fortunate enough to study and work with several professors who shaped my scholarship and my thinking. Franz K. Stanzel, who was my doctoral advisor at Karl-Franzens-Universität Graz, was tolerant enough to let me kick against the pricks at a time when junior scholars were expected to follow a beaten track. Jürgen Peper was a remarkable intellectual mentor, whose expansive vision of research was responsible, more than anything else, for my decision to pursue a career in American Studies. Peter V. Zima greatly influenced my views on theory and gave me respect for the power of academic prose. I have especially appreciated the intellectual exchange in his dissertation reading groups. Franz M. Kuna, chair of the Department of English and American Studies when I joined it and a true cosmopolite, introduced me to the larger academic world. Franz was a wonderful friend and thoughtful reader of many of my writings, in whatever incarnation.

Glen and Rhoda Love shaped my thinking in a different way. They hosted my family and me during our first extended stay in the United States, and their friendship and care helped me form a matrix of private associations and desires attached to what one might call the "symbol" of America. That symbol may often be "usurped" by the United States (the efficient land of smiles and courtesies, and of commerical television), but just as often it is claimed by Europeans in their search for the "possibility of America," of a land of equal opportunity, personal rights, pluralism, community and hope.

Gerhild, my wife, has her own story to tell. What follows is a first installment in payment of the many debts I owe her: "Thou hast turned for me my mourning into dancing." This book is dedicated to her.

Preface

Edgar Allan Poe has traditionally been seen as an alienated outsider, an isolated voice in opposition to a society that refused to heed his unearthly visions of "Madness and more of Sin, and Horror." More recently, Poe has been seen as a writer shaped by a capitalist publishing industry, producing texts for a mass of anonymous readers whom he at once despised and depended on for his survival. *The Monetary Imagination of Edgar Allan Poe* goes beyond both these views to offer an account of Poe's relation to the world of banking and money in antebellum America and thus shine new light on an author whose reputation, it seems, has never been higher.

This book is all about money, banking, and the literary imagination. I contend that Poe was an obsessive — if not entirely coherent or consistent — student of the acrimonious debates about America's money, Andrew Jackson's "bank war," the panic of 1837 and the ensuing depression, and the nation's inability to furnish a "sound and uniform currency." These controversies and issues preoccupied many of Poe's contemporaries and shaped a great deal of America's political life in the antebellum period. Poe likewise was every bit as concerned with earthly visions as with unearthly ones.

This book tries to demonstrate that the chaotic world of banking and money of Poe's time is a persistent theme in his work. Evidently, the chief vehicle for making this case is "The Gold-Bug," Poe's famous tale of the recovery of Captain Kidd's treasure by a reclusive amateur naturalist and bankrupt Southerner. But Poe's creative efforts do not end here. A few years before, he had written "Peter Pendulum," which in its revised version, "The Business Man," contains an open attack on "the frauds of the banks." Just as noteworthy is a little-known poem titled "Epigram for Wall Street," as well as the much better-known "Eldorado," provoked by the discovery of gold in California. This momentous event likewise spawned an elaborate hoax about turning lead into gold, "Von Kempelen and His Discovery." In an indirect way, the discovery of gold in California also is behind Poe's ridicule of the hullaballoo over the release the new $1 gold dollar of 1849. And there are many of Poe's writings that reveal this author's concern about the monetary situation of his time.

Claiming that money and banking is a persistent theme in Poe's work is, needless to say, considerably stronger than saying that Poe set his stories in the midst of a world where monetary stability was of great concern to many of his readers. Writers generally use the cultural materials at hand to produce their work, but that practical necessity is quite different from "investing" in those materials as a thematic backing of their creative efforts. Money and banking are social orders within which other discourses, including literary discourses, are pursued. These orders do not determine literary output so much as they are locales of unresolved conflicts in beliefs and values.

In Poe's case, the primary conflicts shaping the relationship between his art and the economic and financial context were those of class and market. Poe, who was without independent means, was especially vulnerable to market forces, including to those working on the literary market. Because his readers constituted a national rather than a regional or sectional audience, he increasingly expelled politics from his writings. Whereas his censure of the world of money and banking is overt in his early satires, it is more subdued in "The Gold-Bug," and almost an undercurrent in writings that enter into and historicize the discovery of gold in California.

This shifting back and forth between negation and affirmation is further compounded by Poe's predilection for hoaxes and other forms of overt manipulation. Caught up as he was in a cultural logic of hoaxes, he relentlessly worked against stable understandings of his writings. Thus, in Poe's writings much is concealed, though his art also reveals while it conceals — in this instance, a deeply felt desire for an authority that would guarantee a measure of permanence and continuity also to the currency.

A currency pledged to permanence and continuity was finally furnished by Abraham Lincoln, at one time a dedicated reader of Poe's tales and sketches but today of course revered rather as America's greatest president. Wielding his "power of regulation," Lincoln saved the Union not just militarily but also economically. Under him, the United States government at long last provided the kind of "sound and uniform currency" that in Poe's writings often take on the appearance of a code that can only be deciphered by those who know the monetary context from which they emerged. Poe seems to have viewed the monetary context as a *fait accompli*, and his writings constitute a material record of this. The present book explores this record, which is the record of a world that has disappeared, though its spirit lives on in other incarnations. We may no longer worry about suspensions of specie payments, but the great confidence game of a currency backed by nothing more than trust lives on.

Chapter 1 begins by attending to the "money question," which from the outset revolved around the issues of how America's currency was to be regulated and what was to constitute it — gold, silver, or paper. I also discuss in this chapter the rise of commercial banks, whose mysterious practices led to numerous bankruptcies as well as to widespread poverty, a fate that Poe knew only too well. One of the bank practices that were little understood at the time was the suspension of specie payment in exchange for paper bills. This practice, which banks were allowed to do by state law, also ushered in the panic of 1837. The results of this economic cataclysm were felt across the entire nation. It comes as no surprise that it also influenced Poe's writings. Yet in seeing Poe predominantly as a writer of madness and horror, critics have ignored Poe's world — the world of Andrew Jackson, a world of banking collapse, financial panic, monetary insecurity, and grinding depression.

Discussing the history of Poe scholarship, I will address a few of these readings more directly, though I am more interested in scholarship that does take into account the social and political meanings of Poe's writings and thus contributes to resituating Poe's work in the nation's monetary and financial history.

My account of the social and political meanings of Poe's writings carries over into Chapter 2, where I reopen the question of the relation between Poe's writings and the world of money and banking by considering traditional identifications of value with substance, together with the debates this identification gave rise to — from their origins in Britain to the constitutional debates in America and, finally, to Emerson's pronouncement that a paper currency is employed when there is no bullion in the bank vaults. In "The Gold-Bug," Poe enters into and turns these identifications inside out. This is obvious already from the numerous words and phrases in the tale that suggest the world of money and banking — from "gold bug" meaning a supporter of the gold standard, which entered the English language through Poe's tale, to "stamp," "seal," or "signature," which are all known features on paper money, and, finally, to references to green and red "tints." It is little known that Poe added these references only in a later version of the tale; it is probably even less known that the additions allude to inks of those colors that at the time were used as anti-counterfeiting devices on bank bills.

The intertextual reference to counterfeiting reveals the problem that bedeviled the antebellum period, that is, the problem of confidence. Politically, the issue was divisive: to establish a measure of confidence, the Whigs sought to strengthen the power of the central government, including the right to issue notes. The Democrats, enthralled by Jackson, could envisage only gold and silver, which they considered nature's money. Given the divisiveness of the issue, the two-part structure of "The Gold-Bug," which leaves the treasure episode unfinished, can be seen as a mark of Poe's inability or unwillingness to make potentially divisive statements in his creative works. Nevertheless, my discussion in this chapter will move into the direction of confidence or trust — as a central theme in "The Gold-Bug," as the *conditio sine qua non* of a paper money economy, and, in the form of certainty grounded in a reliable authority, as one of the era's deepest desires.

To reconstruct the importance, both for Poe and for his contemporaries, of trust or confidence (and, by extension, of permanence and continuity) is one of the central concerns of this study. In Chapter 3, I extend these ideas by addressing historic events such as the Baltimore bank riots of 1835. A shift of focus to events of this kind seemed justified because in the vast scholarly literature on Poe we have astonishingly little about the dull realities of banking and politics. Yet events such as the Baltimore riots in a number of ways left their marks in Poe's writings. Given his tendency to suppress politics in his writings, however, to identify these marks is a thankless task.

Poe certainly had come to believe that he could sell his writings to a national audience only by excluding politics from his writings. How, then, do we best grapple with many of Poe's writings from the 1830s, which for all intents and purposes are openly political? The upshot, in my view, is that these are mostly works of negation. Indeed, from "King Pest" to "The Philosophy of Furniture" and, finally, to "Mellonta Tauta," there is nothing but disgust with Jacksonian democracy. Does this mean, then, that Poe's relation to Jackson's political opponents was frictionless? I will return to this question in greater detail. Here I would say only that Poe never saw as an option a move *into* politics, though he had no compunction about using politics to his personal advantage. Poe on many occasions tried to get the attention of politicians, including of John Tyler, of whom he had at least two favors to ask — his magazine project, and a government position. Although Poe did find ways to get near Tyler, neither one of his strategies to plead and further his cause with the president got him anywhere, though "The Gold-Bug" at least won him a cash prize as the best tale with money as a subject.

Chapter 4 builds on the complicated history of "The Gold Bug" to show how Poe's interest in and concern about everyday matters eventually steered him to literary politics. His engagement reached from the issue of an international copyright to technical innovations. Such issues call up the material conditions of the commercial writer in general as well as his own inability to make a living from writing in particular. I resist the view, however, that Poe discontinued his preoccupation with the world of money and banking. Even "The Domain of Arnheim," generally read as a piece of landscape writing in celebration of Southern life, thematizes that world. The tale's central character, Ellison, clearly is not a Southern gentleman so much as he is a man of action who turns his immense wealth into capital to be invested.

Other writings of the time are more overtly satirical, including "The Business Man" and "Epigram for Wall Street," both from 1845. Poe's continued interest in the world of money and banking is also evident from his hallucinating, shortly before his death, that he had been arrested on charges of passing a counterfeit bill. But my larger purpose in this chapter is to provide a connection with the discovery of gold in California. This momentous event provoked Poe into writing a poem, "Eldorado," an elaborate hoax about turning lead into gold, "Von Kempelen and His Discovery," and a derisive commentary on the new $1 gold dollar of 1849, the introduction of which was part of an effort to return the country to a hard-money track.

Poe's monetary imagination did not arise from thin air, and so in Chapter 5 we turn to the past — Poe's past — in order to better understand the causes and origins of the world of money and banking Poe lived (and suffered) through. That world is preserved only in textual or documentary residues. One such document is the United States Constitution, which spells out that the states can make "silver and gold a legal tender in the payments of debts," but only the national government had the authority to "coin Money, regulate the Value thereof, and of foreign Coin." The wording establishes the United States as a "hard" money country and, more importantly, that the federal government had power over the states. This state of affairs for instance led to the chartering of "national" banks, in the form of the two Banks of the United States. Both institutions were at once attacked by anti-federalists and, later, by Jacksonian Democrats. This chapter therefore would not be complete without a focus on Jackson's bank war, as well as on attempts, by Federalists, National Republicans, and Whigs, to reinstate a national bank of issue.

I also discuss in this chapter the fact that in 1841 the death of President Harrison and the selection of John Tyler as his running mate deprived the Whig Party of the chance to carry out the mandate it had received in the election of 1840. When Tyler became president, he opposed nearly everything that the majority of Whigs sought and, with his reelection in mind, set to purging Whig appointees from federal offices, replacing them with states' rights men, most of them Democrats. Poe, who had desperately sought office from Tyler, was left empty-handed. As a result, the sympathies he may have had for this president instantly melted into air, and Poe's anger and frustration, which from the 1830s had been directed against the follies of Jacksonianism, now provoked him into writing literary hoaxes which, like paper bills from the commercial banks, promised value even as they flaunted their worthlessness. Yet deep down, Poe, who once claimed that he had in fact "battled" for Harrison, seems to have retained sympathies for Harrison's policies, above all for his plan for a national bank of issue. The currency coming from such a bank, I argue, might well have been the fulfillment of one of Poe's much deeper desires, a desire for permanence and continuity.

One final note. Monetary discourses can perform their differential function only by positing some larger social unity. Abraham Lincoln, who later refashioned himself as the "Whig in the White House," to use Gabor Boritt's words, was capable of positing such a unity in the form of the patriotic national state. Thus in the Epilogue, I reiterate that the problem of a stable currency that Poe could only name and rehearse in his writings was resolved through the introduction of a federal paper currency as part of Lincoln's economic nationalism. In antebellum America, both the political situation in general and the instability of monetary differences in particular had made such a mission impossible.

In the long run, Poe's unique response to the crisis of America's money alienated him from nearly every other writer, intellectual, or public figure of the time — from Jacksonian Democrats advocating a populist reliance on gold and silver, from partisans of the Whigs, who were themselves divided over the question of a national bank of issue, from journalists and writers contributing to William Gouge's *Journal of Banking* and similar publications, which were mostly anti–paper money, and from cultural critics like Ralph Waldo Emerson or the historian Charles Bullock, who exclusively grounded property in land and precious metal and, by associating prosperity with social harmony, continued the English conservative tradition that before the Revolution had been adopted by Tory Loyalists.

The introduction of greenbacks by the Lincoln administration meant that the value of the new notes rested entirely on the credit of the nation. While this was a decisive step, putting to rest many uncertainties, a large number of people in the postbellum period remained suspicious of the sign of the *diabolus* on paper money, that is, its irredeemability. The political and ideological contradictions connected with redemption kept the money question boiling, though public — federal — paper money was here to stay, unredeemable and exclusively based on credit, that is to say, on trust. This fact alone, I would hasten to add, illustrates Poe's acute sense of money and banking, which made him enter into and historicize a tradition that had been drowned out in the bank war only to return as the new order of the age.

Poe took advantage of his creative powers to revisit, in his writings, the fundamental issues of the world of money and banking of his time: the absence of a national bank of issue constituting a reliable authority; the flood of worthless bills from commercial banks that created an endless series of problems; the acrimonious controversies involving outmoded theories of representation; and the discomfiting awareness that the Jacksonians' hard-money politics echoed the hard-money advocacy of the pre-revolutionary loyalist Tories. The link between Poe's writings and the world of money and banking — written, as it were, in invisible ink on a message left by a pirate — completes the case for Poe's representative status, both as an exemplary writer and as a shrewd and original commentator on the malaise of the age.

Prologue

"Y'all Don't Know; But Poe Know"[1]

That Edgar Allan Poe was a man whose entire biography seems like a series of unfortunate events is beyond doubt. The discovery that poverty was Poe's raven, ceaselessly tapping at the door, nevertheless was intensely personal. It was also precognitive, in that it preceded historical knowledge, even the possibility of it. But Poe's poverty was not self-incurred; it was a result of the world he lived in, Andrew Jackson's America, a world of banking collapse, financial panic, monetary insecurity, and grinding depression that had a particularly devastating effect on the publishing industry. That insight prompted a desire to recover history by transcending the barriers between past and present, by trying to understand and thus to give meaning to the past. By focusing closely on Jackson's America, I discovered that the money issue was more convoluted than had been thought, as politics and personality had cobbled together monetary institutions that, though inherently flawed, lasted until the Civil War. All of this deeply preoccupied Poe, but how he saw and responded to his time in his writings cannot be explained without reference to personality: the early death of his mother left Poe deeply wounded; unable to mourn her loss, he tried to overcome the "disconnect" between his emotions and the rest of the world by efforts to recapture the maternal object, for instance in the form of an imaginary treasure taken out of the earth. By the same token, the absence of a father, depriving him of stability and continuity, left its mark on how Poe saw and responded to the country's general monetary situation, which during the antebellum period was singularly chaotic. For if there is any constant in Poe's response to the money question, if not in his entire career, it is in a deeply felt desire for a trustworthy authority that would guarantee a measure of permanence and continuity. Such, then, was my adventure with Poe, the banks, and America's money, and although its record does follow a rough chronology, it also reflects a ceaseless back and forth between discovery and recovery, each shedding light on the other, complementing each other, in an almost endless series of refractions.

Although money and banking was a persistent theme with Poe, his story and his writings not only echo and mirror but also transform the various currents and undercurrents. This calls for a caveat: what happened in the past is never the whole story, and neither is what occurs in literature, which is probably the reason we often forget it once we are finished reading. What we are much less likely to forget are the possibilities and ideas which literary works infuse us with as they take us all the way through imaginary cases. Certainly these possibilities and ideas become lodged in us with greater clarity than any actual event, and so we take them into consideration a great deal more. Suddenly, then, it felt right to have woven together Poe's writings and the social, economic and political undercurrents that dragged the ship of state this way and that, as it tried to find a safe harbor for its monetary policy. Tapestry weaving surely offers a way to fuse style and idea, form and matter. Nevertheless, it just as surely represents a challenge to traditional conceptions between experience and knowledge and thus I can foresee at least two possible objections. One is that, like the Herr Professor Diogenes Teufeldröckh from Thomas Carlyle's *Sartor Resartus*, one professes *die Allerleiwissenschaft*, all sorts of knowledge or things in general. Having dwelled for so long outside the bureaucracy of theory, however, I felt entirely comfortable adopting a bird's eye (or, rather, a weaver's) view of many fields of knowledge instead of being absorbed by a single discourse. Exchanging the rigor of narrative for a tapestry moreover provided a means to remaining true to my aim: to preserve a heightened intensity in the encounter with the past.

My commitment to restore Poe to the historical context of money and banking in Jackson's America has made for a book that is short on theory and long on efforts to let the actors speak for themselves and to listen to the various ways in which they spoke to one another. Hence the second possible objection, that without a strict adherence to narrative rigor only the author of such a study will be able to recognize the subject of reconstruction. The reading I have constructed, I would hasten to add, includes efforts to enhance our ability to make sense of the political and economic orders within which Poe pursued his literary activities. It is my hope that its tapestry-like structure allows us to see the specific shape and distinctive features of Poe's views of money and banking with greater clarity and understanding. In this regard, this book is deliberately Horatian in its intention and execution. It was written both to persuade literary scholars and historians, and to appeal to non-specialist readers. It offers what I take to be a new interpretative account of Poe's preoccupation with the world of money and banking in antebellum America. In addition, it draws on extensive research in historic magazines, newspapers, and other documents to present interpretive accounts of what other actors had to say about the "money question." Finally, it introduces non-specialist readers to important work on Poe and antebellum culture. In this respect, this book can be seen as an example of what Richard Teichgraeber has called "integrative" scholarship, scholarship that makes connections across disciplines, places more specialized research in a wider context, and then tries to make sense of, draw together, and bring new insight to bear on all the topics — and many of the personalities — involved.[2]

In this book I deal primarily with the period between 1837 and 1862. These were the years when Poe published (until his death in 1849) the writings in which his censure of the world of money and banking was in its fullest force. This also happens to have been a period bounded by two events that shook that world to its foundations: the onset, in 1837, of a financial panic that ushered in the six or so years of the first nation-wide economic depression, and the introduction, at the beginning of the Civil War, of a federal paper currency. To contemporaries, each event must have appeared as a rupture, a point in time when past and present were coming apart; to experience these events thus must have been truly "sublime."[3] Indeed, when in January 1862 the Lincoln administration put into circulation the first greenbacks, the new notes, Stephen Mihm found, were hailed as being issued "by the nation, for the nation, in order to pay for the preservation of the nation."[4] This is a speech act that precisely indicates the extent to which past and present were being separated.

Whereas the present could be experienced via a currency as secure as the nation itself, the past, in contrast, appeared as a protracted period of monetary uncertainty. That uncertainty had been of great concern also to America's writers, from Irving and Cooper to Hawthorne and Melville. With no other writer, however, was it as intense as with Poe. Poe directed enormous creative energy to the economic upheavals that came with the panic of 1837 and its aftermath. His record, we will see, comprises a broad range of writings — from satirical pieces and commentaries, including "The Business Man" and "Von Kempelen and His Discovery," to writings that are rarely if ever seen as in any way connected to the world of money and banking (such as "A Descent into the Maelström" or "The Domain of Arnheim"), and, not to forget, to one of his most remarkable and successful stories, "The Gold-Bug," which for the purpose of this study may be approached as a center of gravity.

This book appears at a time when Poe's reputation as a writer has never been higher, and it may be helpful at the outset to articulate my concerns against scholarship that identifies the potential of Poe's art merely as "a stimulus to unearthly visions."[5] This is not to deny that Poe had a visionary's power that made him capable of seeing things other mortals could not see. Yet Poe, like other artists, never was a visionary all the time; in fact, for most of the time he was in step with his own time, even representative of it. I am likewise concerned about scholarship that narrowly focuses on Poe's alleged ability to fuse divergent and sometimes even conflicting elements into a plausible and coherent unit. Even if this ability were the exclusive benchmark of true art, Poe certainly was not capable of achieving coherence in every instance, and on occasion he even may not have wanted to do so. Confronting Poe's ties with the world of money and banking, for instance, we instantly notice a shifting back and forth of his thoughts. Poe's response to that world, it seems, is best understood as a tendency to play with undecidabilities, thus undermining his own positions and obliterating his political agenda to the point of elusiveness. But the many-sidedness, even contradictoriness, of Poe's response, I argue here, should not detract from Poe's status as somehow a "useful" thinker on and critic of matters of finance and money.

The notion of Poe's "usefulness" as a thinker on and critic of matters of finance and money likely would have pleased Thomas Ollive Mabbott. Writing in the 1970s, this distinguished Poe scholar called attention to Poe's "supreme ability to absorb and transform the 'news' of his own time, of his own place," an ability that was the "rock base of the originality that created his tales."[6] Indeed, Poe is most unusual among American writers for having lived and worked as a commercial writer in London and in major American cities such as Baltimore, Boston, Richmond, Philadelphia, and New York. These experiences taught him not only the hardships of literary labor but also the crucial role of banks and monetary policies in the nation's economic, social, and cultural development. In addition, there was a connection to the world of banking and finance through family relations. William Poe, Edgar's second cousin, was a banker in Augusta, Georgia; George Poe, Jr., a first cousin of Mrs. Clemm's, was a banker in Mobile, Alabama.[7] Finally, Poe's upbringing in the opinionated and financially savvy household of John Allan, a merchant and one-time director of the Bank of Virginia who necessarily was observant of the debates over national monetary policy and banking, made him suspicious of partisan attempts to vilify banks, bankers, and bank notes. Poe, we will see, frequently engaged his critical faculty in the work of negation, yet on many occasions he responded with great creativity to the question of what was to constitute America's money — gold, silver, or paper — and from where it was to be issued — independent commercial banks, state-chartered banks, or a national bank.

The claim that money and banks are persistent themes throughout Poe's writings might seem preposterous, especially if one searches for the telltale signs of such matters as overt themes or topics. Doubtless such a search is instantly rewarded in the case of "The Gold-Bug," which for this reason alone deserves a more prominent position in this study. More often than not, however, the signs of dull realities rarely appear in literary texts as overt themes or topic, but must be searched for outside the narrow level of content, in the world of material conditions, in personality, or in the subtleties of literary form. This, I would hasten to add, applies as well to "The Gold-Bug." The reason for this is a simple one: literary form is not universally given, but is socially determined. Poe was acutely aware of this fact, describing the formal constraints he was laboring under in terms of "the brief, the terse, and the readily-circulated," which he was convinced were bound to take the place of "the diffuse, the ponderous, and the inaccessible."[8] Poe, it should be noted, shrewdly refashioned the publishing requirements of his time into an aesthetics of novelty. In fact, Poe in his writings used novelty as a primary measure of literary value. Paradoxically, there was even a place for truth. Seeking support for his proposed *Penn Magazine*, Poe wrote, a "rigorous independence shall be my watchword still — *truth*, not so much for truth's sake, as for the sake of the novelty of the thing."[9] Novelty, the source of originality or "truth," thus was the reader's sense of the new, and so the production of novelty in fact is only the production of a seeming novelty.

Where, one might ask, is the link between Poe's remarks about a poetics of novelty and this book's focus, which is Poe's relation to the world of money and banking? Poe's remarks, exploring the connection between a poetics of novelty and the commercialization of writing, date from June 1841. Later in that year, "The Gold-Bug" may have originated, and so it seems logical to assume that this most celebrated tale of Poe's tales closely follows his definition of beauty in terms of "unusual combinations."[10] Certainly the fusion of cryptography and treasure hunting is an unusual combination; even more unusual, however, is the range of words and phrases suggesting the world of paper and paper money that is that laced through the story. Indeed, this tale can be read as Poe's somewhat oblique way of capitalizing on the bank war and the debates over the proper form of money. Poe, needless to say, wrote "The Gold-Bug" to further his career as a commercial writer and his magazine schemes. Over and beyond this obvious and understandable motive, however, the tale also registers Poe's attempt to overcome a "disconnect" between himself and the rest of the world and, by extension, the stalemate he faced in his quest for a government patronage.

With "The Gold-Bug," Poe no doubt translates into telling a profound knowledge of paper money — as opposed to gold or silver money — a knowledge that had been and continued to be of significance to American history and culture. Yet Poe's affair of dollars and sense in this instance comes to an end without finishing. A treasure is brought home, where it is weighed and counted, though it is never exchanged for or transformed into circulating currency. About halfway through the tale, the central character begins his account of how he cracked a secret code that directed him to the buried treasure. The abrupt transition from treasure hunt to cipher solving, from "money" to "mystery," appears to repeat in ideological form the suspension of specie payments, which Poe, like many other observers, perceived as mere "frauds." While statements of this kind seemingly identify Poe as a supporter of a gold-based currency, we should bear in mind that the "hard-money men" were mostly Jacksonian Democrats, who had been the butt of Poe's early satires. Then Poe chiefly vented his scorn for the Jacksonians' monetary policies, though it cannot be determined with certainty if he also knew that gold had been the preferred currency of the pre-revolutionary Loyalists, while the patriots firmly supported a paper currency as a symbol of political sovereignty from England. Poe rarely made any explicit political statement, but we may well wonder what he meant when he wrote, in 1840, that in America, "the coins current [are] the sole arms of the aristocracy."[11]

Even if the Jacksonians had not adopted the monetary position of the pre-revolutionary loyalist Tories for their populist agenda, Poe would have had no motive to ground property in land and precious metal, let alone to associate prosperity with social harmony. On the contrary, this natural son of itinerant actors and foster child of a Scots merchant shared in the constant fear, then prevalent, that gold (like silver) disappear from circulation altogether because the metallic value of the coins far exceeded their stamped value. Yet Poe also was not a straight "paper money man" defending the right of all banks to issue paper money. Given the country's miserable banking system, this position probably was only reasonable. Moreover, by the time he published "The Gold-Bug," Poe felt renewed disdain toward the controversies over the nation's money that had raged since Jackson's election in 1828. His impulse, therefore, was not to intervene in behalf of a particular conviction so much as to give the full force of his censure to the endless bickering over money and banking.

A censorious intent alone does not, however, sufficiently explain the form of "The Gold-Bug." The material conditions of Poe's existence provide a further clue. Poe's world was Jacksonian America, a world of banking collapse, financial panics and bankruptcies, and grinding depression. Poe, who was without independent means, was especially vulnerable to market forces, not least to those working on the literary market, the "magazine prison-house," as he called it.[12] Shaped by a capitalist publishing industry from the beginning of his writing career, Poe had few illusions left concerning the role of literature as a means to "diffuse light and to do good." Nor did he have any illusions about the audience as "the enlightened, the fair, the exalted in station."[13] On the contrary, locked into a literary work-shop overseen by profit-driven publishers whom he personified as "fat" editors and propri-etors, Poe had come to produce texts for "a mass of anonymous readers who were distinguished primarily by an act of purchase."[14] The readers' civic virtues, their beliefs, val-ues, norms, and assumptions were of little or no concern.

Life in the "magazine prison-house" had lifelong repercussions for Poe. Although he can be considered as the first American writer to support himself entirely by his writing, he did not earn a living by it.[15] Poverty cast a shadow over everything Poe attempted, and it also shaped his political agenda, which, as Terence Whalen has shown at great length, was increasingly confined to the point of literary production itself.[16] Forsaking the opportunity "to diffuse light and to do good," Poe came to adopt a calculating, aggressive stance both towards writing and towards his audience, whose unfathomable "taste" he measured in terms of gross acts of consumption. Thus in order to succeed in the business of American letters, Poe took to composing his tales "to supply a particular demand."[17] "The Gold-Bug" is a prime example of the application of economic doctrine to the realm of letters. Poe wrote the tale in the period 1841–1843, while he was still living in Philadelphia. First published in June 1843, it won him a cash prize of $100 and earned him a measure of fame. It also was widely reprinted, though it is not likely that Poe was paid for these reprints. "The Gold-Bug" finally appeared, with Poe's corrections, in *Tales* in 1845.

That the tale's theme was popular, Poe knew all along. Reviewing, in November 1841, Samuel Warren's novel *Ten Thousand a Year*, he noted that money is a topic "which comes at least *as* immediately to the bosoms and business of mankind, as any which could be selected."[18] The publishers of the *Dollar Newspaper* also anticipated that money tales would supply a particular demand. They not only selected for their contest three tales that had money as their theme but also copyrighted "The Gold-Bug," their first-prize story.[19] In retrospect, Poe likewise emphasized the tale's commercial success. In a May 28, 1844, letter to James Russell Lowell, he proudly noted, "Of the 'Gold-Bug' (my most successful tale) more than 300,000 copies have been circulated."[20] More importantly, two years after the tale's publication, Poe wrote that he had written it — like "The Raven" — solely to sell, "for the express purpose of running."[21]

How can we account for the popularity of money as a literary theme? Of course it is possible to say that the theme's appeal is "universal." Yet in America of the 1830s and 1840s, there was both widespread fascination with and concern about gold, money, and banks and banking. Economic growth almost went hand in hand with economic crisis; there was an increasingly acrimonious conflict over the Bank of the United States, and there was a reawakened controversy over the proper form of money and who should issue it. It comes as no surprise, therefore, that there are some basic correspondences between "The Gold-Bug," in which the central character converts a coded message into treasure, and the general political and economic context of Poe's time, in which partisan factions were in pitched battle over the proper relation between signs on paper and the gold accumulated in various public and private vaults and coffers.

The correspondences between "The Gold-Bug" and the tale's contexts take on a special significance in more ways than one. The first touches on Poe's personal quest to create some kind of profitable connection between cryptography and politics. It is a matter of record that Poe employed an elusive cipher in his attempt to land a patronage job with the Tyler administration.[22] Possibly, he even gave "The Gold-Bug" its final shape so as to please, curry favor from, and perhaps even counsel the President. The second significance involves the controversy over what was to circulate as money, paper issued by banks or gold and silver coin issued by the federal government. America's money, properly so called, then consisted solely of gold and silver coins, but an increasing number of banks — state-chartered banks, independent commercial banks, along with the Bank of the United States and private institutions that simply did business by what they considered to be a common-law right — issued paper notes that were backed by a varying amount of gold or silver in the institution's possession. Because of the general scarcity of coined money, these notes became the major circulating medium of the time, circulating much as paper money does today.

The "paper system," its general usefulness notwithstanding, instantly became the object of diverse attacks. Independent banks in the antebellum period were for-profit operations, with annual dividends ranging from 8 to 10 percent. Solvent banks vastly increased their currency, because in the absence of gold and silver coins at par in circulation their bills were likely to stay in circulation and not be redeemed. It was in a bank's economic interest to keep bills in circulation, for the longer they were in circulation the longer the bank had free use of its funds. And if bills became lost or otherwise were never redeemed, they became pure permanent profit for the bank. Profits also were reaped from issuing notes without proper backing. Overall, then, the problem with commercial banks was that many of them were trying to work wonders with insufficient capital. The practice always contained the danger, noted by Bray Hammond, of taking the valid concept that a paper currency was as good as gold and silver as long as it had public confidence, and turning it into a "monetary burlesque of Pauline theology, faith taking the place of works."[23] While notes from commercial banks were mainly attacked for the instability of their value, notes from the Bank of the United States, in contrast, were attacked both as a means to enrich stockholders and, because of the restrictions imposed on their circulation, as a hindrance to economic progress. The attacks on the banks also resurrected older disputes over the proper form of money itself: supporters of paper money came to defend the right of banks on all levels to issue notes; the hard-money men, in contrast, staunchly advocated reliance on gold and silver coins issued by the federal government.[24]

Poe capitalized on the conflicts over class and monetary politics by selling a "capital tale" to what he hoped was a *national* readership. In pitching to such an audience, he necessarily had to expel politics from his writing. Poe habitually did this, though his refusal, in "The Gold-Bug," to intervene in behalf of a particular conviction is particularly striking. On one hand, it appears to register the historic irony that gold had once been the preferred currency of the loyalist gentry, the Tories, while the patriots had wanted a paper currency, which they linked with anti-royalist protest and, ultimately, with the issue of political sovereignty from England. On the other hand, Poe's ambivalence makes more poignant the actual thesis and source of originality both of "The Gold-Bug" and of other of his writings. The following chapters explore this thesis, which I will here simply summarize as a concern with a stable and reliable currency. Such a currency necessarily would be a national one, and it would include paper money, serving both as a much-needed medium of exchange in everyday commercial transactions and as a social and cultural arrangement of value resting upon trust. Naming or, even, rehearsing the problem of course is not the same as solving it. Poe, we will see, could find no practical way to articulate the promise of a "sound and uniform currency."

A "sound and uniform currency," named and rehearsed by Poe in his writings, was finally furnished by Abraham Lincoln, at one time a dedicated reader of Poe's tales and sketches but today of course revered rather as America's greatest president. Lincoln, the savior of the Union, was in a position to wield "the power of regulation" and thus saved the Union not just militarily but also economically.[25] What the sixteenth president of the United States strove for was a national economy stretching from sea to shining sea, with railroad transportation and telegraphic communications making it possible to send goods and people to and from most if not all places in the Union in a reasonably timely fashion. A new form of federal paper money fueled Lincoln's ambitious project. This money eventually was *fiat* money pure and simple, with no provision for exchanging the paper bills for gold or silver coins. The notes' wording merely stated that they were "a legal tender for all debts public and private." Gone were familiar obligations like "will pay to the bearer *on demand.*"

The new notes — called United States Notes, Legal Tender Notes or, more colloquially, "greenbacks" — were put into circulation pursuant to the Act of February 25, 1862. Lincoln, whose portrait appears at left of the $10 note, was the first President to appear on federal

Ten-dollar United States note, 1862, face, portrait of Lincoln at left; the note's back was printed in green, hence the nickname "greenback" (American Numismatic Association Money Museum).

paper money. Selecting him was a patriotic act, as well as a political one. Impressing the image of the ruler on money — what Michel Foucault termed the "mark or image of the Prince"[26] — had been done almost from times immemorial, yet it had never been done in the United States. Nor had it ever been done in such vast numbers. Almost twelve millions of these $10 notes circulated, together with more than two million of the earlier Demand Notes, which also bore Lincoln's portrait. Their repeated use reinforced the notes' acceptance by the public and popular culture. Through them, it was demonstrated that Lincoln was the representative of the nation, in contrast to Jefferson Davis, whose portrait was printed on Confederate currency.

When the first greenbacks came off the printing presses, Ward Hill Lamon, Lincoln's friend, found the president "in high spirits ... and [he] seemed to feel happier than I had seen him for a long time."[27] It comes as no surprise that the President felt that way: for the first time in American history a uniform currency was available, a currency, as George Wood had envisioned it in 1841, that would "enable a person to travel, either for business or pleasure, from one end of the Union to the other, with funds which can be easily carried, and will pass current at par wherever he goes."[28] George Wood's vision faithfully registers the monetary uncertainty that plagued the entire antebellum period. That uncertainty had been of great concern also to any number of American writers, from Irving and Cooper to Hawthorne and Melville, though with no other writer was it as intense as with Poe. Poe's financial struggles throughout his brief life and career are notorious; they also impelled Poe to respond creatively to the economic upheavals of the time, producing a considerable number of satirical pieces and commentaries and, not to forget, one of his most remarkable and successful stories, "The Gold-Bug." Yet the tale's immediate popularity speaks, not just to contemporary readers' predilection for money-digging stories, but also and more directly to the financial panic of 1837 and its aftermath.

The panic of 1837, Reginald McGrane found, "marked the close of one epoch [...] and the beginning of a new era. It engulfed all classes and all phases of economic life within its toils; and for seven long years the people of this land struggled to free themselves from its

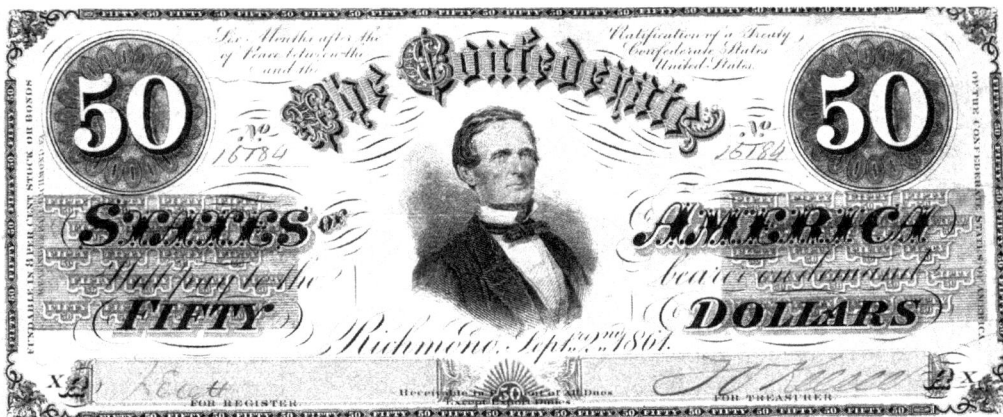

Fifty-dollar Confederate currency note, 1861, face, portrait of Jefferson Davis at center (courtesy National Numismatic Collection, Smithsonian Institution)

oppression."[29] Although McGrane wrote this before the economic cataclysms of the twentieth and twenty-first centuries cast a shadow over previous crises, the panic of 1837 nevertheless holds its place as one of the most severe depressions in American history. Historians generally agree that the panic resulted mainly from an overexpansion of business, combined with the extension of loans to many persons who could not pay them. In the East, a housing bubble drove up real-estate values by a hundred and fifty percent; in the West, there was over-speculation in public lands, intensified by railroad building. The depression was made worse by the over-issue of worthless bills from commercial banks, which drove up inflation, and, not to forget, by the unfortunate policies of the nation's chief executives — Andrew Jackson's war on the Second Bank of the United States, which triggered the rapid proliferation of commercial banks that began issuing increasingly worthless notes, Martin Van Buren's inability to cope with the depression, and John Tyler's vetoes of congressional bills that called for the re-establishment of a national bank of issue.

Tyler's actions sparked massive riots outside the White House from enraged Whig party members, who had not forgotten that this long-time Democratic Republican had been elected Vice President on a Whig ticket.[30] The President's actions also added fuel to contemporary debates about paper money and coined money, pitching the "paper money men" (as the supporters of paper money were called) against the "gold bugs" or "bullionists" (as the supporters of gold money, in opposition to paper money, were called). The debates, which chiefly concerned the relationship between the substantial thing (gold, silver, or paper) and its sign (precious coins or paper money), did not fail to attract Poe's attention. Poe also must have noticed that the "paper money men" defending the government-controlled issue of paper notes often were partisans of the Whigs. By contrast, the "hard-money men" advocating an ostensibly populist reliance on gold and silver coin were almost exclusively Jacksonian Democrats. The historic irony in this situation is considerable: *before* the Revolution gold was the preferred currency of the loyalist gentry, the Tories, while a paper currency had come to be associated with political sovereignty from England, hence with the increasingly rebellious patriots.

Poe's awareness of this shift in political commitments was acute. By the time he published "King Pest," one of his early tales, he felt a thorough disdain for the hard-money policy of Jackson and, as well, of Van Buren, Jackson's handpicked successor, whose platform during the 1836 presidential campaign likewise included opposition to re-chartering the Bank of the United States.[31] Another tale, "Hans Phaall," constitutes a kind of allegorical parody of the life and times of Jackson, then President of the United States and the leading figure in the acrimonious dispute over a national bank of issue.[32] Contemporaries also recognized as a satire of Van Buren and his Democratic party machine Poe's story "The Devil in the Belfry," first published in Philadelphia's *Saturday Chronicle*, a weekly newspaper, on May 18, 1839, much as they could make sense of Poe's burlesque misquoting, in July 1838, of a Spanish poem to read "Vanny Buren ... Pork and pleasure."[33] And, not to forget, there was "The Man Who Was Used Up." First published in *Burton's Gentleman's Magazine* of August 1839, this tale likely echoes a slogan used in ridicule of Van Buren — "Van, Van, is a used-up man."[34]

No account of the monetary history of the ante-bellum period would be complete without reference to "Hard Times" tokens, a distinctive group of monetary tokens that kept appearing from 1837 until the depression effectively ended in 1844. These tokens, which had no semblance of authority behind them, did what the mock shinplasters in imitation of paper bills did, though on a much smaller canvas. One type combined satirical pieces with sarcastic allusions to the sentiments or words of politicians of opposing parties. Whig-leaning supporters of the Bank of the United States for instance issued quite a number of them in order to lampoon Jackson's monetary practices. One of the earliest anti–Jackson tokens, from the fall of 1833, derided the president by paraphrasing words from his bank veto message of July 1832. The words, "The Constitution as (I) understand it," are combined with an image of a donkey on one side and a caricature of Jackson emerging from a treasure chest with a sword in one hand and a bag of money in the other. This was a reference to the fear, subsequently reported in the *Albany Argus* on October 1, 1842, that the liberties of the Union were threatened by a "union of the purse and the sword in some hands," a reference in this instance to the following administration of Van Buren. Presidential power over the nation's money and the military has been the subject for concern at intermittent intervals since that time. The donkey or "jackass" was a favorite symbol of stubbornness, as Jackson's opponents called this President's firmness of character.[35]

The suspension of specie payment, in May 1837, by numerous commercial banks also triggered a mass issue of tokens, at the same time as it seems to have provoked Poe into writing "Peter Pendulum," a satire of ruthless egotism and greed that he published in revised form as "The Business Man" in 1845. Many critics have considered "The Business Man" as Poe's most typical literary reaction to the crisis of 1837.[36] While one might disagree with this estimation (as I certainly do in this book), it nevertheless testifies to Poe's relation to the world of money and banking. Notice but, as material evidence of that world, a token issued later during the depression, on which the wrecked ship *Experiment* represents Van Buren's monetary policy, criticized as "executive experiment" by his Whig opponents. On the obverse, the majestic sailing ship *Constitution* alludes to Whig leader Daniel Webster's nickname, "Defender of the Constitution," which originated from a speech Webster gave in the United States Senate in January 1830. The term "experiment" was first used in 1833 by Jackson's Treasury Secretary Roger B. Taney to describe the placement of federal funds after their removal from the Bank of the United States. Opponents to Jackson's policies

Hard Times token 1841, in support of Daniel Webster, "Defender of the Constitution," and condemning Van Buren's monetary policy as "Experiment" (American Numismatic Association Money Museum).

instantly derided the use of this term. The token in question re-uses the term to mock Van Buren's Sub-Treasuries or Independent Treasuries, another "experiment" that this President had managed to introduce in modified form in July 1840.[37]

This particular token, which was probably issued in Baltimore, dates from 1841. Late in that year, "The Gold-Bug" likely began to take shape. Memory of Tyler's veto of the congressional bank bills, which had caused all the Whigs to resign from the President's cabinet (the lone exception was Secretary of State Daniel Webster, who was in Europe at the time), was still fresh then. Just as fresh must have been Poe's memory of his own naïve and misguided attempts to secure a government clerkship under the Tyler administration. At the time Poe's tale may not have developed much beyond "the kernel of an idea," and composition began in earnest only in August or September of the following year, with Poe probably completing it by the middle of October of 1842.[38] "The Gold-Bug" was finally published in June 1843 — in Philadelphia's weekly *Dollar Newspaper*, whose prize for the best story with an "*American*" subject it had won.[39] By that time, about a third of the nation's banking capital had been destroyed; a great number of the established banks had been liquidated or closed entirely, among them the Bank of the United States of Pennsylvania, the former Second Bank.[40]

As Richard Caton Woodville famously showed in his paintings of everyday life, people were carried away by what was being reported in the newspapers; on more than one occasion, they remained uncertain of what they were hearing.[41]

People were hearing many things, about new technological marvels, including photography, about new means of communication and transportation, but also about issues such as immigration, women's rights, temperance, religious zeal, slavery, capital punishment, the annexation of Texas, and the war with Mexico. And they were hearing about the dizzying issue of monetary instability, which did not go away until speculation had been checked

Richard Caton Woodville, *Politics in an Oysterhouse*, 1848, oil on fabric; original size 16 × 13in (The Walters Art Museum, Baltimore).

and "cheap money" abolished.[42] Dramatized by the bank war, the issue captured the imagination of the people, fired the enthusiasm of intellectuals, and tightened class lines and political allegiances. One argument people were hearing was that only gold and silver had a substantial value. In the eyes of the "hard-money men" paper therefore was a most inappropriate and downright misleading symbol. While the "paper money men" would howl over this, considering paper an appropriate symbol in its own right and the right of the banks to issue paper money as self-evident, they could not deny that, as a sign, paper was "insubstantial" insofar as the material counted for nothing as a commodity and thus appeared downright "ghostly" in the economic system of exchange.

The Monetary Imagination of Edgar Allan Poe concentrates on the social meaning of Poe's work, in which the world of banking and money is a persistent theme. An account of the forces and relations at work in the material environment is essential if we want to grasp Poe's writings in their historical and material specificity. Yet a mere account of historic events, places, or persons does not *per se* establish context. As Fredric Jameson remarked, history is "*not* a text, not a narrative, master or otherwise, but [...] is inaccessible to us except in textual form."[43] Contexts, that is to say, are themselves preserved only in textual or documentary residues. Contextualizing Poe, then, is to use these residues to make sense of the seemingly isolated facts, events, or ideas in which his writings are situated. Whether or not the results of such analysis must be represented in a straightforward narrative is a matter of dispute. Also matters of dispute are the many troubling issues connected with contextualization. This is not the place to spell out all the issues in detail. Suffice it to say that the unified context in which what is to explained can be meaningfully placed is inherently unstable, if not fractured or even antagonistic.[44] Rather than construct a unity of meaning in which Poe and his work would become comprehensible, I decided to allow both Poe and the other actors to speak for themselves and to attend to the various ways in which they spoke to one another. One consequence of this is a plentiful harvest of quotations. Another is, I believe, a sensitivity to questions that are plainly posed by their own announced concerns and by the manner in which those concerns were pursued. This sensitivity preserves the differences that separate us from Poe and his contemporaries. It should make it possible to apprehend their writings and utterances, not in terms of our own cultural anxieties and needs, but "on a horizon of meaning that they have opened themselves."[45]

To give an example of Poe's writings opening a horizon of meaning. As a commercial writer, Poe struggled to make a living, so he needed a bank only very rarely, attempting instead to create funds in his own brain. Poe had strong views not only of the publishers he depended on but also of his readers. His ideal readers, for instance, would have "minds which not only retain *all* receipts, but keep them at compound interest for ever."[46] Terms like "receipts" and "compound interest" belong to the discourse of money and banking. There is even a direct link between these terms and a particular type of currency, the Compound Interest Treasury notes, which constituted a special form of federal paper money that could be redeemed only after specific periods, and were declared legal tender for their face value only. In addition, terms like "receipts" and "compound interest" direct us to Poe's valorization of intellectual power, that is, to his life-long attempt to turn his intellect into a "specialized, non-alienable form of capital."[47] Poe exhausted himself by producing an endless series of entertainment commodities that were condensed, easily circulated, and just as easily consumed. Yet what he really wanted was for his intellect to become a productive force that could expand without limits and thus would help drive out the popular tales that, like the reports about buried treasure, had attained "universal currency."[48]

Poe's search a gold standard of literary value, against the nothingness of mere paper puffery, implies the depth and power of economic forces to influence the thoughts and literary productions even of a writer who was too often considered as out of step of his time.

To demonstrate this, I thought best to begin with the introduction of a federal paper currency by the Lincoln administration, which put an end to the monetary uncertainties that had begun with the constitutional debates and that lingered on until the Civil War. During the entire period, financial crises were the order of the day, and Poe lived through several of them. One such crisis, the Panic of 1837, occasioned his celebrated tale "The Gold-Bug," and so the debates about America's money, which were particularly acrimonious during times of economic upheaval, reopen an entire set of questions about the meaning, not only of this tale but also of other of Poe's writings — both of his satirical pieces and commentaries which, like "The Business Man," "King Pest," and "Von Kempelen and His Discovery," are obvious choices, and of writings that, like "A Descent into the Maelström," "The Cask of Amontillado," or "The Domain of Arnheim," are most unlikely to be treated in a book that explores Poe's preoccupation with the world of money and banking. Altogether, I explore five themes in detail, each identified in the titles of the substantive chapters into which I have subdivided the book.

1

Poe, the Critics and the Question of America's Money

"The Gold-Bug" begins with an account of the bankruptcy of a Mr. William Legrand, a Southern gentleman who in many ways seems to resemble Poe himself, his forswearing of all business practices, and his voluntary exile, in the company of his black servant Jupiter, to a remote island off the coast of South Carolina. There, on Sullivan's Island, which Poe knew well from his duties as a soldier at Fort Moultrie in 1827–28, Legrand keeps himself busy by searching for "entomological specimens," that is, for bugs or beetles. A golden-colored *Scarabaeus* beetle sets him off on a wild treasure hunt. Incredibly, the hunt is successful. Legrand, whose "dreams about gold" leave both Jupiter and the unnamed narrator deeply worried about the man's mental state, is finally rewarded with the "real" thing, gold, as he and his two companions unearth an "oblong chest of wood" that contains, in gold coins, "rather more than four hundred and fifty thousand dollars." Additionally, there are hundreds of objects, also in gold and exceeding "three hundred and fifty pounds avoirdupois." This is close to 160 kilos and would alone have been sufficient for Legrand "to make [his] fortune" as well as "to reinstate [him] in his family possessions."[1]

In most of Poe's stories, events seem suspended in historical time. "The Gold-Bug" is different in this respect, with its dates seemingly faithful to the theoretical demands, articulated much later by Mary McCarthy, of "the fact in fiction."[2] Thus it is worth speculating *when* Legrand lost the possessions into which he expects to be reinstated. The story proper begins about "the middle of October 18 —," on "a day of remarkable chilliness." The tale's opening sentence, however, effects a move further back in time: "Many years ago..."[3] We know that Poe completed the tale in late 1842, so "many years ago" may as well suggest the late 1820s, the time of his service at Fort Moultrie and the beginning of Jackson's bank war. Alternatively, the phrase may refer to the period 1819 to 1820. This was the time of the first major bust in the industrializing nineteenth century. Banks failed and factories closed then, and the word *panic*, pertaining to the economy, entered the English language. To choose these years as a setting bestows on Legrand's bankruptcy also a distant echo of the near-bankruptcy of Poe's foster father, John Allan, in London. London was then the world's capitalist center, the place where young Edgar lived for several years and where all the gold in the world seemed to gravitate towards.[4] Each setting is plausible, as each time period was one of economic upheaval, marked by numerous bankruptcies and fortunes lost, and, in a wider context, creating constituencies for hard and soft money, a national bank, free banking, or no banks at all. These questions were not merely word games or technical distinctions. The "money question" became a fiercely contested public debate, polarizing social groups and shaping the political process of American society.[5]

From the outset, the "money question" revolved around the issues of how America's currency was to be regulated and what was to constitute it — gold, silver, or paper. For reasons I have discussed in the prologue, I also consider in this chapter the rise of commercial banks, whose mysterious practices led to numerous bankruptcies as well as to widespread poverty, a fate that Poe knew only too well. One of the bank practices that were little understood at the time was the suspension of specie payment in exchange for paper bills. This practice, which banks were allowed to do by state law, often had dire consequences on the everyday lives of people. A result of the contradictory interests of "hard" money as opposed to "soft" money, the suspension of specie payment also marked the beginning of the panic of 1837. The effects of this economic cataclysm were felt across the entire nation. While the disastrous consequences on the everyday lives of people are legendary and well documented, the impact the panic had on Poe's writings is much less well known. Who would have thought, for instance, to approach "The Descent into the Maelström" as a kind of economic fable, well worth reading for the social and political implications of the "speculation" that sets its action in motion? Or, who ever noticed that the doomed American empire in "Mellonta Tauta" is specifically described as a hard-money country? Finally, why should Poe's intention in "Von Kempelen and His Discovery" — to exercise a "check to the gold fever" — be understood as directed exclusively against human folly or moral deficiency? But consider that "Von Kempelen," as a socially symbolic act may well target President James Polk, who deliberately used California gold to steer the country back to a hard-money track. In seeing Poe predominantly as a writer of arcane and mysterious lore, critics have ignored Poe's world — the world of Andrew Jackson, a world of banking collapse, financial panic, monetary insecurity, and grinding depression. Yet my discussion of the history of Poe scholarship, while addressing a few of these readings more directly, moves into another direction, to scholarship that does take into account the social and political meanings of Poe's writings. It is the interest in this scholarship I join in with my own efforts towards resituating Poe's work in the nation's monetary and financial history.

The Money Question

At the beginning of the economic crisis in 1837 Ralph Waldo Emerson ventured that a paper currency was employed "when there is no bullion in the vaults."[6] Although any number of banks were then doing business with insufficient capital, this New England sage was at best partly right in his diagnosis. A major reason for the continued use even of depreciated paper money was that specie coins kept disappearing from circulation into bank vaults or private coffers, or else were being exported abroad to be melted down for a profit. The practice has become enshrined in the colloquialism about the American eagle taking wings and flying away.[7] A print, drawn and engraved by W. Charles around 1808, also takes on the selling of undervalued specie coins for a profit. The print caricatures Philadelphia merchant and financier Stephen Girard, here called "Stephen Graspall, Banker and Shaver," as saying: "I declare I have not seen such a thing [as a dollar coin] since I sold the last I had

Surely my eyes do not deceive me—It certainly must be a DOLLAR!—
I declare I have not seen such a thing since I sold the last I had in my
Vaults at 18 per Cent premium—If thou art a real DOLLAR
do drop in my till and let me hear thee Chink—As I have
been sued for payment of part of my notes in Specie I
must collect some to pay them for quietness sake or the
game would be up at once—

STEPHEN GRASPALL.
Banker & Shaver.
Paper Wholesale &
Retail
NB ☞ No foreign Bank
notes taken on
Deposit except such
as are about 5
per cent above
par.—

W. Charles Del et Sculp

THE GHOST of a DOLLAR or the BANKERS SURPRIZE

"The Ghost of a Dollar or the Bankers Surprize," print, lampooning the selling for profit of under-valued specie coins; drawn and engraved by W. Charles, Philadelphia 1813?, 34 × 26 cm (courtesy American Antiquarian Society).

in my vault at 18 per cent premium." Behind him hangs his signboard, advertising "Paper Wholesale and Retail. No foreign bank notes taken on deposit except such as are about 5 per cent above par."[8]

In order to make coins reappear in circulation, many states passed laws prohibiting banks from issuing bills with denominations under five dollars. The Maryland legislature even imposed a penalty of five dollars on "any person who shall pass such notes of banks not chartered by this state." The desired effect — to "get rid of an amazing quantity of filthy rags," to use the words of a contemporary observer — was never achieved. Given the scarcity of specie coins, people just had to rely more and more on paper money. Supporters of "hard" money nevertheless continued to condemn the issuance of paper money. One group comprised writers and journalists like Hezekiah Niles, in whose *Weekly Register* the screed about "filthy rags" appeared.[9] Another group was made up by cultural critics like Emerson, for whom paper money evoked the dangers of big cities and the treacherous instability of urban societies rife with confidence men and swindlers.[10]

Other supporters of "hard" money included Democratic politicians like Thomas Hart Benton, whose extreme aversion to paper money earned him such nicknames as Old Bullion and the Gold Humbug. And there was Andrew Jackson, whose farewell address of March 4, 1837, is a grandiloquent defense of his various attempts to "restore the constitutional currency of gold and silver" against the evils he thought were inherent in a "paper system [...] founded on public confidence, having of itself no intrinsic value [and thus merely encouraging a] wild spirit of speculation."[11] All of them — cultural critics, middle-class reformers, and Democratic politicians alike — had yet to wait for a time when, as New York wholesale dry goods merchant William Earl Dodge proudly noted, "we never think of looking at bank bills."[12] That time arrived with the relative stability of the post–Civil War period, when the national currency finally brought Americans together through what the political scientist Eric Helleiner has called "a common economic language with which to communicate."[13]

The aversion, on the part of cultural critics, middle-class reformers, and Jacksonian Democrats against paper money cannot be separated from the country's general monetary situation, which during the antebellum period was singularly chaotic. Under the Constitution neither the federal government nor the states were in a position to issue paper money. Private banking companies incorporated by individual states, over which the federal government had little or no control, took up the slack. So did quasi-banks that were not chartered but did business by what they considered to be a common-law right.[14] Jackson's veto of the re-chartering of the Second Bank of the United States further increased the number of commercial banks issuing notes. Finally, the decision of some states, notably New York, to grant bank charters to all comers in accordance with general laws of incorporation, prompted what Edward Pessen has called "a frenzied race for riches" through investment and speculation.[15] Yet without the notes from all these fiscal entities, borrowers (especially in the West and South) would have found it difficult to obtain loans from savers (who were located mostly in the East), and more of the nation's capital would have remained stored up unproductively in unused land or inventories of livestock and produce. Also without these notes, the "currency" in large parts of the country would have continued to consist of "a rag-tag mixture of foreign and domestic coins, land warrants, tobacco warehouse receipts, even animal pelts" — most inefficient substitutes that only increased the cost of business transactions. So great was the hunger for currency that even counterfeit notes circulated widely with little attempt to suppress it, alongside the bills of distant and failed banks. Merchants and retail traders routinely accepted almost anything that even remotely looked like money, passing it along on the maxim "If you buy the devil, the sooner you sell him, the better."[16]

Overall, paper money in the antebellum period underwrote and stimulated a dramatic increase of the domestic product. While the opportunities for fraud and other wayward practices enraged "gold bugs" and hard-money men, the plain economic truth was that America needed banks and bank notes for economic expansion. "The soft-money advocates were right," Daniel Walker Howe found. A ready-flowing supply of paper money, however imperfect, was better than a limited quantity of specie currency. And a disorderly banking "was better than no banking at all." [17] Indeed, during the antebellum period the ambitions of businessmen and local civic leaders alike led to a dramatic increase of the number of note-issuing banks — from a few dozen by 1810 to hundreds by 1830, to thousands by 1850, with the value of circulating notes going up from $62 million to $140 million by 1837, to some $200 million by 1850. [18] The proliferation of these banks as well as of other fiscal entities such as insurance companies, railroads, and turnpikes led bankers to referring to the entire period as the "halcyon days" of free banking, when there was a bank at every cross roads. [19] In those days, every bank issued its own notes, and there soon was a multiplicity of excellent note designs, which later gave rise to the kudos that banknote engraving was "the only true American contribution to the arts." [20] For contemporaries, however, the increasing number of banks and similar institutions often brought only a flood of worthless bills that pushed up inflation. As Charles Francis Adams wrote in *Hunt's Merchants' Magazine* of July 1839, "the soundness of bank paper depends [...] upon the will of the banks themselves. They may keep it good if they will listen to prudent counsels; and they may depreciate it if they do again as they did before. We have hopes of the best, not entirely unmingled, it must be confessed, with fears for the worst." [21]

The best, Adams remarked in a follow-up article, could only be realized once "the power of regulation" had been secured. [22] The worst meant holding on to the present system of an ever-growing number of commercial banks of issue. That system also bore an increasing risk from the forger. The risk was increased almost exponentially in light of widespread illiteracy, unfamiliarity with printing of any type, and the fact that genuine notes were often issued for fraudulent purposes. Especially vulnerable to counterfeiting were the South, the Southwest, and the West, which were more short of specie and correspondingly more dependent on paper money than the rest of the country. By mid-century, counterfeiting was so rampant that, some writers estimate, at times roughly forty percent of the money in circulation was counterfeit. In 1856, an article in the *New York Herald* noted that there were some 1,317 banks in operation in the country, with counterfeit bills known to exist of all but 463 of these. Another survey, of 1859, listed some 9,916 different genuine notes *and* some 5,400 different kinds of counterfeit notes in circulation. Murray Bloom, a historian, has referred to the entire period as "the Age of Counterfeit." [23] In such an age, many sound-looking bills quite literally were, to borrow an expression from Marx, "worthless tokens." [24] Accepting them was risky, not least for the unsuspecting poor, to whom what Poe called "the gift of deciphering written characters" was "little less cabalistic than the art of inditing [i.e., of setting something down into writing]." [25] Paper money thus often was the happiness the rich bought from the poor — "the prosperity that the designing man [the speculator] steals from the unwary" [26] — yet it also was not always a boon to the rich but might easily lead to bankruptcy. This fate lies at the core of "The Gold-Bug."

Bankruptcy also lies at the core of *The Haunted Merchant*, an 1843 novel by Charles Frederick Briggs, whom Poe was to meet in New York in 1844, starting to work for his *Broadway Journal* early in 1845. [27] In contrast to Briggs's novel, Poe's tale is about a fortune regained, though all is not well that ends well. For instance, were the happy money-finders to use the treasure for paying their dues to the United States government, the revenue officers likely would refuse them. The reason is that under the "specie requirement" of 1846, all dues to the United States government should be paid in gold. But this is a moot point, as the treasure in the tale is all "gold of antique date and of great variety," at the same time as there is "no American money." The point about American money is driven home more forcefully by the unnamed narrator's seemingly casual remark that, three or four loose pieces of silver coin excepting, there is also, like in King Solomon's household, "not a particle of silver" in the treasure.[28] Gold as well as silver had originally been designated as American money, but silver coins tended to be scarce, and gold coins were even scarcer. Treasury Secretary Alexander Hamilton had proposed gold dollars as early as 1791, and the Coinage Act of the following year established the dollar as the basic unit for the nation's monetary system, yet gold dollars were omitted when the U.S. Mint was established. Gold coins of higher denomination were struck, though the $10 piece, the United States Eagle, was last minted in 1804 and rarely seen thereafter.

Until the discovery of gold in California in 1849, the American $5 half eagle was the highest denomination of federal gold seen in circulation with any degree of frequency, but it was encountered not nearly as often as the Spanish doubloon or *ocho escudo* piece. Although large quantities of $5 coins were minted and a smaller number of $2.50 quarter eagle gold coins were also struck, nearly all of them were exported and melted at their destination, which in most cases was London. In effect, federal gold coins were not seen in general circulation after 1820. The reason was that from the outset American gold coins were worth more than their stamped value. This fact eventually became of considerable concern to American lawmakers. In December 1830, a United States Senate committee report stated, "The fact that we have no gold coins in circulation, is not the intended effect of our institutions."[29] Also not an intended effect was that the absence of gold coins was giving rise to the vastly expanded use of paper money.

United States eagle, 1799, *left:* obverse and *right:* reverse (American Numismatic Association Money Museum).

At the time the financial experts, including Treasury Secretary Samuel D. Ingham, only imperfectly understood the situation, and erroneously claimed that the failure of gold coins to circulate was the effect of the quantity of paper bills in circulation. The real cause, of course, was that gold was undervalued in relation to silver. America's lawmakers in the end did come to see it in this way, and by the Act of June 28, 1834, the authorized weight of gold coins was reduced. Later in the year, quarter eagles and half eagles, which had been absent for a generation, were available at par. Two years later, Treasury Secretary Levi Woodbury reported that more gold had been coined in the twelve months preceding than in the first sixteen years of the existence of the U.S. Mint, and more since revaluation than in the thirty-one years before.[30] The revival of gold also was part of a political program to completely displace small-denomination paper notes. Although there were even measures, both on the national and on the state levels, to ban notes below $5, there was not a real rush for the new gold coins, and they were seen only occasionally in the market. America's public continued to use small-denomination notes for most local and regional business transactions. Using paper bills for smaller transactions also did not change when, by Act of Congress of January 18, 1837, the weight of gold coins was again reduced, to 25 and ⅘ grains to the dollar. A year later, $10 gold eagles of the lighter-weight standard were struck. While their introduction had no influence on paper money, the new coins quickly became the standard coins for settling international transactions. They maintained their status until, following another amendment, the $20 double eagle was introduced in 1850. The year before, America's first $1 gold coins had been put into circulation, exciting much fanfare — and a derisive commentary from Edgar Allan Poe.[31]

In "The Gold-Bug," Legrand promises Jupiter "a present of a silver dollar" for climbing further up an "enormously tall tulip tree."[32] It is unclear whether the coin in question is a Spanish silver dollar — the *ocho reales* piece — or an American one. Neither the one nor the other would have been much by way of compensating the aged servant for the arduous task of climbing up some sixty or seventy feet from the ground, one or two "narrow escapes from falling" included. An American silver dollar would have been a rarity, though. They were last minted in 1804 and were seen only occasionally until 1836, when minting was resumed. During the entire period, the most frequently encountered federal silver coins were half dollars, of the Capped Bust type, designed by John Reich and introduced in 1807. These coins likewise continued to be in use until 1836.[33]

All these efforts by the Mint notwithstanding, until 1836 specie coins in circulation throughout the country were mostly of foreign silver and gold — Spanish and Mexican dollars and doubloons, British Sovereigns, Brazilian *reis*, and French *francs*. Likewise, the specie that banks kept as backing for their paper currency was "largely in foreign coin," a practice that was widely reported in the press.[34] It was only after 1836 that American gold and silver coins in circulation rose — from $4 million, all in silver, to $28 million, including nearly $10 million in new gold coins. At the same time, some $80 million in bank bills were in general circulation, plus some $20 million held in bank vaults.[35]

Poe explicitly marks American money as an absence in "The Gold-Bug," even though it is entirely gratuitous to mark what is self-evident. As the coins in the treasure chest are all "gold of antique date and of great variety," necessarily they are *not* American. Nor could they ever have been, as the historical Captain Kidd was hanged in 1701, long before there was any such thing as "American money." The sentence "There was no American

United States Silver Dollar, 1795, *left:* **obverse and** *right:* **reverse (American Numismatic Association Money Museum).**

money" thus should be probed for its narrative function. As an index to what is not the case in the contemporary world, it may well be an allusion to the fact that during Poe's time federal gold and silver coins were rarely if ever seen in the channels of commerce. And once these coins did come back, they still traded at a premium. In New York in 1837, for instance, it cost $1.10 to $1.11 in bank notes to buy two silver half dollars.[36] Beyond its function as social comment, therefore, Poe's laconic remark reveals a deeply felt need for a circulating currency that would serve as a *stable* medium of exchange in everyday commercial transactions.

Paper money of course can satisfy the need for a stable medium of exchange. In theory at least, such money could assume many guises. State-chartered or independent commercial banks were authorized to issue paper, whereas the so-called "private banks" unofficially issued notes by what they considered to be a common-law right. This caused great confusion in commerce and tended to impair the reputation of all notes. Not that their reputation ever was too good, as the notes in circulation were not always backed by tangible assets, at least not fully, and many banks were notorious for being highly leveraged. As a consequence, paper bills hardly ever traded at par with gold or silver, usually trading at 7 to 10 percent but on occasion as low as 15 to 30 percent of par, and thus had to be kept *in* circulation to prevent further losses to those who received them.[37] In addition, at a distance, particularly outside the state, all paper bills traded at a discount. Paper money from another state was considered as *foreign* money, including in bank records, statements, and other accounts, and area merchants and others who received such issues sold them at a discount to brokers who then returned them for redemption. Awareness of this historic curiosity is conveniently captured in Poe's correspondence. On November 22, 1840, John Tomlin, a minor author who helped drum up support for the proposed *Penn* magazine, wrote to Poe to inquire if "Tennessee money is current in the ordinary business transactions of your city [of Philadelphia]." Tomlin went on to note, "It is possible that I may thro' the Branch of the Union Bank at this place, obtain a check on some one of your Banks. If Virginia, N. Carolina or S. Carolina money is more current in Philadelphia, than Tennessee, I shall certainly obtain the one that you mention, as preferable."[38]

If bank bills in antebellum America were subjected to wide variations of value and integrity, the chaos was further aggravated by the fact that businessmen and entrepreneurs until the passing of the Free Banking Laws in 1837 and 1838 were at the beck and call of state politicians, who more often than not were following their own interests and thus kept at bay ordinary citizens who were attempting to obtain bank charters. To give an example of the practices then common, the first president of the New Hampshire bank was none other than John Taylor Gilman, the governor of the state of New Hampshire. For years Gilman saw to it that no other bank was chartered in the state. Similarly, in Massachusetts the state held most of the stocks in the Union Bank and the Boston Bank, making sure that new banks would not dilute their profits. The continuing blend of banking and politics lasted until 1837, when the Free Banking legislation permitted citizens to incorporate banks of issue, on condition that they deposit securities with the state treasurer.[39]

The country's miserable monetary situation affected the entire nation. Under the Constitution, the states could make only gold and silver "a legal tender in the payments of debts," and so they were effectively eliminated from the note-issuing business. Conceivably at least, the federal government could issue and control paper money in two different forms, specie-backed money or credit money declared legal tender by an Act of Congress. However, each form then seemed prohibited by the Constitution, which had granted the national government only the right to "*coin* Money." To add to the predicament, lawmakers in Congress were thwarting the introduction of another form of paper money, the so-called Treasury Notes. Notes of this type had been issued by the Federal government in 1812 and then again in 1837 and 1838, but in 1844 the House Means and Ways Committee, which then was dominated by Whig Party members, declared that they were in effect bills of credit (that is, money in the form of debt) and that Congress, in issuing them, had overstepped its powers.[40] Congress apparently had not overstepped its powers when in 1791 the First Bank of the United States was chartered as a bank of issue, legitimized by the constitutional "general welfare" clause. In 1811, however, the lawmakers refused to renew the bank's charter, though they came round in 1816 when they authorized another central bank of issue, the Second Bank of the United States.[41]

In 1836, the financial and economic crisis following Jackson's bank war put an end to the Second Bank. Like the first central bank, the Second Bank was an anomalous institution: though set up as a private corporation with private stockholders, the federal government had shares in it; moreover, its charter made it the exclusive recipient of federal deposits, free of interest. From its inception, therefore, the Second Bank was under attack. Agrarian interests, for instance, claimed that its "paper system" enriched the wealthy stockholders at the expense of small merchants and entrepreneurs. Speculators, in contrast, charged that the bank's conservative monetary policy unduly restricted the money supply and thereby stood in the way of progress. The two positions clearly contradict each other, much as the contention that the wealthy were the exclusive defenders of a paper system must seem ironic, given that during the colonial era wealth had been inseparably wedded to gold. The real reason for the discontent must be sought in the bank's concentration of economic power, which indeed was unprecedented in American history. For Hezekiah Niles, the bank's power was greater by far than any power "we would grant to any set of men, unless responsible to the people."[42] Jackson's bank war, all the references to democracy and the "common man" notwithstanding, at least in part was geared up towards restricting the bank's power, including its note-issuing power, and preventing it from obtaining a new charter.

Jackson's triumph over the Second Bank of the United States was paradoxical. Although Jackson posed as a hard-money man, his policy of shifting government deposits to state banks marked the beginning of a liberal money policy that promised entrepreneurs (and speculators) a greater availability of paper bills. Yet once the BUS' charter had expired, in 1836, there already were so many commercial banks issuing bills that Jackson was forced in July to issue his Specie Circular requiring payment in gold or silver for public lands. The edict — one of Jackson's last official acts — was designed to protect the federal government against fraud and to weed out unsound paper bills, but it only produced a run on specie accompanied by the hoarding of sound bills. All this further undermined public confidence in commercial banks and their notes. Under Jackson's successor, Martin Van Buren, the country began to feel the dire consequences of Jackson's financial policies. Interest rates went up, businesses failed, and the cotton industry collapsed because Britain stopped the import of cotton. The predicament of the currency at once leads us back to the question that dominated American political discourse at the time — who should control the currency, the government at any of its levels, or the citizens, and in what form — gold, silver, or paper?

These issues were unresolved at the time, and so we are led forward to a key theme of "The Gold-Bug" — money in the form of treasure. The way the treasure is to be searched for — in a most complex way, by solving a cipher — seemingly symbolizes the disappearance of actual gold, which insofar as it is withdrawn from circulation also becomes detached from its linguistic sign. To put the matter somewhat differently, the inflationary use in the tale of the word "gold" only precipitates the disappearance of gold as a substance at the same time as it foregrounds its potential as a sign. The significance we can deduce from this distinction derives from the difference between use-value and exchange-value. The term use-value or intrinsic value refers to the utility or usefulness of a particular object; the term exchange-value, in contrast, refers to the power of exchanging that object for other goods or services. It is this latter power, the power of the sign, which under a capitalist regime creates the surplus value that is the basis of the accumulation of wealth.

Poe and Political Economy

Poe had a most profound understanding of political economy, and so he probably was aware of the distinction between use-value and exchange-value when he writes, in his "Marginalia" for November 1844, "knowledge breeds knowledge, as gold gold."[43] Assuming that he was aware of the distinction, we may follow Terence Whalen's argument that the allusion to the gold that breeds yet more gold refers "not to the mere metal but to the medium of exchange which, under given capitalist relations of production, facilitates the creation of surplus value and the theoretically limitless accumulation of wealth."[44] It is worth noting that in the terminology of political economy, a medium of exchange that creates surplus value and enables the accumulation of wealth is called "capital." The matter was well known at Poe's time, especially in the South, which was then unusually well schooled in the discipline of political economy. Henry C. Carey, a political economist and, later, chief economic advisor to Abraham Lincoln, summarized his understanding of capital in *Hunt's Merchants' Magazine* for April 1841 in the following way: "Currency is capital seeking investment."[45] Poe seems to have understood this, indicating, in "The Gold-Bug," not merely the amount of the treasure, but also its exchange value. The former is given as weight, at "three hundred and fifty pounds avoirdupois." The latter is given in dollars, estimated by the happy money-finders at "a million and a half of dollars," which is equal to at least thirty million dollars in today's depreciating currency. The precision in Poe's account is also a neat reminder of the invention, around 1840, of the word "millionaire" to describe those five percent of white males who then owned some seventy percent of the real and personal property. For the rest of the population, of course, amount as well as exchange-value verges on the miraculous, as if Poe had wanted to mystify the notion that the treasure — "our golden burthens" — constitutes capital.[46]

Critics and readers alike have been puzzled by the fact that "The Gold-Bug" is so neatly divided into two roughly equal parts. Somewhere in the middle of the tale, when the treasure has been brought securely home and is duly counted and weighed, Legrand begins his narrative of how he was able to solve the cipher and thus find the treasure. "When, at length, we had concluded our examination, and the intense excitement of the time had, in some measure, subsided, Legrand, who saw that I was dying with impatience for a solution of this most extraordinary riddle, entered into a full detail of all the circumstances connected with it." Not a word is lost about what the happy money-finder does or intends to do with the treasure. Of course we remember Legrand's triumphantly optimistic remark that the "bug" was to make his "fortune," which would then "reinstate [him] in his family possessions."[47] Nevertheless, we can only guess how that will be achieved, or wonder whether it will be achieved at all. Poe's play with undecidability once again undermines his own position, destabilizing the representation (and its reception) even though the issues that Poe thematizes are most real. Yet the very undecidability sends back at least the possibility, as the reviewer of the *Tales* of 1845 noted, of the "absolute necessity of each [material] to the whole."[48]

The injunction to stabilization contained in the reviewer's remark warrants a closer look at the logic of the story, which unfolds in more ways than one. Permitting an oedipal narrative, we might say that the continuation of the story beyond the finding of the treasure is foreclosed by the repetition of past experiences. A presumed oedipal logic, of course, must conceive of Poe's life in terms of the psychoanalytic prototype of the bereaved child that is unable to mourn the loss of a parent. More precisely, the source of "The Gold-Bug" must be seen in "'an unfulfilled longing for the maternal object.'"[49] Yet recapture of the maternal object, in the form of a treasure taken out of the earth, that is, out of the mother's womb, only succeeds if there is a father to assist, that is to say, a representative of the outside world. The absence of such a figure leaves the protagonist immobile or paralyzed from reliving the pain.[50] In "The Gold-Bug," paralysis is imagined as the hoarding of the treasure, which is never spent or invested. At the same time, Poe's representation of some neurotic disorder is the cause of the story's peculiar form, which is best described in terms of a symmetry of improbabilities, in which the improbable coincidences that lead to the discovery of the gold repeats the equally improbable series of misfortunes that brought about Legrand's bankruptcy and subsequent self-chosen exile. The narrow-minded narrator fails to grasp this symmetry, which in turn allows Legrand to bring his mystification to a close.

The narrator's mystification ("kidding") cannot be separated from Poe's relationship with his presumed readers.[51] Poe disliked what he saw as his readers' conventionality, narrow-mindedness, even vulgarity, at the same time as he depended on them for his financial support. Consequently, he came to seek, not a regional, local, or partisan readership, but a *national* one. In his attempt to speak to a national audience, Poe persistently avoided bearing the risk of political speech in his writings.[52] To take the story beyond the *finding* of the treasure would not only reveal a metatextual message; it also would make a political statement, as the gold necessarily would be turned into capital. At the very least, it would convey some useful information about a medium of exchange that at once generates value and puts in motion the accumulation of wealth. Through the abrupt transition from treasure hunt to cipher solving, from "money" to "mystery," much is concealed, though as so often in Poe's writings, the art reveals while it conceals — in this case, an entangling alliance with the freewheeling capitalism of the time. Yet Poe's art also conceals while it reveals, so that in the end Captain Kidd's buried loot is not capital but only "potential capital" that the idiosyncratic Legrand refuses or is not allowed by his creator to put into productive circulation.[53]

This estrangement from productive society calls for a reconsideration of Legrand's status. Because Legrand is not finally turned into one of those "worshippers of Mammon" who exclusively measure esteem by wealth, Poe retains for his central character a mixture of the aristocratic, the erudite, and the reactionary. Poe's poetic choice has led critics to see a resemblance between Legrand and the writer himself—"well educated, with unusual powers of mind, but infected with misanthropy and subject to perverse moods of alternate enthusiasm and melancholy."[54] The assumed resemblance between the author and his central character, however, obliterates the differences between Poe and Legrand, which are just as obvious. Legrand, it is worth recalling, comes "of an ancient Huguenot family" from New Orleans that "had once been wealthy."[55] Poe himself was neither of Huguenot descent, nor had his family ever been wealthy.

Somewhat closer to his author is Legrand's astounding knowledge both of natural history and secret writing, and, not to forget, his seemingly tacit acceptance of "the peculiar institution," which had found a visible expression also on Southern currency, on notes from commercial banks, on Confederate notes, and — in somewhat modified form — on bills issued by Southern banks during the Reconstruction period.[56] Poe, it should be stated at once, was *not* a slavery advocate, though mindful of Southern sensibilities he was an occasional critic of abolitionism and did in fact make several statements about slavery. Probably the most scandalous of these statements held, albeit in a somewhat dodging way, that "the slave himself is utterly incompetent to feel the *moral* galling of his chain."[57] Yet Bernard Rosenthal, Joan Dayan, David Leverenz, and, more recently, Eve Dunbar are wrong in their estimation of Poe's Southern-ness because their interpretations are based on a review that Poe did not write.[58] And even if Poe was a Southern gentleman and an anti-abolitionist, he was also a frequent reader of the news, and a professional writer. On the other hand, Poe did write "The Gold-Bug," with its representation of Jupiter, said to be "a perfect picture [...] accurately drawn."[59] Yet Poe carefully specifies, at the very beginning of the tale, that Jupiter is not a slave, but is actually free, having been "manumitted before the reverses of the [Legrand] family."[60] This piece of narrative shrewdness, Terence Whalen found, is owed to Poe's recognition of the political divisions over slavery in the national audience.

Poe may have exploited conventions about the mysterious affection between white masters and black slaves. Nevertheless, in "The Gold-Bug" he is most careful to evade any scandal caused by such a portrayal: he makes Jupiter free, and although Jupiter on several occasions refers to Legrand as "master," never once in the entire tale does Poe use the word "slave."[61] Poe thus had it both ways: he could pander to the "average racism" of his audience at the same time as he neutralized the sectional conflict over slavery. In other words, the crucial yet subtle change in Jupiter's legal status made it possible for Poe to create "a sanitized South that could circulate freely in the national literary market."[62] Obviously, Poe must have found such a strategy convenient because whatever Southern views he might have harbored or voiced, he could scarcely have ignored the emergence of a capitalist economy. Nor could the fact that he was the natural son of itinerant actors have blinded him to this emergence, especially when one recalls that his foster father was an immigrant from Scotland who was naturalized only in 1804.[63] The city of Richmond, moreover, was itself unusual within a Southern plantation economy. Of course there were tobacco factories that had any number of slaves in their workforce, but Richmond also had iron foundries, sawmills, nail factories, and, in its vicinity, huge deposits of bituminous coal.[64]

Such circumstances not only contradict the image of Poe as a conservative Southerner. In fact, capitalist relations of production, the creation of surplus value, and the theoretically limitless accumulation of wealth constituted a ferment that eventually found creative expression in various forms of signification. If Poe was capable of *representing* racism, he was just as capable of *representing* the ingenuity and resourcefulness that human greed — lust for gold or, again following Marx, worship of the "Lord of commodities" — is capable of spawning. It is also worth noting that in Legrand's bug for gold, which appears to drive the man almost to madness, traditional dislikes of money are echoed, from Aristotle's verdict that its accumulation is unnatural to its association, in Christendom, with the sin of avarice. The bug itself constitutes a connection with death and violence, as the money diggers not only encounter a hideous human skull in a tree with the meat gobbled by birds but also unearth two skeletons. The skeletons presumably are the remains of two helpers murdered by the legendary Captain Kidd when the treasure was buried, and so the bones cannot be separated from the treasure, but are buried with the gold itself, in the stolen coins and, even more so, in the jewelry, finger rings, and other golden relics of the pirate's victims. Finally there is, via the *Scarabaeus* beetle, the "gold-bug" of the title, the association with dung or excrement. Although from this association might follow the conventional Christian association of lucre with filth, or the Freudian association of shiny metal with feces, for our purposes it is more fruitful to note that dung is not at first sight of any intrinsic value.[65] The same can be said about the "ideal" cryptographic drawing that the treasure-hunting protagonist exchanges for gold, about paper money that is not backed by precious metal or other tangible assets, or about Poe's literary papers that this poor author could only wish to exchange for cold hard cash.

Captain Kidd's booty doubtless would have meant an end to Poe's own financial worries or, as this tormented genius put it in an 1841 letter, the necessity to "coin one's brain into silver, at the nod of a master."[66] Poe wrote this at the end of the financial crisis of 1837, which was felt across the entire nation. Jackson's Specie Circular of July 1836, designed to protect the federal government against fraud and to eliminate unsound paper bills, had only produced a run on specie accompanied by the hoarding of sound bills. Public confidence

Henry R. Robinson, "The Times," lithograph portraying the hardships brought about by the panic of 1837 (Library of Congress, Prints and Photographs Division, LC-USZ62–8844, 32.7 × 48.4 cm).

in commercial banks and their notes declined dramatically. When Van Buren became president, the dire consequences of Jackson's financial policies hit the country with full force. In March stock prices on Wall Street fell across the board. By May, there had been about a hundred bank failures in New York alone, causing a loss of about $15 million. By the end of the year, across the nation over six hundred banks had closed their doors forever. With no credit available, new businesses could not be created, bankruptcies were recorded by the tens of thousands, and business losses — compounded by Britain's stoppage to cotton imports — were registered at $741 million. Almost ninety percent of the factories in the East shut down, resulting in mass unemployment. Cargo ships were idled, almshouses were filled beyond capacity as the prices for bread, meat, fuel, and rents skyrocketed, and countless families went hungry and froze in the winter of 1837–1838. In New York's Chatham Square riots erupted as the swelling ranks of the city's poor broke into a warehouse storing flour. A lithograph that Henry R. Robinson executed from a cartoon by Edward Williams Clay provides a sarcastic commentary on the depressed state of the American economy, particularly in New York, during the panic of 1837.[67]

Clearly in Robinson's lithograph the blame is laid on the treasury policies of Andrew Jackson, whose hat, spectacles, and clay pipe with the word "Glory" appear in the sky overhead. The artist illustrates some of the effects of the depression in a fanciful street scene that emphasizes the plight of the working class. A panorama of offices, rooming houses, and shops reflects the hard times. The Custom House, carrying a sign "All Bonds must be paid in Specie," is idle. In contrast, frantic customers mob the Mechanics Bank next door, which displays a sign "No specie payments made here." Although writers are not among the principal figures in Robinson's print, they and their families went hungry too, the Poe family not excepting. In the aftermath of the panic, writing was devalued to such an extent that books sold at a quarter of the price of 1820; poetry became, as Poe ruefully remarked in 1842, completely "unsaleable."[68] To make matters worse, magazine publishers even discontinued paying for contributions.[69] In his desperation, Poe begged James Kirke Paulding, then Secretary of the Navy in the Van Buren administration, for a clerkship already in July 1838, when he felt that he "could not possibly live by literary labor" alone.[70]

Poe may not have been able to live by literary labor, though continue to write he did. In many of his writings of the time, moods of fear and apocalyptic fantasies of the world's end prevail, constituting a clear measure of the extent to which economic forces and constraints shaped his creativity also at the level of literary form. "Ligeia," for instance, seems merely a tale about unmerited love. Yet Poe inserts into it a poem, ostensibly composed by the lady Ligea herself, which dramatizes a gala night at a theater. The performance is "a play of hopes and fears," yet the actors in it are "mere puppets [...] who come and go / At bidding of vast formless things / That shift the scenery to and fro, / Flapping from their Condor wings / Invisible Wo!" That play, the poem concludes, is a "tragedy, 'Man,' / And its hero the Conqueror Worm."[71] The sinister outlook on a dismal future is continued a year later in "The Fall of the House of Usher," which again contains a poem, "The Haunted Palace," likewise published separately at a later date. The poem begins by invoking a "fair and stately palace" standing in "the greenest of our valleys." The days of the palace's glory are long past, however, and all that visitors now see is a "pale door" through which "A hideous throng rush out forever / And laugh — but smile no more." "Usher" traditionally has been seen to reflect Poe's interest in the metaphysics of mental disturbances, especially of the main character, Roderick Usher, who is described as suffering much "from a morbid acuteness of the senses." It is quite plausible, therefore, that the poem uses a conceit to represent Usher's tottering mind, and we may safely assume that Poe did not intend "Usher" primarily as a commentary on the time. Yet given Poe's own penury and the socio-economic and political situation at large, Roderick Usher's pronouncement, "I dread the events of the future, not in themselves, but in their results," generates a ripple of meaning that adds weight to the particulars of social reality, extending even beyond the personal and the familial, the "House" of Usher, whose cultural order was rendered obsolete under the conditions of Jacksonianism, to the nation at large, in which the "hideous throng," once suppressed but now become ungovernable, erupts in the form of a mob, "rush[ing] out forever."[72]

The social and political meanings of Poe's writings in the aftermath of the panic of 1837 come to the fore in "The Colloquy of Monos and Una." Written in 1841, this fictitious philosophical dialogue looks back upon "wild attempts at an omni-prevalent Democracy." The unholy experiments, seen as a violation of human nature, come to an end in a "fiery overthrow," that is, in a "purification which alone could efface [the earth's] rectangular obscenities." The tale has as its motto "Mellonta Tauta," which Poe ascribes to Sophocles, rendering it as "These things are in the future."[73] The motto is a consummate symptom of Poe's outlook on politics at the time, especially on Jacksonian democracy, which he saw as one of the undisputable evidences of decline. Poe never ceased to pursue this topic, publishing, in 1845, "Some Words with a Mummy," which mocks Jacksonianism through an allegorical rendering of Egyptian history, as well as, in 1849, a satiric tale titled "Mellonta Tauta." The title links it with "The Colloquy of Monos and Una," the tale about the downfall of the earth that Poe had republished in his *Tales* of 1845, thus adding weight to the satire of Jacksonian "democracy" as "a very admirable form of government — for dogs."[74]

I will come back to Poe's satirical renderings of Jacksonian democracy in chapter 5. At this point, I will continue with "A Descent into the Maelström," which likewise dates from 1841. At first sight, this tale is one of pure adventure, an account of an imaginary voyage ending in a horrifying disaster. Only one man survives the shipwreck, left, like Coleridge's Ancient Mariner, to tell the tale to the afterworld. From him we learn, less about the mysteries of life than about the first cause of the disaster, which has been entirely economic: the men's fishing boat, we are told, ventured beyond the "usual grounds [where] fish can be got at all hours, *without much risk*." Thus the daring risk-takers seek out the "choice spots over here among the rocks [which] not only yield the finest variety, but in far greater abundance." As the lonely survivor confides to the narrator, what motivated the venture in the first place was simply "*desperate speculation* — the risk of life standing instead of labor, and courage answering for capital." It was not, therefore, the tragic heroes' *hubris* that, by way of punishment, precipitated them all into the abyss. The all-embracing range of what they confront in the ocean's depth — "fragments of vessels," "building timber," "trunks of trees," as well as "pieces of house furniture, broken boxes, barrels and staves" — is not cathartic so much as it is a fitting analogy to the economic cataclysm Poe and his contemporaries were then experiencing — the panic of 1837 and its aftermath.[75]

We can also relate to the general mood inspired by the panic of 1837 and its aftermath Poe's "Eleonora," a kind of paradise lost fantasy in which the hero leaves behind forever his memories of the beloved Eleonora "for the vanities and the turbulent triumphs of the world." Yet this tale, which also dates from 1841, does not speak to the financial crisis and its aftermath so much as to the political upheavals that accompanied the succession to the presidency of John Tyler. "Eleonora," which was first published in the *Gift* on September 1, 1841, and was subsequently reprinted in a number of newspapers and magazines, also appeared in the *Madisonian*, Tyler's official press organ. Although it is not known who had the tale included, the plan certainly was to get the president to read the piece.[76] At the time, in late September 1841, Poe indeed was desperate to catch Tyler's attention, both for a government sinecure and for support for one of his magazine projects. Poe then was threatened by unemployment and poverty, and, following his dismissal from the *Southern Literary Messenger*, was deeply disenchanted as a writer. Earlier in the year, therefore, he once again had tried to get off the ground a magazine of his own. Yet the *Penn Magazine*, as it was called, only "would have appeared under glorious auspices ... as advertised, but for the unexpected bank suspensions."[77] Preparations for the new magazine had begun in late May 1840, shortly before Poe lost his employment at *Burton's Gentleman's Magazine*. Poe's prospectus appeared in a number of periodicals throughout the summer and early autumn. In addition, Poe tried to solicit support for the magazine from a large number of private individuals, relatives and friends included. By mid–October of 1840, the project began to sputter. In early December Poe, who then was bedridden by a severe illness, decided to postpone the first number of the magazine until March 1841. On February 20, 1841, the *Saturday Evening Post* announced that Poe had been "forced, at the last moment, to abandon finally, or at least to postpone indefinitely, his project of the *Penn Magazine*."

Suspensions of specie payment by the commercial banks were common during the entire period, though Poe's reference, in his letter to Snodgrass, probably is to the suspension by the United States Bank, on February 4, 1841. The action produced a panic and a run on the other Philadelphia banks, most of which also stopped payment, followed by banks in the South. By the early summer of that year, there was widespread fear. The United States Bank or, as was its correct name, the Second Bank of the United States, had become a local institution under a Pennsylvania charter in February 1836, a casualty of the bank war, which according to Robert Remini was "the single most important event of Jackson's entire administration."[78] The bank's official name then was Bank of the United States of Pennsylvania, though "of Pennsylvania" was never printed on its bills, which led people to believe that the notes were from the Bank of the United States of 1816, the genuine Second Bank of the United States. The look of the bank's notes too suggested this, as they bore panels of portraits of national figures at each end, and a view of the bank building in Philadelphia at top center. Following the suspension of specie in February 1841, the Bank of the United States of Pennsylvania filed for bankruptcy, and its notes — then issued mostly in very high denominations — became worthless.[79]

In late summer, some fifty disenchanted Philadelphians founded the "Anti-Chartered Monopoly Association," for the purpose of preventing "promises to pay [from passing] as money." The association was not only radically anti-paper money in its politics, but did not even find acceptable a fully convertible currency. Their efforts, however, had no practical effect. By March 1842, both the once highly regarded Girard Bank and the Bank of Pennsylvania also had been ruined, along with a number of other local and regional institutions. *Niles' Weekly Register* reported that the currency of the affected banks was discounted up to 60 percent when received in payment.[80] The bank failures and the ensuing economic crisis only added to Poe's "pecuniary embarrassments," which were so grave at the time that in June he considered legally declaring himself bankrupt. Poe was not alone with his plight, though. As one Philadelphian wrote: "Everybody has become poor; there is no business,

$1000 note from the Bank of the United States [of Philadelphia], 1840, face: a local institution pretending to be a national bank (American Numismatic Association Money Museum).

there is no money ... nobody can pay debts."[81] A case thus can be made that both Poe's indigence and his concern about a viable medium of exchange, together with the easy credit availability that such a medium entailed, drove the "The Gold-Bug" story into the obsessive money-finding plot. In other words, what may have begun as a tale about solving a cipher eventually involved a search for money, as if the actual disappearance of gold and silver could be compensated for through the appearance of an imaginary treasure.

Imaginary treasures belong to the realm of magic, not to the real world. Appropriately, in Poe's tale the treasure is discovered in a dream world "excessively wild and desolate, where no trace of human footstep was to be seen [...] a species of tableland, near the summit of an almost inaccessible hill, densely wooded from base to pinnacle, and interspersed with huge crags that appeared to lie loosely upon the soil."[82] The *locale* never was a trivial matter for Poe, but always had "the force of a frame to a picture."[83] The "moral power" it exerts in this instance stems, not from Poe's faithfulness to the "geographical peculiarities" in and about Sullivan's Island, but from his use of the "sublime." Poe's use of the sublime at once recalls the European romanticism inspired by Salvator Rosa and James Thomson and the piously nationalistic rhetoric of the American sublime, in the landscape paintings of the Hudson River school as well as in the travel writings of William Bartram and in the poetry of William Cullen Bryant. In 1829, Bryant published a sonnet to Thomas Cole, one of the landscape painters of the Hudson River school, upon Cole's departure to Europe. Cole's eyes, Bryant states, shall see the light of distant skies, yet the painter's heart shall bear to Europe

> A living image of our own bright land....
> Lone lakes — savannas where the bison roves —
>   Rocks rich with summer garlands — solemn streams —
>   Skies, where the desert eagle wheels and screams —
> Spring bloom and autumn blaze of boundless groves.

Elizabeth Phillips, citing the poem in part, adds that contrary to what critics have said, Poe was not averse to the idea of an American sublime.[84] Planning, near the end of his life, a book on "The Living Writers of America," Poe noted that "distant subjects" are "in fact the most desirable.... The true poet is less affected by the absolute contemplation than [by] the imagination of a great landscape."[85]

In "The Gold-Bug," the sublime involves both the landscape and the treasure buried in the land. Yet the treasure, being pirate money, is useless for being buried, hidden away, instead of being in circulation, fueling the economy and binding people together. Hidden treasures have their place in caves in the mountains, as in European folktales involving dwarfs; in Poe's "Von Kempelen and his Discovery," the treasure is under the bed; in "The Gold-Bug," it is in a pit. For psychoanalytic critics like Marie Bonaparte, the earth of course symbolizes the mother. A treasure that is buried in the earth thus may be said to be *in* the mother's "bowels" or womb. Any encounter with it therefore entails a regression to an earlier stage of development.[86] In "The Gold-Bug," regression is strikingly evident from the emotions displayed by the money-finders once the "treasure of incalculable value lay gleaming before [them, flashing upwards] a glow and a glare that absolutely dazzled [their] eyes" — amazement, excitement, and stupefaction, emotions so powerful that the narrator has no words for them and therefore "shall not pretend to describe them."[87]

The passage about the treasure's glow and glare shows that the source of the money-finders' fascination lies in the appeal that the gold has to their aesthetic sense, not in its utility. Such a desire, which insists on the priority of gold's aesthetic attraction over its usefulness, is, as William James argued in the *Principles of Psychology*, "entirely primitive."[88] As if to emphasize the instinctual or primitive status of the desire for gold, Poe not only has the narrator left speechless. Jupiter too is "thunder-stricken" so that presently he falls "upon his knees in the pit, and, burying his naked arms up to the elbows in gold, let them there remain, as if enjoying the luxury of a bath."[89] Once the treasure is brought safely to Legrand's island home, there "deposited [...] just as the first streaks of the dawn gleamed from over the tree-tops in the East," Legrand and the narrator likewise are enjoying a bath of sorts, as they examine and scrutinize what they have unearthed. Conceivably, the treasure, now that the earth no longer holds it, can become the key to the outer, social reality, the realm of the fathers. This is not what happens, though. Instead, the treasure remains sitting in its new hiding place, there to be endlessly counted but never to be exchanged for or transformed into circulating currency, that is, into capital.[90]

"The Gold-Bug" and the Critics

Capital or rather, the "want of capital," hampered Poe's proposed *Penn Magazine* from its inception.[91] I draw attention here to Poe's use of the language of political economy because it so conveniently guides us to the persistence of the money theme in his writings. To most critics the thought must seem preposterous. Although no single human can grasp the vast amount of scholarship that interest in Poe's writings has spawned, it is possible to make out some general trends. As regards the writings I deal with here, "King Pest," "The Devil in the Belfry," and "The Business Man" predictably have been read as satires, of Jacksonian politics in general and of Franklin's *Autobiography* or Washington Irving's *History of New York* in particular.[92] "A Descent into the Maelström," just as predictably, is generally described as an archetypal sea voyage, the descent itself being very much a spiritual or psychic one.[93] Spirituality also permeates most criticism of "The Domain of Arnheim," with an emphasis on the sublime and a transcendentalist view of nature.[94] Such readings fully correspond with the image of Poe as a dark romanticist engaged in arcane and mysterious lore. Yet Poe himself seems to have directed his readers towards quite different truths, truths that cannot be found "at the bottom" but rather "at the top," that is, in more "palpable places." Poe wrote this in 1831, prefacing his collection of poems. Later in his career, he was even more explicit concerning the "errors" in the search for truth: "[I]t is the nature of Truth in general, as of some ores in particular, to be richest when most superficial."[95] Scholarly works that explain the political and historical references in "Mellonta Tauta" seemingly meet the promise of richness derived from superficiality.[96] Even these readings, however, present difficulties, especially since they tend to neglect the "palpable places" that reveal Poe's ties to the world of money and banking. Readings of "The Gold-Bug," in contrast, are exceptional in this regard. While there is, of course, an accumulated mass of Poe lore ignoring the social and political meanings of this tale, more recently scholars have taken into account those meanings. Thus, my discussion of the history of Poe scholarship will address more directly a few readings that gaze into the "huge abysses" provided by this celebrated tale, before it moves into another direction, to scholarship that describes "The Gold-Bug" as most in step with its time and thus opens a way to resituate Poe's work in the nation's monetary and financial history.

While "The Gold-Bug" was immediately popular with the reading public and has continued to be one of the most popular stories in the world, a number of critics have expressed reservations. D. H. Lawrence in his *Studies in Classic American Literature* for instance dismisses the story as merely one of "those mechanical tales where the interest lies in the following out of a subtle chain of cause and effect. The interest is scientific rather than artistic, a study in psychological reactions."[97] Of course, Lawrence has a point, as part of the story's appeal does lie in the intricate play of solving a puzzle without a crime and, as well, in the psychological dynamics played out between Legrand and the unnamed narrator. W. K. Wimsatt speaks more admiringly about "The Gold-Bug," referring to the story as the brilliant climax to Poe's cryptographic writings, aimed at capitalizing upon the curiosity about ciphers that this writer had aroused through a number of articles published respectively in *Alexander's Weekly Messenger*, the *Southern Literary Messenger*, and *Graham's Magazine* between 1839 and 1842. Thus, the story supposedly originated from Poe's desire to reveal, in spectacular fashion, the solution to a simple substitution cipher.[98] Wimsatt here refashions ideas that already had been articulated by early reviewers and critics. *Graham's Magazine*, for instance, in an unsigned review of Poe's *Tales* claimed that "'The Gold Bug' attracted great attention at the time it appeared, and is quite remarkable as an instance of intellectual acuteness and subtlety of reasoning."[99] The London *Literary Gazette*, containing Martin Tupper's long critique of Poe's *Tales*, called "The Gold-Bug" a "'bit of ingenious calculation' [that] parallels the deciphering of the Rosetta stone."[100] London's *The Critic* was less friendly, remarking that the tale "is only interesting from its strangeness. It tells of the discovery of some hidden treasure, by the solving of certain enigmatical figures. Viewed with the moral, the tale *may* be useful, as showing what a patient, earnest mind may accomplish."[101]

Rufus Wilmot Griswold, in his memoir of Poe, which he prefaced to his edition of Poe's *Works* of 1850, likewise saw "The Gold-Bug" in line with this author's efforts in cryptography: "[The tale] is one of [Poe's] most remarkable illustrations of his ingenuity of construction and apparent subtlety of reasoning. The interest depends upon the solution of an intricate cipher."[102] Indeed, Legrand's explanation of how he cracked the code that will lead him to the buried gold is stupefying, his disclaimer notwithstanding.[103] Yet solving the cipher is only one part of the story. The other part, the finding of the treasure, is no less stupefying. Richard Hull concedes as much, even though his interpretation of this part of the story merely is in terms of a "literalized figure of speech, a gold-colored bug that physically bites Legrand."[104] Because of being bitten, Legrand has no eyes to see anything but "the gold of which [the bug] is the index."[105] Legrand's narrowly self-absorbed drive for wealth obliterates both beauty and whatever moral sense he may have had. It also makes him believe that he can turn the design, drawn by himself, of a specimen into the real thing, gold or specie. This is no less an achievement than to transform from accidental to necessary the relationship between the paper with the design on it and the treasure.[106]

It goes without saying that the tale's structure contains many divergent and sometimes even conflicting elements. Critics generally have admired the skill with which Poe forged from these elements a plausible and coherent unit. For J. O. Bailey, for instance, it is "perfectly fascinating," if only "hocus-pocus, evident to anyone who undertakes to weigh and measure what Poe pretends to weigh and measure so carefully."[107] While Barton St. Armand concurs with this view, he is careful to add that everything has been fused into an aesthetic whole. The story, this critic argues, achieves plausibility and coherence less through the "purely mental legerdemain" that Poe cast over it than through his extended use of alchemy. Alchemy or, rather, the golden visions of the alchemists, for Poe serve to fuse the divergent and conflicting elements of the narrative into a larger whole. Poe's use of alchemy, Armand points out, includes references to a number of "planetary metals," including tin, the symbolic name for which is Jupiter.[108] In addition, the tulip-tree that Legrand's servant is ordered to climb constitutes "a ready-made physical representation of the spiritual process [the alchemist] was mastering through his art," and thus is a most appropriate symbol of the money-seekers' "quest."[109] Characteristically, their quest entails a "deciphering of the secret formula which details the secret of the process." Overall, then, Poe's tale seems to rest on "the magic ingredient of faith and the occult theoturgy of the alchemists."[110]

There is no hint of an "alchemical multiplication" in Jean Ricardou's semiotic study of the tale, though this critic also treats "The Gold-Bug" as "a text with its multitude of problems," in which Poe set forth exploring the reader's comprehension of the content and meaning of the story. The meaning, Ricardou claims, is the *linguistic* "gold" to be found in the story. Legrand finds it because he is an astute observer of signs and a reader of underlying meanings, of the "laws of the text" that generate the meaning Poe's ideal readers also seek as if it were a fabulous treasure.[111] In James Mathews' reading of the tale, Legrand finds an entirely different kind of gold: gold, Mathews claims, "in Poe's symbology always stands for an imaginative and metaphysical state, a realm of supernatural beauty and placidity, attained at great risk and travail."[112] Thus, Mathews compares Legrand's quest to one described in Scripture — "the kingdom of heaven is like unto treasure hid in a field; the which when a man hath found, he hideth, and for joy thereof goeth and selleth all that he hath, and buyeth that field."[113]

Kidd's treasure is not hid in a field, and Legrand also does not sell all that he has, and least of all does he buy the field, though he may indeed find his soul's fulfillment when he discovers the treasure. For Mathews, that is, the true treasure that Legrand finds is not Captain Kidd's booty but the satisfaction and gratification he gains through applying his mind to the solution of an impossible enigma. For this reason the tale ends without any reference to how the happy finder will use the treasure. Legrand's pursuit of the treasure thus is symbolic of an inner search, a search in which Jupiter serves as a kind of guardian, while the narrator stands in as a more pragmatic helper, the only one Legrand can trust. Ultimately, therefore, the treasure is "transcendental," a symbol as much of Legrand's "imperishable self" as of his "imaginative powers."[114] Does the discovery of the treasure then make Legrand a visionary? Daniel Hoffman appears to think so, arguing that Legrand is "Poe's version of the genius of the age," whose "sole occupation is to understand the universe, not for its utility [...] but because his curiosity will not be assuaged until he himself has mastered the secrets written into the world by the Author of its so far uncracked code."[115] To treat "The Gold-Bug" as a prime example of Poe's investigation of a general universe of signs is also on the agenda of an article by Daniel Kempton. Yet Kempton, though he builds on Hoffman, Ricardou, and Michael Williams, denies that the quest for textual gold constitutes a *celebration* of the powers of the mind. Like in the Dupin stories, Poe's explanation of the mystery relies not so much on "logical reasoning" than on "artful rhetoric" and, to an even greater extent, on "*chance*, whose prodigious intervention has favored [Legrand] through the adventure." Kempton points, *inter alia*, to the serendipities of weather, the coincidence of discovering an unknown genus of beetle *and* a dirty scrap of parchment, and, finally, the remarkable congruence between Legrand's sketch of the beetle and the outline of a skull. Overall, then, it is merely "poetic justice" for this extraordinary series of events to "culminate" in the most fantastic accident of all: "the discovery of gold *by mistake*."[116]

Whatever the merits of these readings, none of them takes into account contemporary discourses about America's money. Nor do readings that treat "The Gold-Bug" as a detective story or, more precisely, as one of mystery, a puzzle without a crime, dealing with the discovery of pirate loot after deciphering a piece of cryptographic writing.[117] To resituate the tale in America's monetary and financial history thus is to depart from critical orthodoxy, at the same time as it is to reveal a writer quite different from the familiar one of "Madness and more of Sin, and Horror."[118] Larzer Ziff summarizes traditional views of Poe when he writes, in 1981, that Poe's poems and tales "are rarely set in a recognizable part of America, bear no conscious relation to the habits of abstract speculation that marked much of its literature, bypass explicit moral themes, are *unconcerned with social matters*, and adhere to a 'literary' diction that is confected."[119] Although Ziff's description is not entirely wrong, in the present study I indicate that Poe was never removed from American contexts and contradictions. Poe may have produced the *appearance* of isolation, but that is an artistic achievement that needs to be looked into in its own right.

While Poe may have been America's most exotic writer, he also wrote, as early as 1832, "Every author should confine himself to matters of experience."[120] This statement is particularly trenchant when we consider Poe's development as a commercial writer, which shows a grasp of political economy that calls into question the seeming universality and timelessness of his literary output. Poe's early poetry may have been more insulated, thanks to a living tradition, though in the aftermath of the panic of 1837, it had become "unsaleable."[121] It is no surprise, then, that Poe's output of poetry declined by nearly ninety percent. His production of the relatively more marketable tale, in contrast, more than doubled between 1837 and 1843. In other words, Poe's tales cannot be attributed to an autonomous or even diseased mind but are, as Terence Whalen points out, "in many ways the rational products of social labor, imagined and executed in the workshop of American capitalism."[122] Whalen takes great pains to draw out the true conditions of this workshop by following Poe through the many struggles to get his fiction published. The present attempt to restore Poe to his own culture likewise addresses embodiments of capital, though not so much in the publishing industry as in the realm of money and banking. During the period in question, this particular realm likewise generated enough power to influence Poe's thoughts, feelings, and creativity.

In Poe's "The Business Man," for instance, the swaggering narrator declares that he would not have any one "play the possum" with him. The declaration seems like a distant echo of a motto that was widely used on revolutionary paper money issued by the state of Georgia between 1776 and 1778. The bills in question (actually, "certificates for the support of the Continental troops") were denominated in dollars. They were graced by the image of a coiled rattlesnake, its head raised, and the inscription NEMO ME IMPUNE LACESSET ("No one will provoke me with impunity").[123] The motto is better known as that of the Scottish Order of the Thistle. Originating during the English Civil War, it was added to the Royal coat of arms of Scotland during the reign of Charles II. Poe used the English version, in slightly modified form, in a letter to William E. Burton in June 1840. Six years later, the motto reemerged, again in slightly modified form ("lacessit" instead of "lacesset"), in Poe's elaborate revenge fantasy "The Cask of Amontillado," as the family motto of the Montresors. Poe might have come to know the motto through his foster father, John Allan, whose family belonged to the venerable Scottish order.[124]

Poe also could easily have made sense of the Latin motto, having received an excellent scholastic training thanks to the efforts of John and Frances Allan. According to Poe's earliest memories, he also spent long hours as a boy on the second floor of the mercantile establishment of John Allan and Charles Ellis, where in addition to books he found all kinds of popular magazines, from the *Edinburgh Review* to the *London Ladies' Magazine*. He also spent much time downstairs, working as a messenger and dry goods clerk for the Ellis and Allan firm.[125] If, as Whalen suggests, John Allan had entertained notions that Poe one day would embark on a mercantile career of his own, this worthy merchant must have felt disappointed over Poe's decision to become a writer.[126] Poe, for his part, unforgivingly portrayed Allan as a methodically materialistic businessman, who was intensely hostile to art: "If there is anything on earth I hate," he has the Business Man declare, "it is a genius. Your geniuses are all arrant asses — the greater the genius the greater the ass — and to this rule there is no exception whatsoever."[127]

Despite such bitter lines about John Allan, who Poe thought ignored or, worse, even despised his genius, Poe *was* transformed into a strange synthesis of art and commerce, a public intellectual transformed into a commercial writer. Yet Poe came to deeply despise commercial publishing. His contempt is given full expression in a sketch titled "How to Write a Blackwood Article," which establishes with obvious relish the following wisdom as the "leading principle" of magazine publishing: "when manuscript can be read it is never worth reading." In the sketch, which Poe wrote in 1838 and first published in *The Broadway Journal* of July 12, 1845, the narrator, the vain and pompous Signora Psyche Zenobia, receives instruction on how to "compose" a successful magazine article. One sure method is to take "a pair of tailor's-shears," and several papers, such as the "Times," "the "Examiner," and "Gulley's New Compendium of Slang-Whang." Then it is cutting out and interspersing, and another article "of the genuine Blackwood stamp" is ready to go. Further (and equally hilarious) instruction touches on incidents — including "*bizarreries*," "intensities," and articles of the "sensation stamp" — and tone — ranging from the didactic, enthusiastic, natural, common-place, laconic, and elevated, to the "interjectional" ("the best of all possible styles where the writer is in too great a hurry to think"), the metaphysical and, not to forget, the "heterogeneous" (in which the adept is free to "Hint everything — assert nothing"). "Piquant expressions," preferably in foreign languages, are to be interspersed also, as they lend an air of the knowledge of a language, as well as of one's general reading and wit.[128]

Clearly in "How to Write a Blackwood Article" Poe directs his scorn against an America that refuses to support serious writing because of its narrow focus on making money. Yet the panic of 1837 also sharpened Poe's understanding of the relation between literary production and production in a more general sense. As an editor with the *Broadway Journal*, he singled out *Hunt's Merchants' Magazine and Commercial Review* for the wide range of information it provided for merchant capitalists doing business in an expanding market. *Hunt's* was decidedly pro-paper money and pro-national bank in its editorial policy, facts that cannot have escaped Poe's attention. But Poe not only commended the magazine for its commercial utility and its views on monetary policy; attempting to fill up the columns of his own magazine, he often listed the entire table of contents of the latest issue of the magazine.

> The Value and Prospects of Life in the United States — The Cotton Trade — The System of Mutual Insurance examined with Reference to the Question of Individual Liberty — Maritime Law, Piracy and Financiering — Electricity as the Cause of Storms — The March of Our Republic — The Consular System — Pot and Pearl Ashes — and The Progress of Population in Boston. Besides these papers we have Mercantile Law Cases — Commercial Chronicle — Commercial regulations, etc. etc. — and several pages of judicious literary criticism.

Poe quoted this particular table of contents in *The Broadway Journal* of December 27, 1845.[129] By that time, *Hunt's* had been running for more than six years. Thus, Poe must have noticed essays such as Charles Francis Adams's on the "State of the Currency," "The Government and the Currency," stories on the South Sea Bubble, on "Railroads East and West," several reviews of George Tucker's 1839 book *The Theory of Money and Banks Investigated* (in which the reviewer passionately denounces the "party-ridden house of Congress," seeking in its stead "an upright and independent bank direction"), as well as Tucker's own essay in favor of a national paper currency. Poe also must have come across statistical tables of the principal gold and silver coins of the countries with which the United States then entertained commercial contacts (and which Poe may have remembered for the inventory of the treasure chest in "The Gold-Bug"), lists of the "free" banks formed under the General Banking Law, as well as reports on the coinage at the U.S. Mint or the increase of banking. Last but not least, Poe must have found Daniel Webster's call for keeping commercial paper money "within just bounds," several pleas respectively for a "national paper currency" and a "convenient national currency," plus the tables of bank suspensions that *Hunt's* also printed.[130]

It is probably too far-fetched to suggest that Freeman Hunt's monthly provided Poe with the "kernel of an idea" for "The Gold-Bug."[131] At the very least, however, the variety of articles in the magazine, which clearly represented the interests of the larger merchants, echoes the variety of conversation topics at the Allan dinner table. In addition, the range of information provided by *Hunt's* must have brought back memories of the economic education Poe received when Allan had moved the entire family to England in 1815, where they spent the next five years observing the turbulences and upheavals in what was then the leading industrial country in the world. Attempting to rebuild his business after the War of 1812 and the Napoleonic wars, John Allan confronted all kinds of social ills that had arisen during the depression. Two years into his stay, Allan told a correspondent, "you can have no idea of the distresses of this country since the termination of that long Contest which in its continuance had drenched Europe with blood."[132] For Allan, these were not so much idle remarks as trenchant observations that would have a direct impact on the success or failure of his business. For young Edgar, they provided an introduction to political economy as an important, all-encompassing discourse. His familiarity with this discourse served him well once he confronted the changed conditions of literary production in the aftermath of the panic of 1837.

Restoring Poe to his own culture through a reconstruction of the material conditions that impacted on this writer, Terence Whalen continues the efforts of other scholars to disabuse us from celebrating the separation of Poe's "art" from historical and social "reality." One such effort stems from Marc Shell, whose fine work on "The Gold-Bug" may be summarized in one sentence: "'Humbug' is a good name for the gold bug in 'The Gold-Bug' and for 'The Gold-Bug' itself."[133] In the nineteenth century, the verb "to bug" (or "to hum-bug") was a transitive verb meaning to deceive, to impose on, or to hoax. Yet critics have consistently classified the bug whose bite causes the "gold fever" in Poe's tale as if it were a specimen of beetle for entomological investigation. In doing so, Shell argues, these critics are like Legrand in his initial classificatory researches.[134] The categorization into species, however, is debunked in the tale, dismissed as one of several species of "sober mystification" with which to quietly "punish," not just the incredulous narrator for his lack of trust but also, by extension, readers and critics.[135] If they mistakenly believe that the bug is real, in the end they have to accept that indeed it is a thing that is not really what it pretends to be — like the gold of the hard-money advocates that also is not the money it pretends to be.[136]

Poe's Legrand, Marc Shell found, not only beats the entomological critics to the method of endlessly classifying, but he likewise beats the psychological ones to the method of classifying madness. Of course it is tempting to categorize the bug in the same way that one would classify the affliction that the spider in the epigraph to the tale is said to cause — the dance of the tarantula. In such a case, the gold bug might be classified as a species of "dung beetle," justifying the connection of gold with feces, lucre with filth. At the time of Poe, the noun "bug" meant "madman," and thus a psychoanalytic reading also might tend to classify the particular affliction from which Legrand, and possibly Poe, suffers.[137] Yet as Shell cautions, the gold bug is a "tricky symbol that debunks ordinary classification of both physical and mental things."[138] Shell's reasoning in this instance is similar to the very first critical response to Poe's tale in the *Philadelphia Forum* of June 27, 1843. In the response, which was titled "'The Gold-Bug' — a Decided Humbug," a certain "D" claims that "*humbug* beyond all question is at last the 'Philosopher's stone,' in the discovery of which so many geniuses have heretofore been bewildered."[139]

The discovery did not seem to bewilder political cartoonists of the period who connected both entomological and psychological investigation with the logic of monetary policy, thus connecting the tale's internal economics (Legrand's use of a gold bug impressed on paper to find gold) to external economics (the debates over what was to constitute America's money). Typically, in 1837 Henry R. Robinson issued a cartoon lithograph titled "N. Tom O'Logical [cf. entomological] Studies: The Great Tumble Bug of Missouri Bent-On Rolling His Ball," which is labeled "Expunging Resolution" with the line beneath reading "Solitary and alone." The cartoon ridicules Missouris Senator Thomas Hart Benton's unflinching support of President Jackson, who in 1834 had been criticized by the Senate for dismissing the Secretary of the Treasury in favor of a backer of his own anti–BUS and hard-money policy, which included the removal of federal deposits from the Bank of the United States. Benton and others who supported Jackson proposed to expunge the critical resolution from the senatorial record in 1837.[140]

In the same year, Robinson produced a caricature in the form of a joke note or "mock shinplaster." The word dates back to the Revolutionary War, when soldiers found that the Continental currency they were receiving as payment purchased very little but were great to bandage leg wounds. Hence "shinplaster" — what one used to bandage one's scraped or wounded shin. The word dropped out of favor but was revived during the 1830s to describe small-denomination scrip notes issued as supplements by commercial banks when President Jackson decreed that federal funds be transferred to them from the Bank of the United

States. Most such small notes, which ranged from 6¼ cents upward, circulated only in the area in which they were issued. If these notes were worth little at the time they were issued, they quickly became worthless, as they had backing no stronger than the financial credit of the issuer, which often was nil. The nation was flooded with these fractional notes, which for a time also drove out from circulation all subsidiary coin, like the copper half cent. It was in response to this unintended consequence that Jacksonian Democrats advocated the use of hard currency, or specie, of which there soon was to be a severe shortage eventually leading to the suspension of specie payments in 1837.

Robinson's satirical note depicts Jackson's treasure hunt for the gold that "real" notes were supposed to represent. The President is seen riding a pig headlong towards a precipice, followed by his devout ally, Senator Benton, on a donkey. Both are seen in pursuit of the "Gold Humbug" butterfly, a symbol of their efforts to restrict the ratio of paper money in circulation to gold and silver supplies. As Jackson reaches for the butterfly, he cries "By the eternal!! I'll have it, Benton!" Benton, of course, shouts encouragement, "Go it thou Roman!! A greater man ne'er lived in the tide of times!!" In contrast, president-elect Van Buren, riding a fox, cunningly strays from the two men's disastrous course, saying "Although I follow in the footsteps of Jackson, it is expedient at this time to deviate a little!" Thus he follows a downward path towards the bank — the Second Bank of the United States, against which Jackson had led his famous "war." From below the precipice, Nicholas Biddle, the Bank's president, sights Van Buren.

Robinson's mock shinplaster is dated May 10, 1837, the day of the emergency suspension of specie payments by New York banks. Poe was living in New York then, though how or whether he managed to maintain his household there seems wholly unknown. What we do

Henry R. Robinson, 50 cents, mock shinplaster ridiculing the Jacksonians' hard-money policies, 1837 (Library of Congress, Prints and Photographs Division, LC-USZ62–1582).

know is that after about a year in New York, Poe left for Philadelphia, probably in the spring or early summer of 1838.[141] The literary odd jobs Poe at first had in Philadelphia could only make him more miserable, however. Poe had been miserable enough already in New York, where he had arrived with the manuscript of *The Narrative of Arthur Gordon Pym*, whose eponymous hero begins the narration by telling us that his "maternal grandfather [...] had speculated very successfully in stocks of the Edgarton New-Bank, as it was formerly called." Poe had published two installments of *Pym* in the *Southern Literary Messenger* early in 1837, but revised them slightly and continued expanding the story in New York. In May, Harper and Brothers announced that Poe's first book of fiction was nearly ready for publication, but the economic cataclysm of the same month forced the publishers to delay the book's final appearance for more than a year, until July 1838.[142]

Poe's financial situation remained precarious even after the publication of *Pym*. He may have made a little money from the American edition of the novella, but for the two pirated English editions, he of course received nothing. Poe seems to have received twenty dollars for two pieces thereafter, yet from the end of January 1837, when he left the *Southern Literary Messenger* for New York, to the early summer of 1839, his total earnings were less than a hundred and fifty dollars, or roughly sixteen cents a day.[143] When seen in the context of Poe's near-shipwreck, Robinson's joke note has a direct bearing on "The Gold-Bug." The futile hunt, by Jackson, Benton, and Van Buren, for the gold that "real" notes are supposed to represent (the "gold humbug") becomes a vital clue in any attempt to determine the logical place of the gold bug in Poe's tale. Ontology provides the clue. "A humbug is a thing that is not."[144] For Poe's contemporaries, connections between ontology and political economy were important. The discussions, I have suggested, centered around the question how, if at all, paper money represented anything substantial.

"If the currency consists of the precious metals, it has an intrinsic value," George Wood wrote in *Hunt's Merchants' Magazine* of April 1841; "if of credit [paper], its value arises from its representing other property, viz, the specie in the vaults, and the other funds and assets of the bank." If that is the case, Wood argues, paper becomes "an article of value," ceasing to be "a mere sign of value." In other words, paper money must be fully convertible, lest it depreciates. Wood's arguments clearly reflect the fear, founded on experience, that paper money from the commercial banks was not always fully convertible. His theoretical base is David Ricardo, whom he quotes at length:

> A currency is in its most perfect state when it consists wholly of paper money, but of paper money of equal value with the gold it professes to represent. The use of paper instead of gold substitutes the cheapest in the place of the most expensive medium, and enables the country, without loss to any individual, to exchange all the gold which it before used for this purpose for raw materials, utensils, and food, by the use of which both its wealth and its enjoyments are increased.[145]

The question of representation indeed was a crucial one among political economists at the time, repeating in ideological form the debate about the relationship between symbols and things. In Poe's tale, the search for species in the physical world (including the search for bugs) and the study of species in the internal world of the mind (including psychological species like insanity) thus goes beyond merely connecting nature and psyche, or things with our ideas of them. The search for species and specimens turns into a search for specie in the sense of precious coins.[146] Yet the precious coins that Legrand and his fellow money-diggers find are old, of antique date, and cannot therefore form a circulating currency, which, following George Wood, "is that commodity of value which circulates through society, and in its circulation is used in paying for property sold, and in the liquidation of debts."[147]

The political implications of the uselessness as currency of the coins from Kidd's treasure probably were not lost on Poe's readers. If they were, Poe's strategy to persistently expel monetary politics from his writings to ensure their marketability across the entire nation would have paid off. Nevertheless, Poe could not afford any permanent estrangement from the real world of money and banking, though the disdain he felt toward the debates over the nation's money rather provoked him into satirizing the controversies. The result was an elaborate hoax hinging on the word "humbug." The radical Democrat Samuel Young in 1840 called "humbug" the paper dollars that the banks were issuing in lieu of specie, reversing Henry Robinson's earlier use of "gold humbug," which implied a critique of gold money. Poe, using the word "humbug," puns on both of these meanings. Following Marc Shell one more time, the word "humbug" thus is "a good name for the gold bug in 'The Gold-Bug' *and* for 'The Gold-Bug' itself."[148]

Gathered together, the various strands of this chapter provide what may be a surprisingly straightforward answer to the question raised at the outset: why does Poe, in "The Gold-Bug," stress so emphatically that there was "no American money" in the treasure? The evidence explored here reveals a paradox about the monetary situation in antebellum America. Although gold and, to an extent, silver were hailed as "real" money, gold and silver coins, having taken wings and flown away, simply were not available in real life. Paper bills, in contrast, were available in quantity, though they were often — and for good reason — derided as "filthy rags." If the precariousness of America's money in the aftermath of the panic of 1837 accounts for the absence of American money in "The Gold-Bug," the unearthed treasure also is not an unqualified boon: on a theoretical level, the treasure is capital seeking investment only potentially; within the logic of the tale, it is merely a "golden burthen."[149] Certainly with "The Gold-Bug," Poe responded to the economic upheavals of the time most directly, yet other writings, too, reveal his preoccupation with the economic and political situation that I have tried to make better sense of in this chapter. Altogether in these writings, the future appears as much worse than the present, and Poe supplies powerful images for this estimation — of a devouring maelstrom; of a house torn apart and sinking into stagnant water; of a fiery overthrow (in "The Colloquy of Monos and Una"); and of humans as mere puppets, at the beck and call of a conqueror worm. Was Poe, then, unable or unwilling to provide any alternative to these visions of cataclysm? Did he conceive of disaster as the only option for the future? Put differently, would "The Gold-Bug" have become such a popular story if it provided only bad news for its readers? Any adequate understanding of Poe's position on the money question must bring clearly into view that "The Gold-Bug" is about a treasure found, and so we might legitimately ask if Poe did not also provide a glimpse of a brighter monetary future in this tale, if not in others of his writings.

2

Captain Kidd's Treasure
and the Paper System
Questions of Trust

Poe in many ways responded to the predicaments of America's money and the miserable banking system of his time. This estimation applies with particular force to "The Gold-Bug." To appreciate this response, I considered it best to begin my search outside the narrow level of content. Identifying the telltale signs of real-world pressures in the realm of literary form, however, seemingly contradicts the tale's palpable theme or topic—the search for money, which has long been accepted as the major theme. "The intent of the author," Thomas Dunn English, possibly after a discussion with Poe, wrote in the *Aristidean* for October 1845, "was evidently to write a popular tale: money, and the finding of money being chosen as the most popular thesis."[1] Poe himself was acutely aware of the theme's popularity, writing, in *Graham's Magazine* for November 1841, of Samuel Warren's novel *Ten Thousand a Year*: "[A] main source of the interest which this book possesses for the mass, is to be referred to the *pecuniary* nature of its theme. From beginning to end it is an affair of pounds, shillings, and pence—a topic which comes at least *as* immediately to the bosoms and business of mankind, as any which could be selected."[2] The claim that the search for money is the tale's overt theme or topic thus seems beyond dispute, the more so as in the case of "The Gold-Bug" supply meets demand, the logic of which transforms this popular tale about money and the finding of money into a prime example of the application of economic doctrine to the realm of letters.

It would be easier to continue with the complex relations between "The Gold-Bug" and American capitalism if one could in good conscience ignore other efforts to elevate this tale above other histories and stories about "money-seekers." These efforts do not generally attend to the conditions of literary production that tinged and modified this celebrated tale. They are, for instance, silent on the competitive pressures due to gross literary overproduction, much as they are silent on Poe's extreme caution, motivated by the search for a large nation-wide audience, in relation to the more controversial issues of the time. Not surprisingly, therefore, readings that narrowly attend to the literary merits of "The Gold-Bug" generally are linked to the author's status as an exceptional genius. Charles Baudelaire for instance noted that Poe's tale was "above the common intellectual level." This estimation is supported, if inadvertently, by a reply, to charges of plagiarism, in the *Dollar Newspaper* for July 19, 1843: "The man who should write a tale upon the subject of finding money, and propose, at the same time, to be original in his *theme*, must be a fool. But every one knows that the truest and surest test of *originality* is the manner of handling a hackneyed subject."[3]

What unites Baudelaire, the writer of the reply, and modern critics such as Marc Shell is the conviction that the tale's true originality lies outside the mere *seeking for* or *finding of* money but is rather internalized in the mode of the telling and in its symbols. Already Thomas Dunn English noticed as much, when he writes that the bug, "which gives title to the story, is used only in the way of mystification, having throughout a seeming and no real connection with the subject."[4] What is mystified is at first sight the connection between the gold and the skull and the skeletons, between gold and death and violence. Ignoring this connection, it is quite possible to explain away the gold as purely metaphorical, the outcome, for instance, of Poe's romantic fascination with death.[5] Again by ignoring the connection, the golden bug becomes a mere representation, "an avatar of the philosopher's stone," the perfect "seed" that is both "revived and multiplied in the form of treasure."[6] Yet the adeptness in the philosophy of alchemy that Poe put to work in his tale produces rather a reversal of the process. The completion of the *opus magnum*, the great work, lies not in the transmutation of something base into gold so much as in the — implicit rather than explicit — transmutation of treasure into a circulating currency.

The notion that a treasure can be transformed into a circulating currency links "The Gold-Bug" with traditional identifications of value with substance, together with the debates this identification gave rise to — from their origins in Britain to the constitutional debates in America and, finally, to Emerson's pronouncement that a paper currency is employed when there is no bullion in the bank vaults. In "The Gold-Bug," Poe enters into and turns these identifications inside out. Indeed, that tale is replete with words and phrases suggesting the world of money — from "gold bug" meaning a supporter of the gold standard, which entered the English language through Poe's tale, to "stamp," "seal," or "signature," which are all known features on paper money, and, finally, to references to green and red "tints." It is little known that Poe added these references only in a later version of the tale; it is probably even less known that these additions allude to inks of those colors that at the time were used as anti-counterfeiting devices on bank bills. The intertextual reference to counterfeiting reveals that the problem that bedeviled the antebellum period was one of confidence. Confidence was, however, a politically divisive issue: to establish a measure of confidence, the Whigs sough to strengthen the power of the central government, including the right to issue notes. The Democrats, enthralled by Jackson, could envisage only gold and silver, which they considered as nature's money. Given the divisiveness of the issue, the two-part structure of "The Gold-Bug," which leaves the treasure episode unfinished, acquires a special significance: it marks Poe's inability or unwillingness to make potentially divisive statements in his creative works. Yet as we will see, references to trust abound in this tale. My discussion thus will move into the direction of trust — as a central issue in "The Gold-Bug," as the *conditio sine qua non* of a paper money economy, and, in the form of certainty grounded in a reliable authority, as one of the era's deepest desires.

Money Never Is Money: Uses of Kidd's Treasure

That Captain Kidd's hoard is not an unqualified boon is suggested by certain words in the tale itself. When the party of money-finders reaches Legrand's hut for the second time, they, in a state of fatigue, "deposited" their "golden burthens."[7] A "burthen" or "burden" of course means a load, any load, including one of gold, as is evident from the mid-fifteenth-century *York Mystery Plays*. In its figurative usage, the *Oxford English Dictionary* describes the word as a load of labor, duty, responsibility, blame, sin, despair, or sorrow, the latter appearing in Chaucer's translation of Boethius. In addition, the word means a kind of tax, an obligatory expense, whether due on private account or as a contribution to national funds, pressing heavily. None of these meanings is entirely pleasant, and each contradicts the sensuous pleasure and sheer exuberance the money-finders exhibit when the treasure first lies before them, "gleaming." Clearly the finding of the treasure takes place in a magical setting, in a temporality so alien to history that it constitutes a separate place: Never-Never Land. Yet the anti-climactic depositing of the treasure also does not take place in the real world. In this detached island world, the unearthed gold thus is at best a store of value, but not a medium of exchange. As a mere commodity, it is a "thing" that is subject to the laws of supply and demand and thus is as "insensible" in the economic system of exchange as paper.[8]

The pirate's treasure, insofar as it does not constitute a claim against goods and services, is not money in the sense of capital or currency. Poe seems to have sensed this when he has his money-finders "*deposit*" the gold. Of course, after hours of physical labor the men must have been only too glad to be able to put down their heavy burden. Yet when they are said to "deposit" it, one cannot help but think of banks, the usual place for placing — depositing — money at interest. Poe's pun — if that is what is constituted by the conjunction of "deposit" and "burthen" — thus points to the economic commonplace that any "treasure" is useless until it is returned to society, there to become money. Henry C. Carey, describing the mechanisms of pricing in *Hunt's Merchants' Magazine* of May 1840, expressed the point in the following way: "Prices are dependent upon the relation existing between the amounts of property of every description in which the owners of unemployed capital may invest it, and the amount of capital seeking investment, and constituting currency."[9] Carey's choice of words — "capital," "currency" — implies that money, regardless of its substance, involves something more than its physical qualities. Money, in fact, never *is* money; it always *becomes* money as a variety of social and cultural arrangements accrue. To phrase the matter differently, anything can become money by usage, that is, by virtue of a communicative situation in which there is trust and confidence between those who place currency into circulation and those who use it, for instance to make payments with.

Ralph Waldo Emerson, in the section of his *Conduct of Life* titled "Wealth," wrote that all money, whether coin or paper, is "representative." Therefore, the "value of a dollar is social, as it is created by society." The statement was insightful. It spells out that the value of a given monetary token is not absolute, but the product of all kinds of social negotiations. Neither paper bills nor coins have any value beyond the contexts in which they circulate. Their value derives from social consensus and use, which is why, for instance, "a dollar in a University, is worth more than a dollar in a jail."[10] America's "gold bugs" never saw money in this way. In their logic, gold always already *was* money.[11] Conversely, to say that paper money also was money meant to accept that something is made out of nothing. According to the gold bugs, this is an achievement that only God and his great opponent were capable of. There was one exception to this widely accepted rule — the realm of aesthetics. Already Sir Philip Sidney, in his humanist treatise on the social function of poetry, claimed that the poet, thanks to "the vigour of his own invention," grows "in effect another nature, in making things either better than nature bringeth forth or, quite anew, forms such as never were in nature."[12] Romantic artists in the nineteenth century likewise were fascinated by the generative power of the human intellect, what Poe called the "poetical excitement."[13] If, as many of his contemporaries believed, Poe indeed was "a dreamer," producing "imaginations wild, reckless, metaphysical, delighting in paradox, reveling in the marvelous," we may find convincing the evaluation, by a modern critic, that it is "actually Legrand's romantic imagination that helps to accomplish the multiplication of the gold bug into Captain Kidd's treasure."[14]

Legrand's intellectual glow-worm, however, also accomplishes the multiplication of the gold bug into the *Scarabaeus* beetle and, via the insect, into the financial institutions that render treasure from paper.[15] *Scarabaeus* beetles have a habit of rolling up a ball of dung, in which they have laid their eggs. From them, larvae develop, and finally the young beetles hatch. For the ancient Egyptians there was a strong resemblance between the dung ball being pushed around and the sun as it appears on the horizon every morning. Hence, *Scarabaeus* beetles were put on one level with the god of the rising sun, *Chepre*, and representations of them appeared on jewelry and amulets, or else in graves, made of clay or soapstone, symbolic of the pledge that life arises ever and ever again. What the Egyptians did not know was that the *Scarabaeus* beetles they held sacred develop from larvae. Hence they assumed that there must be a creation out of nothing, *ex nihilo*. The rendering of treasure from paper likewise has been seen as a creation out of nothing. Goethe, in dealing with the devilish deed at issue in the paper money scene orchestrated by Mephistopheles, wrote in the second part of *Faust*: "Such currency, in gold and jewels' place, / Is neat, it bears its value on its face."[16]

In Andrew Jackson's America, the idea of creating something out of nothing served as ideological ammunition in the debates over the nation's money. William Gouge, one of the staunchest hard-money men, in his *Journal of Banking* of December 8, 1841, reprinted a poem satirizing *ex nihilo* creation:

> "Ex nihilo nihil fit," was once
>   A maxim much in vogue with some;
> But few indeed can *now* maintain
> That "nothing can from nothing come."

The reason that this assumption was no longer valid is, of course, paper money:

> For though the ancients could convert
> *Their* gold to rags, (as we are told,)
> Yet we, in times more civilized
> Can make from rags the best of gold.[17]

To accept the transformation by magic of flimsy paper into concrete capital—at the time a truly alchemical vision of wealth creation—meant to take on the entire Aristotelian tradition, which firmly held that finance merely makes something out of nothing, or out of nothing natural.[18] Aristotle abhorred the value-generating properties of money when it is used in trade, loaned out against interest, or used for purposes of speculation. Yet notwithstanding the demonization of money that came with Aristotle and the Aristotelian tradition, open, profit-oriented monetary systems did evolve, and the philosopher's distinction between *oikos* (the "rule of the household") and *chrematistos* (an open economic system comprising trade, debt, and speculation) was no longer viable. It became an ideal, not a lived or livable reality. Reality spelt paper money, which was here to stay. As a result, from the eighteenth-century onwards public discussion came to focus on the disturbing manner of representation and exchange in the form of paper money.

The debates at first arose in Britain, where suspicion towards money that was printed on otherwise worthless pieces of paper met with the forced recognition of the purely symbolic nature of such money. Daniel Defoe, attending to John Law's scheme of a bank that would issue paper notes to borrowers against the security of lands owned by the state, in 1720 dismissed paper credit as a "chimera"—that is, "an inconceivable Species of meer Air and Shadow, realizing Fancies and Imaginations, Visions and Apparitions, and making the meer speculations of Things, act all the Parts, and perform all the Offices of the Things themselves; and thus in a moment their Debts are all vanish'd, the Substance is answer'd by the Shadow, and [...] the name of the thing is made an Equivalent to the Thing itself."[19] Defoe was not merely interested in what John Law was doing in France. His pamphlet also was to serve as a warning to his fellow Britons not to take financial matters lightly. The 1720s in Britain indeed were a period of monetary scandal. Yet the period also saw the increasing influence of a new moneyed, mercantile class that was taking over power from the established, landed one. Social change thus spawned any number of moral attacks on paper money. Characteristically, Alexander Pope in his "Epistle to Lord Bathurst" in 1733 satirized such money as the root of all kinds of social evils and its devastating effect on personality: "Blest paper-credit! Last and best supply! / That lends corruption lighter wings to fly!"[20]

The debates fueled by the supposed unreality of wealth based on paper money did not escape the colonists across the Atlantic. In 1730, Ebenezer Cooke, a poet from colonial Maryland, took up the subject in his burlesque poem *Sot-Weed Factor Redivivus*. The piece marks an important departure from the English conservative tradition of satirizing paper as incompatible with the supposed securities of land and precious metal. Slyly advertising *Sot-Weed* as "Waste Paper" (meaning not only "trash" but also "accounting book") and "Home-Spun Weeds" (suggesting a measure of sovereignty from England), Cooke goes on to urge the colonial authorities to abandon both their false hopes in the importation of gold and silver and reliance on the traditional tobacco currency ("Indian Weed ... secure in bags"); the future, Cooke suggested, lay in "Paper made of Rags."[21] Cooke never received the attention he would have deserved, though another colonist, John Wise did. Wise, a native of Roxbury, Massachusetts, who became a Congregationalist divine and political leader, wrote in support of a land bank the year after Law's scheme collapsed. Arguing that such a bank's bills would stimulate economic growth, Wise claimed that "we [...] can turn other matter into Silver and Gold by the Power of thought as soon as any other People."[22]

In the writings of American colonists such as Cooke or Wise paper money becomes associated with a theory of value that resists the traditional identification of value with substance. Whereas essentialist fictions explain money primarily through its physical qualities, Cooke, Wise, and others accepted that money was derived from a great number of social and cultural arrangements, including from debt. The theory itself was not spelt out until much later, and the popular use of paper money at first was only an emergency measure resulting from the chronic shortage of metallic money. Thus contingencies of economic exchange rather than theoretical deliberations or political convictions drove most if not all

American colonies to embracing paper money to solve their monetary and economic problems. Theory and political debate came later, explaining or attending to a *fait accompli*. In
this regard, no one came closer in influence to Benjamin Franklin, who clearly saw that the
value of paper (the material substance on which monetary engravings are printed) had nothing to do with the notes' value as money. Franklin thus was quite prepared to see all types
of money as commodities, though as regards paper money he kept insisting that the notes
were to be respectively backed by land, by gold or silver, by loans, or by actual or potential
government power and commitment. That being the case, paper money would make people
associate one with another, would enliven and quicken social intercourse, turn over products
and ideas, encourage the poor and ensure that the rich spread their wealth about them by
buying things and employing people, and, not to forget, would act as a magnet to new settlers.

Franklin laid down many of his ideas about money in a 1729 pamphlet entitled "A
Modest Enquiry into the Nature and Necessity of a Paper Currency."[23] The pamphlet was
well received in America. It was printed all through the colonies, and within a decade
Franklin had secured contracts to print paper money for at least three of them — his home
colony of Pennsylvania; the colonies of Delaware and New Jersey; and, finally, an entire
country, the United States of America. Yet Franklin not only established the matrix of land,
debt, and paper money that was to shape American life for more than a century, he also
went before a British parliamentary committee in 1767, trying to convince the colonial over-
lords of the advantages of paper money for the colonies. Paper money, Franklin argued, had
swept away "the extreamly inconvenient method of barter ... gave new life to business, [and]
promoted greatly the settlement of new lands."[24] The British were unconvinced. For them,
using paper money to bolster colonial economies made no sense. Not only was the point
of having colonies to provide raw materials cheap to the mother country; the British also
suspected that paper money would release unruly and uncontrollable ambitions among the
colonists. It turned out that they were right on this point. Twenty-some years after the
British Parliament put a ban on paper money the War of Independence had been won —
by the unruly and uncontrollable American colonists.

The unruly and uncontrollable colonists may have won their war of independence, yet
they did so in a truly unique way, as never before had a people gone to war without money
to pay for it. The Continental Congress, assembled in Philadelphia in May 1775, had no
authority to impose taxes, while the states were unwilling to do so in any measure that
would have been adequate to paying for the enterprise. Thus a finance committee recommended that Congress issue bills of credit. Beginning in June 1775, the "Continental Currency" was issued. The currency notes essentially were the earliest symbols of the sovereignty
of the United States. Building national identity only made up one semantic network, however, while other such networks were constituted by the desire for economic and political
stability. Whereas the national symbolic became a true success story, the latter became a
disaster. Legally, the "Continentals," as the bills came to be known, were money that had
the form of debt. The problem was that they were printed in such excessive numbers that
the result was hyperinflation. By 1782, one needed $7,500 in Continental paper bills to get
$100 in silver.[25]

Under the Constitution, the United States repaid its debts to foreign nations for their
aid during the revolutionary war. Payment of all federal debts also was reassumed. Of the

One-dollar Continental currency note, May 10, 1775, face, motto "DEPRESSA RESURGIT" ("Though oppressed, it rises"), original size 10.49 × 13.73cm (American Numismatic Association Money Museum).

Continental currency, however, only a tiny fraction of their face value was redeemed — at a rate of $100 in bills for $1 in coin. Even this came to an end by March 7, 1793, after which the bills no longer had any official exchange value. It is no surprise that the ill-begotten Continentals came to be remembered as "omens of public bankruptcy." Souring many Americans on the idea of a paper currency for generations to come, the Continentals also precipitated a profound shift in political commitment. The Jeffersonians were not only united in their distrust of banks in general, which they feared were undermining the power of the government; they also followed Thomas Jefferson's suspicion that banking was imitative of British manners and institutions and thus a further threat to America's Republican heritage.[26] Their fears and suspicions only became exaggerated and vulgarized in the Jacksonian era. Thus by the 1830s, paper-money advocacy, which from the 1730s had served to link the currency question with anti-royalist protest and the movement toward political sovereignty, had shifted to the Whig Party, usually considered to represent the wealthy business community; by contrast, the hard-money advocacy of the pre-revolutionary Tory Loyalists had been adopted as the monetary politics of the Democratic Party.

Typically, in August 1839 Charles Francis Adams, grandson of John Adams, son of John Quincy Adams, and a staunch Whig, denounced "the proposition of an exclusively metallic medium" as "monstrous," as the ill-fated work of "one class of politicians [who are] least of all qualified to judge of its probable operation."[27] Just as typically, William Gouge adopted for his *Journal of Banking* Alexander Pope's satirical lines on "paper credit," which allegedly lends corruption "lighter wings to fly."[28] Gouge's partisan intervention came during the administration of John Tyler, when the introduction of Treasury notes was a serious option. When the bank war began in the early 1830s, William Leggett, a leader of the Loco-Focos faction of New York's Democrats and a supporter of Jackson's hard money policies, likewise adopted a position that seemingly was indistinguishable from the Tory loyalism of the pre-revolutionary era. "A cheap [and] most effectual method of disseminating the principles of those opposed to incorporated rag-money factories," Leggett wrote in the New York *Evening Post*, "would be for them to write upon the back of every bank-note which should come into their possession, some short sentence expressive of their sentiments. For example — 'No Monopolies!' [...] 'Jackson and Hard Money!' 'Gold before Rags!' and the like."[29]

Leggett's enthusiasm was fueled by the introduction, beginning August 1, 1834, of new gold coins, whose gold content had been reduced and which therefore were exchangeable at par with paper bills. The Act, which was largely the work of Senator Benton, did not have the desired effect, though. As in earlier times, many of the new coins instantly disappeared from circulation. At the same time, gold minted before August 1, 1834, and of heavier weight, continued to sell at a premium over paper money. The financial and economic crisis following Jackson's war against the bank put an end to the experiment in 1836. Two years earlier, observers such as Leggett had envisioned or at least hoped that the new gold coins would signal the end of paper money. Such visions or hopes were not realized, though Leggett, by proposing that paper bills be turned into political leaflets, at least recognized that these texts offered new possibilities of public communication. Paper bills, though they were derided as rag-money, derived special power and appeal from the fact that they could address a broad and impersonal readership anonymously. The mock shinplasters likewise addressed such a readership, parodying the fractional currency that had come into circulation because of the shortage of hard money that accompanied the limited-currency policy Leggett endorsed and that continued beyond the immediate context of 1834.

By the time of the great panic of 1837, genuine as well as mock bills were part of a whole network of written and printed words proliferating across their spatiality — like street signs, handbills, trade cards, sandwich-board advertisements, parade banners, and daily newspapers in which political cartoons found a congenial home. Leggett's ironic awareness of paper dollars as handbills, together with the presence of mock shinplasters and hard times tokens are good reminders that money never was simply an economic issue. It also was a cultural issue, linking unrelated people and objects in networks of circulation and exchange. Money thus constituted a powerful symbol of the way of life that came with modernization and modernity. This way of life was by definition contradictory, and so was the new paper money. Based as it was on debt secured to a greater or lesser extent by real assets, paper money not only depended on trust and confidence but also invited the possibility of fraud or, at the very least, serious disappointment. It is no exaggeration to say that such money depended on credulousness. To phrase the matter differently, modern money — currency — depends on promises, and promises, as the saying goes, are also made to be broken.

Emerson's dictum that a paper currency is employed "when there is no bullion in the vaults" does not bear out its general application, though it seems justified in a number of cases. The law in most states provided that currency could be issued up to five times the amount of specie actually owned by a bank and in its possession, but some banks violated this limit and issued more. During the 1842 bank riots in Cincinnati, Ohio, inspectors found that the Miami Bank had some $224,000 of notes in its vaults, of which $218,000 was of its own notes; the amount of specie was $1,261.[30] A number of banks took to borrowing specie from other banks and exhibited it to the bank commissioners as capital stock paid in. An extreme case is reported from Michigan, where the Jackson County Bank in 1838 placed before the commissioners "a goodly number of ponderous and well-filled boxes, but on opening them and examining their contents was found covered with [Spanish] silver dollars, but below was found nothing but nails and glass."[31]

Another widespread practice was to cheat by calling bank drafts "specie." There were also a number of banks whose stock was held by persons who, unable to pay for it, hypothecated it to the bank as collateral security for stock notes that were discounted to meet the installments of paying in as they were called for. Still other banks never even organized and never went into the banking business. Their owners simply ordered large quantities of bills from a printer, which they sold at deep discounts to exchange brokers, usually in New York and other large cities farther south. From there, the notes were sent — by the carpetbag full, hence the term "carpet-bagger" — to some distant state to get them into circulation there. If they could not be exchanged for commodities in which there might be a profit, a deal was struck with the courier from another exchange broker for an exchange — usually on a quid pro quo basis — of notes from another bank.[32] Practices of this kind, which are also known from legally chartered banks, usually engendered warnings and notices in newspapers and magazines. For instance, *Niles' Weekly Register* on October 1, 1836, printed a notice from the Paterson *Intelligencer* about an application to the New Jersey state legislature to incorporate a company for the manufacturing of sugar from beets, and with banking and trust powers. *Niles'* professed to "eschew this alliance of the root of evil with the beet root. The cultivation of the last [...] will no doubt prove profitable and advantageous. But if they are to be raised by a *beet bank*, we fear more attention will be paid to it than to the beet-beds."[33]

News accounts of this type may well have attracted the attention of Poe, who once noted that "Lucian, in describing the statue 'with its surface of Parian marble and its interior filled with rags,' must have been looking with a prophetic eye at some of our great 'moneyed institutions.'"[34] In society at large, news accounts about wayward bank practices certainly contributed to a general mood in which, following Bowers, "one would be hard pressed today to find a single cogent contemporaneous explanation by a national writer to advance the issuance of more paper money."[35] One such explanation —*pace* Q. David Bowers — was articulated in a contribution to *Hunt's Merchants' Magazine* of April 1841. Its author, George Wood, saw the advantages of paper money quite clearly:

> Paper money is carried without difficulty. It is easily counted. The loss of wear and tear of a specie currency is all prevented by the use of paper. The loss of specie in the transportation is saved by the use of paper [...] Paper sunk is no loss to the community at large. Another advantage of a paper currency is its flexibility — its power of expanding and contracting from time to time, so as to accommodate itself to the business wants of the community.[36]

Wood's defense of paper money is entirely utilitarian. While he emphasizes its convenience, he says nothing about the theoretical issue that was plaguing contemporaries. It was gold supporters like William Leggett, a partisan of Jackson's Democrats, William Gouge, financial advisor to President Jackson, or Condy Raguet, a well-known Philadelphia observer of finance and the likely originator of the term "fraudulent banks," who were offended by the fact that paper, which unlike gold does not possess a substantial value, could be a carrier of currency. They thus demanded its abolishment.[37] Especially when there was an economic crisis, the issue, which was merely the logical result of the increasing degree of abstraction that accompanies progress in a monetized economy, heated up time and again. The tendency, by Poe and his contemporaries, to base the distinction between paper money and gold or silver money on the relationship between substance (paper, precious metal) and sign or symbol (the inscription or imprint on a coin or bank note) had other consequences as well. Supposing that the inscription disappears from a coin, it may be a coin no longer, yet it is still a valuable commodity.

In "The Gold-Bug," this question comes up in the narrator's account of "several very large and heavy coins, so worn that we could make nothing of their inscription." When, however, the commodity disappears, is the inscription still valid, as is paper money, which is only symbolic? In Poe's tale, this question is merely hypothetical, as we are told that there was "no American money."[38] No mere hypothesis, however, is the distinction between paper money and gold or silver money. It entails the question whether the shadow that is paper money can become as valuable as, or even more valuable than, the substance that is precious metal. An answer to this question cannot be had from Legrand, who is not only blind to "the loveliest thing in creation" — the sunrise — but at first is just as blind to the mechanics of currency, though Poe is not. True, Poe said at one point that the social, political, and cultural world could do no more than "momentarily repress" the development of art, whose principles "lie deep within the immortal nature of man, and have little necessary reference to the worldly circumstances which surround him."[39] On the other hand, it may be well to trust, not the artist, but the art, for "The Gold-Bug" does involve contemporary discourses about money, Poe's poetic credo or posing notwithstanding.

Green and Red Tints: Monetary Discourses in "The Gold-Bug"

Contemporary discourses about money are evident in "The Gold-Bug" from a multitude of words and phrases that suggest the world of paper or paper money. We may begin with the "dirty foolscap" on which Legrand makes his "rough drawing," which points beyond its literal meaning of a cap worn by fools or jesters to a watermark for paper and, additionally, to writing- or printing-paper.[40] The piece of paper in question (the "scrap") only has the "appearance of paper," but in reality is a "parchment," a term that was widely used to denote paper money, down to scrip notes and small-denomination bills.[41] The form of the parchment, we are told, is oblong, or at least was so originally, as Legrand does not fail to observe. If this suggests some meaning, it is yet another reminder that large, rectangular pieces of paper with numerals, phrases, and images on them have served as paper money at least since the beginning of the modern era. Thus it is entirely appropriate that the "scrap" bears a mark. Legrand, because he "perceive[s]" the mark, is finally led to the buried treasure, while the incredulous narrator and, by extension, the reader, are quite literally left wearing a fool's cap. There is another telling incident when Legrand, who almost crumples up the paper to throw it into the fire, has his attention suddenly riveted by the drawing, examines it carefully and, "presently took from his pocket a wallet, placed the paper carefully in it, and deposited both in a writing-desk, which he locked." Equally suggestive of the world of paper money is Legrand's realization that "Matters of little moment are rarely consigned to parchment," just as they are also not consigned to the paper used for currency: in each instance, there is a "record of something to be long remembered and carefully preserved," hence some special "meaning — some relevancy."[42]

One detail of the paper's (the "vellum's")[43] surface even appears as a "signature." Moreover, when Legrand turns the paper over, the sketch of the beetle he has made is revealed, as if it were the back design of a piece of paper money.[44] The narrator, who finds himself "not a little puzzled at what [his] friend had depicted," does not see the design of the beetle but sees, instead, a "death's head at the corner diagonally opposite." This death's head, the story continues, "had, in the same manner, the air of a stamp, or seal." Stamps or seals are known symbols of permanence and features that are well known also from paper money, down to the dollar sign ("$"), which first appeared on United States obligations in 1837 and which would certainly answer Poe's description of an "ominous insignium."[45] Also known features of paper money are various forms of cipher writing or inscriptions. Critics have attacked Poe for the supposedly inaccurate ciphering and cryptography in Captain Kidd's message. However, these critics miss an important point. Often so-called "errors" were purposefully incorporated in paper money inscriptions in order to trap or deter counterfeiters.[46]

All details on the parchment's surface are brought to light only by subjecting the paper to heat. As Legrand explains to the incredulous narrator, they had been applied to the paper by certain "chemical preparations" that respectively yield green or red "tints."[47] Green and red are complementary colors, as Goethe had established in his theory of colors. It is quite possible that Poe, whose interest in science and related matters is well known, was familiar with Goethe's theory. More important than an assumed familiarity with a particular theory, however, is the fact that Poe added the passage about the tints only to the revised version of 1845.[48] This version also contains another addition referring to coloring. As Legrand is about to explain the invisible ink to the narrator, he submits the re-heated paper to his friend's "inspection." The 1843 version continues like this: "The following characters were rudely traced between the death's-head and the goat." In the 1845 version, Poe inserted the phrase "in a red tint," so that the final passage reads as follows: "The following characters were rudely traced, *in a red tint*, between the death's-head and the goat."[49]

What significance — political, economic, or otherwise — are we to deduce from Poe's later insertion of the "tint" passages into the text of "The Gold-Bug"? Poe had written about secret writing in *Alexander's Weekly Messenger* and the *Southern Literary Messenger* as early as 1839, and he continued the series in *Graham's Magazine* from July to December 1842. Additionally, he drew on the article "Ink" from Abraham Rees's *Cyclopaedia* for information about an invisible writing fluid.[50] Poe may not have had any practical experience with invisible inks when he composed "The Gold-Bug," and in fact may have mistaken green for blue.[51] This oversight, if it is one, even corresponds with Poe's use of color words in his writings. Both in the tales and in the poetry the words "white" and "black" appear the most frequently. "Red," too, has a wide range of use, often to intensify the horror of a given situation, but greens and blues Poe uses very little, and they are insignificant even in his poetry. The word "blue," for instance, is used mostly in a very conventional way, as in "blue eyes" or "blue skies;" "green," in contrast, appears mostly in landscape pieces, such as "The Land-scape Garden." The appearance of "green" in "The Gold-Bug" thus seems to attach to this color a much greater importance than a tabulated percentage can reveal.[52] A link can be established, for instance, between Poe's references to coloring in the revised version of the tale and the invention of photographic methods in the 1840s. The invention not only led to a flourishing market in portrait photography but also instantly caught the attention of counterfeiters, which gives a quite unexpected twist to Susan Sontag's argument that "To photograph is to appropriate the thing photographed."[53]

Accounts of daguerreotype images on exhibition had appeared in the American press in early 1839. In September, *Niles'* published the first account in the United States of the process, a mere month after its inventor had first described it. A year later, the first photographic manual was published in the United States. In 1843, the Cincinnati *Sun* wrote that "a process of daguerreotype has been discovered in that city, for imitating bank notes, &c.," which if true, would achieve quite a "revolution in the credit system." A revolution indeed, as a certain Jack Cantar, who on more than one occasion described himself as "nothing more nor less than a Scientific Counterfeiter," diligently researched patent reports and thus also speculated on the possibility of using the daguerreotype process for the purpose of counterfeiting bank notes.[54] Yet the daguerreotype did not yield a negative image from which multiple positive "prints" could be made. Although inventors in the early 1840s discovered both how to make facsimile copies of original photographs and how to transfer images on the daguerreotype onto a metal plate, in the long run daguerreotyping was superseded by other processes. The most notable of these were the calotype, a negative-positive process using a paper negative which was introduced in1841, and the collodio-type wet plate process, a negative-positive process introduced in 1851, which uses collodion impregnated with halide and a glass plate that is sensitized by immersion in a silver nitrate bath. Especially the surfacing of fake bills using calotype photography created a panic in the business community. These new notes all but obliterated the distinction between real and fake, as even bank-tellers had to admit that the signatures they were perceiving were their own.[55]

Five-dollar note from the Monmouth Bank, 1841, orange FIVE counterfeit detector (Courtesy National Numismatic Collection, Smithsonian Institution).

The growing concern over photographic counterfeits is evident from a number of articles in the *National Police Gazette*, the *Bankers' Magazine and Statistical Register*, as well as in a number of counterfeit detectors and bank note reporters from the mid–1850s. An article in *Harper's New Monthly Magazine* summed up the counterfeiters' increasing technological sophistication in the following way: "Give the photographer a camera, a few dollars' worth of chemicals, and a quire of paper, and he could produce fac-similes of any note without limit. No matter how perfect the engraving, or how elaborate the machine work, he could in a few minutes make a copy exact to the minutest point."[56] Efforts to prevent counterfeits had led to the addition of a second color to the faces of the notes by the early 1800s. Following the invention of photography, colors were again tried, as photography then could not reproduce colors. Back printing was applied in a color different from that used on the face; parts of the face were printed at first in blue, then in red and orange, which long enjoyed great popularity — until it was discovered that green was much more of a challenge to photographers than any other tint.[57]

Green is not a basic color but results from the blending of two basic colors, blue and yellow, the one generally standing for transcendence, the other for the sun and radiance. The resulting tint, green, is a balancing color that is neither hot nor cold, unlike red, which is a "powerful" color, said to raise the blood pressure and the heartbeat, thus making people work faster, often to the point of exhaustion. Poe's reds, of course, are special, symbolic less of life and love than of horror, blood, and sudden death. His greens, in contrast, are used for all kinds of vegetation, or as an apparently humorous color. (He rarely, if ever, associates greens or blues with nature and its poesy.) In a more general sense, however, green is associated with the social world, the world of the fathers, even with prosperity. The use of green on paper money therefore constitutes a symbolism that seems quite appropriate. During Poe's time, however, the use of green on paper money was not an unmixed blessing. Counterfeiters could still remove the colored tints, make any number of photographic copies of the remainder of the note, and then restore an imitation of the colored parts. Although an additional process was thus rendered necessary for the production of a photographic counterfeit, this was not a difficult one, and the labor, the article from *Harper's* added, "was more than repaid by the security which was supposed to be given to any note printed in colors."[58]

Given the counterfeiters' increasing technological sophistication, the manufacture of an indelible colored ink became an urgent desideratum for the legitimate bank note producers. This was long held to be impossible, and the *New American Cyclopaedia* claimed until the 1850s, "No tint has yet been discovered which may not be chemically removed from the paper."[59] Here the worthy cyclopedia erred. In 1857 a Dr. Sterry Hunt registered patents for an allegedly anti-photographic green overprint — called *Canada Green*. The patent claimed to make the photographic copying of bank notes impossible, as the green-imprinted sections appeared as black blobs on photographic prints. In addition, the ink allegedly could not be erased without destroying the texture of the paper. Hunt sold the rights to the Patent Green Tint — as it was officially designated — to the Montreal representative of the banknote-producing company of Rawdon, Wright, Hatch and Edson, who quickly sold them to Tracy R. Edson, the firm's president in New York. Edson lost no time promoting the ink as the wonder of the age, including on colorful cards to banks. At one such bank the cashier was so impressed by the ink that he instantly recommended paying a surcharge to imprint the bank's next order for new bills. Many other banks did the same,

62 The Monetary Imagination of Edgar Allan Poe

though the idea soon died out when news spread that the Associated Banks for the Suppression of Counterfeiting, an industry group, had submitted the Canada Green to testing and found that an amateur could remove it easily.[60]

All the bad press notwithstanding, in 1861 a reporter for *Harper's New Monthly Magazine* visited the holder of the Patent Green Tint, which was then the American Bank Note Company, to gather information for an article. A year later the article appeared in print, chockfull with information provided by the company's president, Tracy R. Edson, but without a word of the ink's failure in tests. The federal government also appears to have been oblivious to the tests, as it had awarded a lucrative paper money contract to the company the year before, agreeing to a surcharge of $5 per 1,000 impressions of this tint added to currency sheets. The tint has been in use on American paper money ever since, allegedly affording "a perfect security against photographic counterfeits."[61] The ink's ingredients are, of course, a carefully preserved secret, though the concoction itself quickly earned the notes on which it was used their lasting nickname, "greenbacks."[62]

Both the original company of Rawdon, Wright, Hatch and Edson and its subsequent owner had their base in New York. The city of Philadelphia also was home to a number of banknote-producing companies, among them Murray, Draper, Fairman and Co., which a year after the Bank of the United States had begun operation in that city had printed more than $150,000,000 in bills for the bank's main office as well as its branches.[63] In the same year, 1818, the company changed its name to Murray, Fairman and Co., following Draper's departure. Other Philadelphia companies were Draper, Toppan, Longacre and Co. as well as Underwood, Bald, Spencer and Hufty and their various successors, which at one time had in their employ Jacob Perkins and Asa Spencer, two pioneers in the field of banknote-engraving.[64] Was Poe aware of their good work as inventors? It is impossible to determine the issue with certainty. We do know, however, that Poe was always excited about new scientific inventions, including the daguerreotype, which in 1840 he enthusiastically described as "the most important, and perhaps the most extraordinary triumph of modern science." He presciently added, however, that the consequences of this "process of photogeny (from Greek words signifying sun-painting) [...] cannot, even remotely, be seen," though they certainly will, as with any new scientific invention, "exceed, by very much, the wildest expectations of the most imaginative."[65]

Poe also knew John William Draper, a professor at Hampden-Sidney College and, later, one of the best-known professors in the Medical School of New York University and a leading scientist of the time. In 1836 Thomas W. White published Draper's *Introductory Lecture to a Course of Chemistry and Natural Philosophy*; White also published the *Southern Literary Messenger*, with Poe as editor. Poe noticed Draper's book and reviewed it in the August 1836, issue of the *Messenger*, reprinting a lengthy excerpt that he praised for its "unusual interest and beauty." In all likelihood, Poe would have said the same about Draper's improvements in the chemistry of Daguerre's photography, which shortened exposure time enough to make possible, in 1839, the first daguerreotype portrait.[66] Poe's first portrait, the so-called "McKee" daguerreotype, named for its last identified owner, Thomas J. McKee, presumably was taken in 1842. The origin of the "McKee portrait" is obscure, although, since Poe was living in Philadelphia at the time, it seems probable that it is the work of a Philadelphia daguerreotypist. The daguerreotypist's identity is unknown, though it is not impossible that it was the famous photographer Mathew B. Brady, whom Poe may have known during his Philadelphia period and whom he also may have met in Washington in March 1843.[67] What is beyond doubt is that Poe knew Professor Thomas Wyatt, whom he met in 1839 and to whom he largely owed his considerable knowledge of natural history. Also beyond doubt is that Poe was familiar with Sir Humphrey Davy's "Researches Concerning Nitrous Oxide," which Poe drew on for "Von Kempelen and His Discovery," his prose comment on the California Gold Rush.

The word "tint" in its technical use in engraving describes the effect produced by a series of fine parallel lines more or less closely drawn to produce an even and uniform shading. Thus, "tints" are used also on pieces of paper money, either as a ground of the whole surface, or on the parts that have to be completed in writing, as a security against counterfeiting. An older usage of "tint"—in the sense of color, hue, or tinge—comes from the world of painting. Poe had some acquaintance with painting, as is evident from sundry comments, including comments on the daguerreotype.[68] Poe also made use of the painterly meaning of "tint" in two tales he wrote shortly after his wife Virginia around the middle of January 1842 had shown the first symptoms of the disease that eventually killed her. Both tales were published in *Graham's Magazine*, the one before, the other after Poe's resignation from it. "Life in Death" (which was subsequently titled "The Oval Portrait") concerns a painter and his Virginia-like bride, "a young girl just ripened into womanhood," whom the painter has subjected to long, debilitating hours of posing in creating an oval portrait of appalling "*lifelikeness*." The painter will not or cannot accept that his bride is dying. He "*would* not see that the tints which he spread upon the canvass were drawn from the cheeks of her who sate beside him." Not even as he puts his last stroke on the painting can or will he recognize her death. "And then the brush was given, and then the tint was placed; and, for one moment, the painter stood entranced before the work which he had wrought; but in the next, while he yet gazed, he grew tremulous and very pallid, and aghast, and crying with a loud voice, 'This is indeed *Life* itself!' turned suddenly to regard his beloved—*She was dead*!'"[69]

The painter's evasions and self-deluding questions—"'But is this indeed Death?'"— have been read as symbolizations of the romantic *doppelganger* motif, though Poe scorns them in the second of the two tales, "The Masque of the Red Death." Here the entire countryside is tinged by a deadly illness: "Blood was its Avatar and its seal—the redness and the horror of blood. There were sharp pains, and sudden dizziness, and then profuse bleedings at the pores, with dissolution."[70] Like the painter, and like Poe himself,[71] Prince Prospero tries to banish the bleeding doom he sees. His country half wasted by the plague, he seeks refuge behind the sealed doors of his luxurious abode, there frolicking with his host of friends. Yet for all the barricades, there appears a "shrouded" figure at the masque, its clothes "dabbled in *blood*." Prospero draws his dagger but falls dead. "And now," the story concludes, "was acknowledged the presence of the Red Death," which henceforth will be holding "illimitable dominion over all."[72] Steeped in blood, disease, and injury, and concerned with the attempt to defend oneself against what is most feared and unwanted, both tales seem to play out Poe's refusal to hear anything about the danger of his wife's condition. Similarly, in the obsessive hunt for treasure seems to be played out a refusal to hear anything about the dangers of a gold currency, which stem from its dependence on the market price for unminted gold. Once the price for the metal rises, gold coins will be hoarded and disappear from circulation; when the price falls, producers will discover that they cannot bring the metal to the mints even if they wish to do so. In effect, therefore, gold (like silver) coins are *never* exchanged for their nominal value but only for their relative value.

If Poe did not want to hear anything about the danger of his wife's condition, this is understandable in light of this author's biography. The refusal, in "The Gold-Bug," to hear anything about the dangers of a gold currency, however, is not necessarily Poe's own. Rather, it registers contemporary debates about money that Poe absorbed into his story. For instance, Poe's central character is directed to the buried treasure, that is, to supposedly "real" money, by the details on the "dirty foolscap" on which he has made his "rough drawing" of the gold. Yet he finds the pirates' legacy not only by accident or chance, or because of his superior skills in logic and ratiocination; at least to an equal degree he finds the treasure because he *trusts* these details, the authenticating marks. By contrast, the narrator, to the annoyance of Legrand, is full of suspicions. Upon receiving Legrand's note, which urges him to come "*to-night*, upon business [...] of the *highest* importance," he is at first puzzled by its intention: "What 'business of the highest importance' could *he* possibly have to trans-act?" Mindful of Legrand's bankruptcy, he cannot understand that Legrand's use of language extends beyond the literal, commercial meaning and thus mistakes it for madness, as "this freak of yours [...] the bug business (good God!) [...] an aberration of mind," or, more benignly, as an example of one of the "innumerable Southern superstitions about money buried."[73]

Far from being a chance detail, the presence of "trust" in "The Gold-Bug" constitutes a point of mediation between culture and society. Trust is not only essential for economic transactions, including the working of a currency. Trust is also the basis for human bonding, and thus extends to the bond between author and reader. Yet Poe's work rarely allows itself to be trusted, as it ceaselessly insists that there is nothing outside the fiction that reflects on the action of language within it.[74] This tendency, the result of a cultural logic of hoaxing that relentlessly works against stabilization, all but unhinges an understanding of the nar-rator's saying that he "contracted" a friendship with Legrand. It is of course possible, and must have been quite common in Poe's time, to use the verb "to contract" in the sense of forming, entering into, or becoming engaged in a relation of friendship or, as in our case, a relation of "intimacy." But Poe must have been aware also of the word's primary meaning, which according to the *Oxford English Dictionary* is that of entering upon a convention or treaty, or a legal or business engagement. In this sense, a contractual intimacy is a contra-diction in terms, and thus no intimacy at all.

Poe uses "contracted an intimacy" in the very first sentence of "The Gold-Bug." Such a sentence, he elsewhere laid down as one of his cardinal principles of composition, must tend to "the outbringing" of "a certain unique or single *effect*."[75] In "The Gold-Bug," the "outbringing" registers two levels of meaning, the one personal, the other theoretical. As regards the former, we can say that from the beginning, a shadow is cast over the two men's friendship, which, instead of drawing them close, keeps them apart. For Legrand, the nar-rator is "the only one we can trust," though his trust is not reciprocated. The narrator, caught up as he is in his logic of substantiation, cannot see that there is something in the paper after all, and so remains under the spell of the gold bug, or rather, the gold humbug, meaning the thing that is not. Legrand, too, at first has no eyes to see anything but "the gold of which [the bug] is the index."[76] His fixation on a distant goal leads him to believe that he can turn the design, drawn by himself, of a specimen into the real thing, gold or specie. Seemingly, the relationship between the designed paper and the treasure is transformed from accident to necessity, though it is well to remember that the bug design was not originally on the paper; the skull was. If there is any transformation, then, it involves Legrand turning the pirate's sign into the design of a death's-head beetle. This is not the only transformation, though. The story as a whole hinges on a transition plot. This truly alchemical transformation (albeit not a hoax) works on several layers at once — death is transformed into life, nature into culture, gold into paper, the realm of the mother into that of the father, custom and tradition into law, fictive fantasies or conditions into possibilities and, last but not least, there is a transformation of consciousness. Each of these transformations is important: without them, the point would be that of the gold bugs, that is, to show that nothing ever acquires value, that no money can become good and true unless it already is good and true, and therefore that nature's money, like Captain Kidd's treasure, must be made of gold.

The point about gold as "nature's money" directs us to the theoretical level. The "effect" brought out by Poe's use of a legal discourse ("contracted an intimacy") may as well involve a legal theory of money. Such a theory holds that money proper originates only with the legal institutions of societies "freely bonded by *contract*" and characterized by property rights and laws, including laws governing debt. A full-fledged "legal explanation" of money was put forward by Gunnar Heinsohn only in the early 1980s, but since has received attention through a number of translations into English. Put simply, the model rests on the distinction between possession and property. Only property is governed by laws and thus can be legally transferred and circulated — "alienated," in William Blackstone's terminology; possessions, in contrast, cannot.[77] Money, adherents of a legal model argue, derives from the burdening of property rights, that is, from establishing legally defendable titles against property. If implemented, the model disabuses us from explanations that connect money with religious practices (money as a substitute for the sacrifice of animals) or with the principles of possession that are characteristic of traditional communities (money as a medium of exchange tied to household management, or *oikos*, in Aristotle's terminology). Non-legal explanations of money are entirely appropriate for self-sufficient economies; hence, they are aligned with agriculture, a labor theory of value, and with the gold standard. "Legal explanations" of money, in contrast, correspond with profit-oriented economic systems, systems that are known for extensive commerce and, concomitantly, for trade, debt, and speculation, in short, for all kinds of activities in which money is made to yield a "crop" or "litter," and which are therefore condemned as *chrematistos* by Aristotle and his followers, from Thomas Aquinas to Karl Marx.[78]

Although property rights and defendable titles have been of importance in American literature and thought, throughout the nineteenth century legalized social contracts together with their institutions in general met with distrust.[79] What chiefly concerned American writers and intellectuals were disorder and excess or, beyond those, the complete collapse of the monetary system and the social order buttressing it. In literary writings of the time, therefore, money often is shown to lead a life of its own, with no one knowing how to control it. In Charles Brockden Brown's novel *Arthur Mervyn*, for instance, a yellow fever epidemic constitutes a condemnatory analogy to the monetary economy and, especially, to the wealth accumulated by speculators. Such gothic indeterminacy necessarily obliterates economic causes and effects, much as it elides institutions and laws that not only stand behind, but even make possible monetary speculation. In James Fenimore Cooper's *The Pioneers*, a historical novel of 1823, money likewise appears to be beyond people's control. Thus in the preface, the "author" resorts to family history, anchoring value in land as the only true source of wealth and influence. Thus also, Oliver Edward is discovered, not as a woodsman and hunter who with the help of Natty Bumppo searches for silver that could be coined into specie money, but as the legal heir to a portion of the property of Judge Temple, the power holder in town and the present owner of vast tracts of land. The intellectual stance displayed by writers such as Brown or Cooper is ideological, Nadja Gernalzick has demonstrated, the result of a complete "disregard for issues of property and rights," a disregard that ultimately silences discourses about money and monetary theory which, following Adam Smith, see the individual pursuit of monetary self-gain as the very foundation of happiness and prosperity in society.[80]

In light of Gernalzick's diagnosis, Poe appears truly radical, even though, due both to his upbringing in the Allan household and to his experience as a commercial writer and self-described magazinist, Poe was much more familiar with commerce and economics than with the law. Poe not only prided himself on his understanding of economic theory, but also developed an explicit distinction between intrinsic or use-value and extrinsic or exchange-value. Poe likely found this distinction in the writings of Adam Smith, who observed that the term "value" can refer to either the "utility of a particular object" or the "power of purchasing other goods which the possession of that object conveys."[81] But whereas Smith sought to preserve both meanings of value, Poe seems haunted by the possibility that use-value will be utterly subsumed into exchange-value, thereby transforming the market into the ultimate arbiter of literary taste. The possibility both repulsed and fascinated Poe, for although he often spoke out against salability as the true test of literary merit, he was nevertheless fascinated by the consequences that would ensue if the laws of supply and demand came to dominate all walks of life.

Exchange-value indeed is the crux of the matter. In suggesting that the design of the gold bug on the paper is a link (an "index") in a sequence that leads inevitably to the gold Poe is saying, to adopt the idiom of the time, that a shadow is the cause of a substance rather than the other way round.[82] According to the "gold bugs" or, to use the English term, "bullionists," this is the ostensibly absurd position of the "paper money men." The term "paper money men" belongs to Thomas Love Peacock, the English satirist and friend of Percy Shelley who in *Paper Money Lyrics* lampooned the pieties of political economists as well as the ill-fated practices of bankers. Peacock wrote *Paper Money Lyrics* in response to the March 1837 panic in England, which caused shock waves in America as well. The year 1837 also saw the publication, again in England, of Thomas Carlyle's *The French Revolution*, a book that mocked as a sign of his own times what the author identifies as "the Age of Paper" in late-eighteenth-century France. Continuing the English conservative superstitions against paper money, Carlyle calls the period an age of "Bank-paper, wherewith you can still buy when there is no gold left."[83] Poe was familiar with Carlyle, though not necessarily with *The French Revolution*. He also does not seem to have known Peacock's *Paper Money Lyrics* or, for that matter, *Melincourt*, an early novel, which contains Peacock's famous warning against "this fatal bubble of paper money."[84] Poe does speak, however, in one of his "Marginalia," of an earlier poem by Peacock, "Rhododaphne" (1818), as "brim-full of music." He also republished portions of the poem in the *Southern Literary Messenger* in June and July 1843, though he ascribed it, not to Peacock but to the Virginia poet Richard Dabney.[85]

As regards the term "gold-bug," it seems clear that the monetary sense of it entered the English language from the title of Poe's tale. The *Oxford English Dictionary* distinguishes two different meanings of "gold-bug": (a) a gold-beetle (a name for various beetles of the families *Chrysomelidæ* and *Cassididæ*, thus similar to the *Scarabaeus* of Poe's tale); (b) a plutocrat or millionaire; and a political nickname for an advocate of the gold standard.[86] The *Oxford English Dictionary* does not in this instance provide quotations by date, referring only to Funk and Wagnalls's *Standard Dictionary of the English Language*, which also does not have dated entries.[87] Even less informative is *Webster's Third New International Dictionary of the English Language*, which only says that the word "gold-bug" means an advocate or supporter of the gold standard.[88] More useful are dictionaries of American English or Americanisms. Craigie and Hulbert's *Dictionary of American English* lists altogether three meanings: 1. a fictitious insect (with reference to Poe's story); 2. an advocate of the gold standard; a money baron (first used in this sense in an article for the February 21, 1878, issue of *The Nation*); and 3. a gold-beetle.[89]

Essentially this is also what Mathews's *Dictionary of Americanisms* tells us: 1. any of the various beetles having a golden luster; also "The Gold-Bug," the title of a well-known story by Poe; 2. an advocate of the gold standard; also a badge or emblem worn by one of these; hence "gold-buggism."[90] By the 1870s, the term "gold-bug" was specifically applied to scheming financiers like Jay Gould and Jim Fisk, who speculated "bullishly" on the performance of the greenbacks against gold, as well as to those who wanted to base the national currency on gold, to the exclusion of silver. The economist David Wells, for instance, wrote in *Practical Economics* (1883) about the "'gold-bugs,' speculators and monopolists [who] were everywhere hostile to the circulation of silver."[91] As the debates over the nation's money intensified, the term "gold-bug" became more derogatory. It came to be applied especially to the supporters of a gold standard within the Democratic Party. This group — mostly urban businesspeople and professionals — supported President Grover Cleveland's repeal of the Silver Purchase Act in 1893, and in 1896 they created and supported the National Democratic ticket of John Palmer. Also in that year, supporters of the Republican presidential candidate William McKinley, another staunch supporter of the gold standard, began to wear gold lapel pins and other paraphernalia in their struggle against the "silver menace."

What supporters of the gold standard called the "silver menace" was closely tied to William Jennings Bryan, who at the Democratic national convention in Chicago on July 8, 1896, declared the silver question the paramount issue. Bryan became famous for concluding his speech with the words, "You shall not press down on the brow of labor this crown of thorns, you shall not crucify mankind upon a cross of gold."[92] The speech reflected the popular feeling about gold, which in the populist literature of the time came to be connected with "financial slavery to Great Britain and the Rothschilds."[93] The xenophobic sense of victimhood in works like Warder's, while dimly echoing the anti–British protests of the pre-revolutionary patriots, cannot be separated from the quest for an alien "other" who could be made responsible for economic meltdown. Ready to hand was an offensively anti–Semitic rhetoric that became characteristic of text and imagery in the silverite literature of the time. George W. Warder for his part viciously attacked the "millionaire goldbugs," who in his view "belong to that nation who were the original worshippers of the golden calf."[94]

Fictions of Speech and "Bad" Use of Language

Advocates respectively of gold and silver may have formed a mutually despising company, yet throughout the nineteenth century they were united in their hostility against a paper currency. If the "paper money men" thought that purely symbolic money could supplement or even replace specie, this was merely to succumb to what David Wells excoriated as a "mere fiction of speech and a bad use of language."[95] Wells's pronouncement echoes sentiments from before the Civil War, when analogies such as "paper is to gold as word is to meaning" had come to exemplify both the distinction between substance (thing) and shadow (sign) in monetary theory and the understanding of symbolization and linguistic representation.[96] A trope of decline in Ralph Waldo Emerson's "Nature" is a good example of the use of the analogy of paper being to gold as word is to meaning in antebellum America. In his essay, the New England sage bemoans the fact that in his day and age, "new imagery ceases to be created, and old words are perverted to stand for things which are not; a paper currency is employed, when there is no bullion in the vaults."[97] Washington Irving not much later made quite similar distinctions in describing the inflation in France during John Law's paper money scheme in the 1720s: "Promissory notes, interchanged between scheming individuals, are liberally discounted at the banks, which became so many mints to coin words into cash; and as the supply of words is inexhaustible, it may readily be supposed what a vast amount of promissory capital is soon in circulation."[98]

For many people in the nineteenth century, then, the form of paper money based on credit was marked by a clear dissociation of sign and thing. Paper money based on credit identified paper as a mere sign, hence as mere "currency;" to view paper as a thing (a commodity) would have established it as "money," meaning as possessing intrinsic value. I will come back to this distinction in Chapter 5. At this point, I will continue with the correspondence between the dissociation of sign and thing and the felt dissociation of word and meaning in "bad" use of language. In "The Gold-Bug," Marc Shell has found, the only "bad" use of language is in the form of the malapropisms and puns of Jupiter, Legrand's black servant. Jupiter's speech thus is "the real 'goole'" in Poe's tale.[99] The word "goole," which occurs about nine times in the tale, may well be a survival of an older pronunciation of "gold" as "[guld]," though the additional "e" makes the word sound like "goolah," which is the name linguists apply to the dialect spoken by African Americans living on the sea islands and tidewater coastal strip bordering South Carolina and Georgia.[100] In Jupiter's Gullah speech, the bug's being without "antennae" comes out as there being "*no tin in him.*"[101] Obviously, if there is "no tin" in the bug, it is a "bug of real gold" or "solid gold."[102]

Legrand no doubt thinks that the bug is of real gold ("I shall arrive at the gold"); however, the "no tin" also can be understood as there being "nothin' in" the bug, meaning that it is hollow. And if there is "nothing in" (or "nothing to") it, it is a mere insubstantial sign that, like paper money, at best is only an "index" to something substantial. Jupiter's speech also brings into focus a charge that frequently was brought to bear on the "paper money men"—their unholy quest to become rich by manipulating the paper money ghosts. Thus Jupiter's "goole" also illuminates connections between the devil, gold, and God: God and gold are heard or seen in "my golly" and "Lor-gol-a-marcy." The "ghoulish" devil is echoed in "goole," much as Satan—"sartain"—confers the "debbil's own lot of money." This money is "not done by human agency," a statement that typically was applied to paper money.[103] Jupiter, when he pays for the digging tools Legrand instructed him to purchase, has to give "the debbil's own lot of money" for them. And when Legrand suggests that the design of the skull on the paper was "not done by human agency," we can only conclude that ultimately, it is the "goole" ("ghoul" or *ghul* in Arabic), the grave-robbing spirit, who with the help of "dat d — d bug" finds the gold.[104]

Another word from Jupiter's gullah lexicon, "gose," has been read as meaning "ghost," and thus as a reference to a phantom or a ghoul. Indeed, Jupiter, the gothic storyteller inside the tale, describes Legrand as going about "wid de head down [...] and as white as a gose." While ghosts are generally represented as white, so is a "goose," meaning the bird, as in Aesop's fable about the goose laying the golden eggs. The connection with the fable only further removes the tale about gold from fictional realism, at the same time as it adds weight to the theme of greed overreaching itself: "One day," the fable reads, in Joseph Jacobs's English rendering,

> a countryman going to the nest of his Goose found there an egg all yellow and glittering. When he took it up it was as heavy as lead and he was going to throw it away, because he thought a trick had been played upon him. But he took it home on second thoughts, and soon found to his delight that it was an egg of pure gold. Every morning the same thing occurred, and he soon became rich by selling his eggs. As he grew rich he grew greedy; and thinking to get at once all the gold the Goose could give, he killed it and opened it only to find nothing.[105]

Assuming that Poe was aware of the fable about the goose laying the golden eggs, his allusion to it may well be taken as a warning against using the treasure as capital. For, to do so would transform it into a medium of exchange that, under capitalist relations of production, makes possible the creation of profit and the theoretically limitless accumulation of wealth. In such a case, the allusion to Aesop refers not to any country simpleton but to all those would-be capitalists who become poor by shortsightedly striving to gain all. There is, of course, another association, as the word "goose" is also used to describe a person who is gulled into accepting counterfeits. It is said that images of that bird appeared also on paper notes from commercial banks. This may or may not have been the case, though in Melville's *The Confidence-Man* a conversation towards the end of the novel turns on a potential goose's attempt to match up the design of a goose in his Counterfeit Detector with the design of a goose on a bank note he is attempting to authenticate. "Stay, now, here's another sign. It says that, if the bill is good, it must have in one corner ... a goose ... I can't see this goose ... I don't see it — dear me — I don't see the goose. Is it a real goose?" To which the confidence man responds: "A perfect goose; beautiful goose."[106]

To the extent that Poe, in "The Gold-Bug," allows for something to be generated from nothing, his interest seems at once economic and linguistic. According to Marc Shell, Poe took his studies of the "omnipotence of money" and of usury — themes that he praised in Nathaniel Parker Willis's *Tortesa the Usurer* (1839), which he called "by far the best the play ever written by an American"[107] — and transformed them in two ways. On the one hand, the transformation resulted in a story about generating gold from a bug or from the design of a bug; on the other hand, the transformation resulted in a discourse whose exemplary means of generating meaning is Jupiter's goolah or gullah punning.[108] In terms of the economics of symbolization, therefore, goolah is the linguistic counterpart of Legrand's productive imagination. As such, it is also its symptomatic externalization, since Jupiter's speech is there for us to see and to hear, as important to deciphering the meaning of Poe's tale as his scythe is to the party's getting to the place where the gold was hidden.[109]

The argument that "The Gold-Bug" connects an economic practice (usury) and a linguistic process (punning) by demonstrating that both make something out of nothing has some validity, but in failing to distinguish between money and currency or, rather, capital, Marc Shell obscures the productive process that only *appears* to create something out of nothing. Though Poe's tale contains an abundance of puns and double entendres, the drawing that leads Legrand to the treasure remains untouched by any inflation of meaning. The value of the pirate's message, that is, can be realized only if Legrand establishes an *unam*-biguous relationship between language and geography.[110] Legrand's attitude towards language is aptly conveyed through the "definite point of view, *admitting no variation*," that he imposes on the text of the pirate's message. When read in this manner, the secret text conveys but a single message, which can allude to "nothing but" and can "refer only to," or else, can "admit, also, of but one interpretation."[111] Other interpretations of the cryptograph are of no use to Legrand in his search for gold and are not, therefore, admitted of. Of course, his observation that a skull is an "ominous insignium," the commonly known emblem of piracy and murder, makes plain enough that there is a symbolic dimension to language and that a "poetical" view is possible. To Legrand's "common-sense" view, however, the pirate's message is a purely correlational code, like the Morse code. In each case, rendering the text intelligible involves merely the mechanical substitution of one character or sequence of characters for another, following a predetermined key. At the end of the day, the new text is strictly identical with the real state of things. In Legrand's instance, it is a string of "landmarks of his own contrivance," which leads directly to the spot where the gold is buried. So far as Legrand is concerned, linguistic signs convey a univocal message, which is at the same time the meaning the author (Captain Kidd) intended and the truth the reader (Legrand) aims to arrive at.

Legrand's view of language, then, may be utilitarian, though whether his discourse is really "pitched at the semiotic level of bee language," as Daniel Kempton argues, is a matter of dispute.[112] Of course, the efficacy of the pirate's message as a vehicle for transmitting information between sender and receiver depends on its "symbolic (semiotic) impoverishment," to use Kempton's phrase, but the same can be said about the efficacy on the messages on paper money. Any piece of paper money is distinguished by its "peculiar properties of representation," which involve iconographic details like numerals indicating its nominal value, seals and stamps of the institution guaranteeing its value, signatures, serial numbers, the decree authorizing its production, the fiscal theory behind it (an obligation like "promise to pay" or a phrase like "legal tender"), and, not to forget, portraits and vignettes.[113] Thus when we see Legrand marching through the dark forest with the designed paper clutched in his hand, it is difficult not to think of Poe's central character as one of the "paper money men." Both the bug and Legrand's design of it somehow lead to the stamp and the signature on Captain Kidd's message and even, as the narrator says, to "a letter between the stamp and the signature," or, as Legrand remarks, to "the text for my context."[114] The relationship between the drawing of the gold bug and the treasure of course cannot be explained in terms of a chain of cause and effect, but that does not make it simply "absurd," let alone homologous to the unproblematic exchange of paper money for specie.[115] The entire story is in fact predicated on the difficulty of such an exchange, and although Legrand does in the end redeem the pirate's note, the "parchment so strangely found, [which] involved a lost record of the place of deposit," he must first expend a great deal of physical and intellectual labor on his journey from secret writing to buried treasure.[116]

The difficulties that accompany Legrand's exchange of paper for gold clearly show the extent to which Poe entered into and historicized discourses about money. So, of course, does the fact that Legrand finds the pirate's legacy only because of his *trust* in the marks he sees on the paper, while the obtuse narrator remains doubtful. The narrator's lack of trust, which also infects his relation to Legrand, about whose "sanity" he begins to harbor "suspicions," also constitutes a breach of the intimacy "contracted," as he begins the tale by remarking, between Legrand and himself. Instead of trusting Legrand and accepting his drawing or representation of the bug, the narrator, like the Queen of Sheba confronting Solomon, demands substantiation: "I must wait until I see the beetle itself."[117] This obvious distrust, Kevin McLaughlin points out, registers "the unwillingness to accept a representation, perhaps a promise, and the insistence that something more substantial be delivered. *In financial terms, this is the insistence on gold, hence the appropriateness of the gold bug in the scene.*"[118] What Poe in his imaginative exploration of paper money seems to suggest, then, is that in economic exchange people must have *trust*. If they do not, choosing instead to pursue the elusive gold humbug, this only shows that they are living in the past, in a time when indeed there was "no American money."

"The Gold-Bug," which the *Dollar Newspaper*'s prize committee pronounced a "capital story,"[119] appeared just before the nation at last surfaced from a seven-year-long depression. The experience of a world of banks collapsing, financial panics, and personal misery had made Poe dubious of partisan attempts to vilify banks, bankers, and bank notes, at the same time as it fired his satirical intent. Yet can we trust Poe's work, in which the unhinging of understanding often seems the whole point of the fiction and its pay-off? The difficulty with Poe, it seems, is that his writings are grounded in a regime of deception that destabilizes all representation (and its reception).[120] This does not mean, of course, that the issues that Poe thematizes were not real in society at the time. Indeed, outside of his celebrated tale, the controversy over what was to constitute the nation's money — gold, silver, or paper — was raging in full force. The question what backs the value of money was of great concern to all parties, as was the authenticity of paper bills from the commercial banks. Commenting on "the fluctuations in [America's] currency" and on "the stability of [its] moneyed institutions," Charles Francis Adams noted in *Hunt's Merchants' Magazine* of July 1839: "The subject of money, considered as a science, is acquiring tenfold greater importance in the eyes of the American public, than it has ever heretofore enjoyed."[121]

Americans in the antebellum period had every reason to closely watch the currency. The absence of paper money issued and controlled by a powerful authority in particular contributed to a situation in which whoever was wealthy yesterday could be poor today, and vice versa. Under the circumstances, it became everyone's vital interest to make monetary transactions as quickly as possible, to avoid long-term transactions, and to learn to take up economic opportunities instantly. "Never Keep a Paper Dollar in Your Pocket Till Tomorrow," read the inscription on a satirical token issued in Connecticut in 1857 by an observer of the difficulties with paper money.[122] A stranger could also spell trouble, especially if he was arriving at a bank's door with a bulging carpetbag in hand, demanding specie to the full value of the many different notes he presented for payment. "It was the redemption problem that bedeviled the antebellum dollar bill," a modern commentator remarked. "A sound bank would redeem its notes at par in gold. But how could you be sure it was sound, unless you tried redeeming its notes? And if everyone tried to redeem its notes, what started as an inquiry would turn into an autopsy when the bank ran out of reserves. If only people could have more confidence."[123]

We find a similar point about confidence in the writings of a contemporary observer. "The evil of the time," Charles Francis Adams remarked in *Hunt's* for December 1839, "is a great want of confidence." This being so, the Whigs sought to strengthen the power of the central government and establish a new national bank that would, for instance, receive notes from commercial banks and return them for redemption, or else drastically curtail the right of commercial banks to issue notes. The Democrats, in contrast, would rather be dead. For them, the crux of the matter was that lawmakers had granted too much power to the banks by special charters. "If their charters were taken away from them," William Gouge observed in February 1842, "not even their own stockholders would trust them."[124] The worst problem of course was redemption, for any bank that resumed specie payment was likely to experience a "run" and have its specie reserves reduced to zero. This would then make people think the bank was on the brink of failure and, by way of a self-fulfilling prophecy, cause its implosion. In terms of economics, therefore, it was doubtless best for a bank to hold on to specie and not pay it out until it could do so with confidence. But this concept, Q. David Bowers notes, "was virtually impossible for lawmakers and newspaper editors to understand. Instead, an otherwise sound bank was 'bad' if it did not redeem its notes in an era of economic stringency."[125]

The problem of confidence, at least in part, was also a matter of the dissemination of information, of publicity. Only "bad" (as well as truly wayward) banks were written about in the newspapers and financial journals like *Niles' Weekly Register*, *Hunt's Merchants' Magazine*, Gouge's *Journal of Banking*, or *The Mercantile Advertiser*. Properly conducted institutions, in contrast, attracted little notice. Nor did activities that were considered normal practice. Nevertheless, Poe and his contemporaries did have enough reasons not to trust people and paper dollars. People trying to create a new town tried to drive up real estate values on land they owned. Often enough they sold sections of land they knew were worthless. Others paid for purchases in counterfeit bills. Still others sold useless patent medicine, watered-down whiskey, phony lottery tickets, stolen horses and cattle and, at least in fiction, forged letters and delivered them to rich people, asking them to pay postage themselves.

The scheme of the "sham-post" forms an episode in the revised version of Poe's "The Business Man," which appeared in the *Broadway Journal* of August 2, 1845. The central character, now tellingly named Peter Proffit, discloses without compunction, "Nobody hesitates at paying for a letter — especially for a double one — people are *such* fools — and it was no trouble to get round a corner before there was time to open the epistles."[126] Peter Proffit undoubtedly answers to the Jacksonian ideal of the self-made man, an ideal that Poe sets out to deconstruct, emptying out its meaningfulness as a mere social construct, what Poe describes as a "diddler." Proffitt's operations to defraud other people are all on a small scale — like the diddler's, who might, for instance, accept a genuine fifty-dollar bill as a reward for handing over a pocket book he had allegedly found, though the "large amount" of money in the book is later seen to be merely "'a counterfeit presentment,' and the whole thing a capital diddle." Activities of this kind, and there are many more in the satirical sketch Poe published in the *Broadway Journal* of September 13, 1845, are said to be different only in scale from what true "financiers" then were doing by way of "magnificent speculation." Accordingly, a diddler (the verb "diddle" means "defraud") may be regarded as "a banker *in petto*— a financial operation,' as a diddle in Brobdingnag. The one is to the other, as Homer to 'Flaccus'— as a Mastodon to a mouse — as the tail of a comet to that of a pig."[127]

What conclusions can we draw from Poe's irreverent language? "Diddling," like "The Business Man," does not require much explication; straightforward accounts of frauds are simply entertaining. And they were popular at the time, both in the form of fictitious magazine items fleshed out by narrative illustrations and of life stories peddled about by impostors — in Poe's case, the Yankee hero.[128] Apparently, accounts of frauds also were easy to exploit. As the frontier widened and the cities and towns spread, people moved far and move often, and not only in the West either. No matter how responsibly most of the commercial banks managed the flow of paper money, and also notwithstanding the attempts, by individual states, to regulate banking by introducing stricter reserve and other requirements, the general experience was one of a growing intensity in economic life and a quickening of its pace that also spread to other areas of social life. It is no surprise that modern critics often describe the general experience of the time as one of alienation.

In American literature, the general experience of the time found a heroically sinister expression in Poe, a tragically romantic one in Hawthorne's *The House of the Seven Gables*, and a nihilistically comic one in Melville, whose novel *The Confidence-Man* appropriately is set on a Mississippi riverboat called *Fidèle*. Melville's novel of 1857 — that "most thoroughly American story," as a contemporary reviewer quipped — traditionally has been read as an allegory on the devil boarding the riverboat for the purpose of luring the trustful to their spiritual death. Later criticism has turned on the confidence man's role in exposing the philosophical confusions of his victims. It is worth recalling, however, that Melville's largely unpopular novel was suggested by the exploits, in 1849, of a shyster by the name of William Thompson, whose appeals for "confidence" gave a philosophical twist to the wiles of the swindler at the same time as they provide the link with paper money. As all kinds of paper bills, genuine notes, ghost notes, counterfeit ghost notes, and phantom notes, are peddled about the ship, the reader learns one rule for telling the confidence game: watch out for the man who walks away with the dollar bills. With the introduction, in one of the novel's final scenes, of an old man poring over a counterfeit detector, the reliability of this sign system is put into question as well. As the old man notices, searching for authenticating signs on the dollar bills in his possession, "there's so many marks of all sorts to go by, it makes it kind of uncertain."[129]

Uncertainty is the predominant mood also in Hawthorne's 1851 novel, *The House of the Seven Gables*, which this author wrote at one of the peak periods of land speculation and social mobility. For Hawthorne, the instabilities of a market society constituted a monstrous threat to property (actually, possessions), and he took to the form of the romance to defend this traditional institution. Perhaps the central point in *The House of the Seven Gables*, Walter Benn Michaels found, is "the implicit comparison between the impoverished capitalist and the dispossessed aristocrat. The capitalist who loses everything loses everything, whereas the nobleman, losing everything material, retains his nobility, which has a 'spiritual existence.' This title cannot be bought or sold; unlike the land you have 'hewn out of the forest,' it cannot be stolen either. Aristocracy's claim to land is unimpaired by the inability to enforce that claim."[130] Hawthorne knew, of course, that in "this republican country" there no longer was any aristocracy. Hence, loss of wealth constitutes a deeply felt "tragedy."[131] His fictional alternative is a world in which not everything is for sale, alienable. Yet if romance brings back a time when land was not yet a commodity, not yet subject to speculation, it does so at a price. Certainly, through the romance form Hawthorne was able to domesticate the social dislocations he was witness to. Yet by obliterating the distinction between past and present, change itself becomes foreclosed. In the end, "mere business" (the acquisition of wealth, together with the speculative thrills this entails) is transformed into "inheritance," at the same time as mimesis (fictional realism) is transformed into a fairy-tale.

The moral and epistemological dilemmas that writers such as Melville, Hawthorne, and Poe raised motivated and underwrote one of the era's deepest desires — a desire for certainty grounded in a reliable authority. For the writer of fiction, the problem was insurmountable. There was no authority outside of fiction that the reader could trust. Poe tried to establish such an authority by turning himself into the most relentless, unsparing, and, on occasion, even abusive critic. He attacked Carlyle and Emerson as "conventional," and he dismissed Margaret Fuller's style as "a triple-distilled conventionality." Cooper hardly fared any better, for Poe saw the popularity of any writer merely as an index to their belonging to a world of "busy-bodies, toadies, quacks."[132] The Young Americans, Poe charged, were merely adhering to "the gross paradox of liking a stupid book the better, because, sure enough, its stupidity is American." By the same token, he heaped scorn on the Transcendentalists and literary Bostonians for the simple reason that, "self-bepuffed," they praised one another's work.[133] Poe, in short, saw himself as the nation's only real critic, and his opinion on literary matters as something like a "gold standard of literary value, against the nothingness of paper puffery." There was, Jill Lepore concludes, "in Andrew Jackson's America, a literary bubble, and Edgar A. Poe was determined to bust it."[134]

In the world of money, a measure of certainty had been provided by the promise of specie money. While that promise, coming as it did from commercial banks, often was merely illusory, specie at least could be associated with the substance of value. Paper money could not, and thus was inherently problematic. With some people the conviction, going back to the days of the South Sea Bubble of 1720, that paper money was "the devil in specie," a "nothing" pretending to be "something," prevailed. On the level of theory, then, the fact had to be confronted that paper counted for little or nothing as a commodity or thing; as a representation of value (a sign), paper money therefore was insubstantial. Such money accordingly was dismissed as an appearance or shadow. A number of American (and European) writers during the first part of the nineteenth century explored the theoretical relationship between aesthetic and monetary theory, considering a connection between economic symbolization in paper money and aesthetic symbolization in literature. A comparison for instance was made between poetry, fiction and the promises to pay made on paper bills. The logic of appearances of idealistic thought and fiction, each operating without material guarantees, was linked with paper money, which likewise operates on the tension between promise and delivery. To put the matter differently, the way a mere shadow or piece of paper becomes credited as substantial money was seen as quite similar to the way an artistic appearance is taken for the real thing by a willing suspension of disbelief.[135]

A willing suspension of disbelief certainly was needed in order to overcome the prevailing monetary theories. These theories conceived of paper money only as a medium of exchange. Insofar as they were based on possession, the theories were essentialist, necessarily connecting to a gold standard. Such money is appropriate for a closed economy — one governed by the Aristotelian "rule of the household"— though it is unfit for an open system with extensive commerce and all that it implies — trade, debt, and speculation. In an open system, money derives from the burdening of property rights, though this scheme presupposes a stable institution of power. In its absence, how could anyone trust the paper bills that were passing from hand to hand? During Poe's lifetime, the predicament remained unresolved. As there was no authority of power that people could trust, the tension, inherent to paper money, between promise and delivery could only be discredited as a "distortion" of the "natural" understanding of the relationship between symbols and things. Only with the establishment of a stable institution of power would the idea become acceptable that true money represented what it could purchase, not the specie or other "thing" it could be converted into. Such an idea marked a radical departure also from traditional aesthetic thought, towards a logic of appearances that, while operating without material guarantees, nevertheless was economically sensible.

Economic sense does not mean political expediency, though. No matter what the position was on the money issue, it was always a political position. As such, the "money question" was simply too divisive politically to be articulated in a tale for a mass market. Poe's "affair of dollars and sense" thus breaks off at midpoint, to continue with Legrand's account of how he cracked the secret code that led to the discovery of the buried treasure. Under the circumstances, it is difficult to imagine what other form Poe might have given to "The Gold-Bug." Put differently, Poe did fill his tale with any number of words and phrases suggesting the world of money — such as "gold bug" for a supporter of the gold standard, "stamp," "seal," and "signature," for known features on paper money, and, finally, green and red "tints" as intertextual references to counterfeiting. Yet notwithstanding all these signals, Poe undermined his own position by not telling us what the money-finders will do with the unburied treasure. By once again playing with undecidability, Poe left to his readers the thankless task of untangling the knot comprised of gold, paper, and signs. And it is this thankless task that will be taken upon in the chapter to follow.

3

Capital Stories
Poe, the Banks and Politics

"The Gold-Bug" differs from most tales about buried treasure insofar as the presumed "money-seekers" are rather "money-finders."[1] At the time, this was not a customary topos in America.[2] It also was not customary to describe a money-seeker's "chief amusements" as "gunning and fishing, or sauntering along the beach and through the myrtles, in quest of shells or entomological specimens."[3] Legrand, it should be noted, wanders at a "beach" only in the J. Lorimer Graham copy of the last manuscript, with revisions about 1849. Both the original version printed in *Dollar Newspaper* of 1843 and the one of *Tales* of 1845 have the central character conducting his search at a "bank." Perhaps Poe wanted to downplay the explicitness of the financial theme in the new edition; perhaps he had become disgusted with banks, "our great 'moneyed institutions,'" with their "surface of Parian marble" and their interiors "filled with rags;" perhaps Poe even calculated that later readers would notice the change and be alerted to it as a deliberate signal emphasizing the money theme. Be that as it may, a "desire to avoid the mundane" is hardly a sufficient reason for Poe's revision, just as romantic irony is not a sufficient reason for Poe to break off the money-story at mid-point, continuing with Legrand's explanation of how he cracked the code on the parchment.[4]

Of course, many instances in Poe's life and writing may be seen in terms of a "willing-reluctant shuffle of retreating advance and advancing retreat." Kenneth Silverman uses these words to describe Poe's courtship of Sarah Helen Whitman,[5] though they just as well apply to Legrand's retreat into cipher solving as Poe's way to bridge an autistic gap with a secret code. In the case of "The Gold-Bug," however, any explicit reference to the financial theme necessarily evokes the monetary politics of the Jacksonian Democrats, which almost uncannily resembled the hard-money advocacy of the pre-revolutionary Tory Loyalists; by the same token, a majority of Whigs, usually considered to represent the prosperous business community, had become paper-money advocates, a position that during the colonial era had been linked with anti-royalist protest and the movement toward political sovereignty. How could Poe, who in his writings avoided partisanship at all costs, resolve this knot? Historic irony was compounded by everyday realities, as gold money, whose value as money was derived from its "intrinsic" value as commodity, kept disappearing from circulation. The distinction between what gold *is* and what it *represents* is possible only when gold is thought of as looking *like* money. Phrased differently, what allows gold finally to become money is to think that it is not in itself money but only looks like money. The thought may strike one as paradoxical, though as Georg Simmel explains in his *Philosophy of Money*, "The more [money] is really money in its essential significance, the less need there is for it to be money in a material sense."[6] All these ideas — the historic irony of shifting political positions as well as a new way of thinking about gold as money — were too divisive politically to be articulated in a tale for a mass market, and so Poe's "affair of dollars and sense" is held in abeyance, set aside for the time, or deferred to convention: abeyance, from Anglo-French *abeiance*, desire, from *abaher*, to gape at or after. We as readers are rapt, waiting for the further realizations the tale seems to promise, though we are only left with the thankless task — a task that is comparable to Legrand's solving the cipher — of untangling the knot comprised of precious metal, paper, and signs.

The task of untangling the knot comprised of precious metal, paper, and signs is a thankless one largely because of Poe's tendency to shun, both in private and in public, the issues that contemporaries regarded as political. As a critic, Poe proclaimed that "political allusions" have "no business in a poem."[7] Poe wrote this in 1844, at a time when he certainly had come to believe that he could sell his writings to a national audience only by jealously excluding from them political explicitness. Yet as I gathered and worked through the material that testifies to a depoliticized Poe, I found that many of Poe's writings from the 1830s are openly political. At the same time, I would hasten to add, they are works of negation, as I was unable to find a single piece in which a character follows a trajectory of action motivated by political circumstances. In fact, from "King Pest" to "The Philosophy of Furniture" and, finally, to "Mellonta Tauta," there is nothing but disgust with Jacksonian democracy. This should not be taken to mean that Poe's relation to Jackson's political opponents was frictionless. Poe to an extent shared the Whigs' fears of lawlessness, and he supported their efforts to reestablish a national bank of issue; on the other hand, Poe could only have been unhappy with the Whigs' professed positions of elitism. Yet what I want to propose in this chapter is that Poe never saw as an option a move *into* politics, though he appears to have had no compunction about using politics to his personal advantage. Poe on many occasions tried to get the attention of politicians, including of John Tyler, for whom he professed to have the highest respect. Whether this is true or not, Poe had at least two favors to ask the President — one was support for his magazine project, the other a government position that would provide a secure income. Poe found two ways for getting near Tyler, the one a cryptogram that he dedicated to the President, and the other "The Gold Bug." Yet neither one of Poe's strategies to please and further his cause with the president got Poe anywhere, though "The Gold-Bug" at least won him a cash prize as the best tale with money as a subject.

Politics Invisible?

Regardless of whether beach or bank, Legrand in "The Gold-Bug" discovers a paper that leads to the gold that he could exchange for commercial papers. The ostensible topic of the tale thus may well be the search for buried treasure, a truly sensational subject that Poe could count on his readers would like and that, true to his own literary beliefs, he treated in a heightened style. Yet Poe did not take the story beyond the finding of the treasure, but continued instead with Legrand's narrative of how he solved the cipher and thus found the treasure. I have dealt with the Oedipal logic underlying the division of the tale into two parts in a previous chapter.[8] Framing the tale within America's monetary history, however, its actual thesis and source of originality is not so much the plight of the bereaved child that is unable to mourn the loss of a parent as a concern with money as currency. Were Legrand in fact to make use of the unearthed treasure by engaging in the social world, he would have to exchange the gold for currency. Of course, to attempt to exchange the "gold of antique date and of great variety" for gold or silver coins would have been gratuitous, as in real life such coins were scarcely seen or, if they were, tended to be withdrawn from rather than kept in circulation. Similarly, the conversion of the gold for depreciating paper bills would be begging for the very bankruptcy that had motivated the treasure hunt in the first place. There is, however, a third possibility, not explicitly spelled out, but rather in the form of an unspoken desire, a presentiment. That possibility comes in the form of a stable paper currency that would serve not only as a much-needed medium of exchange in everyday commercial transactions but also as a social and cultural arrangement of value resting on the general trust that people have both in an institution of power and in one another.

In order to lend plausibility to this thesis it is necessary to go back in time, to the year 1811, when John and Frances Allan took in young Edgar. In that year, the mercantile firm headed by his foster father and Charles Ellis likewise confronted a financial and economic crisis. Based in Richmond, Virginia, Ellis and Allan had been closely observing the congressional debates over proposals to renew the charter of the first Bank of the United States. Like the majority of well-to-do merchants, they looked to the bank to provide a sound and uniform currency. When Congress refused to renew the charter, Ellis and Allan informed their customers that, "the fate of the U. States Bank seems to be decided.... We consider the existence of that institution at an end."[9] The end envisaged by the two partners in business lasted until 1816, when the institution returned as the Second Bank of the United States. The resurrected bank played a major role in the business affairs of Ellis and Allan throughout Poe's childhood. Later, when Poe was struggling to become a commercial writer, the bank was a key player in the political affairs of the nation and especially in the presidency of Andrew Jackson, whose "war" against the bank put an end to it when its charter expired in 1836. Later still, as Poe was seeking a clerkship under the Tyler administration, the mere idea of a national bank of issue prompted a crisis in the Whig Party and the near collapse of the Tyler presidency.

Poe's upbringing in the Allan household not only provided him with a supreme economic education as well as an introduction to political economy as an important, all-encompassing discourse. It also brought him in direct contact with the world of banks and banking. Poe was not quite sixteen years old when the *Richmond Compiler* reported that John Allan had been elected to the Board of Directors of the Richmond branch of the Bank of Virginia, of which Allan's uncle William Galt, one of the wealthiest men in the State of Virginia, was already a director. Two years later, Poe's foster father, from whom young Edgar had become increasingly estranged, was appointed director of the Bank of Virginia and its ten branches.[10] The Bank of Virginia was chartered on January 13, 1804, with a capital of $1,500,000. The institution was profitable in its early years. Its currency traded at par with gold and silver, which was not common at the time. Following the panic of 1837, the bank was in difficulty, including a loss of $540,000 in uncollectible loans made by the paying teller. Like other banks, the Bank of Virginia was prohibited from issuing any bills under the $5 denomina-

Twenty-dollar note from the Bank of Virginia, Richmond, 1836 (courtesy National Numismatic Collection, Smithsonian Institution).

tion. To make transactions more convenient, it issued odd denominations such as $6, $7, $8, and $9 in addition to such values as $10, $20, $50, and $100.[11]

Although the Bank of Virginia was troubled by the panic of 1837, many other banks fared much worse during the economic turmoil. Whenever they felt that they no longer could meet their customers' demands of exchanging their paper bills into precious coins, they suspended such payment. The Virginia legislature passed a rule that, contrary to earlier law, banks could issue bills denominated at less than $5 up to a total value of six percent of their capital. Most banks resumed specie payment in due course. Then in 1841 the collapse of the Bank of the United States of Pennsylvania sent shock waves through other states, and many banks again suspended, including those in Virginia.[12] In Cincinnati, Ohio, several banks that had suspended became the "objects of assault," *Niles' National Register* of January 22, 1842 reported. The banks were "forcibly taken possession of, and their books, papers, notes and fixtures were destroyed and thrown into the street."[13]

Bank riots were also reported from New Orleans and several other cities throughout the nation, engendering reports in the *Register*, in Gouge's *Journal of Banking*, as well as in numerous newspapers. Poe may well have taken notice, as he too was much concerned about the frequent suspensions of specie payments by banks during the administrations of Jackson and Van Buren. It is possible, though not proven, that Poe was present when in August 1835 creditors and note holders ran riot in Baltimore, following the failure of the Bank of Maryland. The bank, which had gained its charter as early as 1790, had recklessly expanded in the early 1830s, circulating paper bills far exceeding its means to redeem them. By 1833, the bank's currency had become unacceptable to many in the financial community. A year later, the bank failed, leaving holders with paper with a face value totaling more than $1.5 million. The bank's officers promised a full explanation, which never came. When the riots began, people went out of control in the city for almost a week, destroying houses and personal property of the former bank officers. *Niles' Weekly Register*, which then was published in Baltimore, followed the events in detail.[14]

Baltimore was then the third largest city in the United States and a site of glory that was as important for the arts and culture as it was for commerce and politics. In 1832, both

Andrew Jackson and Henry Clay were nominated as presidential candidates by their respective parties there. Poe had taken residence in this city in 1831, following his dismissal from West Point. Two years later, he ends a letter to the editors of the *New-England Magazine* with the words: "P.S. I am poor."[15] Another two years later, Poe goes on record as being "*very* poor." In March of 1835, Poe applied for a position as a teacher in the Baltimore Public Schools, though apparently he did not get the appointment. As John Pendleton Kennedy wrote Thomas White on April 13, "I told [Poe] to write something for every number of your magazine [the *Southern Literary Messenger*], and that you might find it to your advantage to give him some permanent employ. He has a volume of very bizarre tales in the hands of——[Henry C. Carey], in Philadelphia, who for a year past has been promising to publish them. He is at work upon a tragedy [*Politian*], but I have turned him to drudging upon whatever may make money."[16] Grinding poverty later drove Poe to accept a position offered him at *Graham's Gentleman's Magazine*, though the deferral of his plans for the *Penn Magazine* was largely because of the bank suspensions.[17]

Poe left Baltimore for Richmond, Virginia, in early August of 1835. He never again made a home in Baltimore, but thought fondly of the city and often passed through on business and to visit family and friends. The bank riots of August 1835 probably were the most alarming such situation in American banking history, though there were many more bank failures to follow. The panic of 1837 had in its wake a general loss of confidence in paper bills, which already had begun to lose value. One reason for the depreciation of paper bills was inflation caused by the dramatic proliferation of commercial banks issuing notes; the other was Jackson's Specie Circular, which ordered land offices to only accept gold or silver in payment except from actual settlers. The land boom was over almost instantly, yet Jackson's edict also resulted in an unprecedented run on specie and the hoarding of sound bills. In the long run, interest rates went up, banks and businesses failed. The financial crisis had immediate consequences for Poe. His worsening financial situation has been mentioned, as well as the sad fate of his planned *Penn Magazine*, which from its inception was hampered by Poe's "want of capital." In addition, as editor of *Burton's Gentleman's Magazine* Poe had to inform other writers that "Mr. B[urton] with nearly, if not every, publisher of the country" had been obliged "to discontinue paying for contributions."[18] Poe was not one to easily forget, let alone forgive, past grievances. Towards the end of "Peter Pendulum" (probably written in early 1840, and published in revised form as "The Business Man" in the *Broadway Journal* of August 2, 1845), he has the narrator declare that he might suffer "no one to play the possum" with him. However, there was nothing he could do against the mysterious practices of the banks. "The frauds of the banks of course I couldn't help."[19]

I have dealt with the issue of "fraudulent banks" in Chapter 2. When the Baltimore bank riots made the headlines, Poe wrote "King Pest," ridiculing the monetary policies of Jackson and Van Buren. In this tale, which unfolds in "the parish of St. Andrews," the man with the bandaged leg recalls Thomas Hart Benton, the Missouri senator who led Jackson's fight for gold and against paper money. The gaunt and tall King Pest—the "president of the table"—of course points to President Jackson, who then was often lampooned as King Andrew. One of the drunken sailors who, fleeing from the "Jolly Tar's" landlady "down a dark alley in the direction of St. Andrew's Stair," seems to have been intended as Martin Van Buren.[20] Supporters of gold money derisively called small-denomination paper notes "shinplasters." In contrast, Senator Benton, Jackson's congressional ally, was nicknamed

"Old Bullion," and the elusive gold coins he chased came to be called "Benton's mint drops."[21] In fact, all of Poe's early satires suggest affinities with Whiggish positions, which then included support of paper money from a national bank of issue. Yet Poe is also on record for temporarily associating himself with the *Democratic Review*, a political-literary magazine that John O'Sullivan had founded in 1837 in order to champion Jacksonian democracy, hence also hard-money policies. Also a matter of record is that Poe called Richard Adams Locke "one among the few men of *unquestionable genius* whom the country possesses."[22] Locke was a newspaperman from England, whose popular daily, the *New Era*, supported both Van Buren's Independent Treasuries and the disuse of all paper money from government payments.

How does one explain such seeming inconsistencies? It is tempting to see in them the — quintessentially American — dream of politics without partisan conflict, and of politics without political parties. That dream, Sean Wilentz wrote recently in *The New Republic*, already ran deep in American political culture of the revolutionary era and the early republic.[23] George Washington, in his Farewell Address of 1796 had given expression to the classical formulation of American anti-party thought. Parties were not "natural" but "artificial" and intolerable — "of fatal tendency," Washington wrote, and duly warned of their "dangers" and of the "fury of party spirit."[24] Thomas Jefferson, too, in his inaugural address of 1801, stressed "difference of opinion" rather than "difference of principle," concluding, "We are all Republicans, we are all Federalists," united in "common efforts for the common good."[25] In each instance, however, the professed neutrality of political ideas served a strategic point *within* the larger political process: Washington could play the critical role of embodiment of the Constitution only by being nonpartisan; Jefferson's conciliatory animus was to placate the Federalists, who rightly suspected that the Jeffersonians' "democracy" was undermining their own claim to being the nation's natural, disinterested, wise, and virtuous rulers.

Poe's version of post-partisanship is different. If Poe generally avoided referring to the more controversial issues of the day, he clearly did so because he had learned that divisive political questions might be harmful to his success in a mass market. It was in order to succeed with a national audience that Poe took such great pains to fashion himself as a politically neutral author. The writings he published in the *Democratic Review*—a series of "Marginalia," respectively in November and December 1844 and in April and July 1846—cannot in good conscience be said to reveal any partisan bias. In April 1848, he even expunged the promise to include, in each issue of the proposed *Stylus* magazine, "a Retrospect of our Political History."[26] This move clearly testifies to Poe's disenchantment with politics, yet already in an earlier letter to Thomas H. Chivers, Poe had disavowed partisan politics altogether, declaring that his "political views" had "reference to no one of the present parties."[27] This may simply be a diplomatic disclaimer, if not a dim echo of a letter George Washington wrote to Henry Knox, the Secretary of War, speaking of the "difficulty to one, who is *of no party*."[28] It is more plausible, however, to see in the letter to Chivers further evidence that neither Poe's life nor his writings betray a greater degree of political involvement. This is surprising, as both his upbringing and the experiences he made would make one rather expect this. Poe of course did advocate a number of progressive reforms, but as his career wore on, he would concentrate his political energies on the field of literary production. "I am a literary man," he wrote to his friend Frederick William Thomas.[29]

Presumably one can be "a literary man" in more ways than one. Poe's ideal literary man seems to have been Freeman Hunt, whom he also considered a friend. In January 1845, Hunt both announced the establishment of the *Broadway Journal* and inserted a "puff" for the new magazine by citing the journal's prospectus. Praise for the journal's "discriminating and just" criticisms came in the April issue. In addition, Hunt favorably mentioned Poe's *Tales* in the August 1845 issue of his *Merchants' Magazine*, and published an equally appreciative review of *The Raven and Other Poems* in the January 1846, issue. For his part, Poe on several occasions commends *Hunt's Merchants' Magazine* as "the most valuable journal of its kind," praising it for its "perfect nationality" or "strict *nationality*." Freeman Hunt, he observes in December 1845, "is neither a Northern, a Southern, an Eastern, or a Western man. He is an inhabitant of the United States — if you please, an Alleghanian. He speaks to the whole people — and very effectively, because usefully, to all."[30] Poe, it seems, lost no chance to trumpet the *Merchants' Magazine*. While he most certainly did so in return for Hunt's flattering attention to his own new magazine, if not for Hunt's repeatedly calling him a "genius," he would hardly have done so if he had not felt at least a measure of proximity to the mercantile interests in general and the pro-paper money positions in particular that were represented in the magazine's pages. However, praise for Hunt speaking to "the whole people" also reveals the extent to which Poe had learned to avoid partisan politics when he entered the magazine business. In this business, in which the publishing industries and the primary commercial functions of the cities came together, success or failure was starkly a matter of the salability of literary commodities across the boundaries of class, taste, political affiliation, and region.

Already the prospectus for the *Southern Literary Messenger*, which beginning in 1837 appeared on the cover of many issues of the magazine, promised that "*Party Politics* [...] as far as possible," would be "jealously excluded." A few years later, Poe's co-editor at the *Broadway Journal* warned about the dangers of embracing "horrifying because unprofitable doctrines."[31] This prudent stance, Terence Whalen notes, was perhaps a legacy of the business protocol Poe had learned from John Allan. Allan, ever mindful of the exigencies of commerce, had warned William Galt, Jr., about the pitfalls of mixing business with politics: "[Y]ou will recollect you are to have no Political Opinions, as you go to America as one of its foster Sons it is but right you should be neuter. No man will blame your attachment to the country which gave you Birth, but prudence dictates that you should not say anything about the Government, but the best is to let Politics alone altogether."[32] At the time, Poe was living in London with the Allans, and so it is quite likely that Allan gave similar advice to his foster son.

Poe's calculating approach to the literary market makes any attempt to read politics back into his work extremely "vexing," as Whalen aptly puts it.[33] For one thing, a "depoliticized" Poe is not simply a construct of modern critics; a "depoliticized" Poe in many ways was depoliticized from the start, and Poe's writings evidence this by their ambiguities and contradictions. It is blatantly obvious, for instance, that in none of Poe's major works is there a character following a trajectory of actions that is motivated by *political* circumstances. Thus to identify Poe as either a "paper money man" or a "gold bug" is as misleading as to say that he was a Federalist, a Whig, or a Democratic Republican. For one thing, Poe did not enter directly into the political debates about America's money, which he seems to have despised, though his friend John Pendleton Kennedy did. This Baltimore novelist in 1840 published *Quodlibet*, an allegorical attack on the supposed follies of Jacksonianism — its glorification of majority voting, its cant of the common man, its vilification of "aristocrats," and its demagoguery. What according to Vernon L. Parrington is "one of [America's] few distinguished political satires" tells the story of the rise to prosperity of the Borough of Quodlibet, following the removal of the "Deposites." Yet its rows of shops are all built on speculation, and its Patriotic Copper-Plate Bank, which issued unlimited numbers of bank notes as fuel to the economy, fails and the cashier runs away to Europe. Its end, nevertheless, is attributed by the Jacksonians to the secret politics of the Whigs.[34]

Although Poe, through his work as a commercial writer, managed to make politics almost invisible, he could not afford any permanent estrangement from the controversial issues of the real world. Poe was, as Evert A. Duyckinck noted in his diary years after the writer's death, "sensitive to opinion," and his writings especially from the late 1830s offer many glances at the state of American society.[35] What Poe saw generally made him dejected and often gave rise to images of fear and horror. Already "Ms. Found in a Bottle," which dates from 1831–1833, is replete with images of bottomless abysses, and in the end — "Oh, horror upon horror"— the ship, "amid a roaring, and bellowing, and thundering of ocean and of tempest" is in fact "going down!"[36] Poe's poetic use of shipwrecks is obsessive, indicative of the power the conventions of romantic art had on his writing, though mindful of his "supreme ability to absorb and transform the 'news' of his own time, of his own place,"[37] a symptomatic reading of the catastrophe seems in order. Rather than postulate an unearthly vision that disengages us from historic reality, such a reading seeks to construe the tale's "ship" in terms of the traditional metaphor of a "ship of state." In doing so, a link is established between the political subtext of "Ms. Found in a Bottle" and the Hard Times token on which the wrecked ship *Experiment* represents Van Buren's monetary policy.[38]

"Shadow — A Parable" is written from the point of view of a deceased person, who remembers an encounter, during a nightly meeting with friends, with the dead. There is at first much merriment, yet it all takes a turn for the uncanny by "the boding and memory of Evil," which the frolickers are unable to shut out. They must wish they were able to, though, as "The year had been a year of terror, and of feelings more intense than terror."[39] It is tempting to read "Shadow — A Parable" as yet another story of abstract speculation, the poetic rendering of a voice from beyond the grave, though the year of the tale's composition —1834–1835 — should caution against too much emphasis on a metaphysics of terror. There had indeed been plenty of "news" of his own time and place for Poe to absorb and transform in the tale, most notably the election of Andrew Jackson to his second term and Jackson's bank war that was in full swing then. The general mood is somewhat different in "Silence — A Fable," though Jackson still looms large over this piece from 1832 to 1835, which is conveyed to the first-person narrator by a demon. The demon tells of coming, in a landscape of dreary morass, upon a rock that bears the inscription "DESOLATION." On the rock stands a solitary man, "tall and stately in form," with the "features of a deity," a "brow lofty with thought," and an eye "wild with care; and, in the few furrows upon his cheek I read the fables of sorrow, and weariness, and disgust with mankind, and a longing after solitude."[40]

Does "Silence — A Fable," then, constitute an allegory of a general world-weariness that is completely unconcerned with social matters? One would have to answer in the affirmative, were it not that Poe called this piece a fable. Yet is it really a fable of world-weariness?

No motives are given for the man's sorrows. On the other hand, there is a textual detail, easily overlooked perhaps, but sufficient to read the piece as a political fable. The man standing on the rock is "wrapped up from his shoulders to his feet in the toga of old Rome." A toga is not just any piece of clothing, but constitutes a key symbol of American republicanism, which constructed Roman virtue above all in terms of resistance against tyranny. John Tyler, for instance, during his presidency claimed the toga of Roman virtue for his imagined role in the political struggle over the destiny of America's money. Poe of course could not yet know this at the time of the tale's composition, though memories were still fresh then of Henry Clay's loss, in the 1832 election, against an incumbent Andrew Jackson. Clay, for all his pretensions to Roman virtue, lacked public appeal, while Jackson interpreted his reelection as the people's reward for his war against the Bank of the United States, a war that he continued to pursue with great energy.[41]

Poe republished both "Shadow — A Parable" and "Silence — A Fable" in his *Broadway Journal* in 1845. By then, his satirical impetus against Jacksonianism was more forceful than ever, though he had made any number of derisive pronouncements before. In "The Philosophy of Furniture," for instance, Poe connected the corruption of taste he found in contemporary America with the relentless pursuit of money and wealth. "We have no aristocracy of blood," he wrote in 1840, "and having therefore as a natural, and indeed as an inevitable thing, fashioned for ourselves an *aristocracy of dollars*, the *display of wealth* has here to take the place and perform the office of the heraldic display in monarchical countries."[42] In his attack on the habit of marking social status through a competitive display of one's possessions Poe anticipates Thorstein Veblen, who later called this habit "conspicuous consumption." Yet Poe also rails against "democratic capitalism," which he saw as mere social climbing and craving for rank in society. Although Poe has been said to be full of ambition, he nevertheless denounced the debasement of values that he observed as "an evil growing out of our republican institutions, that here a man of large purse has usually a very little soul which he keeps in it. The corruption of taste is a pendant of the dollar-manufacture."[43]

Poe first published "The Philosophy of Furniture" in *Burton's Gentleman's Magazine* in May 1840, and then slightly revised it for publication in *The Broadway Journal* in 1845. Four years later, he returned to the theme of "dollar-manufacture" in "Mellonta Tauta," a futuristic satire that was first published in *Godey's Lady's Book* in February 1849. In this slight piece, Poe explores the idea that something indeed can be made from nothing. The notion was central to the debates about paper money; hence "dollar-manufacture" can be taken quite literally. Of course, to make something out of nothing is not an achievement that human beings are capable of accomplishing. While this had been held true generally, Poe's reference to Lucretius, *De rerum naturae*, is telling: "Ex nihilo nihil fit," he quotes, adding that this "long established axiom" now has been "rejected" as "untenable." Indeed by Poe's time, to make something out of nothing seemed possible both in the realm of aesthetics and in the world of finance.[44]

"Mellonta Tauta" was the first work of fiction Poe had published for two whole years. Set in the year 2848, it records a present where mile-high balloons transport hundreds of passengers at high speed, and looks back satirically on a past in which the ancient "Amriccans" built what they called churches — "a kind of pagoda instituted for the worship of two idols that went by the names of Wealth and Fashion."[45] The balloon-ride begins, appropriately, on April Fool's Day, marking the intent of parodying philosophical positions like the belief in human perfectibility and other cherished myths of Poe's time. Today, the piece is remembered mainly for containing Poe's most absolute attack on Jacksonian democracy. The "Amriccans," we are told, lived in egalitarian chaos, in "a sort of every-man-for-himself confederacy, after the fashion of the 'prairie dogs' that we read of in fable." In this strange land, "Every man 'voted,' as they called it — that is to say, meddled with public affairs — until, at length, it was discovered that everybody's business is nobody's, and that the 'Republic' (so the absurd thing was called) was without a government at all." "Mellonta Tauta" is a kind of thought experiment. Poe had set up its terms already in "The Sphinx," published in *Arthur's Ladies' Magazine*, January 1846, in which the narrator's host declares that, "To estimate properly [...] the influence to be exercised on mankind at large by the thorough diffusion of Democracy, the distance of the epoch at which such diffusion may possibly be accomplished, should not fail to form an item in the estimate." If by 1848 Poe felt that no one who saw democracy from a distant future would consider it feasible, he was looking abroad as well. His "*Mob*" in "Mellonta Tauta" is described as a foreign monster "said to have been the most odious of all men that ever encumbered the earth. He was a giant in stature — insolent, rapacious, filthy; had the gall of a bullock with the heart of an hyena and the brains of a peacock."[46]

Poe rarely wrote about current political affairs, but in the case of "Mellonta Tauta" he clearly had been alarmed by the popular uprisings in Europe during 1848, the culminating year of the "Hungry Forties" there, and the year that brought *The Communist Manifesto* with its sinister promise, "A spectre is haunting Europe."[47] Given the difficulty of determining Poe's political allegiances, it is worth noting that America's major political parties responded rather differently to the revolutions in Europe. The Democrats, by invoking the principle of the sovereignty of the people, were able to welcome the surfacing of new nations on the ruins of Old World despotism. The Whig Party, in contrast, displayed ambivalence, wavering between sympathy for humanitarian reformers in Europe, and attachment to legal order and dismay over mob rule.[48] These differences take on special significance insofar as Poe presents "Mellonta Tauta" as "a translation, by my friend, Martin Van Buren Mavis, (sometimes called the 'Toughkeepsie Seer,') of an odd-looking MS. which I found, about a year ago, tightly corked up in a jug floating in the *Mare Tenebrarum* — a sea well described by the Nubian geographer, but seldom visited, now-a-days, except by the transcendentalists and divers for crotchets."[49]

The "Toughkeepsie Seer" in Poe's "Mellonta Tauta" is a barely disguised aside on the spiritualist author Andrew Jackson Davis of Poughkeepsie, New York, who by the 1840s was much admired for his alleged skills in reaching the beyond or, as Poe contemptuously phrases it, the Sea of Darkness (the "*Mare Tenebrarum*" of the tale). Of course, the "Andrew Jackson" in Davis's name also could not have failed to attract the attention of politically savvy readers, especially since it comes coupled with a reference to "Martin Van Buren." The historic Martin Van Buren, as Poe must have remembered only too well, not only was Jackson's handpicked successor. Van Buren also had been utterly unable to cope with the economic depression in the aftermath of the Panic of 1837. Tellingly also, Poe represents "Amricca" as a hard-money country. Among the relics that antiquarians salvage from the ruins left by a disastrous earthquake is "a leaden box filled with various coins."[50] The money discourse of Poe's own America resurfaces again in an oblique reference to Missouri senator Thomas Hart Benton, who in the story appears as "the great Amriccan poet Benton," whose

line "solitary and alone" of course identifies him as the hard-money man and staunch supporter of Andrew Jackson. Benton used the phrase "solitary and alone" in his famous
"expunging speech" of January 14, 1837. The speech referred to the condemnation, by the
Senate, of President Jackson for his insistence on removing federal deposits from the Bank
of the United States. Jackson had sent a formal protest on April 17, 1834. The Senate formally
refused to receive this and it was not until almost three years later that Benton found it possible to defeat the "bank ruffians," as he called the supporters of a national bank of issue.
His speech in the Senate concludes thus: "Solitary and alone, and amidst the jeers and
taunts of my opponents, I put this ball in motion ... I [now] demand the expurgation of
that sentence [from the journal of the Senate]."[51]

The notion of literally "expunging" the Senate's record struck many people as improper.
The feeling certainly did not go away when the financial policies of Jackson and Benton
made worse the effects of speculation and overexpansion in the panic of 1837. Early in the
year Henry R. Robinson came forth with cartoon titled "N. Tom O'Logical Studies: The
Great Tumble Bug of Missouri Bent-On Rolling His Ball," which is labeled "Expunging
Resolution" with the line beneath reading "Solitary and alone." By then Benton's phrase
had become a household phrase. In October, the *United States Gazette and Democratic
Review* published a picture showing Benton at the debate in the Senate and uttering the
well-known words. The *United States Gazette and Democratic Review* was an influential
magazine that Poe knew well, and we can reasonably assume that he saw the portrait and
the caption. He may also have seen Robinson's cartoon, as he had come to New York in
February 1837, in the hope of a paying job. Certainly the effects of Jacksonian financial
policy did not make Poe a partisan of the Democrats. The "great Amriccan poet Benton,"
then, is used by Poe to give expression to his disenchantment with popular democracy,
whose "civilization" has collapsed, like the balloon "Skylark" that carries the antiquarians
over the ruins in the year 2848.

Whereas Jacksonian Democrats are the butt of Poe's satirical efforts, other public figures
seemingly get a much better press. One is George Washington, about whom we learn that
the corner stone for a monument to his memory was laid, "with appropriate ceremonies on
the 19th day of October, 1847, the anniversary of the surrender of Lord Cornwallis to General
Washington at Yorktown, A.D. 1781." Poe tells the story through the foolish narrator "Pundita," who observes that the state of the excavations show that the monument itself was
never built. Poe was living in New York then, and so the reference clearly is to the monument
proposed by the Washington Monument Association of New York. A subscription had
started in August 1843, though the collection of money was slow. A public festival for the
laying of the cornerstone was to speed things up, but the attempt to solicit contributions
turned out to be as spectacular as it was futile. The New York *Herald Tribune* of October
20, 1847, gives the whole account, which Poe may well have read as he was at work on the
story. Poe also may have been aware of the Washington National Monument Society, which
went ahead with its own plans, even though the Washington, DC, monument for a long
time seemed to be always building, too, never to be completed.[52]

While the cornerstone to the Washington monument was to remain, like Senator Benton, "solitary and alone," the nation's father, always the embodiment of the dream of politics
without partisan conflict, and of politics without political parties, remains unscathed.
George Washington is not the only one to have been spared Poe's satirical lash. At the end

of the tale the narrator, who is about to stuff the whole tale into a bottle as the balloon is about to hurl them all into the sea, declares, "from a hasty inspection of the fac-similes of newspapers [...] I find that *the* great men in those days among the Amriccans, were one John, a smith, and one Zacchary, a tailor."[53] Presumably, "John, a smith" is a reference to John Smith, a nephew of Joseph Smith, Jr., the founder of the Mormon Church and the author of *The Book of Mormon*. In 1848, John Smith, along with Heber C. Kimball, reached Salt Lake City, Utah, to join Brigham Young, who had become the leader of the largest Mormon group, the Church of Jesus Christ of Latter-Day Saints. Many magazines at the time, the *Dollar Newspaper* included, carried pictures and sensational reports of the doings of Smith and his faithful, so a reference to Smith is not a real surprise.[54] What is truly surprising is that in "Mellonta Tauta" Poe seems to also articulate sympathies for the Democrats' political adversaries. "Zacchary, a tailor," without doubt evokes the name of Zachary Taylor, who was the last Whig to win a presidential election, when in November 1848 he defeated Lewis Cass, the Democratic candidate, and Martin Van Buren, who then stood for the Free Soil Party.

Zachary Taylor had been born into the Virginia plantation gentry and tried in the recent war with Mexico. In 1848, he aligned himself with the Whig Party, though he disagreed with the party's stand on protective tariffs and costly internal developments in manufacturing and large-scale agriculture. Always tight-lipped about his political beliefs, Taylor declared himself a firm nationalist, for whom neither sectional nor partisan division secession were proper ways to resolve national problems. In addition, Taylor professed belief in a strong and sound banking system for the country, holding that Jackson had willfully and impudently destroyed the Bank of the United States in 1836. Taylor was, however, realistic enough to concede that, thanks largely to California gold, the idea of a national bank issuing paper bills "is dead, & will not be revived in my time." The statement, together with his declaration that he would never be "the slave of a party instead of the chief magistrate of the nation," did not make him many friends with Whig leaders in Congress, though each might have resonated with Poe, who seems to have taken it lightly that the excitement attending Taylor's election thwarted his plans for a possible lecture in Lowell, Massachusetts.[55]

What also might have resonated with Poe was the Whigs' defense of principles and prejudices that ostensibly upheld an individual's dignity and rights, including discipline, order, self-control, and principled conviction. All this, Poe states with a measure of bitter sarcasm, was gone by 2848. In "Mellonta Tauta"—the Greek phrase means "These things are in the future"—the narrator celebrates the future as "an age so enlightened that no such thing as an individual is supposed to exist." In this day and age, it is "the mass for which the true Humanity cares." Accordingly, when a man is knocked overboard from a small boat, he, "of course, was not permitted to get on board again." Nor are "War and Pestilence" regarded as "calamities" any longer.[56] The depressing outlook—in which "democracy" and "the masses" appear as a violation of the natural order by human nature in all its perversity[57]—testifies to the degree of Poe's abhorrence of the Jacksonians' political rhetoric, with their populist celebration of the rights of the multitude and of the wisdom and sagacity of the common man. Poe's manifest loathing links "Mellonta Tauta" to his first attempts at political satire in the 1830s, such as "King Pest," "Hans Phaall," "The Devil in the Belfry," "The Man Who Was Used Up," and other short pieces.

One of these short pieces is "Four Beasts in One." Poe wrote it in 1833 as "Epimanes" and published it under the better-known title only in the *Southern Literary Messenger* of December 6, 1845. The piece faithfully registers comments, by contemporary observers, on Jackson's taking office in March 1829. Whereas the President's supporters saw the event as the harbinger of a bright Democratic millennium in which at long last "the people" would rule, his opponents saw only darkness in the rude, illiterate mob that seemingly expected a personal part in running the country. For one observer it was evident, therefore, that "[t]he reign of King 'Mob' seemed triumphant."[58] This commentator, like many others who regarded the rise of the underclasses with fear and loathing, eventually gravitated towards the Whig Party. So apparently did Poe, in whose "Four Beasts in One" the incredulous bystander professes to see "nothing but a tumultuous mob of idiots and madmen, who are busy in prostrating themselves before a gigantic cameleopard, and endeavoring to obtain a kiss of the animal's hoofs." In a later scene, the courtiers are seen deserting the King when danger threatens, a reference, in this case, to E. W. Clay's cartoon of Jackson's cabinet, titled "Rats Leaving a Fallen House." Poe's portrayal of the beasts turning on their masters thus can be said to mark the beginning of this author's habitual denunciation of that mysterious collectivity known as "the mob." Many critics, including William Charvat and Michael Gilmore, have been repulsed by what they considered as Poe's apparent ideology, the more so as Poe has been identified with a screed, published in 1836, against the "lawless appetite of the multitude for the property of others," an appetite, it is emphasized, that erroneously "calls itself liberty."[59]

The passage in question is part of a review of James Kirke Paulding's *Slavery in the United States*, published in the *Southern Literary Messenger* of April 1836, together with a review of *The South Vindicated from the Treason and Fanaticism of the Northern Abolitionists*, an anonymous work generally attributed to William Drayton. This proslavery essay from the *Southern Literary Messenger* often has been used to determine Poe's conservative politics and alleged racism, though it was attributed to Poe mistakenly. The essay's real author was Nathaniel Beverley Tucker, a law professor at the College of William and Mary, who violently opposed any form of central government as well as any form of democratic politics. Tucker also was the author, in 1836, of *The Partisan Leader*, the first secessionist novel, which assaults Jacksonianism at the same time as it glorifies John C. Calhoun. Although Tucker's authorship of the Paulding-Drayton review has been known since 1924, some seventy years later the essay was still called Poe's "greatest love poem."[60] The Paulding-Drayton review also influenced Ernest Marchand's estimation of Poe as a social critic. Writing in 1935, Marchand unforgivingly criticizes Poe as a defender of "the South's peculiar institutions" and, as well, as hostile to "democracy, industrialism, and reform."[61] Indeed, "Slavery" does cite the French Revolution, trying to persuade readers that only the ownership of property can bring true happiness. Property, the reviewer claims, is that thing at which "all men aim, and their eagerness seems always proportioned to the excitement, which ... may for the time prevail. Under such excitement, the many who want, band themselves together against the few that possess; and the lawless appetite of the multitude for the property of others calls itself the spirit of liberty."[62]

To insist on property (actually, possessions) as a precondition of happiness of course would make Poe an enemy to "democracy, industrialism, and reform," much as it would identify him unequivocally as a partisan of the gold standard. But Poe did not write "Slavery." The tendency towards resolving textual ambiguities by speaking to the alleged beliefs of the alleged author, however, seems ineradicable. David Long, for instance, begins his remarkable essay on Poe's political identity by aligning Poe with the Whigs. Like Poe, Long argues, the Whigs needed the fiction of a popular "mob" as an ideological base for their elitist program. They too wished to make a heterogeneous audience assailable in some identifiable political opponent. In addition, they too assumed the viewpoint of the deeply offended citizen who nevertheless feels compelled to speak the honest but unpalatable truth. All this, Long claims, points to a deep malaise that had invaded American culture by the 1840s, though to acknowledge the malaise would not have been politically viable. Poe, however, did acknowledge it, and thus became so disenfranchised both from and with the Whigs that in the end he was debunking the ideological complex that most resembled his own. The vengeance with which Poe joined the Whigs' laments allowed him to transform it, yet at the cost of reducing himself to a majority of one. From this position, he described degeneracy and decay as part of human nature, a condition he saw as inescapable. Poe's anxiety, Long found, was so intense that it defied social categorization; so personal that it demanded original expression; and so literal to his mind that often in his writings the shadow became the substance. In all of this, he probably testified to the reality of the Whigs' worst nightmare: the violation of the natural order by human nature in all its perversity, and hence, the likelihood that the political order would change suddenly and violently.[63]

While there are numerous instances in Poe's biography of avowed elitism and a declared hostility towards democracy, we should nevertheless not take his pretensions towards elitism and outsiderdom at face value. For one thing, they are often balanced by his denunciations of editorial coteries, publishing cliques, and scribbling leisured gentlemen, "a class proverbial for conservatism." Moreover, Poe seemingly was capable of distinguishing between manufactured public opinion and the wisdom of "the people." This ability is evident from his characterizing his audience, not as the "mob" or the "rabble" or the "uncultivated taste," terms that he also used, but as a "demagogue-ridden public."[64] Importantly, Poe characterized the publishing industry itself as a kind of demagoguery, distorting and manipulating public opinion. Thus, Poe's diatribes against "the "mob" suggest that there must have been at least two such mysterious collectivities, one slowly emerging from the general process of capitalist development, the other conjured up in response to the uncontrolled expansion of the literary market. To the extent that Poe's scattered remarks on the "mob" reveal any anxiety, therefore, it is an anxiety over his economic reliance on a mass audience, with its dangerously unpredictable tastes.

A case can even be made that Poe's professed fear of and contempt for the "mob" at least in part was an aesthetic problem. As Alexis de Tocqueville remarked, in a democracy "men are all insignificant and very much alike." This "general similitude" of individuals, Tocqueville added, by lessening the likelihood of their idealization, renders them unfit as "objects for poetry."[65] In other words, the social and cultural conditions of a democracy lead to the disappearance of the tragic hero, though neither Tocqueville nor Poe observed that inevitable result. What we do know is that Poe, in search for suitable "objects for poetry," seems to have despaired over "the fact," as he saw it in 1849, "that the air of a Democracy agrees better with mere Talent than with Genius."[66] If this is to say that greater equality results in a lack of differences, Poe came to embody the tension between the — imagined — advantages of a cultural elite and the exigencies of a more egalitarian, capitalist society in which he had to survive by his writing.

Difficult as it may be to get to the bottom of Poe's true political sentiments, there are nevertheless many occasions when he advocated governmental intervention in the economy, just as he often took a polemical stand on chiefly aesthetic grounds, mediating "conservatism" with irony and satire. In light of such inconsistencies, Ugo Rubio's characterization of Poe as a "transgressive conservative" seems apposite.[67] Although this formulation is easier to admire than to apply, it does shed some light on Poe's political beliefs and behavior. In a letter to Frederick W. Thomas, for instance, Poe muses that, should Robert Tyler, the president's son, be induced to become interested in his proposed *Penn* magazine, the magazine "might be made to play even an important part in the politics of the day." Poe's idea of something like an American equivalent to *Blackwood's* of Edinburgh certainly is interesting, given his customary reluctance to adopt a political position.[68] Also of interest is that in the course of 1845 Poe revised "The Gold-Bug," adding the passage about the green and red "tints" at the same time as he deleted a direct reference to the financial world by making Legrand walk along a "beach" rather than on a "bank." By that time, Poe had become a contributor to the *American Whig Review*, a political-literary journal that lasted from 1845 to 1852. The question, raised also by David Long, is what the appeal was of Poe's literary agenda to a *national* political organ? Moreover, given the Whigs' hope in a strong centralized government that would exert a tight control over the nation's money, what was the appeal to Poe's views about the money question?

An "Honest Statesman": Edgar Allan Poe and John Tyler

As champions of a government-controlled paper currency, the Whigs were fundamentally opposed against the "gold humbug" of Jackson and Van Buren. Yet the mainstay of Whig monetary policy had become extended credit availability that chiefly benefited the business community, even if such a policy prompted — as it certainly did in the eyes of their political opponents — extravagant speculation and overtrading. It is no surprise that the Democratic Republicans accused the Whigs of merely addressing themselves to human greed or, in the words of Samuel L. Young, "of cupidity; as though sordid interest alone was the controlling element which actuates mankind." Young, a radical Democrat and member of the state senate of New York, is here riding an all-out attack on the Whigs' use of the regulation of money and credit as a means of promoting the interests of the privileged in the society. "This," Young argued, "is simply the principle of monarchy, carried directly into the banking system, and indirectly into the national government."[69]

Young's fellow Democratic Republicans already in the 1830s had suspected the Whigs of using the Bank of the United States in an effort to subvert the government of the people. Thus for the Democrats, the mere presence of a government-controlled bank issuing paper dollars ("humbugs" in Young's words) for specie was enough to "defile the Temple of Liberty," as an orator thundered at a Democratic gathering in 1837. At the other extreme, at a Whig party convention held in Massachusetts in 1837, Jackson's vetoing the renewal of the Bank of the United States' charter was denounced as the beginning of all evil: "Under a pretence of a design to return to a currency which shall be all specie, we are likely to have a currency in which there shall be no specie at all. We are in danger of being overwhelmed with irredeemable paper [from the commercial banks]— mere paper— representing, not gold and silver,— no, Sir,— representing nothing but broken promises, bad faith, bankrupt corporations, cheated creditors, and a ruined people!"[70]

The Whigs also accused the Democratic Party of subverting the "platform of the Constitution," of undermining the "elements of the government," and of deriving its policies from "the uncertain sanctions of popular will."[71] Through their rhetoric, the Whigs projected a chaotic, even catastrophic future for a nation that was clearly bound for a vertiginous descent into the maelstrom. The only solution that seemed to offer itself for the Whigs was to re-establish a strong centralized government, in the sense of a stable center of power that would act in a socially significant way by holding on to the "American System" of tariffs, internal improvements paid for by the federal government, and a national bank. Charles Francis Adams was not the only Whig voice to see a national bank as "the only device which we have ever yet been able confidently to believe a means of preserving the currency in the Union perfectly sound." For Adams, preservation and control were synonymous: the premier object of a national bank, he concludes in August 1839, is "to control and regulate what can be controlled or regulated in no other manner."[72]

The Whigs' advocacy of a central bank may have been motivated by a desire to effectively control the currency, yet it also compelled Americans into a war of public virtue against bank corruption, to use the rhetoric of American republicanism.[73] As the Democrats saw it, only they could lead the forces of right because they had found the bank as extravagantly powerful, corrupt and corrupting in its doings, dangerous to the nation, and unnecessary to its prosperity. "If we sum up in one grand total all the woes to which paper money, banking, and the over-extended system of credit growing out of, have given birth, we shall pronounce it to be the most tremendous of the plagues which the Almighty in his wrath has suffered to afflict degenerate men." Excessive as this rhetoric was, its purpose was to add weight to the conviction that only the Democrats could restore the government of the country "to its primitive simplicity."[74] The measures the Democrats sought in the bank war— especially the Independent Treasury System to hold the federal government's receipts— would separate banking business from politics. This argument may well have been behind President John Tyler's decision to twice veto the proposed reestablishment of the Second Bank, though it does not explain why the congressional Whigs in 1844 suppressed attempts at federal paper money. But which side, if any, would Poe take?

The "paper money men" were mostly partisans of the Whigs. On occasion, they defended the right of all banks to issue paper notes, though more often than not they called for a new national bank of issue. By contrast, the "hard-money men" advocating an ostensibly populist reliance on gold and silver coin were mostly Jacksonian Democrats. The historic irony in this situation is considerable. Gold had been the preferred currency of the pre-revolutionary gentry, the loyalist Tories, at the same time as paper money had come to be associated with political sovereignty from England, hence with the patriots. Even the ill-fated Continental Currency—"paper-wasted, rag-born, kite-faced"— had been explicitly put in allegiance with "*whiggism*," in contrast to hard-money's alleged "bias to *Toryism*."[75] Yet from the beginnings of the new republic, the Jeffersonians not only distrusted banks in general, but also suspected that banking was imitative of British manners and institutions and thus threatening America's Republican heritage. By the 1830s, the idea of a national bank of issue had shifted to the Whig Party, usually considered to represent the wealthy business community; by contrast, the hard-money advocacy of the pre-revolutionary Tory Loyalists had been adopted as the monetary politics of the Democratic Party.

Poe's awareness of this shift of allegiances was acute. Just as acute was his awareness that gold coins were sold for a profit when the price of gold rose. In addition, he knew that at other times gold coins disappeared into vaults, were pulled from circulation just like the legendary Captain Kidd's treasure. By reversing the appellation of the phrase "humbug," from its populist reference to the paper dollars that the banks were issuing in lieu of specie to "gold humbug," Poe clearly implies a critique of gold money or, at the very least, a satire of the acrimonious debates of the time. For a "humbug," regardless of its referent, is a thing that is not, like Legrand's "dreams" about gold. Ultimately, of course, it does not really matter whether the money is of paper or of gold, as money — independent of its substance — is a social construct that always already implies an abstraction. The enterprise the *American Whig Review* had embarked on likewise was an abstraction, a social construct that Poe may have thought was merely trying to make something out of nothing. Indeed, the construct of an ideal body politic that Poe found spread over the journal's pages was one that was stitched together from relics of a distant past — standards of "knowledge and confidence" that spelled out the need for discipline, order, coherence, self-control, and principled conviction, such as the conviction that property and power belonged together. It is no surprise, then, that Poe's attitude towards the Whigs and their journal became mocking, if not derisive. Nowhere is this more strikingly obvious than in "Some Words with a Mummy," in which the narrator concludes, "I am convinced that everything is going wrong."[76]

These pessimistic sentiments are conventionally attributed to Poe himself. A letter Poe wrote to James Russell Lowell on July 2, 1844, also seems to bear this out: "I think that human effort will have no appreciable effect upon humanity [...] Man is now only more active — not more happy — nor more wise, than he was 6000 years ago."[77] Critics also refer to "The Balloon-Hoax," which Poe published in the same year and in which he satirized not only human gullibility but also the contemporary infatuation with the idea of progress. Yet the general context of the statement in his letter to Russell suggests that Poe was not giving expression to his own political and philosophical convictions so much as he was striking a pose. Earlier in the letter, he writes that he had "rambled and dreamed away whole months," awakening, only at long last, "to a sort of mania for composition."[78] Assuming that Poe's professed aloofness towards schemes of human perfectibility was merely affected, it may well have been, as Terence Whalen suggests, part of "a larger effort to portray himself as an impractical and somewhat tragic romantic visionary."[79]

Though others took him seriously, Poe without doubt understood that he was fashioning himself as a romantic poet, whose whole existence had been one of "the most utter unworldliness," and whose only pleasure was "solitary communion with the 'mountains & the woods' — the 'altars' of Byron."[80] This is a pose that can hardly be beaten. Poe's life may have been tragic, but it was about as unworldly and solitary as the paper bills passing from hand to hand then. In actual fact, the epithet "unworldly and solitary" is a much better fit for some of Poe's characters, such as the first-person narrator in "Berenice," whom the realities of the world affect only "as visions, and as visions only, while the wild ideas of the land of dreams became, in turn,–not the material of my everyday existence–but in very deed that existence utterly and solely in itself." It is, however, one thing for the narrator to begin his account by lamenting, "Misery is manifold. The wretchedness of earth is multiform," but it is quite another to ascribe such seeming universality and timelessness to Poe himself. True, Poe wrote at one point, "Truth is often, and in very great degree, the aim of the tale."[81] This may be an important principle for writing in a romantic vein, but such expressions do not per se constitute a true record of a writer's thoughts or convictions. Any writer works under certain constraints, which may well be poetic constraints. The latter are felt all over Poe's poetry. This is no surprise as Poe, who wanted to live and be appreciated as a poet, had inherited a living tradition of poetry. Indeed, the epithet "unworldly and solitary," so suggestive of a seeming universality and timelessness, applies well to "The Haunted Palace," through the "pale door" of which "A hideous throng rush out forever / And laugh — but smile no more." As a poem standing alone, "The Haunted Palace" may well have no other end than itself, while inserted into "The Fall of the House of Usher" it works as a dramatic monologue whose end is to represent Usher's "disordered brain." Yet the poem is not nearly as timeless and universal as its seems, and neither is the tale into which it was later inserted; on the contrary, there are good reasons to link the lost days of glory to the nation at large, from the "legitimate" terrors of Jackson's America to the house that soon was to be divided in fact.[82]

Nor is "The Conqueror Worm" entirely devoid of social symbolism. Coming to us as a "play of hopes and fears" that turns out to be merely a "tragedy, 'Man,'" the poem does seem to disengage the reader's mind from reality, as if to protect the reader from its remarkable lack of meaning and its cast of characters without individuality or free will. Yet the poem's composition at a time when Poe had realized that he could not possibly live by literary labor alone reveals the extent to which economic forces and constraints shaped his creativity also at the level of literary form. Mindful perhaps of the poem's reach beyond the ideal, Poe in 1838 inserted it into "Ligeia," though he gave it its final form only in the Lorimer Graham copy of *The Raven and Other Poems*.[83] Poe also revised for Lorimer Graham "The Dream-Land," which was first published or composed in 1844. The poem, which together with the two previous ones Poe considered "my best poems," is notable for its apocalyptic vision of "Mountains toppling evermore / Into seas without a shore." The dream-land may even constitute an "Eldorado," though not for an ordinary traveler who gets there by a "route obscure and lonely, / Haunted by ill angels only."[84] It is difficult to see in such lines anything but a stimulus to unearthly visions. Indeed, an imaginative order administered only to the other side of space fully corresponds to the conventions of romantic poetry, with its juxtaposition of thinking and feeling, and a diction that insists on dreams as the only "true" reality.

Poe, in fashioning himself as a romantic poet, took his clue mostly from Samuel Taylor Coleridge. That Poe was familiar with the writings of Coleridge at an early time is shown by his eulogistic praise of him in the preface to the 1831 edition of his poems. Poe found particularly attractive Coleridge's principles of aesthetics, especially the principle that art, to endure, must deal with experiences common to all humans, hence must possess a universal interest. He also borrowed from Coleridge an interest in exploring the limits of consciousness, an interest that reached a peak when he gave human attributes to his raven. Moreover, in Poe's estimation the *Biographia Literaria* was "the most deeply interesting of the prose writings of Coleridge," and he found in it a most valuable depository of wise quotations. In imitation of Coleridge, of whom five volumes of "Marginalia" have been published, Poe titled some of his own reflections and fragmentary material "Marginalia," publishing them

King Andrew the First, lithograph on wove paper, 1833 (original size 31.7 × 21.4cm) (Library of Congress, Prints and Photographs Division, LC-DIG-ppmsca-15771).

from 1845 to 1849. Finally, Poe appropriated Coleridge's philosophical voice, which apparently suited as well his mystical turn of mind.[85]

Poe's rendezvous with romanticism came to a grand finale in 1848, when he dedicates "Eureka" to "the few who love me and whom I love—to those who feel rather than to those who think—to the dreamers and those who put faith in dreams as in the only realities."[86] By that time, however, Poe's vision of Ultima Thule had shrunk to a mere memory of a personal dream inspired by Coleridge at a time when Poe still had hopes to be able to survive as a poet. Poe had since turned to other forms of writing, not out of inclination so much as out of sheer necessity, when as a consequence of the economic crisis that began in 1837 poetry had become "unsaleable."[87] Once Poe shifted his creative energies to literary forms that he hoped would be more marketable, he exchanged the image of the romantic outsider for that of the entrepreneur. The new role also compelled him to expunge politics from his writings, the more so as he wanted to reach out to a national audience. In doing so, his prose necessarily became almost indistinguishable from the romantic universalism and otherworldliness of the poetry. Yet writings such as "Some Words with a Mummy," in which the narrator concludes, "I am convinced that everything is going wrong," do not simply convey an unearthly vision that disengages us from historic reality. Notwithstanding the affected world-weariness, the tale at once expresses its author's disaffection and disguises the ideological affiliation and discrepancies between himself and the Whigs.[88]

Poe may have become thoroughly disaffected from party politics in his later years, though until the time of "The Gold-Bug" his political sympathies appear to have been with the National Republicans or Whigs, as the descendants of the earlier Federalists had come to be called. The Whig Party's origins and name have their roots in a speech Henry Clay gave on April 14, 1834, in which he compared the resistance to "King Andrew's" (that is, President Andrew Jackson's) usurpation of power to the English Whig party that rose in opposition to George III.[89] Identification of Jackson as "King Andrew" was a commonplace at the time, as is evident from an 1833 political cartoon by an unknown artist. The cartoon shows Jackson, in regal costume, standing before a throne in a frontal pose reminiscent of a playing-card king. He holds a "veto" in his left hand and a scepter in his right. The Federal Constitution and the arms of Pennsylvania (the United States Bank was located in Philadelphia) lie in tatters under his feet. A book "Judiciary of the U[nited] States" lies nearby. Around the border of the print are the words "Of Veto Memory," "Born to Command" and "Had I Been Consulted."

Throughout the 1830s and 1840s, many Southern conservatives sought refuge in the Whig Party, where a number of their concerns—about Jacksonian reformism and demagoguery, fears of "the mob," and the uncertainties of the currency—found a national voice. There is, however, no need to assume that Poe felt a deep sympathy for the ruling elites. True, Poe had studied at the University of Virginia, that is to say, in the neoclassical shadow of Monticello, whose owner he never ceased to admire. Thus he noted in 1846, "Jefferson's assertion that in this country, which has set the world an example of physical liberty, the inquisition of popular sentiment overrules in practice the freedom asserted in theory by the laws," was only too true. On the other hand, to take Poe's aristocratic pretensions at face value is to ignore the fact that John Allan's business dealings put him in conflict with both Southern plantation owners and Northern industrialists; moreover, Poe's status as a self-described "poor-devil author" sheds a glaring light on the precarious nature of his class position, which clearly also does not fit the image of a relapsed Federalist. And while Poe's affiliation with the Whig Party does make some sense, for Poe, the Whigs in the end were at best the lesser of two evils in a political system that he had come to despise.[90]

The Whig Party had its origins with the earlier Federalists, who as a party were pretty nearly destroyed by their resistance to the War of 1812, though Federalism survived into the presidency of John Quincy Adams. By that time, 1825 to 1829, the Federalists had reinvented themselves as the National Republican Party. Economically, they had put in place the "American system" of a national bank, tariffs, and internal improvements such as highways and canals, funded by the sale of public lands. Ideologically, they were held together by the firm conviction that society was governed best by an aristocracy, though not so much a hereditary one as an aristocracy based on property. Daniel Webster put it most massively in a speech in the Massachusetts constitutional convention. Power "*naturally* and *necessarily* follows property," he declared in 1820; for this reason, a "republican form of government rests, not more on political constitutions, than on those laws which regulate the descent and transmission of property."[91] Yet a political credo based on property and education was made obsolete by the ascendancy of popular democracy, which came to the forefront with the election of Andrew Jackson in 1828.[92] And just as the Whigs — Federalism had transmogrified one more time — became culturally marginal as defenders of principles and prejudices in opposition to "democracy" and "the masses," internal factionalism and their inability to deal with new issues such as nativism, prohibition, and anti-slavery, eventually pushed them into a marginal position politically. Although the Whigs in the 1840s adopted the Jacksonians' common man rhetoric, the whole enterprise soon proved unreal and outmoded and the Whig Party, having failed to capture the White House respectively in 1844 and 1852, fell apart. By 1856, there was virtually no Whig organization left anywhere.[93]

The end of the Whig Party would not have been much of a loss to Poe. His ambitions to control both words and their meanings and his audience had put him at ideological odds with ideologues who stubbornly clung to words and meanings that had outlived themselves and to which a majority of the people would no longer submit. Poe did, however, profess his sympathies for John Tyler, for whom, "personally, & as an honest statesman," he claims to have had "the highest respect."[94] Poe wrote this in September 1842, at a time when he was at work on "The Gold-Bug," and not much after Tyler's veto of two national bank bills and the first Tariff Bill of 1842, which alienated all members of his cabinet. A majority of Whig Party members even considered Tyler's acts at once as a "betrayal" of his Party to the Democrats and as gestures of radical negativity, a departure from all trodden paths.[95] Not surprisingly, New York's Democrats in particular chuckled, some even vowing to vote for Tyler for president at all future events. The Democratic press likewise responded with "pleasure and delight" to the "gratifying intelligence" of Tyler's veto. In contrast, a Whig-leaning paper such as the *Baltimore American* expressed "feelings of regret and disappointment."[96]

The business community in New York was particularly outraged; the New York correspondent even for the Washington *Madisonian*, Tyler's official press organ, could not conceal his disappointment: John Tyler, he writes,

> might have been a little more favorable towards us forlorn "bank whigs," who are yet convinced that a national bank, or at least a national currency, of some kind, is desirable and necessary. I see nothing in the message controverting this, but on the other hand nothing affirming it. Must we ever tumble along with a currency with which a man cannot buy a lodging at night with the

par money he started from home in the morning? I wish the president had indicated more fully a desire to do whatever may be constitutional to remedy this vexatious, ruinous inequality. At this moment the notes of the best New York city banks, which are as solid as the rock of Gibraltar, will not be taken for passage on a New England rail road. How long must we endure this?[97]

Whatever the response, President Tyler, a long-time advocate of states' rights, had vetoed the bank bills as unconstitutional extensions of federal power. His decision thus was not radically negative so much as it was a logical consequence of the debates over the proper form of money. In its issue of December 14, 1841, the *Madisonian* defined money as "*metal coined for the purpose of commerce.*" The paper's wording directly echoes the United States Constitution, which had incorporated the framers' idea of the United States as a hard-money country. In the spirit of the sacred document, the *Madisonian* rejected the notion that paper bills could be money: "Nothing can be more absurd," the editorial insisted, than to talk about "'*paper*' money, as though '*paper*' was a species of '*metal*,' instead of a vegetable substance.... Paper is not metal; neither is money paper; though they have long been confounded, most confoundedly."[98] In other words, at stake was both the question whether there should be a national bank of issue and the question whether paper bills were to be viewed as things (that is, as commodities or money) or as mere signs (that is, as currency). The *Madisonian*'s distinctions seem clear:

> Bank notes, or Bank issues, or Bank paper, or by whatever name Bank promises may be designated, is not, never was, nor can be, MONEY: though it may be a commercial "currency," (which is a "circulation" of paper,) and a substitute for "MONEY," or, more properly speaking, a *token*, a mark, or sign, in lieu of money — a mere counter in the great game of human commerce and civilization.[99]

Clearly, then, there is in the *Madisonian*'s editorial a tangle comprised of precious metal, paper, and signs that in many ways resembles the tangle of puns, ambiguities, and allusions Poe set up in "The Gold-Bug." It is less clear, however, that the distinctions made any practical difference. Whatever the rhetoric used in the debates over the proper form of money, it meant very little when it came to monetary policy. Even the writer for the *Madisonian* appears to have known this, concluding that the "great desideratum now is a CURRENCY for commercial and universal circulation, whose basis is MONEY—gold and silver."[100] The statement is crucial, as it meant that the question for Tyler was not whether there would be a paper currency, but how the federal government was to regulate the relation between the marks or signs of specie and specie itself. As demonstrated by this brief outline, there are some basic correspondences between "The Gold-Bug," in which the central character exchanges a coded message for treasure, and the general political context of Poe's time, in which partisan factions bitterly debated the proper association between a system of signs (paper money) and the specie that was stored in public or private vaults. In this context, Tyler's explanation, in his annual message to Congress of December 7, 1841, that the most pressing task for his administration was that of "furnishing a corrective for the derangements of the paper medium," is particularly telling.[101] The message openly hints that, unlike the "gold humbugs" around Senator Benton, Tyler did not object to paper money per se. Although for the "speculative philosopher" the only logical conclusion was "that the paper system had probably better never been introduced," the "practical statesman" could no longer be concerned with the debates over the proper form of money. The choice between hard money and paper had been made and so Tyler in his speech rather emphasized the "wise regulations" designed to keep "plainly apart from each other private and public funds."[102]

The "wise regulations" Tyler envisaged were aimed at the commercial banks, which were issuing paper money that was de facto irredeemable, as the government had no leverage to force them to resume. Whereas Old Whigs like Nathan Appleton wanted a resurrected Bank of the United States to curtail the right of commercial banks to issue notes, Tyler's alternative was the Treasury notes, which were backed by specie deposits and fully redeemable. The notes, which were receivable in government dues, would constitute a "sound paper medium" at the same time as they pretended to be "wedded to no theory" but solely to look to "the advancement of the public good."[103] Jacksonians in general objected to Tyler's plans, though a Congressional report of February 1842 came to quite similar conclusions. The report was quite explicit about gold and silver being "natural" money, while it also concedes that these metals were commodities, thus subject to market fluctuations. It therefore deems a fully redeemable bank paper best. Mindful that the federal government was neither in a position to prevent the states to charter banks, nor capable of compelling banks to redeem their notes, the report recommends an "Exchequer Board" within the Treasury to oversee and issue paper money.[104]

Poe, like Tyler, also did not enter into a comparative analysis between hard money and paper, though "The Gold-Bug" *is* concerned with money as currency and, in particular, with the ways a paper currency might function. In one way, a sound paper currency would constitute a much-needed medium of exchange in everyday commercial transactions; in another, it would constitute a social and cultural arrangement of value resting upon trust — on the general trust of people in one another as much as on trust in an authority of power that, through its regulatory control, would guarantee the currency's stability. Such positions at the time were finding expression in a number of articles in *Hunt's Merchants' Magazine*, which Poe followed closely. It does make sense, therefore, to identify John Tyler as Poe's "closest counterpart in national politics," though when in March 1843 Poe's suit to secure a clerkship under the Tyler administration expired, this doubtless put an end to whatever elective affinities there may have been. Until then, however, Tyler did stand in as Poe's new "capital" reader, the one who, because of his particular take on the money question, would be capable of disentangling the knot of gold, paper, and signs that Poe had tied in "The Gold-Bug," and who, moreover, might appoint him to a government job.[105]

John Tyler: Poe's "Capital Reader"

Poe had a regular income from his association with *Graham's Magazine*, but after only four months on the payroll he felt nothing but "disgust" with his situation, not to mention with the saccharine fiction and poetry he was made to endure.[106] His plans for launching the *Penn* magazine likewise remained in stalemate, even though in late November of 1840 he had tried to enlist the wealthy and prominent Nicholas Biddle, a former president of the Second Bank of the United States. Poe called on Biddle's country estate on the outskirts of Philadelphia. Biddle agrees to subscribe to Poe's magazine, upon which the grateful writer presents him with a copy of his *Tales of the Grotesque and Arabesque*, inscribing it "For Mr. N. Biddle, with the author's respects." On January 6, 1841, Poe writes to Biddle, asking him to contribute to his proposed magazine, *The Penn*, thus adding prestige to the project.

In a way, then, Poe once again tried to capitalize on the bank war to further his own venture, though Biddle, broken by the bank war, did not oblige.[107]

Hope of a different escape from the prison-house of literary production arose through Poe's friend Frederick William Thomas, a popular novelist and songwriter. Thomas also was a partisan of the Whigs, giving speeches on behalf of the party, and it was on one such occasion that Poe first met him in Philadelphia in the summer of 1840.[108] A short time afterwards, Thomas obtained a clerkship in Washington under the new Tyler administration, probably as a reward for his services in the Harrison campaign.[109] In the spring of 1841, Thomas suggested that Poe might enjoy such a sinecure himself, at the handsome salary of $1,500 per annum. For Poe, this friend's gesture seemed to be offering a way out of what a few years previously he had bemoaned as his "miserable life of literary drudgery."[110] Poe felt elated, suggesting to Thomas that he even had "some slight personal acquaintance" with Tyler, probably through his work on the *Southern Literary Messenger*, where Poe had had his first full-time job in the publishing business, at $10 a week; Poe added that he was a Virginian like Tyler, and that as a writer he was happy to see a tendency in the new administration to appreciate letters.[111]

The word "letters" should not be understood too narrowly. When Poe had befriended Thomas, the two men, together with Jesse Erskine Dow, a journalist and Democratic radical, frequently met, discussing "literature, politics, and cryptograms."[112] Poe soon discovered that there was a connection between cryptography and politics, which he might exploit. Thus, there were discussions of ciphers written by Aaron Burr and, more importantly, Poe's own cryptogram, submitted to *Alexander's Weekly Messenger* in 1840, containing a partisan account of the Battle of Tippecanoe.[113] Poe's guess that cryptography possessed certain political applications took a more serious turn during his attempt to land a government patronage. In "A Few Words on Secret Writing," published in *Graham's Magazine* in July 1841, Poe suggested that cryptography was a skill highly valued and generously remunerated by governments: "Good cryptographists are rare indeed; and thus their services, although seldom required, are necessarily well required."[114]

The idea that cryptographists would be in demand on the labor market may have been wishful thinking, but Poe nevertheless thought he could advance his quest for patronage by solving his own cipher, either in the press, or in a public lecture, or, better still, in a personal meeting with President Tyler or his family. To achieve the latter goal, Poe made use of Tyler's dramatic political style, in particular of the tendency to portray himself as a martyr for a noble cause. Explaining his veto of the second bill for a national bank, for instance, Tyler told the House of Representatives, "I have been actuated by no other motive or desire than to uphold the institutions of the country, as they have come down to us from the hands of our godlike ancestors, and [...] I shall esteem my efforts to sustain them, even though I perish, more honorable than to win the applause of men by a sacrifice of my duty and my conscience."[115] On other occasions, Tyler located his political ancestors in ancient Rome; he posed as a stoical Cassius, quoting Shakespeare's Brutus, and he relished being seen as Marcellus. Yet no other figure better symbolized Tyler's pose of resistance to tyranny than Cato, a name that referred to several historical personages and literary characters. One of Tyler's political allies, for instance, Tennessee Judge Hugh Lawson White, was known as the "Cato of the Republic" or the "American Cato." The epithet in this case had been taken from Joseph Addison's *Cato*, which was one of the key literary sources for American republicanism. In its depiction of defiance against tyranny this play of 1712 also became the perfect model for Tyler's imagined role in the political struggle over the destiny of America's money.[116]

Poe, considering the ability to solve a cipher as a rare and lucrative form of genius, published, between July and December 1841, altogether four articles on secret writing in *Graham's Magazine*. In the fourth and final one, he reprints a letter from one "W. B. Tyler," which contains two ciphers. The letter claims that these cryptograms cannot be solved without the "proper key." [117] Since, the code has been broken and the cipher solved, independently by Terence Whalen and John A. Hodgson. The identity of "W. B. Tyler" also has been revealed, as an alias adopted by no other than Poe himself. The coded message, however, is not by Poe, but is a quotation from the final act of Addison's tragedy. The implications of the quotation, a soliloquy in which Cato stoically awaits the defeat of republican rule by Caesar's superior forces, together with Poe's authorship of the letter, are indeed serious. The cryptogram, Whalen suggests, indicates, "among other things, that Poe used the pseudonym Tyler to encode a message uniquely suited to please and comfort President Tyler."[118]

Cryptography was not the only strategy Poe used in his attempt to land a patronage job with the Tyler administration. On September 25, 1841, the *Madisonian*, which was then edited by Jesse E. Dow, himself a minor poet and one of Poe's friends, printed Poe's "Eleonora."[119] It is unclear just who had the tale included in Tyler's official press organ, though getting the president to read Poe was certainly the plan. Poe must have been truly desperate to catch Tyler's attention, so much so that in his inquiry to Frederick William Thomas, he even advanced that his "political principles" had always been, "as nearly as may be, with the existing administration."[120] Poe's awkward and naïve approach convinced no one, not even Poe himself. In a follow-up letter, Poe asked that Thomas on his behalf see John Pendleton Kennedy, a novelist Poe knew from his years in Baltimore. Kennedy, who had been elected on a Whig ticket, was now serving in Congress and thus might be able to find the ear of the secretary of war. "I would be glad," Poe wrote in desperation, "to get almost any appointment — even a $500 one — so that I have something independent of letters for a subsistence."[121]

Thomas was fond and admiring enough of Poe and thus tried repeatedly to speak to Kennedy, even met Kennedy during the summer, though nothing ever came of it. "I know very few of the 'bigbugs' here," Thomas wrote Poe from Washington, though he added, by way of encouragement, "but I think I have skill enough to commit your merits to those, who [...] will be more skilful advocates of your claims."[122] By the end of November of 1841 Poe, not having heard from his patron in a long while, gave up on him. Thomas persevered, though, and even got to speak to Tyler's son Robert, who had literary ambitions of his own and valued Poe's critical opinions. But no job came of this either, nor was there support for the projected magazine. Although Poe remained unrescued from his unloved work at *Graham's Magazine*, in early April of 1842 he resigned from the magazine's staff. This step, so impulsively taken, may have placated Poe's ego, but it did nothing to improve his financial prospects, and by the summer of the same year he once again tried to obtain a government post. The new plan, which again was Thomas's idea, was to place Poe not in the nation's capital, but in the Custom House in Philadelphia. In late April, supporters of President Tyler were beginning to make a demonstration with a view to nominate and support him for another term. Within the coming week the President took steps to reward his faithful by appointing them to offices in the city's customhouse. One highly visible backer of Tyler was Poe's associate and later enemy Thomas Dunn English, who was appointed to a different office in September, as a reward for his active support.[123]

Appointments of this kind are evidence of a clear about-face in Tyler's policies. At the beginning of his administration, Tyler had opposed the "spoils system," whereby the victorious party in an election rewards its followers by appointing them to government offices. Following his break with the Whig Party, however, Tyler sought to build his own political base by appointing officials who would be sympathetic to his presidency, in the hope to organize a third party that would stand behind his candidacy in the presidential elections of 1844. That party also was to have included Tyler backers who previously had been Democrats, though the high-handed manner of the Whig faction around Thomas Dunn English and Thomas S. Smith, the new Collector of the Port of Philadelphia, eventually alienated most of them. These former Democrats subsequently formed a group that called itself the "Tyler Democratic Association," announcing their support for the "Jeffersonian republican principles of government" as practiced by Presidents Jefferson, Jackson — and John Tyler.[124]

Tyler's decision to fill the Custom House in Philadelphia and other cities with his supporters clearly was to have a direct effect on Poe, who was led to believe that he would be appointed to one of the anticipated vacancies. To Poe, such a post promised both a regular income and enough time for literary pursuits. Poe would have been in good company, as about a dozen or more literary figures of the time found employment in the United States Customs Service, most notably Hawthorne, Melville, and George Bancroft, the greatest American historian of his day and eventually an enthusiastic Jacksonian Democrat. The prospect of finally securing a reliable income inspired Poe, who was convinced that it would give him "new life" and relieve him "of all care as regards a mere subsistence."[125] In early June 1842, Poe writes his friend James Herron, "I have the promise of a situation at our Custom House. The offer was entirely unexpected & gratuitous. I am to receive the appointment upon removal of several incumbents — the removal to be certainly made in a month. I am indebted to the personal friendship of Robert Tyler [President Tyler's first son]. If I *really* receive the appointment all may yet go well."[126] It did not, and after weeks and weeks of useless waiting, and once again *"desperately* pushed for money," Poe went in person to see the new Collector of Customs, Thomas S. Smith, presumed to be a loyal Tyler man, only to meet with new frustrations. Poe let it be known that his political views had "reference to no one of the present parties," a statement that for anyone only remotely familiar with the existing spoils system must have seemed unwise, to say the least.[127]

Thomas S. Smith was appointed to the office of collector of customs on September 10, 1842. He replaced Jonathan Roberts, who was a personal friend of President Tyler but had refused to make the removals and appointments that the President requested. Already the rumors of the impending removals created considerable anxiety and excitement. Newspapers regularly commented on the issue, which pitched the incumbents — mostly Whigs who were loyal to the party's foremost spokesman, Senator Henry Clay — against their presumed successors — supporters of the Whig ticket during the election of 1840, but now loyal to President Tyler. Tyler had intended to remove Roberts from office as early as May, but he cautiously bided his time, knowing that most members of Congress, being Whigs, would object to his plans. Poe probably knew of the situation before Thomas wrote him, since it was fully covered by the Philadelphia papers. From about mid–September until mid–November, Poe's hopes rose and then again crashed. He expected to be sent for, but in the end was told that no more appointments were to be made. In a letter of November 19, 1842, Poe called Smith both "a scoundrel" who had treated him "most shamefully" and "a Whig of the worst stamp [who] will appoint none but Whigs if he can possibly avoid it."[128] Above all, Poe felt deeply insulted. The whole affair not only put out of reach a much-needed job, but also mortally wounded his feeling of entitlement, his sense, as years earlier he had written to James Kirke Paulding, of "the station in society which is my due."[129]

Poe did not give up yet, though his hopes now solely rested on the possibility that the United States Senate would reject the nomination of Thomas S. Smith, as it had rejected many of President Tyler's previous nominations, and that another Collector of Customs would be installed in office. Towards the end of January 1843, Poe was still waiting "for some definite action of Congress on Smith's case," as he writes Thomas, and began to make plans to settle the matter by a personal visit to Washington. When the Senate in its session of March 3, 1843, finally did reject Smith's appointment, confirming in his place Calvin Blythe, a Democrat who had held the post during the Van Buren administration and who had been replaced by Jonathan Roberts in 1841, Poe was ready to leave for the nation's capital. Once again, he was "in sad need of means" and therefore left "in great haste," and on two missions. One was to speak to Robert Tyler and the president himself about the post at the customhouse. The other was to seek patronage for his projected magazine. Following an agreement with Thomas C. Clarke, publisher of the *Philadelphia Saturday Museum*, the *Penn* magazine was now called *The Stylus*; as a showpiece, its premier issue was to have contained "The Gold-Bug."[130]

Poe's trip to the nation's capital was a disaster. Poe "went on a spree, called on President Tyler with his cloak inside out, and got into a quarrel with Thomas Dunn English."[131] A week later, Poe returned to Philadelphia jobless and penniless. The trip, which had begun in difficulty, thus ended in disgrace. Although Poe tried to repair the damage, offering his apologies to all around for the offense he had given and even enlisting Nathaniel Hawthorne in his magazine schemes, his efforts were wasted. Still he has hopes for the position in the Philadelphia Custom House. He asks Thomas to write to the new Collector immediately, enclosing, if possible, a line from Robert Tyler.[132] The new Collector, Calvin Blythe, was instantly "beset with an army of eager applicants for office," a Philadelphia paper reported on March 16, 1843.[133] In late March, Poe, disappointed in Thomas's apparent inability to get a line from the President's son, himself wrote Robert Tyler to request a letter of recommendation that he could present to Blythe. Tyler wrote back instantly, saying that it would "gratify" him "very sensibly, to see you appointed by Judge Blythe. I am satisfied that no one is more competent, or would be more satisfactory in the discharge of any duty connected with the office."[134]

Judge Calvin Blythe, Collector of Customs in Philadelphia, did not appoint Poe. Yet just as this hapless author was exchanging letters with Robert Tyler, the *Dollar Newspaper* announced details of a prize story contest. The *Dollar Newspaper*, a typical "family newspaper" aimed at a popular audience of high morality and of limited literary sophistication, is remembered because Poe won the first prize with "The Gold-Bug." The original announcements of March 29, 1843, have been long lost, but the date is established by a report in the Baltimore *Sun*:

PRIZES.—*Important to Literary Writers*—*Very Liberal Offers and No Humbug.*—We perceive by an advertisement in the last number of the Philadelphia Dollar Newspaper, that the publishers have come out with an offer of $200 for the three best stories that shall be furnished them by the first day of June next. One hundred for the best, sixty for the second, and forty for the third best. The only conditions imposed upon the writers, are that the subjects of the stories shall be American, and that they shall not be less than a certain length. This exhibits a liberality rarely met with among the publishers of our weekly sheets.[135]

Poe had originally sold "The Gold-Bug" to *Graham's Magazine* for fifty-two dollars, but later retrieved it from the magazine's owner, George Rex Graham, and then entered it in the *Dollar Newspaper's* contest.[136] Poe must have completed the story and sold it to *Graham's* prior to the date the contest was announced. Katherine Rex Burgin, a young niece of Graham, remembered hearing her uncle read the tale aloud shortly after he purchased it for his magazine.[137] Felix O. C. Darley, a young Philadelphia artist who came to do the illustrations for the story, also remembered Poe reading "The Gold-Bug" to him before it was published. "The form of his manuscript," Darley wrote to G. E. Woodberry on February 26, 1884, "was peculiar: he wrote on half sheets of note paper, which he pasted together at the ends, making one continuous piece, which he rolled up tightly. As he read he dropped it to the floor. It was very neatly written, and without corrections, apparently."[138]

On June 14, 1843, *Dollar Newspaper* announced that Poe was awarded the first prize in its contest for a tale titled "The Gold-Bug." The entry is established by reports in the *Pennsylvania Inquirer* and the Baltimore *Sun*.[139] Interestingly, each of the three prize stories has money as its subject matter — "The Gold-Bug," "The Banker's Daughter," and "Marrying for Money." "The Banker's Daughter" was the product of Robert M. Morris, the editor of the *Philadelphia Inquirer* and, for several years, President of the Commonwealth Bank; Morris probably knew Poe, who in turn seems to have liked Morris's poetry. "Marrying for Money" was attributed to "F.E.F.," who, as the Philadelphia *Public Ledger* of June 19, 1843, reports, was a "lady in New York, whose name does not accompany her production; she is known as a contributor to several of the magazines by initials only." Hiding behind initials was common in that day, not least for women. All three stories were reprinted together in a supplement to the *Dollar Newspaper* dated July 14, 1843, though the latter two likely were never reprinted thereafter.[140]

"The Gold-Bug" first appeared in the *Dollar Newspaper* in two installments, respectively in the June 21 and June 28 issues, with illustrations by Darley.[141] The tale became by far the most popular of Poe's stories, and instantly had, as the physician and editor Joseph Evans Snodgrass wrote on July 8, "a tremendous run."[142] Less than a year later, Poe wrote, "Of the 'Gold-Bug' (my most successful tale) more than 300,000 copies have been circulated."[143] The claim may not be greatly exaggerated. But Poe not only thought that "The Gold-Bug" was his most successful tale. In a letter to Rufus Griswold of February 24, 1845, he writes that he even preferred it to "The Murders in the Rue Morgue" — "I prefer having in [*Tales*] the 'G.B.' to 'Murder in the R.M.'"[144] Following the publication of "The Gold-Bug" in the *Tales* of 1845, Poe even wrote concerning a possible republication in England, "we should undoubtedly give 'The Bug' a more prominent position than it even occupies at present. We should call the book 'The Gold-Bug and Other Tales' — instead of 'Tales,' as its title stands."[145]

"The Gold-Bug," Thomas C. Clarke declared in the *Saturday Museum* of July 8, 1843, is "the most remarkable American work of fiction that has been published within the last fifteen years."[146] Also in July, the *Saturday Courier* published a lengthy article on Poe and his most recent publication, asking, "Is there a man, woman, or child, 'read up,' as they phrase it in American literature, who is unacquainted with Edgar A. Poe? We take it for granted that there is not."[147] The laudation also might have included readers from the other side of the Atlantic. An English piracy, *The Gold Bug*, was published in London in 1846 or 1847.[148] The tale also was translated into French as "Le Scarabée d'or," with Poe acknowledged as the original author, respectively in 1845 and 1848.[149] In 1847, P. Redkin selected "The Gold Bug" for the first issue of the *New Library for Education (Novaja biblioteka dlja vospitanija)*, a journal designed for children and their educators.[150]

Reprints, piracies, and translations were not the only form of tribute to "The Gold-Bug." The tale also made an appearance as a short play, produced at Philadelphia's Walnut Street Theatre. The drama version by Philadelphian Silas S. Steele was titled *The Gold Bug; or, The Pirate's Treasure*. Its first — and probably sole — performance took place on August 18, 1843. While Steele's drama version is little known, it is commonly understood that Robert Louis Stevenson took inspiration from "The Gold-Bug" to write his own treasure-hunting novel, *Treasure Island*, in 1883.[151] A different sign of the success of "The Gold-Bug" is the fact that Poe was accused of collusion with the Committee that selected the prize stories — and of plagiarism.[152] Both charges were later dropped, though it is no secret that Poe habitually used things he found in print, particularly accounts of incidents and events that he believed were based on fact, regardless of how sensational or even impossible they might appear. To Poe, such matters seemingly were more promising than obviously fictional stories or personal experiences.[153] For the money-finding theme in "The Gold-Bug," for instance, Poe drew on Washington Irving's "Wolfert Webber; or, Golden Dreams" from *Tales of a Traveller*; a novel titled *Shepard Lee* by a Robert M. Bird; a semi-autobiographical novel about an English sailor; reports about a shipwreck off the Coast of South Carolina; a story by Seba Smith titled "The Money Diggers"; possibly, a little book by a George Ann Humphrey Sherburne, titled *Imogine*, and, not to forget, the Captain Kidd legend.[154]

To the principal theme of money finding, Poe added two more interests of his own, the one in natural history and chemistry, the other in cryptography. Poe's considerable knowledge of natural history is largely owed to Professor Thomas Wyatt, whom he met in 1839. Another probable source from which Poe might have borrowed is Thomas Green Fessenden's "Remarks on the Scarabaeus Roseus, or Rose-Bug," a front-page article that appeared in the August 31 and September 7, 1827, issues of the *New England Farmer*.[155] For the theme of cryptography, Poe drew on William Blair's article "Cipher" in Rees's *Cyclopedia*, one of like title in the *Encyclopaedia Britannica*, and one titled "Cryptography" in the *Encyclopaedia Americana*. Poe's own essays on secret writing, respectively published in *Alexander's Weekly Messenger*, the *Southern Literary Messenger*, and *Graham's Magazine* between 1839 and December 1841, excited considerable interest, though "The Gold-Bug" is the only piece of fiction in which he made use of this interest.[156] Yet Poe did so with a vengeance, as if to expunge some deeply felt trauma with the help of the formulae of ciphers. Some of this vengeance rests on Poe's puns involving the verb "to bug" (or "to humbug"), which in the nineteenth century meant to deceive, to impose on, or to hoax.

Indeed, a great deal of the tale's meaning derives from puns — on "bug" (insect and madman), "gose" (ghost and goose), "specie" (entomological specimen and gold coin), "goole" (gold and ghoul), and "fortune" (treasure and luck or chance). For Marc Shell, these puns indicate that Poe's interest in the tale was in "a generation of something from nothing that is at once economic and linguistic."[157] Another pun — derived from "kid," and referring at once to a young goat (as it is illustrated on the parchment Legrand finds) and Captain Kidd (the pirate and originator of the coded message)—seemingly contradicts Shell's findings, though it is only by consulting a dictionary that one can move beyond the tale's internal structure. The verb "to kid" according to the *Oxford English Dictionary* means: "To hoax, humbug, try to make (one) believe what is not true." In addition, there is a meaning this dictionary adopted from the 1811 *Lexicon Balatronicum*, a *Dictionary of Buckish Slang, University Wit, and Pickpocket Eloquence*, whose originator was a Captain Grose. Grose's dictionary "of the vulgar tongue" defines the verb "to kid" in terms of "to coax or wheedle ... To amuse a man or divert his attention while another robs him."[158]

Terence Whalen takes great pains to draw out the implications of the "vulgar" meanings of the verb "to kid." For one thing, he points to parallels between Captain Kidd, who murdered his associates, and Legrand, who also is seen standing above the pit, with a mattock in his hand, and, "infected with misanthropy" as he allegedly is, could easily commit yet another crime.[159] Legrand of course does not do this, though his somewhat deficient moral equipment shows in his resolve to "punish" the narrator, "quietly, in my own way, by a little bit of sober mystification." By so diverting the narrator's attention, Legrand satisfies part of the slangy definition of "kid." Yet according to Whalen, Poe also satisfies this definition with the help of a series of linguistic exchanges and substitutions involving such crucial terms as "paper" and "specie." Poe uses the term "specie" with great precision. In fact, he never uses the word for the gold bug, which is described as a "new genus," but not a new species of bugs. Although the word "genus" likewise registers a connection between language and money, Poe reserves the word "specie" for Kidd's cryptograph, which for Legrand was "of a simple species." Ultimately, therefore, it is Kidd's species of secret writing, rather than a new species of insect, that makes Legrand rich. Following Whalen, the central exchange of the story is "code for gold."[160]

The gold that the code is exchanged for is, however, at best a store of value, not a medium of exchange, and also not a measure of value. It is a mere commodity that does not constitute a claim against goods and services, and thus is not money in the sense of capital or currency. In other words, the gold must be exchanged for money, that is, for paper, which was the kind of form current at the time. Poe also exercises much care in applying the term "paper," distinguishing between mere paper and Kidd's scrap. The scrap "had much the appearance of paper," Legrand explains, "and at first I supposed it to be such, but when I came to draw upon it, I discovered it at once, to be a piece of very thin parchment."[161] For Terence Whalen, remarks of this kind are evidence enough to conclude that Poe, with "The Gold-Bug," makes capital of the public's gullibility: Poe at one and the same time sells to and mystifies a mass audience. In doing so, Poe not only robs readers of their time and money, but also deprives them of their cherished myths: that pirates buried their loot, that treasures can be found, and that supernatural forces are at work in the world.[162]

Though I admire Whalen's research and analysis, I find myself in disagreement with his ultimate conclusion. In fact, Poe's calculating approach to the literary market complicates the political meaning of "The Gold-Bug" and of his other fictional writings that enter into and historicize discourses about money. Legrand, I suggested, realizes that "Matters of little moment are rarely consigned to parchment," just as they are also not consigned to the paper used for a well-regulated currency: in each instance, there is some special "meaning — some relevancy." Poe of course was cognizant of the debates over America's money, and so he must have known that "parchment" was a term used to denote paper money, down to the scrip notes and small-denomination bills that Hawthorne referred to in at least two of his own paper-money fables.[163] Poe may have drawn inspiration from Hawthorne's tales, as he admiringly reviewed the collection, *Twice-Told Tales*, while he was at work on "The Gold-Bug." In addition, Poe's avoidance of "paper" in the tale — "not far from the boat was a parchment — *not a paper*," Legrand says — registers the prejudices and anxieties that since the Middle Ages had been connected with the material itself, the degenerative or ephemeral character of which doubled when paper was used to represent value, as in paper money. Indeed the paper money form had created problems of acceptance from the beginning, spawning the most vigorous debates. These debates usually centered on the notes' redeemability or, failing that, on their being backed by something else. The passage in question from "The Gold-Bug" thus may well constitute an aside on the "filthy rags," capitalizing on the demand for pecuniary themes, though in a manner that cannot fully be explained in terms of Poe's "laughing — or kidding — all the way to the bank."[164]

The "scrap" found on the beach bears all kinds of marks or authenticating signs. Legrand, because he "perceive[s]" these marks or signs, is led to the buried treasure, though he is able to redeem Kidd's note only because of his faith in the signs and after he has expended a great deal of physical and intellectual labor on his journey from secret writing to buried treasure. To add to his travails, the happy money-finders are utterly unable to lift the chest out of the pit. Counting the booty is troublesome, too, and must be done with the help of tables of the period, and even then the treasure remains wildly "undervalued."[165] In light of all these exertions, the exchange of paper for gold in Poe's tale seems a parody of convertibility and, by extension, a reminder of the advantages and conveniences of a federal paper money, as they were spelt out by George Wood in *Hunt's Merchants' Magazine* of April 1841. Given a well-regulated paper currency, Wood argued, there was simply "no use for specie."[166] During Poe's time, of course, paper money was not well regulated, and so the Jacksonian hard-money advocates considered the very idea of convertibility as fraudulent.[167]

Just how laborious attempts were to exchange paper money for specie is illustrated by an incident involving the Bank of Morocco, a wildcat bank that did business out of a potato barrel. The story is part of the personal recollections of Alexander Lovett Stimson, an agent for "Adams & Co.'s Express," which in the era of free banking did a profitable business hunting up banks for brokers in a variety of western states. Stimson then was the firm's Indianapolis agent, overseeing a team of messengers that tracked banks and got their notes redeemed. One day a thousand dollars on the Bank of Morocco arrived in Stimson's office and as none of the messengers were available, Stimson agreed to go himself, though even a visit to the state auditor's office only taught him that Morocco was somewhere in Newton County, in northwestern Indiana.

After a lengthy and arduous journey Stimson arrived at two cabins, the one a blacksmith's shop, the other the smith's home. Asking for directions to Morocco, Stimson was told that he was in town already. His next question, whether there was a bank in town, drew considerable astonishment, which only grew stronger when he explained that he had some business with the bank, though he would state this only to the bank officers. The blacksmith then started for the cabin where he lived, explaining that this was the Bank of

Morocco and that he was doing all the business that was done there. Stimson then went ahead, stating that he had a thousand dollars in paper of the smith's bank, for which he wanted gold. The worthy "cashier's" answer was that it was late already and that Stimson would have to stay overnight, though he would be welcome to put his money in the bank vault. Stimson handed over the package of bills, which the blacksmith took to a corner of the cabin where he started taking potatoes out of a barrel and putting them into a basket. When the basket was full, he put the money in the barrel and put the potatoes back, remarking, "'That vault is easily unlocked, but it is as safe as any you have in Lafayette'"— supposing Stimson lived there. The following morning the man retrieved the notes from the barrel, took the rest of the potatoes out and brought up a bag marked "$5,000," from which he counted fifty double eagle gold pieces. He handed the gold to Stimson, who thanked him and offered to pay for his overnight stay. The blacksmith would not take a cent, saying, "'You are the first man who has ever found the Bank of Morocco, and if you will keep the location to yourself, you are welcome to all I have done for you.'" Stimson promised to do so, and started home "well pleased with [his] adventure."[168]

Poe's Legrand too succeeds in his exchange of paper for gold, and his success likewise is owed not to intellect and hard labor alone, but at least to an equal degree to chance, accident or, as Legrand explains by way of an inimitable circular logic, to "Fortune," which "has thought it fit to bestow [a "fortune"] upon me." The discovery of a fortune by Fortune of course sheds some light on Poe's tale of ratiocination, for it reveals that the author himself no longer expected to receive similar rewards in the literary marketplace, at least not for honest intellectual labor. In Poe's ideal economic realm the maxim that "industry pays debts" lacked all conviction, while the solace of Horatio Alger's tales of industry and perseverance was still below the horizon.[169] In their stead, cryptograms function as currency, though the consequences for a fuller understanding of "The Gold-Bug" must be spelled out in greater detail. Poe knew only too well how much time and effort it took to practice cryptography, complaining, in an 1843 letter, that solving them had cost him, "in time, which to me is money, more than a thousand dollars."[170] Similarly in "The Gold-Bug," the value of the cryptogram can only be realized through Legrand's rare gift, his intellectual powers. In economic terms, then, the ratiocination part of the tale adds value to the money-finding part. Popular readers may consume the first part for pleasure. The second part, in contrast, by narrating the amount of decoding that has gone into the treasure hunt lays bare the mechanisms of the conversion of paper into gold. Through the addition of value, therefore, Poe in effect creates a new text, one that enters into and historicizes contemporary monetary discourses.

There is a striking parallel to Poe's valorization of intellectual power in the world of money. One of the obvious differences between "filthy rags" and a well-regulated paper currency is the amount of intellectual labor required to realize value. This is precisely the kind of labor implied in President Tyler's struggle to set right the "derangements of the paper medium."[171] Poe may have exploited popular readers, refusing emotional identification as well as, by relying on cryptography, depriving them of their interpretive powers. It seems, however, that there was at least one reader with whom he must have expected that mystification would not work. This reader was no other than John Tyler, who was easily as cognizant of the debates over America's money as Poe and thus qualified as one of the select few who could in fact "elude general comprehension."[172] Getting the president to read Poe had been part of the plan when the *Madisonian* in September 1841 printed Poe's "Eleonora." We do not know whether Poe himself or one of his Washington friends had the tale included in Tyler's official press organ. We do know, however, that in December 1841 Poe used the "W. B. Tyler" cryptogram for the purpose of getting close to the president. No less suited than the *Cato* passages to please and comfort President Tyler are the subtleties about America's money in "The Gold-Bug." Poe must have known that whatever he had to say about regulating the relation between gold and paper would strike a responsive chord with the President. If Poe composed his last article on secret writing in an attempt to procure a political appointment from the Tyler administration, it is just as plausible that he composed "The Gold-Bug" from the same motive, though there is no sign that Tyler ever got around to reading this celebrated tale.[173]

"The Gold-Bug," like other of Poe's writings, testifies to a depoliticized Poe who jealously excluded politics from his writings. Yet unlike Poe's satirical pieces, which clearly are works of negation, the result of this writer's disgust with Jacksonian rule and with policies that made America's monetary situation singularly chaotic, "The Gold-Bug" pursues a different trajectory. We saw in this chapter that Poe, though he had no inclination to move *into* politics, had no compunction about using politics to his personal advantage. Although his attempts to curry favors from President Tyler failed, Poe nevertheless had his sense of unresolved conflicts sharpened. We shall see presently how some of these conflicts in beliefs and values, specifically those of market and class, precipitated his engagement in literary politics, at the same time as they deepened his preoccupation with money and banking.

4

Poe's Nightmares

Gold, Counterfeits and Literary Politics

Among Poe's tales, none seems to have a more complicated history than "The Gold-Bug." To determine the composition of the tale is particularly troublesome. Poe's manuscript "has not been seen since 1843, and was almost surely lost after printing, but is presumably recorded in [the text published in *Dollar Newspaper*]."[1] Critics generally agree that the tale probably began to take shape soon after Poe wrote, in *Graham's Magazine* for November 1841, of the popularity of Samuel Warren's novel *Ten Thousand a Year*, asserting that "the *pecuniary* nature of its theme [is] a main source of the interest which this book possesses for the mass."[2] Poe's own "affair of pounds, shillings, and pence" was ready some time in the fall of 1842, when he sold the story to George Rex Graham. As an extended tale with unusual internal complexities, we should presume, as Jeffrey Savoye suggests, "that it took Poe a longer time to write, perhaps over the course of two or three months."[3] Poe had left *Graham's Magazine* after the publication of the May 1842 issue. That issue contained "The Masque of the Red Death," the last story by Poe to be published in *Graham's* until 1845. Poe's plans for the *Stylus* magazine were active again, but, "*desperately* pushed for money" as he then was, he could not afford holding material for the magazine. Already in April he had sold "The Pit and the Pendulum." In June and July, he tried to place "The Mystery of Marie Roget" and "The Landscape Garden," though each was at first rejected.[4] It cannot be determined precisely when Poe wrote these tales, but in light of his pressing need for money he likely completed them shortly before the date on which he offered them for sale.[5]

There is another bit of evidence in a handwritten table of contents for Poe's proposed *Phantasy Pieces*. The table lists both "The Pit and the Pendulum" and "The Mystery of Marie Roget," though the two titles are cancelled, possibly because Poe had submitted them for publication elsewhere. Neither "The Landscape Garden" nor "The Gold-Bug" is listed, which strongly suggests that they had not yet been written. Jeffrey Savoye thus is convinced that "by the middle of July 1842, 'The Gold-Bug' most likely had not been brought into existence."[6] Moreover, for the rest of July until early August, Poe's energies likely were focused on his review of Griswold's *The Poets and Poetry of America*.[7] By September 1842, Poe's hopes for a post at the Philadelphia Custom House were still intact, and in a letter from Poe it is mentioned that Graham had made him "a good offer to return." Although Poe did not officially rejoin *Graham's* as an editor, he at least had secured a reliable venue and a consistent source of income. A critical piece by his hand already appeared in the October issue, and Poe probably sold "The Gold-Bug" to Graham right after this.[8]

The presumed date of Poe's selling "The Gold-Bug" to Graham is almost uncannily consistent with the time of year in which the tale is set — "[a]bout the middle of October, 18 —."[9] Jeffrey Savoye concludes, justly I think, that it "probably reflects the time during which it was being written, or at least completed."[10] There are, however, two possible objections. One stems from the fact that the date is also an integral part of the story. As Savoye explains,

> A fire is the key to the discovery of the secret message on the parchment, and as we are told in the introductory paragraphs of the story, a day in the fall being cool enough in Sullivan's Island as to require a fire is a rare thing, emphasizing the serendipity of the events. One may debate the notions of whether Poe selected October to fit with this idea of serendipity, or the serendipity of the events was suggested by Poe himself incorporating an actual cool day in October into the story.[11]

The other possible objection relates to the actual search for the treasure, which is undertaken "about a month *after*" Legrand shows the drawing to the narrator, hence in November. Perhaps one should not make too much of these details. As the debate stands, we may reasonably assume, again with Jeffrey Savoye, that "The Gold-Bug" was "started in earnest in August or September, and finished by the middle of October 1842."[12]

When Poe sold to Graham "The Gold-Bug," he also sold him "The Conqueror Worm," which was published in *Graham's* for January 1843, but Poe bought back "The Gold-Bug" before it could be printed. The date of this event most likely was in January as well. Poe, who had joined forces with Thomas C. Clarke, once again was seriously active on the *Stylus* project. Having recognized the unusual merits of "The Gold-Bug," he planned to use the tale, in two parts, as a "showpiece" in the premier issue, complete with Darley's illustrations.[13] In April 1843, Poe was still trying to get *The Stylus* off the ground, but his plans soon faltered. On June 20, 1843, he wrote to James Russell Lowell that his magazine scheme had "exploded."[14] Less than a week before that, the *Dollar Newspaper* had announced that the first prize was awarded to a story that had been planned in two parts. This fact in itself adds weight to my claim that what may have begun as a tale about solving a cipher eventually involved an obsessive search for money. The successful conclusion of the search thus compensates in ideological form for the perceived absence of real financial comfort — one that would have been a good deal more substantial than the somewhat cold comfort of the prize money of a hundred dollars.

What was a hundred dollars worth in the early 1840s? It is difficult to establish relative values based on today's incomes and purchasing power, though about $10 a week then would have been sufficient to cover weekly living costs. William Poe of Baltimore must have known this, when in a June 16, 1843, letter he expressed his hope that the prize money would come in time to relieve his cousin of his financial worries.[15] Yet neither "The Gold-Bug" nor "The Black Cat," which the *Saturday Evening Post* published in its August 19, 1843, issue, or any other literary venture, not to mention the frequent lectures on American poetry, in a variety of different locations und usually before large audiences, did Poe much good moneywise. Nor did solving ciphers; on the contrary, Poe complains that already it had cost him, "in time, which to me is money, more than a thousand dollars."[16] By the end of August, he approaches Ezra Holden, one of the owners of the *Saturday Courier*, for money he needed for a proposed trip to Richmond. In mid–September, Poe in a letter to James Russell Lowell once again bemoans his "pecuniary troubles."[17] At about the same time, Thomas C. Clarke began to have second thoughts about *The Stylus*, though Poe continued to believe that he might resume the plan next year, under "better auspices."[18] That year was 1844. Poe and his wife Virginia were living in New York then, having left Philadelphia on April 6.[19]

The move from Philadelphia to New York in no way improved Poe's precarious financial situation. This chapter therefore builds on the complicated history of "The Gold Bug" to show how Poe's interest in and concern about everyday matters eventually steered him to literary politics. Poe's engagement reached from the issue of an international copyright to technical innovations. Yet Poe, with a paper-money fable behind him, also continued to be preoccupied with the world of money and banking. Even "The Domain of Arnheim," generally read as a piece of landscape writing in celebration of Southern life, thematizes that world. The central character, Ellison, clearly is not a Southern gentleman so much as he is a man of action who turns his immense wealth into capital to be invested. Other writings of the time are more overtly satirical, including "The Business Man," which attacks "the frauds of the banks," or a poem titled "Epigram for Wall Street." Poe's preoccupation with the world of money and banking is also evident from his hallucinating, shortly before his death, that he had been arrested on charges of passing a counterfeit bill. But my larger purpose in this chapter is to provide a connection with the discovery of gold in California. This momentous event provoked Poe into writing a poem, "Eldorado," an elaborate hoax about the transmutation of lead into gold, and a derisive commentary on the new $1 gold dollar of 1849, the introduction of which must be seen as part of an effort to return the country to a hard-money track.

Poe's Literary Politics

Poe is generally considered the first American writer to support himself entirely by his writing. He certainly did not earn a living by it. Nor did he ever enjoy the privileges and advantages a number of his fellow writers had at the time—Emerson was a clergyman, Longfellow and Lowell were professors, Cooper was a consul in Lyons, Irving a diplomat in Spain, and Hawthorne at first a customhouse inspector and then a consul in Liverpool. For Poe, living was an almost constant nightmare, crystallizing in his conviction that in America, "more than in any other region upon the face of the globe, to be poor is to be despised."[20] Statements of this kind show to what degree Poe as a writer succumbed to the pressures of a capitalist publishing industry. It is no surprise that he increasingly turned his back on the political and social struggles of his day. He did, however, counterbalance his reserve on partisan political issues by concentrating his political energies on the realm of literary production — battling for an international copyright agreement, exploring the potential of alternative printing technologies, and dissecting the magazine business.

Keenly aware of and deeply concerned about the material conditions of writing, Poe linked the "ghastly poverty" and "despair" of so many authors with the lack of an international copyright law. "Without an international copyright law," he wrote to Frederick W. Thomas, "American authors may as well cut their throats."[21] Thus he wholeheartedly approved George Rex Graham's decision to copyright each issue of his magazine. Poe seems to have discussed the issue of an international copyright already with Charles Dickens, during the latter's visit to Philadelphia in early March 1842. Frederick William Thomas became a true ally, who tirelessly advocated the need for copyright legislation in speeches he was giving.[22] Once Poe had settled in New York, he was ready to join the American Copyright Club. Organized in 1843 under the presidency of William Cullen Bryant, the group denounced literary piracy as a crime and promoted enactment of laws against it. Many publishers opposed such laws, arguing that it was contrary to the national interest to pay royalties to foreign authors. The publishers also shrewdly aligned their interest with that of the reading public, claiming that the very absence of copyright legislation made a vast amount of literature "affordable" to a vast audience. Jacksonian Democrats sided with the publishers rather than with the authors. The authors, in contrast, found a champion in Henry Clay and parts of the Whig Party. For Poe, the flood of inexpensive books that were shabbily printed on flimsy paper merely constituted a "quagmire of [...] pamphleteering" that was not significantly different from the flood of worthless paper bills — what critics like Hezekiah Niles called "rag-money" or "trash in circulation" — put into circulation by commercial banks at the time.[23]

Poe on more than one occasion singled out the literary genius as the most tragic victim, who, "From the nature of the Copy-Right laws, [...] has no individual powers" and is about as equal as "the dean and chapter of the see-cathedral, in a British election of Bishops." To make matters worse, the "man of genius" is "imperatively [...] controlled" by the publishers, who are in a singular position to print so as to suit themselves.[24] The direct literary application of Poe's bitter views of the "organized *cliques*" that he saw hanging "like nightmares upon American literature" is summed up in William Gilmore Simms's editorial remarks of November 1845, which Poe reprinted in his *Broadway Journal*:

> In the matter of magazine and periodical writing ... the author is constantly the victim of lying editors and publishers, who beguile him of his writings and abuse him, from their chair of criticism, if he ventures to complain. There is not a professional literary man of the country, who has not a long story to relate, of the arts by which he has been swindled of his contributions by that class of insects of literature, whom Moore compares with the maggot who is said to feed and fatten upon the brains of the elk, — the noble animal perishing finally, the prey of the miserable insect which has fed upon his life.[25]

A generation earlier, the theme of the author as a victim of the capitalist hold on writing had inspired Washington Allston to execute *The Poor Author and the Rich Bookseller* in oil on canvas. Allston was living in Europe then, though his reputation was high also in the United States. Emerson was a declared admirer, Irving was both an admirer and a friend, though Poe mentions Allston only in passing, including in a review of Rufus Griswold's *The Poets and Poetry of America*.[26] There is, it should be noted, a noticeable difference between Allston's unexcited painting, whose effectiveness rests chiefly on color contrasts — while the prosperous bookseller is done in rich, gorgeous colors, the poor author's clothes are all but drab — and the firebrand tone of Simms's remarks. The fact that Poe reprints Simms's remarks testifies both to the intense politicization of the matter and to his own bitter scorn of an America that refuses to support serious writing because of its narrow focus on making money on the quick.

In the mid–1840s, the issue of intellectual property provided a focus also to Poe's thinking about literary nationalism. Calls for a distinctively American literature — which was to make America as independent culturally as it was politically — had been heard since after the Revolution. Adopted by Emerson and other *literati*, with increasing passion these calls had converged with romantic notions of self-development in individuals and nations

Washington Allston, *The Poor Author and the Rich Bookseller*, 1811, oil on canvas, original size 31½ × 28¼ inches, Museum of Fine Arts, Boston, Bequest of Charles Sprague Sargent, 27.220 (photograph © 2013 Museum of Fine Arts, Boston).

alike. Poe had long challenged such views of a genuinely American literature, insisting instead that no true literature could be "national" but the world at large was "the only proper stage for the literary *histrio*."[27] In his own writings, Poe rarely used unmistakably American settings and characters, and if he did, as in "The Gold-Bug," it was hardly ever in a celebratory, nationalistic way.[28] Nevertheless, his removal from Philadelphia to New York brought him to the company of "Young America," a group of strenuous literary nationalists that had found a home in the city's *Democratic Review*.[29]

Although Poe never sponsored the Young Americans' views, being near them pushed him to formulating his ideas about a native literature more fully and more precisely than ever before. Eventually he articulated in the *Broadway Journal* his own brand of literary nationalism, calling it the "nationality of self-respect."[30] Self-respect demanded that Americans not look to English critical opinion to establish the worth of American authors, a position on which indeed Poe was on common ground with the Young Americans. At the same time, Poe's idea was the fulfillment of the hopes of James Kirke Paulding, who was one of the first critics to appreciate Poe. Paulding's hope was that Poe would satirize Americans' tendency to slavishly imitate the extravagancies of current English writers. Which indeed Poe did, explaining that, "irreparable ill is wrought by the almost exclusive dissemination among us of foreign — that is to say, of *monarchical or aristocratical sentiment* in foreign books; nor is this sentiment less fatal to democracy because it reaches the people themselves in the gilded pill of the poem or novel."[31] Critics have often said that Poe was in a sense "unhappy" with democracy, but at least what he wrote in the *Broadway Journal* of 1845 is rather a reprimand to those who do not understand the difference between abuse of freedom and free institutions. Poe also proposed taking American literature away from unimaginative men of wealth. As he formulated the issue in the *Broadway Journal*, an "aristocracy of dollars" had come to govern American literary life; wealth or social position thus "determines an author's success." Poe had originally developed this idea in *Burton's Gentleman's Magazine* in May 1840. Five years later, he adds that the imitativeness of American writing, so much deplored by the Young Americans, itself grew out of an economic situation that left the production of literature to leisured gentlemen, "a class proverbial for conservatism" and the "insipidity of their productions."[32]

According to Poe, existing laws designed to produce "affordable" literature for the masses undermined true democracy, not only by privileging leisured gentleman-scribblers but also by disseminating "aristocratic" writings and by provoking similarly "aristocratic" responses from writers. As a result of the injustices perpetrated against them, true geniuses were alienated from American society. A true literary nationalism, by contrast, would advocate international copyright and thereby afford American writers a living, putting them in this important sense on a par with their English counterparts. Such a form of nationalism would affirm American self-respect not through the use of native subjects and themes but through an exercise of "that nationality [which] will do all it can to procure our authors fair play."[33] Overall, then, Poe was no mere cultural critic, for whom "culture" chiefly represented a kind of court of appeal that was to preside over social processes and practices at the same time as it was to serve as a mitigating alternative.[34] To be sure, Poe in his criticism often brought together discontent with the present, nostalgia for a past state of unity, and an aesthetic view of the world, while otherwise he remained silent on the controversial issues of the day. Yet Poe's whole existence had been shaped by a tyrannical minority of bankers, businessmen, and achievers, and he had come to devote himself wholeheartedly to the material interests of the commercial writer.

Devotion to writers' material interests also brought with it a new perspective on magazine publishing. Poe's earlier ventures had hinged on his ability to attract capital. By 1844, Poe was conspiring to create a magazine through a "radically different" strategy, one that would eliminate all dependence on wealthy proprietors. Under the new scheme, intellectuals would "combine secretly," as he wrote Lowell on March 30, 1844. Some would contribute capital, some would contribute articles, and another member would serve as editor. Such a "coalition," Poe was convinced, "would be irresistible," much as it would be the only way to escape being "devoured, without mercy, by the Godeys, the Snowdens, et id genus omne."[35] Poe's scheme for a new order of literary production, of course, was utopian. The stark realities came home to roost when Edward H. N. Patterson replies to Poe's August 7, 1849, letter: "In publishing a $5 magazine, of 96 pp., monthly,—p page same size as *Graham's* [...] it would be necessary for me to make an outlay of at least $1,100 (this amount including a supply of paper for three months for 2,000 copies). Now, if you are sure that, as you before thought, 1,000 subscribers can be obtained who will pay upon receipt of the first number, then you may consider me pledged to be with you in the undertaking." If Poe agrees to this proposition, he should plan to meet Patterson on October 15, in Saint Louis, where they can "settle on arrangements" for their magazine: "You may associate my name with your own in the matter, the same as if I had met you in person. [...] The first number can be issued in July."[36]

Poe passed away on October 7, 1849, and never saw the words he had ardently sought for so long. On the other hand, Patterson hardly would have met Poe's ideal of a partner, a partner, Poe had written in 1843, "possessing ample capital, and, at the same time, so little self-esteem, as to allow me entire control of the editorial conduct."[37] Nevertheless in 1845, Poe still thought he could loosen the link between capitalism and literary production. At the time, his hopes rested on the seemingly radical potential of "anastatic" printing. He predicted, in an article for the *Broadway Journal*, that with the help of this new invention publishers would be able to turn out unlimited copies at minimal cost. The fundamental principle of "anastatic" printing was making impressions directly from manuscripts that had been transferred onto zinc plates. "Anastatic" printing thus was expected to greatly reduce the material value of a book or magazine and proportionally raise the value of its literary content, which, Poe added, "the copyright laws are needed to protect." The alternative printing method, once fully implemented, would reduce reliance on expensive printing machinery and so would break the capitalist hold on literary production. This in turn would give readers access to a wide range of texts ordinarily kept from circulation by profit-oriented publishers.

The scheme of "anastatic printing," Poe predicts, will "cheapen information," "diffuse knowledge and amusement," and "bring before the public the very class of works which are most valuable, but least in circulation on account of unsaleability." By turning writing into a specialized, unalienable form of capital, Poe hoped that he could liberate himself from *both* capital *and* the mass audience, as he saw these as merely two aspects of the same productive process. Poe also anticipates a number of changes, both literary and social, from "improvement in *style*" and "precision of thought" to the emergence of a genuinely democratic literature. Such a literature would "at once give the ascendancy to the literary value," at the expense of the "physical or mechanical value" of a book. Once Poe's democracy of producers is fully established, the "wealthy gentleman of elegant leisure will lose the vantage-ground now afforded him [and] the humblest will speak as often and as freely as the most exalted."[38]

Poe probably used anastatic printing to "mass" produce, in November 1845, a number of circular letters soliciting subscriptions to the — then already moribund—*Broadway Journal*. More importantly, the class analysis of cultural production that underlies anastatic printing as well applies to the realm of money. The word "anastasis" originally referred to the doctrine of resurrection and thus is a principle of faith or trust, a principle that is fundamental also for a workable paper currency.[39] Ironically Poe's plan, disclosed in his letters to Lowell, to overcome the exploitation of writers by the publishing industry through a secret coalition in many ways resembles the counterfeiters' plotting in order to escape, not so much the law as the monopolization of issuing currency. Another parallel stems from the method itself. Poe imagined that the "anastatic" method would liberate writers from "the imposition of publishers" insofar as it transforms literary production from an industry to a craft.[40] Industry and craft are separated by the measure of value they respectively employ. In industry, value is always relative; the value of a commodity thus depends on its relation to other commodities in the marketplace. In craft, the measure of value is objective, dependent on the amount of labor expended in the productive process. This was the measure Poe preferred for his own compositions.[41] It also was the measure in the production of counterfeit bills. In addition, "anastatic" methods were widely used by counterfeiters in the antebellum period. In order to prevent counterfeiting by this and other nefarious practices, a Christopher D. Seropyan in 1856 published a circular describing his chemical methods. His patented method, which allegedly was endorsed by a professor from Yale, provided for a translucent overprint, announced to be in blue but actually executed in yellow. Subsequent tests found the method utterly useless, and it soon disappeared from usage on bank bills, fading into history, as did the anti-counterfeiting system promoted as "Captain Glynn's Anti-Anastatic Bank Note Paper."[42]

Another parallel between Poe's "anastatic" method and the world of counterfeiting is played out on a more theoretical level, concerning the certainties of established classifications. Counterfeiters assume the public production of paper money into the private domain of their workshops, before they reintroduce their products back into the public domain, thus inverting the established pattern of the public domain as the originator of currency.[43] In a paper money economy, negotiating the difference between the public and the private is, of course, crucial. In the economy that Poe participated in, gold money, though advocated by Jacksonians as the money of the "people," often was hoarded by the wealthy, who also kept shipping coins abroad to be sold for a profit. Yet paper money likewise was hardly the money of the "people." Coming as it did from commercial banks, essentially it was also a product of capitalists and leisured gentlemen. Until the Free Banking legislation of 1837 to 1838 made bank charters more easily obtainable, worthy entrepreneurs were themselves at the mercy of state politicians, who continuously mixed banking and politics. The legislation also added a degree of protection for holders of currency, though there was not as yet any effective control of the institutions by the federal government.[44] As a consequence, what Poe calls "the humblest" were starkly at the mercy of profit-oriented banks, whose practices such as issuing worthless paper bills or willfully suspending the payment of specie Poe considered as simply intolerable. As the narrator declares in "The Business Man," "The frauds of the banks of course I couldn't help. Their suspension put me to ruinous inconvenience. These, however, are not individuals, but corporations; and corporations, it is very well known, have neither bodies to be kicked, nor souls to be damned."[45]

"The Business Man" is the revised version of "Peter Pendulum," which Poe wrote in early 1840; Poe published it in the *Broadway Journal* of August 2, 1845. In January 1845, the New York *Evening Mirror* published a poem titled "Epigram for Wall Street." The poem was first noticed and reprinted by Thomas Ollive Mabbott, and is now generally ascribed to Poe:

I'll tell you a plan for gaining wealth,
  Better than banking, trade or leases —
Take a bank note and fold it up,
  And then you will find your money in
    creases!
This wonderful plan, without danger or loss,
Keeps your cash in your hands, where nothing
    can trouble it;
And every time that you fold it across
  'Tis as plain as the light of the day that
    you *double* it![46]

The poem is unusually good-natured and light-hearted, though one of its puns ("in *creases*"—"increases") deserves special notice for its echo of colonial monetary practices. Early colonial bills were unusually large — about 4 inches wide and 5¼ inches high — too large to be put conveniently into a purse or pocket without folding. People would therefore fold them in half in each direction and then unfold them when spending them. This created creases and splitting along the folds, but people found it convenient when a bill split apart to use a half or a quarter section as change rather than paste or sew the parts together. Some people tore the bills deliberately to make change. This was not quite what the issuers had intended. Thus, colonial authorities for instance in Massachusetts set up a special committee to investigate the sectioning of bills. Connecticut in May 1726 even prohibited the use of sectional bills, but people simply responded by circulating sections on large bills. As of 1735, each quadrant on a note's back was made to read "Quarter of"—as in "Quarter of 2 shillings" or similar appropriate language for other denominations. On later issues, the calculation of the quadrant's value was printed on each of the four quadrants on the back, thus: "Quarter 2s. & 6d. / Seven-pence-half-penny."[47]

While "Epigram for Wall Street" makes light of one of the nation's most pressing questions — the stability of the currency and the authenticity of the paper notes that were passing from hand to hand—a more serious note is struck in a letter Poe wrote to Thomas H. Chivers on August 29, 1845. In the letter, Poe explains that he has "been making all kinds of inquiries about the 'broken' money — but as yet have not found it." The reference to "broken" money concerns Chivers' request that Poe find the Commercial Bank of Florida, on Wall Street, and obtain certain securities so that Chivers will not lose a large sum of money by the coming month.[48] Finally, the question of the authenticity of bank bills takes on an almost deadly urgency when a mere three months before his death on October 7, 1849, Poe talks about the "delusions" he had had to the Philadelphia publisher and engraver John Sartain. Poe seemed to trust Sartain, who recorded years later that Poe had hallucinated that he had been detained in the Philadelphia County Prison, under suspicion of passing a counterfeit fifty-dollar bill.[49] Poe's persecution mania, the result of his drinking to excess, would not have been out of place in David Simon's television series *The Wire*, which captures the texture and mythology of urban decay in post–September 11 Baltimore.[50] During the era of commercial banking, however, a vision such as Poe's often was not a mere delusion. A great number of poor and illiterate people then ended up in prison because they unwittingly passed a counterfeit note received from someone else.

An ever-growing proportion of those arrested on counterfeit charges were immigrants, whose "monetary illiteracy" made it utterly impossible for them to tell "good" notes from "bad" ones. "I have only been in the country 18 months and begin to speak English within the last three months," one French man charged with passing counterfeits said. "I know nothing about the Bank Bills in this country."[51] Certainly, this poor immigrant would not have known anything about a $1 note from the State Bank of Indiana at Richmond that was put into circulation contemporaneously with the publication of "The Gold-Bug." The note, bearing the date June 20, 1843, was a counterfeit in imitation of a genuine note from the Lawrenceburg branch of the State Bank of Indiana.[52] Nor would this poor suspect likely have known anything about a note that originally had been produced by The New England Bank Note Company in the 1830s and was altered from the Stillwater Canal Bank of Maine. As the following illustration shows, the word "Blackstone" is beautifully lettered, though it is spaced too closely to "Canal." Also noteworthy is the misspelling of "Providence" as "Providence." In addition, "Rhode Island" was drawn in (vertically, on the right of the vignette) after "Maine" had been removed.[53]

Counterfeits — and moral panics — had been the bane of America's monetary history from its colonial beginnings. One problem was overproduction, as colonial authorities habitually issued more notes than they were able or willing to redeem. The second problem was numbers. Between 1690, when Massachusetts issued the first bills of credit, and 1789, when George Washington was inaugurated as the first President of the United States, more than 100,000 different bills in many denominations were issued to meet a wide range of financial needs. The third problem was that under the rather primitive technological conditions (printing was done either from an engraved copper plate or by using an ordinary printing press), early paper money was easy to counterfeit or fake. Following independence, the situation hardly improved, as engraving and printing from copper plates continued. Early nineteenth-century reports indicate that up to fifty percent of the money in circulation was fraudulent or, to use the idiom of the time, "bogus." Ironically, solid banks that were well respected and widely known were the most popular targets of counterfeiting schemes, as their reputation pretty much eliminated the need to ask about the legitimacy of the bank and created a level of comfort that would render inspections rather casual. Notes of the Second Bank of the United States, which thanks to the bank's good standing circulated at par

Five-dollar note, altered from the Stillwater Canal Bank to the Blackstone Canal Bank, Providence [sic!], Rhode Island, 1840 (courtesy of Mark D. Tomasko).

throughout the country and therefore were considered "good as gold," often fell into this situation. It is a matter of record that many of this bank's notes are known today only from counterfeits, many of which were produced in workshops run by illicit entrepreneurs across the border in Canada and subsequently passed into circulation throughout the United States.[54]

Altering as well as numerous other practices, including "raising" the denomination of a note, issuing "spurious" notes from nonexistent banks, or "multiplying" notes by cutting them into pieces and patching them together so that four good bills made five fraudulent ones, caused a great deal of trouble. Special organizations tried to fight the crime by paying rewards for arrests and convictions of counterfeiters. Yet authorities until the mid-nineteenth century generally showed little interest and the punishment was not severe enough to deter criminals. Most of them escaped punishment altogether. In 1818, Hezekiah Niles predicted that the United States was on its way to becoming "a nation of counterfeiters." Niles, who had made himself a name with the *Weekly Register*, then the most important financial publication, was horrified at the proliferation of fraudulent paper money. "Counterfeit notes and false bank notes are so common," he wrote in the July Fourth issue, "that forgery seems to have lost its criminalty [sic!] in the minds of many."[55]

Forgery had not lost its criminality in the mind of Poe, as is evident from his hallucinatory vision of being detained in prison under suspicion of passing a counterfeit bill. While it is impossible to determine the first cause or point of origin of Poe's vision, its "*incitamentum,*" there is circumstantial evidence. During the bank-note issuing era, discussions of counterfeits and forgeries were popular at lyceums and other public venues. Frequently, presenters showed examples of currency to the audience, challenging them to tell the difference between the genuine and the fake. Newspaper and magazine editors were quick to report on such events, which they thought were educational rather than mere sensational news. For the most part, discussions of counterfeits and forgeries took place in New York, where currency experts like Waterman L. Ormsby, who also owned a banknote printing company, could be netted as presenters. New York, of course, was also the place where the majority of "infallible" counterfeit detectors were printed.[56]

New York then was solidly in the hands of radical Democrats, in contrast to Philadelphia, which was more of a backwater of American politics, where Federalism was still lingering. Poe's removal from Philadelphia to New York clearly renewed the author's interest in the future of the political process. Some of this interest may be owed to Charles Frederick Briggs, another member of the New York literary scene, though outside the circle of Irving and Cooper. Briggs was an independent ally of the Whigs, and the founder, in 1845, of the *Broadway Journal*. Poe, who brought a letter of introduction from James Russell Lowell, met Briggs in the middle of December 1844, shortly before he left Nathaniel Parker Willis's *Mirror*. Seemingly no less important for rekindling Poe's interest in politics was the actor and artist Gabriel Harrison, who later left several reminiscences of Poe. Harrison likely first met Poe in the fall of 1844, and the two men met through 1847, "when ever [Poe] was in the city." Harrison also mentions the White Eagle Club, a Democratic political organization that flourished during the Presidential campaign of 1844, contributing much to the election of James Polk. According to Harrison, Poe composed a song for the Club, which was used "successfully through the campaign of 1844."[57]

How can we explain Poe's involvement with a Democratic political organization, if such it was? It is a matter of record that Poe wrote the song under a pseudonym, Thaddeus Perley. Moreover, at the time Poe was destitute again, accepting a bag of coffee for the act.[58] And while Poe had emphasized his "earnest desire for the future," it is well to consider his negative political capability, described as "the flexibility of his political commitments."[59] This "flexibility" became of considerable concern to his friends and political allies. Frederick Thomas, for instance, wondered whether Poe's political sympathies had not shifted to the administration of James K. Polk, a Democrat: "What are your politics? Are you friendly to the powers that be," Thomas wrote two years after he had recommended Poe for a Whig patronage.[60] Thomas's suspicion that Poe could easily accommodate himself to either a Whig or a Democratic administration was not unfounded, as Poe repeatedly represented himself as politically neutral, including in a letter to Thomas H. Chivers, in which he claimed that his "political views" had "reference to no one of the present parties."[61]

Contemporary Poe scholars have expanded on Frederick Thomas's doubts about Poe's political reliability, arguing that all his commitments and attachments were unreliable, corresponding to a highly unstable self-image.[62] Moreover, Poe's writings relentlessly insist that there is nothing outside the fiction that reflects on the action inside it. Thus, even seemingly overt political allusions, while they allow themselves to be admired often do not allow themselves to be trusted. The "earnest desire for the future," which emanates from "Some Words with a Mummy," clearly follows an injunction towards stabilization, yet it is less clear whether any stable understanding of it is possible. The tale enters into the defeat in the presidential elections of Henry Clay, the Whig nominee from Kentucky, in a closely contested race, against the Democrat James Polk, from Tennessee.[63] In the tale, there is hope, albeit a desperate one, that the Whigs or their descendants would fare better in the election of 2044 than Clay fared against Polk in November 1844. "Besides, I am anxious to know who will be President in 2045," the narrator says towards the end. With these words, the narrator of course takes back as utterly banal the disillusionment ("I am heartily sick of this life") he has just given expression to. This is surprising, given Poe's general reluctance to make any overtly political statements. As if to downplay the politics, the narrator then dismisses as trivial or absurd virtually every modern "advance," while wisdom is declared a thing of the past.[64] Nevertheless, the narrator cannot finally disengage himself from his democratic identity and his stake in national affairs, and neither could Poe, who continued to labor within and against a system that he professed to despise.

From the Appreciation of Beauty to California Gold

No doubt the impetus to write "The Gold-Bug" had come to Poe by his own grinding poverty, and by the wish to change it for something better. A similar impetus appears to have driven "The Landscape Garden" into an elaborate fantasy of inherited wealth. "The Landscape Garden" is the first of Poe's prose stories of pure beauty, and at least at first sight seems completely devoid of sadness or frustration. Poe probably wrote it shortly after he gave up his editorship at *Graham's Magazine* in the spring of 1842. Pressed for money as he then was, he offered it to the editors of the *Democratic Review* in July, who promptly returned it, so that it was first published in Snowden's *Ladies' Companion* for October 1842.[65] A later version of "The Landscape Garden," known as "The Domain of Arnheim," was published in 1846. Each version, however, displays a sense of nostalgia that is impossible to overlook.

Poe as a boy had known the home of John Allan's partner, Charles Ellis, with its beautiful garden. Memory of Ellis's estate led him to call the wealthy young hero of his tale Ellison, a man who is as "remarkable in the entire and continuous profusion of good gifts ever lavished upon him by fortune." "From his cradle to his grave," the story begins, "a gale of prosperity bore him along. Nor do I use the word prosperity in its mere worldly sense. I mean it as synonymous with happiness." If Ellison can realize his poetic sentiments only because he is wealthy enough to do so, he may well represent the "station in society" Poe felt was his due.[66]

Ellison essentially is Poe's only truly happy character, proof that "it is not impossible that man, the individual, under certain unusual and highly fortuitous conditions, may be happy." The heir to a fortune of "four hundred and fifty millions of dollars," which is about three hundred times the value of the treasure Legrand finds, Ellison truly is in a position to live the good life. Given his appreciation of beauty, his "poetic sentiment" as Poe calls it, Ellison of course could have become a poet, and in a sense he has, though he turns to "improving" the natural landscape through landscape gardening, a pursuit that was much talked about at the time. Poe himself was keenly interested in landscape gardening, which for him signified one of those "liberal pursuits" that wealthy men of taste should be allowed to follow unmolested even in a democracy. Without a "just appreciation of" these pursuits, Poe continues, "our institutions cannot be preserved, or if they can, would be scarcely worth preserving." Not surprisingly, Poe's celebration of "liberal pursuits" appears in a passage about Thomas Jefferson, the Virginia gentleman who in his later years had retired to his private garden estate of Monticello, in whose neoclassical shadow Poe studied the classics at the University of Virginia.[67]

Jefferson in his retirement might well have served as a model for Ellison himself, and it is probably this semblance that has led Thomas Mabbott to suggest that Poe's principles, or conditions, for happiness sound very much like the ideals of a Southern aristocratic gentleman, with the exception perhaps of the dedication implied in having an "object of unceasing pursuit."[68] The object of Ellison's unceasing pursuit is the perfect tract of land for the creation of the perfect landscape. His choice of location--an "elevated tableland of wonderful fertility and beauty"--seems ideally suited for the purpose. The land is traversed by a river, Poe's preferred symbol of life and aliveness; more importantly, however, the land does *not* "startle," "excite," and then "fatigue" and "depress," as do scenes of "grandeur." Poe's choice of words is significant, and not only because it shows that Poe was keenly aware of the distinction between the sublime and the picturesque. Avoiding any reference to the discourse of sublimity in the description of the landscape, Poe redirects the sublime to "the contemplation of" the vast sum Ellison has inherited, and "of the services to which it might be applied." In doing so, Poe not only transcends the aesthetic meaning of the sublime, but also keeps "The Domain of Arnheim" within the boundaries of political economy.[69]

If Ellison realizes his dream by virtue of his enormous wealth, which, even at three percent interest, increases at a rate of "six and twenty dollars for every minute that flew," he does so by investing it. In other words, Ellison is a man of action who turns his wealth into capital. The value of capital, however, is not intrinsic so much as it derives from exchange, from the power of purchasing his "domain." The word "domain" according to the dictionary is a legal term meaning a heritable property; it is derived from the Latin word *dominicus*, of or belonging to a lord, though not in the traditional sense of possession but in terms of a right to property. Ellison's status as a representative of expansionist capitalism, together with his deficient sense of social responsibility, should make anyone wary of identifying either him or his creator as a Southern gentleman. Poe may have projected much of his own personality upon Ellison, though a true Southern gentleman, Joseph Osgoode wrote in 1918, is an exponent of "independent thought, free outlook, original conception, genial humor, unobtrusive yet commanding dignity, exquisite refinement, and sound and penetrating judgment." Osgoode had been intent on restoring the South to a respectable place in American history and accordingly described Poe as a "true type of the Southern gentleman." Vernon Louis Parrington, by contrast, feels almost embarrassed about Poe's alleged social habitus, identifying the writer's determining environment as that of the "indolent life of the planter gentry." William Taylor's later views of Poe as a "son of the South" are, once again, much more self-confidently southern: a Southern gentleman, Taylor claims, must "possess every quality which the Yankee lacked: honor and integrity, indifference to money and business, a decorous concern for amenities, and a high sense of civic and social responsibility." More recently still, James Hutchisson has portrayed Poe likewise as a genuinely southern voice, and he explicitly treats several of Poe's stories as "covert allegories endorsing the ethos of the antebellum South."[70]

It is too facile to dismiss all these ascriptions as so much bunk. Posing as an intellectual aristocrat Poe did on occasion articulate fictive fantasies that associated prosperity with social harmony, though as a writer on the brink of poverty he did not have the status quo to act in that manner. Moreover, he often seems to suggest that there is no alternative to a political consensus that was watched over by the "better sorts of people," though again there was no material base for him to think in that way. This is not to deny that Poe *was* raised in the expectation of becoming heir to one of the wealthiest men in Richmond, and that as a student at the University of Virginia he *did* share in the social lives of the sons of families constituting the South's aristocracy. Yet Poe also was conscious both of his humble origins and of his precarious status as a foster child. When his break with John Allan put out of his reach the social position that he felt was his due, Poe asserted his aristocratic sensibilities with a vengeance. "As a man of the world you will at once understand that what I most need for my work in its commencement [...] is *caste*," Poe wistfully confided to Judge Robert T. Conrad. The word "caste" here reveals Poe's acute awareness of his lack of class distinction. It is not much of a surprise, therefore, that Poe even took to fabricating his genealogy, falsely claiming that his family name was derived from German; or else that his Irish great-grandfather had been a wealthy financier.[71]

Class distinction in Poe's time might be conferred by any special profession, property, or acknowledged hereditary or social rank. Since Poe was so acutely aware of his own lack of such distinction, his professed scorn for an egalitarian democracy and his fear of it at best mimic those of the people of "caste." In their view, government indeed was instituted for the protection of property, much as the interests of property were identical with those of religion and morality. In Jackson's America, however, this already was the theory of a social group on the defensive, a group that necessarily was suspicious of industrialism and, as well, of the various reform movements that were thought to threaten established institutions — reform of prisons, of the position of women, of education, marriage, slavery, and of the currency.[72]

While all kinds of Southern sensibility can be grounded in historic reality, to identify them as Poe's own is to ignore the distinction between professed and real conditions of existence. Poe all too often derived his pronouncements from the words of others, much as he consistently bent his writings to other people's ideological agendas. His calculating approach to the literary market further complicates the political meaning of all his writings, fictional or otherwise. It would therefore be a mistake to resolve textual ambiguity by establishing direct links between the written words and the biographical author. One result of such an approach we have seen in Marchand's account, on the basis of the Paulding-Drayton review that Poe did not write, of Poe's complicity with "the South's peculiar institutions" and, as well, of his alleged hostility to "democracy, industrialism, and reform." In a more recent instance, David Long somewhat obliquely describes the discrepancies in Poe's life and work in terms of "some idiosyncratic and displaced amalgam" of the aristocratic, the erudite, and the reactionary.[73]

Interpretations that personalize, even wrongly personalize, share some common assumptions, Terence Whalen notes. One such assumption is that Poe chose his attitudes freely and knowingly; another, that his political attitudes could be expressed without constraint, or at least without regard to the political divisions in the national audience, and, by extension, that his expressions always constitute a "true" record of his thoughts or convictions. Poe himself seems to have cautioned us against such assumptions when, as early as 1841, he has one of his characters comment on "some trivial discrepancy [...] between what I said and what I had not the courage to say." More to the point, in 1848 Poe wrote, "No man ever will dare write" and no man "*could* ... even if he dared" write anything laying the heart bare. Charles Frederick Briggs likewise sounds a note of caution. Writing in *Holden's Dollar Magazine* for December 1849, Briggs claims that, "Like all other writers, Mr. Poe developed himself in his literary productions, but to understand his writings it was necessary to be possessed of the key of his personal acquaintance. Knowing him thoroughly, you could thoroughly comprehend what he wrote, but not otherwise."[74]

Though there be the risk of incomprehension, the point can be made that Poe did have dreams of an ideal place in society. Although these dreams should not be accepted uncritically, they were nevertheless real, a means to compensate for the sordid circumstances of his life. Seen in this light, it is anybody's guess how deeply disappointed Poe was in his expectation of being heir to one of the wealthiest men in Richmond. John Allan, who might have adopted him, had remarried in 1830 and sired a son by his second wife, Louisa Patterson. Upon Allan's death in 1834, Poe received "not a mill."[75] In view of the wound received it is hardly coincidental that, as Poe assured Mrs. Whitman, the story of Mr. Ellison had in it, not only much of his "soul" but "more of myself and of my inherent tastes and habits of thought than anything I have written."[76] When Poe disclosed himself thus, he was referring to the later version of "The Landscape Garden," known as "The Domain of Arnheim," which he published late in 1846. Poe retained the fifteen paragraphs of the original version, but re-examined the happiness theme under the shadow of his wife's dissolution. With Ellison himself removed from the scene by death, the whole "Paradise of Arnheim," into which the narrator-traveler's craft glides through a fretted gate of burnished gold, seems not so much a representation of anything real as a vision of the afterworld, conjured up by a disillusioned Poe less than three years before his own death. Indeed it is hard to believe that Poe found much reassurance in imagining that death, his wife Virginia's impending death, meant gliding into the domain of supernal life, there to appreciate beauty.[77]

Virginia Poe passed away on January 30, 1847. In the years before, Poe had been able to appreciate beauty in the fashionable salons of New York, which he frequented during 1845 and at least the early part of 1846. His entrée had been insured by the recent fame of "The Raven," which was even more of a popular success than "The Gold-Bug." By this time, Poe had discovered that quality and salability were not mutually exclusive. As the reviewer of *Tales* had noted in 1845, Poe "evidently" intended a tale like "The Gold-Bug" to become a popular success because it "made a great noise when it was first issued, and was circulated to a greater extent than any American tale, before or since."[78] Although Poe was more tight-lipped about the dual critical and popular success of "The Raven," in a letter to Frederick William Thomas of May 4, 1845, he compared the popularity of the poem with the tale, writing: "The bird beat the bug, though, all hollow."[79]

Three years later, a different bird appeared on the horizon, though it is a matter of dispute whether this bird also beat the bug. Some background should help clarify the connection. On January 24, 1848, James Wilson Marshall, a carpenter, glimpsed "something shining" in the bottom of the raceway of John Augustus Sutter's sawmill on the South Fork of the American River. On March 15, 1848, the discovery was recorded in the San Francisco *Chronicle* and other papers. By that time, the ink had barely dried on the Treaty of Guadalupe Hidalgo, its signers utterly unaware of the gigantic value of the territory Mexico was ceding away.[80] The Gold Rush came late in 1848 and in 1849, when headlines in the *California Herald* ran "El Dorado of the United States of America. The Discovery of Inexhaustible Gold Mines in California. Tremendous Excitement Among the Americans," who, thanks to extensive advertising, were already preparing "to migrate to the gold regions."[81]

By 1849, all kinds of people were on their way from "the States" to the California goldfields, yeoman farmers, journeyman workers, and middle-class townsfolk, including a surprising number of professionals and men of letters; one of Poe's publishers, Israel Post, died on the way. Poe himself, Thomas Mabbott claims, "must, at least in imagination, have considered making the journey," though he eventually decided to remain a "*littérateur*," unwilling or unable to "abandon the hopes which still [led him] on for all the gold in California."[82] It is unclear what exactly kept Poe from making the trip to the California goldfields. One clue comes from a review of *Tales*, which describes Poe as feeling "chained down to a wheel which ever monotonously revolves around a fixed centre, progressing without progress."[83] Unable to tear himself from the magazine prison-house, and probably just as unable to raise or borrow the money for traveling to California, Poe took to satirizing all and everything, especially the search for gold by the self-described "gallant knight," over whose heart "a shadow / Fell as he found / No spot of ground / That looked like Eldorado."[84]

Poe's "Eldorado" is an intensely personal poem. First published in the Boston magazine *The Flag of Our Union* of April 21, 1849, it is at the same time one of Poe's last poems. Thus it has been read as a reflection of the artist's conviction that the search for gold was misdirected and that it would be preferable to search, as Poe had done throughout his career, for different treasures, including elusive ones or treasures that possibly do not even exist in this world. For Mabbott at least, "Eldorado" represents "the song of discovery of those who seek for the true gold, for beauty, for truth, for the ideal."[85] Yet in order to find any such, the seeker will have to go "over the mountains of the moon," that is, to the utterly remote and, beyond that, "down the Valley of the Shadow," which in the King James Version of the

Bible appears as "the valley of the shadow of death."[86] Who would want to, or dare, go there? Probably only the "Tom o' Bedlams" would, those harmless madmen who once wandered about England begging. We know about them from *King Lear*, where Edgar pretends to be one of them, riding boldly in the face of adversity, even of death, singing a song and fearing no evil.[87]

However immediate the occasion of "Eldorado," the poem strikes one at the same time as a cry of defiance and as a song of mourning, a mourning of all the losses Poe had suffered, so that the change from the real to the unreal once again suggests a vision of the afterlife.[88] By contrast, "Von Kempelen and His Discovery," Poe's prose comment on the California Gold Rush, seems more light-hearted, resembling more a thought experiment or, following Barton Armand, a "calculated alchemical hoaxing."[89] That the transmutation of base metals into gold would be possible had been the alchemists' dream from early on. In the early nineteenth century, the possibility was asserted by a "Dr. Girianger," a German scientist, according to the article on "Alchymy" in Isaac Disraeli's *Curiosities of Literature* of 1834, which Poe may have seen referred to in 1842.[90] By the time of the Gold Rush, Poe had learned that people were only too willing to believe in imaginary miracles. He concluded that such people might swallow an account of a chemist who really made gold from base metal. Thus his narrator, having recounted Von Kempelen's case, claims that indeed, "*gold can be made at will, and very readily, from lead, in connection with certain other substances, in kind and in proportions, unknown.*" The thought experiment, the alchemical hoax, comes in the final paragraph of the story: "gold now is [...] of no greater *value* than lead, and of far inferior value to silver."[91]

Lead, it should be noted, was the old alchemists' first color, black, which is the color of the *prima materia*, of matter not yet touched by spirit or consciousness. Thus, it was the color of the black beast that, the alchemists would say, must come forward prior to any growth. The second stage was white, the color before dawn, as the horizon slowly whitens. White thus stood for purification, the stage when consciousness is developing. This is an abstract or ideal state, which in order to make it come alive must have blood, what he alchemists called the "redness of life." At that stage, the final one, the sun rises, passion flares up, and spiritual lead turns into spiritual gold. In Poe's "Von Kempelen" there is neither spiritual lead nor spiritual gold. Instead, real lead is turned into real gold — "gold far finer than any employed in coinage — gold, in fact, absolutely pure, virgin, without the slightest appreciable alloy!"[92] Poe had the story finished by early March of 1849; it was first published in *The Flag of Our Union* in the April 14, 1849, issue.[93] About a week earlier, Poe had written to Evert A. Duyckink that his intention had been to create

> a kind of "exercise," or experiment, in the plausible or verisimilar style. Of course, there is *not one* word of truth in it from beginning to end. I thought that such a style, applied to the gold-excitement, could not fail of effect. My sincere opinion is that nine persons out of ten (even among the best-informed) will *believe* the quiz (provided the design does not leak out before publication) and that thus, acting as a sudden, although of course a very temporary, *check* to the gold-fever, it will create a *stir* to some purpose.[94]

Poe's strategy — to exercise a "*check* to the gold-fever" — not only serves to neutralize a general passion for gold. Likewise, it capitalizes on the public's gullibility by pretending that lead can be transformed into gold, thus rendering obsolete all debates over the nation's money. Indeed, these debates would come to an end once the supply of gold increased to such an extent that it lost all value "beyond its intrinsic worth for manufacturing purposes."

Yet Poe also raises the question whether Von Kempelen's "momentous discovery" will be "of service or disservice to mankind at large." At the end of the story, Poe makes his position clear by raising the specter of financial speculation, as the only noticeable results of Von Kempelen's discovery are a two-hundred percent increase in the price of lead and a twenty-five percent increase in the price of silver. Von Kempelen's gold thus is hardly the stuff that dreams are made of, and much the same can be said about Kidd's treasure. As has been suggested, "The Gold-Bug" likewise makes capital of the public's gullibility by at once selling to and mystifying his audience. The strategy robs unsuspecting readers of their time and money, much as it destroys their cherished myths of pirates and buried treasures, and of the working of the supernatural.[95]

"Von Kempelen" no less than "The Gold-Bug" constitutes a gesture of revenge, motivated both by the cultural contradictions of the time, the regime of deception at once indulged in and denied, and by the everyday pressures that impacted on Poe's literary production. Not the least of these pressures stemmed from the unresolved issue of America's money, and so Poe's comment that there is "*not one* word of truth" in "Von Kempelen" is at once a denial of anything outside the fiction that reflects on the action inside it and a distant echo of the obligation to "pay to the bearer upon demand" printed on paper bills from the commercial banks. These banks were not only generally reluctant to have notes — their own as well as good ones from other banks — exchanged for gold or silver; they also wholesaled notes by the bundle to exchange brokers in distant cities in order to prevent their return to their place of issue. For instance, the New Hampshire Bank of Portsmouth, New Hampshire, for a time had its notes payable in Philadelphia, Pennsylvania, which of course made them useless for redemption locally. Perhaps the most unusual caper is reported from a bank in Salem, New Jersey, which paid out notes that to the casual viewer looked as if they had been issued in Philadelphia. The intention was to ship the notes to Illinois. There, as well as in other distant places, Philadelphia bills were apt to be highly valued, while few people would have heard of Salem, New Jersey. Only with a magnifying glass is Salem visible in the bank title on the note's face.[96]

Attending to the "stir" Poe's thought experiment was to create, one such stir centers on the question what if the "the old chimera of the philosopher's stone" had been realized *before* the discovery of gold in California? In such a case, California would look very different indeed. For, if gold is devalued because of Von Kempelen's discovery, what good is there in a rush to California to seek an elusive fortune in the mines there? No less a stir is created when we consider the implications of Poe's thought experiment for the money question. By having his narrator declare that gold is now "of *no greater value than lead,*"[97] Poe is offering, at least implicitly, a way of seeing gold that, identifying it as lead instead of as money, allows it actually to *become* money. In "Von Kempelen," therefore, the logic of the gold bugs — that gold never becomes money; it always *is* money — is turned inside out. No longer marking the continuity between nature and the economy, between "natural" money and no money, the logic now registers the fluctuating price of gold, which for that very reason constitutes it as a most risky form of capital and, more importantly, an even riskier form of backing for a currency. For Poe and his contemporaries, the fact that lead can represent gold only because gold already is a representation, may well have been "stranger than fiction," though had Alexander Del Mar's warning against using gold as commodity money been available then, they might have adopted a different view.[98]

The discovery, in California, of the gold that Spanish explorers of the region had searched for in vain for three hundred years also may have been a truth stranger than fiction, yet it had profound effects on America's money. By 1846, the country's gold coinage had dropped to $4 million; by 1850, it had risen to $31 million, climbing to more than $62 million the following year. As gold coins began to flow from America's mints in large quantities, the price of gold in the world market dropped, while the price of silver in relation to gold rose. Predictably, once the market value of the silver dollar reached $1.05, silver coins began to disappear from circulation. This posed a severe threat to commerce, and so Congress in 1851 authorized the production of the silver three-cent piece. This coin was only ¾ pure silver, and thus was kept in circulation rather than melted down. Thanks to the abundance of gold and the introduction of subsidiary silver, Congress eventually repealed the legal tender status of foreign coins — Spanish-American gold doubloons, Mexican silver dollars, and a host of other coins that had been serving in American commerce for many years. Old and worn money, as well as "thalers" and other "foreign inscriptions" on currency also were eliminated.[99] Poe did not live to see any of this happen, nor did he live to see Congress welcoming California to the Union as the 31st state. Poe also did not come to live through the panic of 1857, which took off when in the summer of that year rumors concerning unsound bank loans began to spread. The problems were compounded by America's trade imbalance, which had reached about $100 million. Soon businesses began to fail, the wreck of the *S. S. Central America* in September disrupted the regular inflow of gold California gold, banks suspended specie payment, and by the end of the year several thousand companies had gone bankrupt.[100]

What Poe did live to see was President James Polk's message to Congress of December 5, 1848, which urged the establishment of a branch mint in San Francisco, so as to save transporting bullion gold to the East coast and shipping the minted gold back to California.[101] Poe also saw the passing of the Act of March 3, 1849, which authorized the minting of the first $1 gold dollars. One-dollar gold coins were not included in the original authorization of the United States Mint in 1792. A trial pattern for a gold dollar was produced in 1836, but circulating coins were not struck until after the discovery of gold in California in 1849.[102] The first type of the 1849 gold dollars is known as the Liberty head or small-sized type. The coins were minted from 1849 to 1854, at Philadelphia, Charlotte, Dahlonega, New Orleans, and San Francisco. They were superseded in 1854 by coins that were larger in diameter and thinner. This type of coin became known as the Indian Princess Head or large-sized type. In 1856, the type was changed slightly by enlarging the size of the head. Minting $1 gold dollars was discontinued in 1889.

The Coinage Act of March 3, 1849, set the weight of the gold dollar at 25.8 grains and its fineness at .900, that is, at ⁹⁄₁₀ pure gold. The gold dollar was instantly popular as a substitute for the silver dollar, which was still produced in small quantities but was rarely seen in commercial channels. The tiny gold coin, in contrast, was produced in considerable quantities and became widely used in the early 1850s. *Thompson's Bank Note Reporter* printed a reproduction of the coin in gold. The *New York Weekly Tribune*, which was then edited by Horace Greeley, ran an enthusiastic report in its issue of May 19, 1849: "THE GOLD DOLLAR.— It has come at last! [a] glittering, diminutive gold drop [...] the neatest, tiniest, lightest [coin] in the country [...] too delicate and beautiful to pay out for potatoes, and sourkrout, and salt pork."[103] The new coin had been eagerly awaited, though the paper's

One-dollar Liberty Head gold dollar, 1849, the object of Edgar Allan Poe's scorn (courtesy National Numismatic Collection, Smithsonian Institution).

conviction that it would "prove a great favorite" and be "generally welcome" is disproved by Poe's comment in the *Southern Literary Messenger* of June 1849: "The Romans worshipped the standards; and the Roman standard happened to be an eagle. Our standard is only one tenth of an Eagle — a Dollar — but we make all even by adoring it with tenfold devotion."[104]

The idea that in the United States money was elevated to the status of a deity already was a commonplace in Poe's time. A few people even might have remembered its origin in Washington Irving's sketch "The Creole Village." The piece, which originated from Irving's frontier notebooks, begun in 1833, appeared in Henry Herbert's annual, *The Magnolia*, in 1837, at the height of the financial crisis following Jackson's bank war. Referring to one of the villages of French and Spanish origin in Louisiana that were bypassed by modernization, Irving writes that, in a word, "*the almighty dollar*, that great object of universal devotion throughout our land, seems to have no genuine devotees in these peculiar villages." He added that, unless some of this almighty's "missionaries" despoiled the idyll and built "banking houses and other pious shrines, there is no knowing how long the inhabitants may remain in their present state of contented poverty."[105]

Critics and intellectuals like Irving considered worship of the "almighty dollar" as potentially dangerous because it would undermine trust and confidence through increasingly anonymous relations between individuals. In these relations, "everything has its price," Thoreau wrote. For Emerson, the price was "duplicity and falsehood." Thomas Cole, one of the landscape painters of the Hudson River school, echoes these views in a didactic poem: "Each hill and every valley is become / An altar unto Mammon, and the gods / Of man's idolatry — its victims we." Cole's poem, which also dates from the 1830s, treats the future of America as fatally entangled with an expanding market economy made possible by the availability of abundant money in the form of paper notes issued by commercial banks, often in excess of the "real" money on deposit.[106] There are remarkable parallels between Cole's poem and landscape paintings of the time, including some of his own, which typically depict an Arcadian America beset by the storms of modernization. What we are confronting in the cultural productions from Irving to Cole, then, are representations, and so the question whether Americans of the nineteenth century really conferred the status of deity to pieces of money is a moot one. At stake was nothing less than the issue of money and value.

Irving, Emerson, Thoreau, Cole, as well as a whole range of other artists and intellectuals, together with journalists and newspaper editors and, not to forget, politicians on all levels of government, were united in their suspicion not of money in general but of paper money. Being contemporaries, they could not fully comprehend that the way in which paper money was so widely accepted, despite its lack of any intrinsic value, was a phenomenon that at once depended on trust and confidence and invited the possibility of fraud or, at the very least, a breach of trust and confidence. "The thrall in which an ideology holds a people," the late Tony Judt explained in a recently published essay, "is best measured by their collective inability to imagine alternatives."[107] Hezekiah Niles's remarks on the convertibility of paper into gold, penned in 1816, illustrate well this inability to imagine alternatives. Bank notes, Niles writes, are "considered in the same light as specie, under the *idea* that they [are] always convertible into it, on demand; and this confidence must be restored before the banks can do a business advantageous to their stockholders or the community."[108]

Niles's point was taken up a generation later, at the height of the Bank War. George Wood, for instance, urged that paper money — the value of which "arises from its representing other property, viz, the specie in the vaults, and the other funds and assets of the bank" — must be fully convertible, lest it depreciates. Predictably, the Jacksonians' position was much more extreme. For William Gouge, chief Democratic theorist on banks and banking, only gold and silver had "intrinsic value." Paper money, which the banks were issuing in amounts of up to three or four times of the value of specie in their possession, was not even representative of value. Such notes, Gouge wrote in September 1841, "cannot represent that which the banks have not, and which is not in the country." At best, paper money was "adscititious," that is, "dependant [sic] on *an opinion* that those who have issued them, have the disposition and the ability to give in exchange for these notes gold and silver, or something else possessing *inherent* value." No nation, Gouge thus concluded, could supplant its "*natural* money [gold and silver], by the use of paper money, without involving itself in distress and embarrassment."[109] In light of such convictions, which often cut across political allegiances and, at least in one case, were also being articulated on the other side of the Atlantic, it is no surprise that only much later in the century was gold seen as an outdated form of money, something that could be amassed or accumulated but not circulated. Conceived of as substance rather than energy, gold money was "an offense to the truth of the future," to borrow from Don DeLillo's novel *Cosmopolis.*[110]

Poe's "Imp of the Perverse"

In "The Gold-Bug," much is made of the absence of dollar coins — "there was no American money" among the coins unearthed by Legrand and his fellow money-diggers. At first sight, therefore, Poe's commentary about the devotion of the $1 Gold Dollar may strike one as coming from an imp of the perverse, inciting its victim to act contrarily only "for the reason that we should *not.*" Gold was available after all, the long-sought-for American money that is as absent in "The Gold-Bug" as it was in Poe's own life, there to be compensated for by an imaginary treasure or by fictive fantasies of inherited wealth. By the end of 1848, some $10 million in gold had been produced in California; by the end of 1851, $220 million. The value of United States gold coins in circulation had increased by a factor of twenty.[111] Gold thus had become a presence, though not in Poe's own life.[112] At best, Poe would compose a romantic vision in which the speaker stands "amid the roar / Of a surf-tormented shore, / and I hold within my hand / Grains of the golden sand —/ How few! Yet how they creep / Through my fingers to the deep, / While I weep — while I weep." At worst, Poe would have none of it, purporting to "perversely" despise any real treasure. "The Imp of the Perverse," which dates from 1845, is the last of a group of pieces that stem from Poe's interest in the metaphysics of mental disturbances — like "Berenice" (1835), "The Fall of the House of Usher" (1839), "The Black Cat" (1843), likewise predicated on a "spirit of perverseness," and "The Tell-Tale Heart" (1843). Yet only in "The Imp of the Perverse" do we find the narrator standing "upon the brink of an abyss," irresistibly meditating "a plunge." Given Poe's physical and psychological state at the time, there is some plausibility to the idea that by so deriding the new coin, Poe staged his own personal apocalypse at the same time as he fortified the hedge against his increasing disillusionment and irrationality.[113]

While Poe's biography doubtless is useful to an understanding of his comment on the gold dollar, external evidence warrants a different reading. Let us recall that at the end of "Mellonta Tauta" Poe has the narrator identify as one of "*the* great men in those days among the Amriccans [...] one Zacchary, a tailor."[114] We may reasonably assume that the reference is to Zachary Taylor, who was both a fervent believer in a national bank of issue and the last Whig to win a presidential election. "Mellonta Tauta" was originally published in February 1849, and so Poe's screed on the gold dollar may well constitute at once a rallying cry for a stable and reliable *paper* currency and a somewhat oblique critique of gold-bug orthodoxy, which had received a new lease on life thanks largely to the discovery of gold in California.[115] Affinities between this "one Zacchary, a tailor" and President Taylor certainly are more than incidental, though as so often in Poe's writings, there is no absolute certainty. It is impossible to overlook the fact that "Amricca's" glorious past is mediated, at least in part, by a Martin Van Buren Mavis, the alleged translator of the original manuscript and the narrator's declared "friend." The name of course alludes to President Van Buren, known both for his inability to cope with economic depression and for his pro-slavery policies. Such details, needless to say, downplay the politics in the tale. While they are proof of Poe's extreme caution with regard to committing himself politically, they at the same time testify to this author's "supreme ability to absorb and transform the 'news' of his own time, of his own place." According to Thomas Mabbott, this particular ability was "the rock base of the originality that created [Poe's] tales, no matter what strangeness they may explore."[116]

For Poe, originality was to be judged by novelty, the reader's sense of the new, and Poe's later reflections on literature are haunted by this concept. Thus in his critique of American drama he writes: "The great opponent to progress is Conservatism. In other words — the great adversary of Invention is Imitation: — the propositions are in spirit identical. Just as art is imitative, is it stationary."[117] If the fine arts in Poe's opinion have failed to "progress," applied arts like architecture advanced insofar as they were informed by a utilitarian spirit. Literature, too, could advance, but only by fusing "combinable things hitherto uncombined."[118] Although this appears to collapse the distinction between novelty and mere conventionality, Poe had insisted, in a review of Thomas Moore's poem *Alciphron*, that "all novel conceptions are merely combinations. The mind of man can *imagine* nothing which has not really existed."[119] This statement has been said to reflect Poe's bitter insight that his audience could not read pure novelty. Dependent on a mass audience, yet driven by the iron laws of literary overproduction, commercial writers like Poe were forced to squeeze novel effects out of worn materials. Invention — the survival of the commercial writer — for Poe thus came to lie in the amount of decoding he required of his readers. Detecting Poe's presence in a text, then, is nothing other than "seeking for the profound in the superficial and speculating upon ciphers of dubious import."[120]

Displacements that need decoding are all too obvious from "The Gold-Bug." One might argue, for example, that Legrand represents the sensitive, disinherited aristocrat in "a democratic shopkeeper's world."[121] Consequently, this character is "infected with misanthropy" and, standing above the pit, a mattock in his hand, could easily commit a heinous crime. While the crime is no more than hinted at, Legrand's deficient moral equipment is evident from his resolve to "punish" the narrator, "quietly, in my own way, by a little bit of sober mystification."[122] An angry and disillusioned Legrand of course resembles his creator, who came to have nothing but disdain both for the monetary debates of the time and for politics in general. Let us also not forget that while Poe was at work on "The Gold-Bug," his prospects for government employment (and for support of his magazine) were drying up fast. "You can have no idea of the low ruffians and boobies," Poe wrote to Frederick William Thomas, "who have received office over my head."[123] Poe may have despised the meanness and pettiness of men "without a shadow of political influence or caste," though politicians and their trickeries fared worse. Poe's withdrawal, after failing to secure a clerkship, from identification with a political party fueled his most bitter satires. For instance, in "Some Words with a Mummy" one of the interlocutors of the revived mummy cannot make the Egyptian make sense of the word "politics." The dilemma is resolved by sketching on the wall, "with a bit of charcoal, a little carbuncle-nosed gentleman, out at elbows, standing upon a stump, with his left leg drawn back, his right arm thrown forward, with the fist shut, the eyes rolled up toward Heaven, and the mouth open at an angle of ninety degrees."[124]

Poe wrote "Some Words with a Mummy" early in 1845, almost three years after "The Gold-Bug." We can therefore consider "The Gold-Bug" as a hinge or fulcrum in Poe's career, the beginning of his journey into night, into the dark, which came to a dreadful closure in the ominous references, in "For Annie," to a state in which "the fever called 'living' / Is conquered at last," and in "Eldorado," to the "valley of the shadow [of death]."[125] Had death, then, been demanded of Poe? Charles Baudelaire for instance remarked that Poe's death was "almost a suicide, a suicide prepared for a long time."[126] In fact, to many who knew or had read about Poe, the writer's death did not come as a surprise, though one wonders just for how long it had been in the making. Could it all have begun in February 1829, when Poe's foster mother, Mrs. Frances Allan, passed away and the young man was too late for the funeral? Or else, around the middle of January 1842, when Poe confronted the first signs of his wife's illness? Perhaps it all began later in that year, when Poe finished "The Gold-Bug" and was seeing his hopes for an improvement of his station in society expire. Or else in 1845, when he revised "The Gold-Bug" at the same time as he conjured up, in "The Raven," all those "fantastic terrors never felt before." Poe's aunt Maria Clemm ("Muddy") in her bewilderment mistakenly used 1845 when she wrote to Neilson Poe, in

1849, "I have heard this moment of the death of my son Edgar. I cannot believe it, and I have written to you, to try and ascertain the fact and particulars."[127]

In "The Gold-Bug," there is a sense not of futility so much as of ambivalence played out as an epistemological/ideological game of hide-and-seek, as if Poe were to insulate his thoughts and convictions against the incursions of general comprehension. We know that Poe had come to despise the debates over the nation's currency, much as he had come to realize that there was no authority of power he could trust. There is "no absolute *certainty*," he wrote in September 1848, defending the poetic method he had employed in "Eureka."[128] Against this rent in consciousness, the feeling of ontological insecurity called forth here, one must set "The Gold-Bug." In that tale, readers are not so much excluded as, at least in part, appeased by being entertained — by Jupiter's "bad" use of language, by the narrator's unmotivated incredulity and, not to forget, by Legrand's efforts towards solving the cipher, what Jupiter inimitably calls the "syphon."[129] Of course, Poe's willingness to appease readers by entertaining them only goes so far. Although Poe had become especially attentive to the literary market, he could not afford any permanent estrangement from what was going on around him. With "The Gold-Bug," then, Poe, while reticent on partisan political issues, did engage his readers in the monetary debates of the time; worked into the text are both the fear that gold and gold-backed money would disappear altogether and the question whether Americans could trust the paper bills that were then passing from hand to hand. Yet Poe would not have been Poe if he had provided easy or clear-cut answers. Not that there were any easy or clear-cut answers to the money question.

In theory at least, Legrand's gold could serve as the backing for quite an amount of paper bills. Yet for such bills to work as currency, behind them there must be a reliable — trustworthy — institution of power. A pirate stuck in the fictional modality of a Never-Never Land would not do, and neither would the free market, which could (and would) do nothing to prevent the fluctuations in the price of gold. The commercial banks, over which the federal government had little or no control, were themselves part of the problem. On one hand, these banks were constantly caught up in power games with state politicians, on whom they depended for the procurement and renewal of their charters. On the other hand, many banks and similar institutions engaged in wayward practices that did nothing to enhance the reputation of the bills they put into circulation. To make matters worse, the unpredictability of the market often enough led to the suspension of specie payment, which banks were permitted to do under state laws for a one-year period. For a time, the Bank of the United States seemed a reliable authority, promising at least a measure of certainty, though that certainty was compromised by easy credit, which in turn gave rise to speculation and overtrading. Moreover, the Bank of the United States was not strictly speaking a central bank, even though the federal government had shares in it, and even though it was authorized to issue notes receivable in payment to the federal government. The bank also was caught up in the partisan politics of the time, and was said by its opponents to control the money supply in favor of the wealthy merchants. For the populist Jackson this had been reason enough to vow to abolish it. In contrast, Frederick William Thomas, one of Poe's few lasting friends, like other members of the Whig Party favored the (re-)establishment of a national bank of issue. Another member of Poe's circle, John Pendleton Kennedy came around too. Although he had attacked commercial paper in *Quodlibet* in 1840, a year later Kennedy, who was then a Whig representative, put himself in opposition to Tyler because of the President's veto of a bill that would have reestablished a national bank of issue.

Kennedy's decision probably cost Poe dearly in his efforts to obtain a government position. Immediately after Tyler's veto of September 9, 1841, Kennedy wrote the "Whig Manifesto," which describes Tyler as "a President without a party." The pronouncement to expel Tyler from the Whig Party was read out on September 13 at a caucus on Capitol Square held by over fifty Whig Party members. On November 23, Thomas wrote to Poe that Kennedy's manifesto "has 'used up' as we say in the West, all the influence he might have had at the White House."[130] Poe's response was that Kennedy had acted "cavalierly."[131] It is hardly too far-fetched to say, therefore, that Poe's sympathies for Tyler were not so much tied to this President's policies as they stemmed from Poe's personal frustrations with the renegade Whigs, including Kennedy, who he felt had betrayed him in his efforts to secure a much-needed source of income. Indeed, the alliances that were forged in the wake of Tyler's veto appear to have made even more convoluted Poe's position on the bank issue. It was none other than Thomas Dunn English who continued to be loyal to Tyler. English, who Poe fell into a quarrel with in 1843 and who eventually became Poe's bitter enemy, provided the verses for a new song celebrating the Tyler presidency. In the final stanza English requests: "Then pledge me again every neighbor, / *Remember old Tippecanoe*; / We are up in a good cause to labor, / And we're headed by Tyler, the true." Supporters of Tyler toasted English at a political dinner celebrating Washington's Birthday held in Philadelphia on February 22, 1842. The happy recipient of such praise went on to write Tyler's biography, published in November 1842, as the Philadelphia Custom House appointments were announced.[132]

The ambiguities and indeterminacies that characterize Poe's position in the debates about America's money clearly resonate with Marc Shell's argument that Poe was not concerned with partisan politics so much as he was engaged in a politics of language of his own, exploring "the implicit ideological relationship between aesthetic and monetary symbolization." For Poe and his contemporaries, Shell maintains, paper money could be no more money than a "shadow could be the substance," or the picture of something the thing itself, as each in its turn constitutes a most "insubstantial" sign. Thus for Shell, "The Gold-Bug" contains an all-out attack on paper money.[133] This is not to deny that the contingent and arbitrary relationship between inscription and inscribed thing that is characteristic of paper money was of considerable interest to Poe. Yet matters of everyday life — what Daniel Hoffman deprecatingly calls the "dull realities" of money, politics, and the social order[134] — impacted on Poe to an equal, if not greater degree, from the suspensions of specie payments by the banks to the value of paper bills passing from hand to hand and, not to forget, the hard-money policies of Jackson and Van Buren, which Poe satirized during the 1830s and, again, with "Mellonta Tauta." Poe's comment, in 1849, on the $1 gold dollar, also registers the discomfiting awareness that the Jacksonians' hard-money politics, while they ostensibly served the "common man," preserved in a different form the hard-money advocacy of the loyalist Tories of the pre-revolutionary era. Thus to argue that in "The Gold-Bug" Poe had made explicit his support of gold, in opposition to paper money, would stretch beyond the point of plausibility the alleged flexibility in his political commitments. So, of course, would the opposite argument, that the tale articulates the position of a "paper money man." To be sure, paper-money advocacy before the Revolution had been linked with anti-royalist protest and the spirit of republicanism. Yet by Poe's time the political commitment had shifted to the Whigs, whose beliefs may have been republican but certainly not rebellious. Moreover, to defend the paper bills from the commercial banks during Poe's time would have been naïve, thoughtless, and irresponsible.

In "The Gold-Bug," the fundamental ambiguity concerning the proper form of money registers both the regime of deception in the culture at large and the instability of monetary differences in antebellum America. Yet what begins as an absolute distinction between gold, silver, and paper ultimately collapses into a startling identification. Poe facilitates this collapse by devising a scene in which his central character promises Jupiter a "present of a silver dollar."[135] This silver dollar might as well have been a Spanish one, as specie coins in circulation throughout the country were mostly of foreign silver and gold until 1836.

In principle, a silver currency would have been an alternative to gold, at least by way of a thought experiment. In reality, however, silver was as inherently problematic as gold, and American silver coins mostly were just as scarce as gold coins. A way out of this impasse offered itself in the form of paper money circulating among a community of trust. Yet paper money cannot circulate among such a community without a new kind of thinking, one that accepts as somehow "natural" a new relationship between symbols and things. Under that relationship, monetary tokens would represent what they could purchase, not the gold or silver they could be converted into. If this was a radical departure from traditional thought, just as radical would have been the idea that only under an institution of power could people trust the paper bills that were passing from hand to hand.

Naming or, even, rehearsing the problem is not the same thing as solving it, and Poe neither would nor could find a practical way to resolve the issue of a stable circulating currency. In "The Gold-Bug," an institution of power that would guarantee the value of the currency is nowhere in sight. Hence the money-finders not only hoard the gold they have found, but also take pleasure in cataloging the antique coins. Clearly to them, precious metal *embodies* value, while paper bills only *represent* it. Nor do paper bills have much weight, whereas gold does, and is duly weighed, at "three hundred and fifty pounds avoirdupois."[136] By making the money-finders not only hoard the treasure but also grasp it with their senses, hold it in their hands, Poe demonstrates that they — like Frank Norris's Trina — are unable psychologically to deal with the issue of representation. For them, gold is the only real money and land — the "possessions" into which Legrand expects to be reinstated — the only stable and secure form of wealth. What none of them sees is that land and other "possessions" are far from stable and secure. Nor do they see that gold, to be money itself, need never be money at all and so, as Walter Benn Michaels notes, "*can* never be money at all."[137] Clearly, in "The Gold-Bug" the money-finders feel threatened by the increasing abstraction and the loss of familiar signs. They consequently turn to establishing quite arbitrary connections between thing and meaning, setting up the *Scarabaeus* beetle Legrand accidentally finds on the beach as the "index" to the treasure. Conversely, in a desperate effort to find support and mainstay, they turn to the hoarding — and counting and weighing — of the gold. It is only logical, therefore, that the story breaks off at mid-point, to continue with Legrand's explanation of how he solved the cipher, "this most extraordinary riddle."[138] The riddle concerning America's money, which is no less extraordinary, remains unsolved.

A major reason that the riddle concerning America's money remained unsolved at the

Silver peso of Felipe V, México, 1739 (Wikimedia Commons).

time was that the discovery of gold in California only hardened the hard-money course the country had been steering since 1846, when Democratic congressmen had initiated a legislative amendment requiring that all payments to the government be made in gold and silver coin. President James Polk in particular had high hopes in gold. Indeed, production figures skyrocketed; at the same time, the value of domestic gold coins in circulation increased dramatically, thanks also to the newly established branch mint in San Francisco.[139] Yet the problem about using gold as commodity money remained: the amount of gold in the world, Alexander Del Mar later explained, is never stable but fluctuates with each new discovery and each new development in technology. At times, newly found gold floods the market unexpectedly. At other times, it comes in very slowly, though the economy may desperately need an influx of fresh money. As a result, gold is never exchanged for its nominal value on coins but always for its relative value as a commodity. Its introduction as a currency thus would only have compounded America's economic problems, and could hardly have been a solution for a debtor nation such as the United States.[140]

Was Poe insightful enough to foresee the vicissitudes of a gold currency? His commentary on the $1 gold dollar seems to suggest this. Notice but the disproportion between the size of the new coin — 13.1mm in diameter — and the degree of devotion — tenfold — that Poe imputes. The disproportion of course intensifies Poe's censure. We saw at the outset of this chapter that Poe's interest in and concern about everyday matters eventually steered him to literary politics; we also saw, throughout this chapter, that he continued to be preoccupied with the world of money and banking. Yet that world was also already the result of history, and so we need to turn to the past — Poe's past — in order to better understand the causes and origins of the monetary situation Poe lived (and suffered) through. For reasons I have discussed in the prologue, a mere account of historic events, places, or persons is not nearly enough. History, Fredric Jameson remarked, is *not* a text," though it is "inaccessible to us except in textual form."[141] Poe's past likewise is preserved only in textual or documentary residues. And it is to use these residues that we move on in the chapter to follow.

5

Fables of Circulation

Poe, Civic Virtue and the "American System"

In "The Gold-Bug," Poe goes a long way to emphasize the absence of American coined money. His professed scorn of the first $1 gold dollar — "adoring it with tenfold devotion" — therefore must seem puzzling. Poe's words, I have suggested, appear to have been dictated by an imp of the perverse. Gold was available after all, so why satirize the new coin? It is as if a portion of Poe's self had become separated out from the rest, seeking to destroy that from which it was separated, including the potential of a capitalist future, together with the original dream of becoming established in society. The material apocalypse in the comment on the gold dollar, as well as in "Eldorado" and "Von Kempelen," thus constitutes, not a fulfillment of Poe's dreams, but a contradiction to his attempts to achieve real financial independence.

While biography doubtless helps to make sense of Poe's scorn of the gold dollar, the narrator's identification, at the end of "Mellonta Tauta," of "one Zacchary, a tailor" as one of "*the* great men in those days among the Amriccans" points into a different direction. The narrator is far from reliable; her very name, "Pundita," reflects Poe's satirical use of the term "pundit" for a pretentious intellectual. Moreover, the story itself is a translation, by a "Martin Van Buren Mavis," described by "Poe" as a "friend," of a manuscript found corked up in a bottle floating in the *Mare Tenebrarum* and dated, appropriately, April 1, that is, April Fool's Day.[1] Yet if there is, in the narrator's name, an allusion to President Van Buren, we may with equal justification presume "Zacchary, a tailor" to be an alias for President Zachary Taylor. Despite Poe's attempt, by means of multiple removals, to render as difficult as possible any identification of presumed beliefs as those of the presumed author, I felt justified to suggest that the seemingly satirical remark about the gold dollar stands as an admonishment to the monetary discourses of the time, at once a call for a stable and reliable *paper* currency and a somewhat devious critique of gold-bug orthodoxy and the shifting political commitments of paper-money men and gold bugs. Such a reading also lends coherence to the grander trajectory of Poe's monetary imagination, a trajectory that stretches from the early satires to the final commentary on the gold dollar, reaching a golden-colored peak with "The Gold-Bug."

Poe's monetary imagination clearly did not arise from thin air, and so we turn to the past — Poe's past — in order to better understand the causes and origins of the world of money and banking Poe lived (and suffered) through. That world, I suggested, is preserved only in textual or documentary residues. One such document is the United States Constitution, which spells out that the states can make "silver and gold a legal tender in the payments of debts," but only the national government has the authority to "coin Money, regulate the Value thereof, and of foreign Coin." The wording demonstrates that the country was to have been a "hard" money country and, more importantly, that the federal government had power over the states. This state of affairs for instance led to the chartering of "national" banks, in the form of the two Banks of the United States, though both were at once attacked by anti-federalists and, later, by Jacksonian Democrats.

This book seeks to resituate Poe within the network of economic and political institutions in Jackson's America, and so this chapter would not be complete without a focus on Jackson's bank war, as well as on attempts, by Federalists, National Republicans, and Whigs, to reinstate a national bank of issue. I also deal in this chapter with the fact that in 1841 the death of President Harrison and the selection of John Tyler as his running mate deprived the Whig Party of the chance to carry out the mandate it had received in the election of 1840. Accordingly, Henry Clay's plan for a comprehensive American System was not enacted, nor was a national bank reconstituted. As president, Tyler opposed nearly everything that the majority of Whigs sought and, with his reelection in mind, set to purging Whig appointees from federal offices, replacing them with states' rights men, most of them Democrats. What were the consequences of all this on Poe, who had desperately sought office from Tyler? We shall presently see that the sympathies Poe may have had for this president instantly melted into air, and that Poe's anger and frustration, which from the 1830s had been directed against the follies of Jacksonianism, now provoked him into writing literary hoaxes which, like paper bills from the commercial banks, promised value even as they flaunted their worthlessness. Yet deep down, Poe, who once claimed that he had in fact "battled" for Harrison, seems to have retained sympathies for Harrison's policies, above all for his plan for a national bank of issue. The currency coming from such a bank, I argue, might well have been the fulfillment of one of Poe's much deeper desires, a desire for permanence and continuity.

Transcending History

Both "The Gold-Bug" and, to an extent, "Mellonta Tauta" contain Poe's most extreme illustrations of America's capitalist future, and obviously such illustrations would have appealed strongly to escape the mediation of capital. From what has been suggested so far, there is, then, a "latent utopian impulse" behind the apocalyptic surface of "The Gold-Bug," if not of other writings as well.[2] Instead of simply resolving the structural antagonism between gold, silver, and paper, these writings portend a signifying environment where individuals are free to exchange in a community of trust. Poe, it is true, had high opinions about solving ciphers, even making use of this skill to further his personal plans for a government sinecure. Yet he also asked, "where is the ingenuity of unraveling a web which you yourself (the author) have woven for the express purpose of unraveling?"[3] Poe thus warns us to confound the ingenuity of a fictional character's ratiocination with that of its author. We also should not forget that Legrand finds the treasure not simply because of his superior skills in logic and ratiocination but because he *trusts* the authenticating marks on the paper.

Far from being a chance detail, the presence of "trust" in "The Gold-Bug" constitutes a point of mediation between culture and society. Trust, that is to say, is essential for the working of a stable currency.

In a more general sense, "trust" is also the basis for human bonding, including bonding between author and reader. Yet Poe's writings rarely allow themselves to be trusted, as they ceaselessly insist that there is nothing outside the fiction that reflects on the action of language within it.[4] This tendency, the result of a cultural logic of hoaxing that relentlessly works against stabilization, is also constitutive to Poe's literary theory. In his later review of Hawthorne's *Twice-Told Tales* and *Mosses from an Old Manse*, published in *Godey's Lady's Book* in November 1847, Poe commends Hawthorne for creating, in his writings, a "bond of sympathy" as the basis for true literary pleasure. Rather than "forcing" an impression upon people, this author, whom Poe represents as "neither a man of wealth nor a quack," brings out "the half-formed, the reluctant, or the unexpressed fancies of mankind," combining them with "the pleasurable effect of *apparent* novelty." Novelty, we have seen, is Poe's premier criterion for literary originality. Yet he also claims, in the review, that Hawthorne is "*not* original in any sense."[5] Thus true originality is a simulation, the production of the "seeming novelty" of a notion that readers appreciate as if it were original with the writer. The effect of seeming or "apparent" novelty serves a final end: the forging of a tie of sympathy between writer and reader. But this, too, is the writer's doing, so that even the bond of sympathy is merely a simulation of an original or authentic relationship. Poe's conviction that the effect of truth is best produced by the simulation of trust is no real surprise, as he habitually disparaged his readers as a "mob," attacked other authors, and was generally skeptical about popularity as a measure of literary value. Even "The Gold-Bug" appears as a simulacrum of a tale about treasure hunting, a copy with no original. There are, nevertheless, premonitions of original or authentic relationships even in this tale — half-formed, reluctant, unexpressed, "utopian," but not "denied," as Whalen suggests.[6]

One such premonition is inherent to the cipher-solving part. Ciphers constitute repetitive structures; writing and solving them can be seen as forms of habitual or repetitive behavior that traumatized people use in their attempts to overcome a "disconnect" between their emotions and the rest of the world. It could be, for instance, that Poe, who was certainly traumatized by his mother's early death, produced ciphers in order to compensate for the autistic gap, thus attempting to establish an original "bond of sympathy" between himself and his readers, President Tyler included. There is another premonition or presentiment, likewise lacking of metaphysical depth. Playing itself out on the textual level, it registers Legrand's trust in the narrator, a trust that remains unreciprocated. Playing itself out on the material surface of culture, Poe's utopian premonition registers, despite the regime of deception in the culture at large, the presence of a reliable — trustworthy — institution of power. If there is any new thinking to be drawn out from "The Gold-Bug" about America's money, then, it is one that links "trust" or confidence both with an institution of power that issues and controls the currency, and with people's relationship to one another.[7]

Poe's vital impulse towards the end of his life may have subsumed the idea of a community of trust to the point of total eclipse, yet in "The Gold-Bug" it still gestures towards its transcendence. We should take this "inherent transhistorical potential"[8] in the tale as the point of departure for a move beyond the paradigm of union the Whigs were trying to sustain in the 1840s, to the Founders of the republic. Critics have noted that Poe was not writing poetry or fiction on topics of figures related to national (or even regional) history. While it is true that Poe never wrote about the battle of Yorktown or Washington crossing the Delaware, and while he generally objected to using topics or figures related to national (or even regional) history in poetry or fiction, he nevertheless was aware of his friend's Frederick W. Thomas's early "War Song of Seventy-Six." George Lippard also was a friend, whose "legends" of the American revolution — *Herbert Tracy* or *The Ladye Annabel* — Poe thought highly of. In addition, Poe wrote a painstakingly detailed review of William Gilmore Simms's *The Partisan*, a historical novel that records the Revolution in South Carolina from the time when the Loyalists were in the ascendant and the British Tarleton swept all before him to the day when Marion — the "Swamp Fox" — and his men saved the state. Simms, Poe wrote in the *Democratic Review* of December 1844, is "immeasurably the best writer of fiction in America." Whether or not Poe's compliment was prompted by one of the characters' preparedness "to fight for his country against her invaders" cannot be decided here.[9] We do know, however, that warfare in South Carolina was intense during the Revolutionary war. Indeed, at the entrance to Charleston harbor lies Sullivan's Island, on which a partially completed colonial fort was intended to secure the harbor and the city. The fort was under the command of Colonel William Moultrie when, on June 28, 1776, several British men-of-war threatened the unfinished stronghold. The British fleet met with stiff resistance and was driven off, with many of the ships severely damaged and many British officers and soldiers dead or wounded. The victory at Fort Sullivan convinced many colonists to join the fight and persevere in the Revolutionary cause. Soon after the garrison was renamed Fort Moultrie, and it was here that Poe served as a soldier in 1827–28.[10]

Poe was generally enthusiastic about American history. Reviewing James Kirke Paulding's *Life of Washington*, he professes to have read the biography "with a degree of interest seldom excited [...] by the perusal of any book whatever." Poe was almost equally enthusiastic about works about Chief Justice John Marshall, the "last of the Virginia Federalists," as Parrington calls him, and the one who in 1816 upheld the constitutionality of the Bank of the United States. Poe also admired Marshall's own five-volume *Life of George Washington*, and he defended George Bancroft, whom he personally knew and whose *History of the United States* was written explicitly to glorify Jacksonian democracy. Poe's own view of Jacksonian democracy was dim, and he on more than one occasion satirically depicted the "despotism" of its "mob" as a lamentable decline of Jeffersonian democracy. About Jefferson himself, Poe had nothing derisive to say. On the contrary, in a review of Jeremiah Reynolds' *Address* on the South-Sea Expedition, Poe praises Jefferson as a "distinguished philosopher" whose "extended views and mental grasp" no one would question. Poe added that Jefferson, that "sage" who had sent Lewis and Clark on their way west, was sorely needed today, as an "apostle of liberty, father of democracy, and strict constructionist!"[11]

Poe's enthusiasm about American history was not exceptional. The antebellum period in general was a time of intensive cultural production during which a genuinely American historical and cultural memory came into being. In this process of culturally constituting the United States, the American Revolution was the "natural" starting point. Biographies as well as history books abounded. Representations of revolutionary figures and events in paintings, lithographs, pictorial histories, and illustrated magazines from the 1830s to the 1850s likewise contributed to an archive that was seminal in the formation of a "usable past." As sites of memory, all these representations helped to define the nation. While they often stabilized larger narratives, on occasion they also contested historical and cultural memories.[12] When Poe reached back into the nation's past for ideological munitions, he generally ignored the practical implications of the American Revolution and instead offered vague, rhapsodic paraphrases of revolutionary slogans, as in his eulogy of Thomas Jefferson. Moreover, to his radical individualism the idea that he could ever stand "in awe" of any of these larger-than-life figures was repugnant, though he might have made an exception with his paternal grandfather, David Poe, the father of the actor David Poe, Jr., Edgar's father.

"Edgar Allan Poe was of gentle birth," John Ingram begins his account of the writer's life, letters, and opinions. "His paternal grandfather, General David Poe, the descendant of an ancient and highly connected family, was born in Ireland, but, taken at a very early age by his parents to the United States, became a patriotic citizen of his adopted country, and greatly distinguished himself during the War of Independence."[13] To wit, in 1779 David Poe, Sr., was commissioned Assistant Deputy-Quartermaster General for the city of Baltimore. There he was noticed for his self-sacrificing efforts in the financially strapped department, allegedly using, in 1780, his own funds for purchasing supplies for the patriot forces. David Poe's rank was that of a major, though the post gave him a courtesy title: he was usually called "General Poe." In September 1814 David Poe, Sr., at age seventy-one, took part in a battle in which the Maryland Militia fended off British troops that were threatening Baltimore. "General Poe," an "early and decided friend of American Liberty [and a] zealous Republican," as the *American and Commercial Advertiser* described him in its obituary, died on October 17, 1816. When the much-revered Marquis de Lafayette, then in his sixties, visited Baltimore in 1824, he found words of praise for Poe's grandfather, choosing to remember him as a friend. Two weeks later, Lafayette visited Richmond, where young Edgar was then serving with the Morgan Junior Riflemen. Not only was Poe's company appointed to ride in the procession that followed the visitor's carriage, but Lafayette himself also later reviewed Edgar.[14]

As Anne Loveland has found, Lafayette's triumphal tour of 1824–25 contributed greatly to a revival of republicanism in the United States, though it is not clear to what extent (if at all) it shaped Poe's political views.[15] It is a matter of record, however, that on May 26, 1827, Poe enlisted in the U.S. Army. His decision was grounded, not in mere romantic admiration for the martial ambitions of a Lord Byron and a Tamerlane, or else in the prospect of family-like camaraderie, but to a great extent in his grandfather's association with the Revolutionary cause. Once enlisted — in the First Regiment of Artillery — Poe soon became responsible for arranging the army's food supplies and thus was closely connected to the quartermaster — work similar to that performed by his grandfather for the Continental Army. In the spring of 1830 Poe was admitted to West Point, from where he soon proudly reported that the military hero General Winfield Scott, a friend of John Allan, had been "attentive" to him, and that he had been "very politely received" by a captain of the academy.

Poe was dismissed from West Point in January 1831. While he claimed to have been General Poe's "favourite grand-child,"[16] his grandfather's legacy never crystallized in the tangible form of a social ideal in his writings, though the legacy of some of General Poe's contemporaries did, if only in an indirect way. For one thing, many descendants of Huguenot refugees, mindful of the persecutions they endured under Louis XIV, were active in the

American Revolution — among them John Jay, Francis Marion, Henry Laurens (who signed the Declaration of Independence for South Carolina), and Paul Revere. The latter began his career as a watercolorist, developing an interest in copperplate engraving only later. Upon the advent of the Revolution Revere, who was then a member of the Sons of Liberty, desperately wanted to enlist, but was more needed as a printer of Massachusetts paper notes. He stayed at the job from May 1775 to October 1787. It is said that he also built the presses to print these notes, including the issue of August 1775, in which he engraved on the back plate the motto "Issued in defence of American Liberty."

The 1775 issue, which was still in shillings denomination, shows a Minute Man holding a copy of Magna Charta in one hand and a sword in the other, which is why among collectors it is known as "sword in hand" money. Of particular interest is the way Revere used this figure to reflect and foster the hardening of colonial sentiment in favor of independence. The scroll carried by the patriot on the 1775 notes says "Magna Charta." This man is fighting to defend the vested liberties of *all* English people, including those in the American colonies. A year later the notes still carried the motto "Issued in defence of American Liberty," retaining the British spelling of the word "defense." However, the words on the scroll are different. They now call for "INDEPENDANCE" (sic!). Colonial sentiment, Richard Doty remarked, had changed considerably between the first and second issue of these notes, whose function was now clearly to foster popular support for seeking liberty as Americans.[17]

America's liberty or, sovereignty from Britain and anti-royal protest, had been linked

Thirty-shilling and Sixteen-shilling Massachusetts notes, back view, respectively December 1775 and November 1776: motto on scroll changes from "Magna Charta" to "Independance [sic!]" (courtesy National Numismatic Collection, Smithsonian Institution).

with a commitment to paper money from the 1730s. Advocacy of gold and silver coins, in contrast, then was a sure sign of a Tory bias. The political commitments shifted after the Revolution, so that by Poe's time gold and silver were on the Jacksonians' populist agenda, whereas paper money advocacy had become a matter of Whig politics. The Whigs' prime constituency was formed by the business community, which included a large number of Huguenots or their descendants. This community thus constitutes a fitting environment for Poe's William Legrand, who is described as coming from "an ancient Huguenot family" that "had once been wealthy." Legrand's views on the money question are never explicitly stated, though he obviously uses paper money to purchase the implements needed for the execution of the treasure hunt. Jupiter, when he makes the purchases, complains that he has to give "the debbil's own lot of money" for them.[18]

It is worth noting that Thomas Jefferson's personal slave was called Jupiter. We can only guess whether Poe was aware of this, though if he was, the correspondence takes on a special significance. Thomas Jefferson was a Southerner, like Poe, and so it is tempting to place Poe's political sympathies with Jefferson and his descendants. But Poe, we have seen, had come to despise the decline of Jeffersonian democracy into demagoguery and the "despotism" of the Jacksonian mob, much as he had put aside his Southernness in his attempt to speak to a national audience. The significance thus lies in Jefferson's choice of name. Distasteful as the habit was of naming the most powerless being after one of the most powerful mythic figures, it reflects the founders' predilection for classical republicanism as a source of inspiration.[19] The Jupiter of Poe's tale, making purchases with paper notes, thus foregrounds the almost uncanny synchronicity between the shifting political commitments of paper-money men and gold bugs or bullionists and the course of the American Revolution. In addition, it foregrounds the fact that the democratic identity and stake in national affairs of some of the Founders articulated itself in deep resentment of the present state of affairs and in fear and even contempt of "the mob."

Doubtless such fears and mortifications motivated the prohibition of state-issued paper money, when in 1789 the balance of authority shifted from the states to the national government. Favoring debtor farmers through a fast-depreciating paper currency had come to be considered as not just "improper or wicked," as James Madison wrote, but also bad for business. Joined to this was the class bias of Alexander Hamilton and his fellow Federalists, for whom "a government of the better sorts of people (one made up of the rich, well-born and the able)" was more desirable than any other.[20] Indeed the hands of these "better sorts of people" are visible throughout the Constitution. States were forbidden to interfere with contracts. The debt of the federal government was recognized, and its payment guaranteed. The national government also was authorized to suppress domestic uprisings, and in 1794, it used this power to put down a group of disgruntled farmers in Pennsylvania, the Whiskey Rebels. Federal judges were appointed for life. United States Senators received a term that was three times as long as that of ordinary representatives, and they would be elected by state legislatures rather than by popular vote. The President likewise received a longer term, and he also would be chosen by an Electoral College rather than by the people. This "national conservative trend," Richard Doty observes, "would continue in the area of money."[21]

The Treasury Department, following its creation by Congress in September 1789, became the focal point of the entire executive branch of government. Its influence from the outset was marked by the sheer size and scope of its affairs. As Wright and Cowen have noted, the department's

> initial headcount, thirty-nine, ballooned to fifty-three within a year. Compare that with the staff of five at State under Jefferson, and three at Henry Knox's War Department. Total salaries for each department also demonstrate Treasury's dominance: Treasury, $43,000; State, $6,250; War, $6,500. Hamilton alone among all the cabinet officers had an assistant, or vice-secretary. More impressively, or ominously depending on one's perspective, Treasury maintained a comprehensive network of agents throughout the country.[22]

The legislative branch of government likewise wielded its authority. When the representatives in Philadelphia were debating what sorts of money would be allowed and be created by whom, their "fiscal conservatism," as Doty calls it, "led to a permanent change in who was responsible for money, and who was not."[23] The delegates from the state of Pennsylvania in particular were opposed to a federal issue of bills of credit, though it is not known how the most prominent delegate, Benjamin Franklin, voted on the matter. Most likely Franklin, who was shrewd and troubled enough to settle for compromise and project completion, deliberately left the issue unclear in order to stop the wrangling and get the Constitution approved. Under it, the states could make "silver and gold a legal tender in the payments of debts," but only the national government had the authority to "coin Money, regulate the Value thereof, and of foreign Coin" (Article I, Section 8, Paragraph 5). The meaning of these wordings led to intermittent litigation for decades to come, including comments today that the Federal Reserve System is a legal, federally incorporated construction for the purpose of evading the language of the Constitution.[24]

George Wood, defending the idea of a national bank of issue, ventured a literal interpretation of the Constitution. His argument, put forth in *Hunt's Merchants' Magazine* of April 1841, was that the Constitution's general enactments in no way forbid the use of bank paper. According to Wood, the stipulation that only specie could be legal tender simply means that the creditor "*is compelled* to take specie in payment and nothing else. But the *voluntary use by the community*, as well debtors as creditors, of paper currency, is not prohibited." Such a currency, Wood continues, of course cannot be issued by individual states, though this prohibition does not extend to the federal government.[25] Interesting as Wood's attempt to legitimate paper money is, especially in its vision of a community of trust, it cannot be denied that the Constitution's wording clearly reflects the framers' idea of making the United States a hard-money country, that is, a country whose currency consisted mainly of gold and silver and thus was fully as impressive as the new nation and the new government.

Alexander Hamilton already during the War of Independence had articulated his firm conviction that finance was critical and that therefore Congress must have control of "coining money; establishing banks on such terms and with such privileges as they think proper; appropriating funds and doing whatever else relates to the operations of finance."[26] Thomas Jefferson had different views on the issue, in particular on Hamilton's plans for the national debt. Jefferson eventually acceded to these plans, though their consequences haunted him until the day he died. He was, however, adamant that "real" property was only land and tangible assets such as gold or silver. In 1792, the year the United States Mint was established, Jefferson charged the Federalists with a scheme to banish gold and silver from circulation and flood the fledgling republic with cheap paper money.[27] Jefferson's attack on the Federalists followed political expediency rather than economic logic and fact. Yet during the constitutional debates James Madison, who had not then joined Jefferson to form the Democratic-Republican Party, also would have nothing to do with paper bills that were founded on public confidence, but had of themselves no intrinsic value. Madison, mindful of the ill-fated Continentals, fiercely opposed Hamilton's plans to create a national bank of issue. In the *Federalist Papers* of 1787, for instance, he called the current "rage for paper money" an "improper or wicked project," whose effects on the "necessary confidence between man and man, on the necessary confidence in public councils, on the industry and morals of the people, and on the character of republican government" was, simply, "pestilential."[28]

Like others of his time, Madison saw paper money as only the beginning of a completely corrupt system of mysterious credit, debt certificates, stock, and deliberate depreciation, based on a legal fiction. Paper implied a promise that might be broken. While there was initially a clause in the Constitution that permitted the federal government to issue paper money, it was quickly eliminated. As a delegate from Delaware said, granting the government the right to issue paper money would be "as alarming as the mark of the Beast in Revelations." It would be better, another delegate urged, to "reject the whole plan than retain the three words 'and emit bills.'"[29] The rhetoric of the constitutional debates in this regard is deceptively similar to the English conservative tradition of rejecting paper money as incompatible with the supposed securities of land and precious metal. Writers from Pope to Burke and beyond warned that if property is the foundation of personality, the "unreal" wealth provided by a paper economy (meaning that nothing is owned except worthless paper) was bound to make personality unreal and words meaningless. Such moral arguments did not reach the ears of those Americans for whom the currency issue was a matter of political sovereignty, and so the English classicists had every reason to look with a mixture of suspicion and disdain at the paper money experiments that many of the American colonists were undertaking.[30] On the other hand, the English classicists were well received by wealthy loyalists in the colonies, who generally opposed any addition to the volume of money in circulation. Distrustful of the idea of a "general" prosperity, these people were ranged against all ventures into paper money.

Typically, Governor Thomas Hutchinson of Massachusetts, who in the late 1740s had been instrumental in wrenching the colony away from its paper money experiments, denounced the system's supporters as an "ignorant majority [...] unrestrained by a superior class."[31] Hector St. John de Crèvecoeur likewise considered paper money scandalous, and so has his ingenuous Farmer James wonder about the strangeness of people who "can live upon what they call bank notes, without working, they think that all the world do the same."[32] Such words clearly stem from a Tory's fear that a paper currency would become the cause of social upheaval, a suspicion that was connected to the aspirations that wealth founded on paper entailed. For Crèvecoeur as well as for Hutchinson and other contemporaries of conservative leanings, the specter of a new type of personality arose from people whose wealth was no longer based on landed property or specie. Paper money thus was branded as "pernicious" and fully incompatible with established social and moral values and with tradition. As Hutchinson wrote in *The History of the Province of Massachusetts-Bay*, "the morals of the country depreciate with the currency."[33]

The Revolutionary leaders who were to frame the Constitution in 1787 did not like paper money any more than the Loyalist Thomas Hutchinson. Indeed, Hutchinson's fears that the proliferation of paper money become a threat to social stability re-emerged with quite a few of the Founders, including Madison, who hoped that ordinary people would have the "virtue and intelligence to select men of virtue and wisdom" as their representatives. If this was not the case, Madison warned in 1788, no government could "render us secure."[34] Madison or, for that matter, John Adams, therefore expected landed, well-educated, and wise politicians — men like themselves — to govern in a disinterested manner and in the name of the public good, transcending "local prejudices" and selfish interests. What remained below their radar was that their currency views were becoming indistinguishable from the hard-money advocacy of the pre-revolutionary Tory Loyalists. Also below their radar remained those self-interested men of the "middling sort" who were no longer interested in being governed by their supposed betters but wanted to do the governing themselves.[35]

For men of the "middling sort" there also was a new kind of national hero: the "self-made man." Poe, in "The Business Man," later emptied out the meaningfulness of this new social ideal as a mere social construct. For the post-revolutionary generation, however, the "self-made man" was the "ideal character," unashamed of his obscure origins, and a strong believer in hard work and ingenuity. This model, Joyce Appleby notes, "developed his inner resources, acted independently, lived virtuously, and bent his behavior to his personal goals."[36] Indeed, the newly ambitious people valued work and not leisure. They also aspired to be property owners, but property for them was not the static land of the gentry or the yeoman farmer. For these risk-takers, who were coming into their own in the 1820s, property was capital and capital was the fuel for dynamic, speculative investment. Many of these "self-made men" were outspoken defenders of the debtor-paper money interests, and thus fierce opponents of a national bank. For them it was self-evident that an individual's quest for wealth and prosperity would enhance the prosperity of the entire nation. "All are people," commented the Federalist-turned-Republican Charles Jared Ingersoll in 1810, echoing Thomas Jefferson's glorification of men who were "not so well dressed, nor so politely educated, nor so highly born."[37] Ingersoll, as well as the "people" he invokes, loyally followed the monetary ideals of Adam Smith, who in *Enquiry into the Nature and Causes of the Wealth of Nations* calculated that a bank might safely loan about five times as much cash as it actually possessed in specie.[38] Smith's currency views were on the moderate hard-money line, favoring the suppression of notes below five pounds. Jacksonians in the 1830s and 1840s found Smith rich in ammunition for their hostility towards business manipulation by the government, which they saw as a mere exploitation of the people.

Adam Smith had based his anti-monopoly stance on the metaphor of an "invisible hand." The conceit denoted market forces that may have been beyond the control and foresight of individuals but were nevertheless benevolent. Critics have shown that this metaphor was borrowed from gothic fiction and the then current discourse of supernatural intervention.[39] Supernatural intervention also was not unknown to the founders of the republic, and there is ample evidence of it in the symbolic constitution of the early republic. A good example is the phrase "*annuit coeptis*," the mark of God's approval of what Americans had undertaken but what had been bestowed by God's grace or, in the diction of the time, through God's providence. The delegates to the Constitutional convention appear to have been more sober, though, and did not therefore entrust the organization of the fledgling republic's monetary economy to mystical, irrational, or ungovernable forces. Tellingly, records of the convention bear testimony not so much to the delegates' moral scruples or class bias as to their fears that if government held power to issue paper money, it simply could not be trusted to avoid inflation. Thus when the delegates had finally thrashed out the Constitution, the document implicitly denied the federal government the right to issue paper money, at the same time as it explicitly denied the individual states the same prerogative. Effective of 1789, therefore, neither the states nor the federal government were authorized to issue paper money.[40]

Many of the delegates to the Constitutional Convention did not oppose government-issued paper money in principle, but would accept it as long as such money was backed by tangible assets such as land, gold or silver, by loans, or by actual or potential government power and commitment. The latter form of backing of course required a measure of "trust" or confidence in the government. Such trust was justified, Benjamin Franklin remarked, if the government was observant of the "Limits beyond which the Quantity [of paper money] may be hurtful."[41] Insightful as Franklin's words are, they did not amount to a full-fledged quantity theory of value, for which Americans had to wait until Ricardo's *Principles of Political Economy and Taxation* made its rounds in the early nineteenth century.[42] Notions of trust did, however, prevail among the colonists already of the seventeenth century. The costs of fighting all those little wars — against the French, or the Indians, or both together — had made the printing of paper money a necessity, and the question of faith in it a matter of principle.[43] Indeed, from the colonial era onward paper money was recognized as a means towards achieving an alchemical effect, at the same time as it symbolized the limits of economic and political authority. Altogether, such money came to weave a web of action and industry around communities that in the minds of the puritan divines were threatened by darkness, disintegration, and lack of faith. Faiths — in a common purpose, in a wholesome future, in divine providence, in the righteousness of one's fellow human beings, in the expectation of redemption funded by taxes — turned out to be just the beliefs on which an undertaking was founded that eventually would meet God's own approval.[44]

Once the undertaking had been completed and independence achieved, American lawmakers returned to the issue of money. On December 12, 1791, the Bank of the United States, chartered by Congress and later known as the First Bank of the United States opened

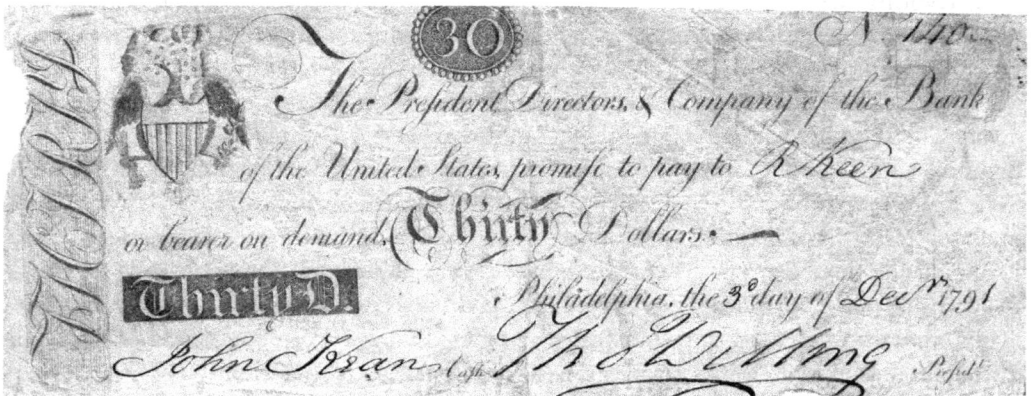

Thirty-dollar note from the First Bank of the United States, 1791 (courtesy National Numismatic Collection, Smithsonian Institution).

for business at Carpenter's Hall in Philadelphia, which was then the seat of the federal government. Madison's congressional speech on the Bank Bill, delivered on February 2, 1791, had not had the desired effect. Just as ineffective was his essay on money and finance in Philadelphia's *National Gazette* of December 1791. In this essay Madison remembered the ill-begotten Continentals, calling them "omens of public bankruptcy" as they had been issued in such large quantities that they soon after gave rise to a "distrust of the *public ability to fulfill their engagements*."[45] Madison's opposition came to nothing against the combined forces of Hamilton and the Federalists who, the constitutional silence notwithstanding, legitimized the Bank of the United States by the "general welfare" clause. Modeled after the Bank of England, the Bank of the United States became a depository for federal funds, a fiscal agent for the government, a facilitator of major commercial transactions, and the largest source of paper money operation in the country, providing something like a uniform currency. Its notes enjoyed a high reputation both at home and abroad, buying the entire Louisiana Territory from Napoleon in 1803.

The Bank of the United States was never as successful as its proponents wished. For one thing, it was not a truly "national" institution, despite the fact that the federal government owned a fifth of the shares, and also despite the fact that its notes were receivable in payments to the federal government. For another thing, fierce opposition instantly beset the bank. Opposition came from two principal sources, from Southern agrarians like Jefferson, who never understood banks but nevertheless claimed that the Bank of the United States was unconstitutional, and from the state banks. Congress' refusal to renew the bank's charter thus was a clear give-in to the national mood of financial free enterprise and state power. There clearly was no room in that mood for the bank's policy of making loans available primarily to established merchants, including the Ellis and Allan firm. Wealthy merchants therefore had much good to say about the Bank and its stable paper money. Small businessmen, ordinary farmers, artisans and craftsmen, as well as less well-to-do citizens, in contrast, exerted pressure on the states to charter private banks that would supply the credit they and their local communities badly needed.

The republicanization of the banking system marked not only a return to a horse-and-buggy view of economic development, but also a victory to hard-money advocates who regarded the Bank of the United States as merely another "paper mill" that, rather than hold other banks in check, actively encouraged them in their "pernicious activity of issuing a paper currency" that would inevitably depreciate.[46] Given the mood of the time, it helped little that the New York *Morning Post* had written, in September 1810, that it was not specie so much as paper that "offers the Government a most indestructible support because it makes the daily bread of every individual depend substantially on the safety of government, whereas money which can be hoarded separates the individual from the public safety."[47] Once the Bank of the United States had lost its charter, almost all of its notes were redeemed. This move makes them excessively rare today; at the time, it whisked more than $7 million in hard cash out of the country to refund foreign stockholders. The result was a national shortage of gold and silver, which led many banks in the country to stop redeeming their notes.

The War against England made the situation even worse. The Democratic Republicans had killed not just any bank but the premier instrument for borrowing money and financing the war effort. Commercial banks, which were grossly undercapitalized, were in no position to take the BUS's place as lenders to the government. Starting with the banks in Baltimore, which had become alarmed by a battle between British and American troops that had taken place a few days before, there was soon a general suspension of specie payment. The situation was of increasing concern to the federal government, which expected and depended on prompt payment of debts, taxes, and tariffs. Only a national bank, Secretary of the Treasury James Alexander Dallas wrote in December 1815, could "relieve the country and the Government from the present embarrassments."[48] John Allan, Poe's foster father, would have been delighted to read this, as he and Charles Ellis had been horrified when the charter was not renewed in 1811.[49] In 1816 Congress did charter another central bank, the Second Bank of the United States. The bank lasted until 1836, when it became a victim to the financial and economic crisis following Andrew Jackson's populist war against the BUS.

"Mob": Poe's Response to Jacksonianism

The "war" against the Second Bank of the United States, which Jackson invariably called "a monster" and "a hydra of corruption," was the direct outcome of the panic of 1819, the pit of the antebellum economy, with the panic of 1837 marking the pendulum. Beginning with the economic upheavals of 1819, bankruptcies and lost fortunes created constituencies for hard and soft money, a national bank, free banking, or no banks at all. In the last analysis, of course, the bank war pitched the supporters of a speculative economy, with fast expansion, enormous gains and enormous risks, that is, the rich and powerful, against the "humble members of society," to use Jackson's words.[50] The words rang loudly in the President's veto message of July 10, 1832 against a bill the National Republicans under Henry Clay had pushed through Congress to renew the Second Bank's charter. In the Jacksonians' rhetoric, Thomas Jefferson's doubts became exaggerated and vulgarized. Banks, Jefferson had said, serve "to enrich swindlers at the expense of the honest and industrious part of the nation." According to the Jacksonians, their political opponents — men like Henry Clay, John Quincy Adams, Daniel Webster, and Nicholas Biddle — wanted to "convert our government into a heartless aristocracy, in which the people are to be transferred, cheated, taxed, and oppressed, that a few may revel on the spoils of many."[51]

Such sentiments of victimhood were enough for a majority of people to vote for Jackson again in the elections of 1832. Distrust, the essence of the Jacksonians' view of government, had paid off. The facts admitted to no such thing, though. The Second Bank of the United States, that "great monetary tie of the Union," as Tocqueville had called it, neither enriched wealthy aristocrats at the expense of producers, nor did its policies unduly restrict the money supply. Instead, the criticism the Bank aroused was largely a function of the unprecedented concentration of economic power it represented. Under the command of Nicholas Biddle, who in the elections of 1828 had voted *for* Jackson, the BUS reached into practically every channel of commerce in the country. In 1830, for instance, the BUS was responsible for between 15 and 20 percent of all loans nationwide, and it had issued more than 40 percent of all the bank notes in circulation in the country. The Bank's capital of $35 million was more than double the total annual expenditure of the entire federal government. In addition, by instructing its twenty-five branch offices to have the bills of commercial banks presented for redemption, the BUS could curtail their limits of credit, thus regulating the entire economy. Finally, the Bank paid interest to holders of its own unredeemed bills, at a rate of

Five-dollar note from the Second Bank of the United States, 1830 (courtesy National Numismatic Collection, Smithsonian Institution).

twelve percent per annum. This made its bills worth slightly more than bills from commercial banks. For all these reasons, commercial banks resented the Second Bank's strength, though they remained quiet about this, just as they remained quiet about the fact that the BUS handled virtually all foreign exchange transactions.[52]

Other elements of the business community had reasons of their own to resent the Second Bank. New York bankers, for instance, wanted Wall Street to replace Philadelphia's Chestnut Street as the nation's financial center; "wildcat" bankers from the West resented the way the Bank monitored their — often wayward — business practices; and "soft-money" entrepreneurs hoped that without a national bank it would be easier to obtain credit. Andrew Jackson, for his part, resented the BUS chiefly for the reason that the people who had control over it were not from his own party, the Democratic Republicans.[53] By seizing on the money question Jackson, who had been elected President in 1828, at one and the same time eliminated political opposition and put himself at the head of a large segment of the American people, those less affluent ones who had not found a political home with the National Republicans and who, moreover, felt alienated and alarmed by the growth of banks and the uncertainties of paper money. Jackson, who willingly accepted his role as "the second Jefferson," united them all against the alleged power of the "moneyed interest" of the Northeast. That interest, derived as it was from the paper currency it was able to control, was represented as the major threat to Jackson's western republic of "the agricultural, the mechanical, and the laboring classes."[54]

During his second term in office, Jackson went out of his way to restrict the Second Bank's power and to prevent it from having its charter renewed. Thus he managed to have some $10 million of government deposits removed. The measure hit the institution's capital hard as the government money comprised almost half of the bank's total deposits; yet by having the deposits removed, Jackson had both the social and the political argument against the BUS covered: he could claim that he had successfully prevented the rich and powerful from ruling the state, making the country safe for a government by the people. He could also claim that he had crushed the rise of independent powers within the state, reserving power over the currency for the national government. The two purposes of Jackson's policy — the one social, the other political — converged in an economic purpose: to prevent periodic depressions.

In order to have a comprehensive statement to fall back on, Jackson had his financial advisor, William M. Gouge, write a long treatise on America's banking system. The treatise culminated on the "ruinous effects" that paper money from the commercial banks had on landowners, farmers, traders, and on all the industrious classes of the American nation. Gouge's book, which was published in Philadelphia in February 1833 as *A Short History of Paper Money and Banking in the United States*, became an instant success. It was sold out within a year, was reprinted in 1835, and had gone into its third edition by 1837. Many of the nation's papers serialized it, William Cobbett published an English edition, and an abridged version was translated into French and printed in Brussels. In America, it captured the imagination of intellectuals like William Leggett and William Cullen Bryant, stimulating them to continue the debate over the currency. In 1835, it earned Gouge a post in the Treasury Department.[55]

Overall, the monetary policy conceived by Gouge was the complete opposite of the Hamiltonian system. Hamilton, in his enthusiasm for a government-controlled paper money had argued that note issue would inevitably lead to an increase of capital. It turned out, however, that this was just the basis for a speculative economy, with all the evils of over-issue and the rise and fall of prices and, not to forget, the intense feelings of insecurity on the part of those with fixed or rather small incomes. The Jacksonian alternative was to exclude banks from control over the currency. Bank paper would continue to exist, for large commercial transactions and in the form of drafts and bills of credit, but the mainstay of "ordinary domestic purposes" and smaller payments was to be "hard" money provided and regulated by the federal government. Once the system was up and going, commercial banks would gradually lose the privilege of note issue. Congress and the Treasury, drawing on their authority to define the kind of money receivable in federal payments, acted accordingly. A Treasury circular of April 1835 banned all notes under $5, and prohibited banks holding federal deposits from issuing such notes. Within a year, notes under $20 were banned, and it became mandatory for banks to immediately redeem all notes. President Jackson, in order to raise public opinion against paper money, made a personal appeal to the states to follow the example of the federal government. Several states, including Pennsylvania, Maryland, and Virginia, already had legislation outlawing low-denomination bills. In 1835, the states of Maine, Connecticut, and New York banned notes under $5; restrictive measures were also passed in North Carolina, Georgia, Alabama, Ohio, Indiana, and Missouri.

One effect of all these measures was the reversal of a joint resolution of Congress of 1816 that had made *all* notes from note-issuing banks acceptable in tax payments. In the economy at large, however, low-denomination notes continued to circulate, and in ever growing numbers. Between December 1834, and July 1835, the Bank of the United States alone enlarged its loans by about two and a half million dollars a month, and its paper circulation by a total of ten million dollars. Other commercial banks rushed to follow, driving up the overall amount of paper money from $82 million by January 1, 1835, to $108 million a year later, to $120 million by December 1, 1836, and $149 million by May 1837.[56] Jackson's administration was watching the speculative mania with increasing alarm. On July 11, 1836, Jackson, in an attempt to end the nation's "mad career" of speculation and inflation issued an executive order that forced deposit banks and receivers of public money to accept only gold and silver coins for the sale of public lands. Jackson's "Specie Circular" was aimed at speculators, as actual settlers were excepted. It ended the land boom almost overnight.[57] Yet Jackson's edict, designed to protect the federal government against fraud and to weed out unsound paper bills, struck a deadly blow against confidence in the economy. In its wake came an unprecedented run on specie, accompanied by the hoarding of sound bills, which further undermined public confidence in commercial banks. Interest rates in the country began to climb, at the same time as real estate values dropped by $40 million in just six months. The Specie Circular also infuriated the business community, which saw it only as the latest example of executive despotism. Roger B. Taney, Jackson's former Treasury Secretary but now on the Supreme Court, backpedaled by vindicating the right of state-chartered banks to issue paper money.[58] Although the Court's decision was a clear victory for "soft" money, it came too late. Barely a month into Van Buren's presidency, a New Orleans cotton broker failed because of contracted credit, then others followed. By April their New York City creditors were failing too, and on May Day the merchant firm of Arthur Tappan and Company collapsed. The Panic of 1837 had begun.

The Panic of 1837 did not merely repeat the one of 1819; it lasted much longer, until 1843, and it did so as a direct result of Jackson's policies. By paying off the national debt, Jackson had returned $50 million to London bankers alone; this sum, together with capital going to the Continent, deprived the nation of much-needed fuel for the economy; by destroying the Bank of the United States, Jackson had left the country without a lender of last resort and had made it next to impossible to regulate the domestic money supply. During Jackson's "third term," that is, under the Van Buren administration, responsibility for regulation fell to the states. At the state level, the Democrats, now deprived of their nemesis, pursued a variety of contradictory policies, which only showed that they were not generally interested in government regulation. Such laissez-faire seems paradoxical, as Jacksonian hard-money supporters had always deeply distrusted banks and had wanted to make sure that government at no level did them any favors. Meanwhile, the Whigs, the party committed to planned economic development, kept reminding people that they were strongly in favor of government regulation and, concomitantly, of government-paper for circulation.[59]

If the depression gave the Whig Party a new lease on life, this is reflected also in a number of articles on money and banking published in *Hunt's Merchants' Magazine*. Charles Francis Adams, bemoaning "the present unregulated state of the currency," in September 1839 calls for "a single bank of issue" as the only workable remedy for the "root of all evil," that is to say, for the government having "relinquished the control over the power to create money."[60] In the April, 1841 issue, George Wood attacks the "derangement of the currency," explaining it as the combined result of speculation through long-term loans extended by the commercial banks, the lack of a fixed ratio of paper money to specie reserves, and the secrecy surrounding bank commissioners' reports. The solution, as George Wood saw it, could only be the re-establishment of a Bank of the United States, whose primary task must be in the "constant control over the excessive issues of other [that is, commercial and state] banks."[61] *Hunt's* published a similar article in its July 1841 issue, by a "Merchant of Boston, Mass.," though the most elaborate plan for a national bank came from a prosperous New

York merchant by the name of W. S. Wetmore. Published in June 1841, when President John Tyler's veto of the congressional bills that called for the re-establishment of a national bank of issue was not yet foreseeable, Wetmore's article suggested a national bank of issue that was fully accountable to Congress, had representatives from each state on its board of directors, had branches in each state, and would issue uniform bills that were fully redeemable by gold deposited at the United States Mint.[62]

All these contributions to *Hunt's* were soberly written, and they all made suggestions towards creating "the safest and most beneficial currency in the world."[63] Quite different voices made themselves heard in the newspapers of the day, which often printed squibs ridiculing political opponents. For instance, the *Virginia Advocate*, a literary journal published in Charlottesville, had the following in an article headed "Who would not be a Jackson man?":

> Have you been seven times spurned by the people when you offered to serve your country, and are you in want of the wherewithal to make the pot boil?— try the hard money tack, and jingle a few Benton yellow jackets at everybody but your creditors, and it's odds if you don't rise to an embassy or a department. It is the short cut to fame, to wealth and power; and one has hardly time to put on a clean shirt before he writes his name [...] on the milky way of 'glory.' [...] The Jacksonian is a crucible which like that of the astrologer, turns all baser metals to gold [...] Oh, what it is to be a Jackson man![64]

Poe might have relished the article from the *Virginia Advocate*, and not just because he wrote and delighted in hoaxes. Poe knew that the Jacksonians' hard-money politics echoed the advocacy of gold and silver of the loyalist Tories of the pre–Revolutionary era. Perhaps this shift in political commitment had brought him at an early age to detest Jacksonian political rhetoric, with its populist celebration of the rights of the multitude and of the wisdom and sagacity of the common man, a term that specifically meant the common *white* man, and one that was not bothered by slavery.[65] Both Poe's aversion to party politics and his generally apolitical stance, including his avoidance of a firm stand on the question of America's money, thus can be seen as a response to Jacksonianism, though this should not be construed as an aversion to politics altogether. Poe sympathized with Jefferson's forebodings that the democracy he had helped to father was destined to fail, and he developed his genius in political satire in response to the political culture under Jackson and his successor, Van Buren. One of the most remarkable examples of Poe's genius is the appeal, at the end of "The Devil in the Belfry," to "restore the ancient order of things [...] by ejecting that little fellow from the steeple." The "little fellow" who fiendishly disrupts the quixotically orderly and punctual Dutch community in the story is associated with things Irish. Martin Van Buren's political power base in New York was based on the well-oiled Irish political machine, and it was Van Buren's triumphant visit, in June 1839, to New York had motivated Poe to make him the butt of his tale.[66]

In August 1841, Poe published "The Colloquy of Monos and Una," in which Jacksonian democracy is represented as undisputable evidence of decline. The reason Jacksonian democracy was not a fit government, Poe suggests, is what he calls the "law of gradation." Applying that "law," universal suffrage appears as a mere "meddling," resulting in fraudulent vote-buying schemes and the inevitable decline of democracy to the despotism of the mob. In "The Colloquy of Monos and Una" the "wild attempts at an omni-prevalent Democracy" come to an end in a "fiery overthrow" that is seen as a "purification which alone could efface [the earth's] rectangular obscenities." The tale has as its motto "Mellonta Tauta," which Poe ascribes to Sophocles, rendering it as "These things are in the future." In 1849, Poe published a satiric tale so named, in which he ridicules "democracy" as "a very admirable form of government — for dogs."[67] Finally, in "Some Words with a Mummy" Poe mocks Jacksonian democracy through an allegorical rendering of Egyptian history:

> Thirteen Egyptian provinces determined all at once to be free, and so set a magnificent example to the rest of mankind. They assembled their wise men, and concocted the most ingenious constitution it is possible to conceive. For a while they managed remarkably well [...] The thing ended, however, in the consolidation of the thirteen states, with some fifteen or twenty others, into the most odious and insupportable despotism that was heard of upon the face of the earth.
> I asked what the name was of the usurping tyrant.
> As well as the Count could recollect, it was *Mob*.[68]

These few examples show a consistent development in Poe's attempts to ridicule political foibles and ills. In addition, they show that the rhetoric with which Poe denounces the political philosophy of Jacksonianism brings back with a vengeance the social ideas of the Federalists of the early republic. Then, Jeffersonian democracy was felt to threaten the prerogatives of those whom John Adams called "the industrious, virtuous, and deserving," on whose spoils "the idle, vicious, and abandoned, will live."[69]

John Adams undoubtedly would have included among "the idle, vicious, and abandoned" anyone who dealt lightly with paper money. As he declared in 1809, "Every dollar of a bank bill that is issued beyond the quantity of gold and silver in the vaults represents nothing and is therefore a cheat upon somebody."[70] This is not merely a Federalist articulating an abstract position on monetary matters. Adams' words directly refer to what is generally considered as the greatest bank fraud in early nineteenth-century America. The fraud involved the Farmers Exchange Bank of Gloucester, Rhode Island. Incorporated in 1804, the bank instantly was caught up in dubious practices, though all this was child's play when compared with what happened when in 1808 the bank came to be controlled by one Andrew Dexter, Jr., a Boston entrepreneur. Soon rumors concerning Dexter and the bank began to circulate and many suspicions were aroused. Finally, in early 1809, the state legislature decided to investigate the situation. The report found that there "is now in the bank $86.46 in specie." Surely this sum did not do much toward redeeming the hundreds of thousands of paper dollars that this bank had passed into circulation. All bills of course became worthless and the state of Rhode Island closed the operation soon thereafter. The incident itself— described in a local paper as "a system of fraud beyond which the ingenuity and dishonesty of man cannot go" — was discussed for years afterwards, though it is largely forgotten today.[71]

Democratic-Republicans like Thomas Jefferson too despaired over the transformations taking place in the realm of the economy. "Pseudo-citizens [...] infected with the mania of rambling and gambling" filled Jefferson with loathing and apprehension, as did the specter of the national debt, Hamilton's legacy, to which Jefferson had acceded only after much soul-searching. A generation later, the Farmers Exchange Bank fraud came to serve, in William Gouge's treatise on paper money and banking in the United States, as a prominent example of the supposedly "ruinous effects" of the paper money issued by commercial banks. Gouge was Jackson's financial advisor, though in this instance the hard-money man was missing an important point. "The superior value of specie over a note issued by a good bank," Hezekiah Niles had commented in his *Weekly Register* for October 5, 1816, "is more in idea than in fact — yet the idea operates as a fact, for coin bears a premium. I would therefore attack the *idea* and lessen the weight of the *fact*."[72]

Hezekiah Niles, it should be recalled, never had much good to say about commercial paper money. He did, however, staunchly back Henry Clay and his "American System" of federally financed internal improvements. His statement therefore should be read against his nationalist stance. What Niles is saying is that ultimately it does not really matter whether the money is of paper or of gold or silver. Money, independent of it substance, involves something more than its physical qualities. It is always an abstraction, the outcome of a large number of social and cultural arrangements. For this reason alone money cannot be reduced to the thing it is made of and yet remains the thing it is. A famous son of the Scottish Enlightenment, James Steuart, knew this long ago. As Steuart wrote in *An Inquiry into the Principles of Political Economy* in 1767, paper money is "no more than a species of what is called credit [and which is] principally useful to encourage consumption and to increase the demand for the produce of industry."[73] In other words, paper money is capital, whose value is not intrinsic so much as it derives from exchange or, as Adam Smith formulated it a decade after Steuart, "the power of purchasing other goods which the possession of that object conveys."[74] John Adams was unable to accept any of this, and neither was Poe, though for entirely different reasons.

Things had not worked out as the Founders had hoped and expected. While Federalists like Hamilton and Adams bemoaned social trends, considering "democracy" a threat to their cherished values of wisdom and virtue, by the early nineteenth century they had become oblivious to the fact that classical republicanism no longer mattered as much as it had in the past. One reason for the decline was that many members of the gentry could not live up to the pretensions of aristocratic status and eventually faced financial ruin, Jefferson and Monroe included. Just as important was the fact that Jefferson, as well as Madison, was a Southerner. If in their politics these men unleashed the forces of egalitarianism and manufacturing in the North, the South — *their* South, as Gordon Wood emphasizes — remained mostly immune to that dynamic culture. The South stood apart, becoming by its own desire a forbidden region. Committed to a patriarchal way of life, many southerners disdained not only work, which they deemed fit only for slaves, but also the pecuniary motifs of merchants and industrialists. While the North became a bustling nation of the future, the South, caught up in a wasteful system of industry and a primitive (and morally reprehensible) system of labor, fell out of step. Bewildered southerners turned to the past, clinging to the agrarian myth of yeoman farmers leading independent, virtuous lives on the land as well as to the patrician idyll of a leisurely life of family, hospitality, books, and slaves on well-kept plantations. Politically, too, the South remained backward, for many Southerners, alarmed by Nat Turner's revolt in 1831, took a dim view of an intrusive national government, Northern abolitionism, and a restless people of "self-made men" who might challenge their defensive order.[75]

While Jefferson saw in agrarian states not only of the West but also of the slaveholding South the "last asylum and bulwark" of the principles of free government, others tried to uphold the Founders' vision of a classical republic by different arguments. Albert Gallatin, for instance, in a memorial to Congress clothed his concern about the non-renewal of the Bank of the United States' charter in the following words: "We know from the experience of nearly forty years, that so long as the bank of the United States has been in operation we have had a sound currency; and that it was thrown into utter confusion, when left to the control of the several states, each acting according to its particular views of the subject."[76] Gallatin, it should be noted, originally was a Democratic-Republican like Madison and an opponent to Hamilton's entire program, though when he was appointed Treasury Secretary in 1801, he found himself holding on to all the main parts, supporting the Bank of the United States that other Jeffersonians, including Jefferson himself, vehemently opposed. Ultimately, however, Gallatin's support was based on a social fiction that may have been valid for as long as he was in office, 1801–1809, though by the time he penned *Considerations on the Currency and Banking Systems of the United States*, in 1831, it was wholly divorced from the realities of social conflict.

What Gallatin's remarkable book registered were standards of "knowledge and confidence" held aloft from the masses for whom the need for discipline, order, coherence, self-control, and principled conviction would have been simply relics from a distant past. The direct literary application of such outdated views is summed up in these comments in reference to the rise of banking in the state of Virginia:

> The currency being specie [...] No people had more cause to rejoice than the people of Virginia, but alas! The Banks came and all things became changed. Like the Upas tree, they have withered and destroyed the healthful condition of the country, and inflicted on the people political and pecuniary diseases of the most deadly character.[77]

These mournful words were aimed at the commercial banks, which were then usually chartered by the states. Yet the lamentation, like Gallatin's *Considerations*, attaches a special meaning to the word "bank," one that is tied to note issue as the chief function of a bank. An attack on "banks" thus meant an attack on the right to emit paper notes. It did not mean doing away with the functions of deposit and discount. At the time, this was a mute point. Democratic Republicans and Jacksonian Democrats had no intention of eliminating the banks but were instead interested in the *form* of credit that would best perform the functions of a sound currency. Federalists and the later Whigs, in contrast, almost exclusively saw note issue as the characteristic banking function and thus charged that the Jacksonians wanted to overthrow the entire banking system, putting in its stead a currency exclusively based on gold and silver.[78]

A speech Senator Daniel Webster of Massachusetts gave on May 25, 1825, is a good example of the special meaning attached to the word "bank." On the implicit assumption that a bank's chief function is note issue, Webster complains bitterly about state banks refusing "payment of their notes, and thus fill[ing] the country with irredeemable and degraded paper."[79] Senator Webster may have had good reasons for his complaint; nor was it without interest. As a Federalist, Webster in 1814 had opposed a bill providing for what would have been an irredeemable currency. Surprisingly, he also opposed a bill for the chartering of the second Bank of the United States. Although the bill provided for the redemption of notes in specie, Webster objected to giving the federal government so large a share in the affairs of a bank. Later, he just as fiercely opposed the "American System," originally devised by President John Quincy Adams and Secretary of State Henry Clay, of protective tariffs, domestic improvements paid for by the federal government, and a national bank of issue, though he eventually gave up his opposition. Following Jackson's bank veto, in 1832, Webster exclaimed in the Senate, "It manifestly seeks to inflame the poor against the rich; it wantonly attacks whole classes of the people, for the purpose of turning against them the prejudices and the resentments of other classes."[80]

If Harrison Had Lived

When Senator Webster delivered his anti–Jackson oration, he had long abandoned the moribund Federalist Party for the "National" Republicans, that is, the Republicans supporting the national administration of John Quincy Adams, in contrast to the "Democratic" Republicans, or later, simply "Democrats," who supported the states' rights policies of Jackson, Van Buren, and Calhoun. With his aspirations for the presidency growing, Webster eventually was ready to join the ranks of the Whigs. While the highest office in the country remained out of reach, President William Harrison appointed him Secretary of State, an office Webster accepted. Yet Harrison died after less than a month in office. John Tyler, his successor, was soon a president without a party, and all his cabinet resigned. Webster hesitated, but after consulting with a delegation of Massachusetts Whigs decided to stay on. As regards a reconstituted Bank of the United States, Webster by 1842 considered this an "obsolete idea," though he continued his struggle for regulating the paper money from the commercial banks.[81]

If Harrison had lived, the Whigs, who then had majorities both in the House and in the Senate, would have been able to push through their plans for a third national bank of issue. The plan had met a first setback when on February 2, 1831 Senator Thomas Hart Benton launched his all-out indictment of the Whigs' plans to renew the charter of the Second Bank of the United States.

> First: Mr. President, I object to the renewal of the charter ... because I look upon the bank as an institution too great and powerful to be tolerated in a government of free and equal laws.... Secondly, I object ... because its tendencies are dangerous and pernicious to the government and the people.... It tends to aggravate the inequality of fortunes; to make the rich richer, and the poor poorer; to multiply nabobs and paupers.... Thirdly, I object ... on account of the exclusive privileges, and anti-republican monopoly, which it gives to the stockholders.[82]

Benton's own policy was clear: no paper money. "Gold and silver is the best currency for a republic," he thundered at the opening of his speech; "it suits the men of middle property and the working people best; and if I was going to establish a working man's party, it should be on the basis of hard money;—a hard money party against a paper party."[83] The words "reverberated" through the hall of the Senate, Arthur Schlesinger, Jr., notes, as Senator Webster hastily called for a vote that defeated Benton's resolution against recharter. But the words — "a hard money party against a paper party" — also reverberated through the country. The speech was speedily reprinted in the press, and pamphlets carried it further across the nation, where it was read excitedly and talked over passionately. And it set the agenda for the partisan battle over the Second Bank, pitching Webster, Clay, and the National Republicans against Benton, the Democrats — and Jackson.[84]

Andrew Jackson shrewdly linked his personal dislike of banks with Western farmer-debtor desires to loosen restraints on the local issue of paper money, while at the national level he continued the hard-money policies of his administration. Thanks to this strategy, he could interpret his reelection — by 219 electoral votes to 49 — as an approval by the people of his war against the Bank of the United States, and he pursued it with great energy.[85] Jackson won the election against Henry Clay, who, for all his charm, had much less public appeal than Old Hickory, though the bank issue had a strong constituency, and not merely among National Republicans. Following the mid-term elections of 1834, dissatisfaction with Jackson's monetary politics led to defections among Democrats and, eventually, to the consolidation of the Whig Party as the chief opposition to the Democrats. Their opposition centered chiefly on the business community, which included not only wealthy merchants and industrialists but also the larger commercial farmers and planters producing export staples, all of whom depended on reliable banking services and a stable currency and credit system.[86] Nevertheless, the election of 1836 went to Martin Van Buren. This election was unique because the Whigs used four different candidates in different regions of the country, in the hope that each would be popular enough to defeat Van Buren in their respective areas. The strategy, which included Harrison and Webster, failed. Thus the Whigs had to wait until 1840, when Harrison wins against the incumbent Van Buren.

Van Buren's platform in 1840 included the dismantling of the American System as well as an endorsement of "hard" money, thus carrying on Jackson's legacy, its echo of the old Loyalists' position on the currency notwithstanding. Jackson's policies, of course, had had the benefit of prosperous times. 1840, by contrast, was a year of hardship in the aftermath of the Panic of 1837, and Van Buren lost primarily because the Whigs reached majorities mainly from commercial areas where all classes had been hurt by the depression. Harrison did not stress the economy in his inaugural address of March 4, 1841. His victory, he made clear, had averted, just in time, the corruption of American republican institutions at the hand of Jacksonian demagogues. "It was the remark of a Roman consul in an early period of that celebrated Republic," Harrison declared at the beginning of his address,

> that a most striking contrast was observable in the conduct of candidates for offices of power and trust before and after obtaining them, they seldom carrying out in the latter case the pledges and promises made in the former. However much the world may have improved in many respects in the lapse of upward of two thousand years since the remark was made by the virtuous and indignant Roman, I fear that a strict examination of the annals of some of the modern elective governments would develop similar instances of violated confidence.[87]

Claiming for the Whigs the toga of Roman virtue in a speech that on a singularly cold and windy day lasted for hours had its price, though. Within days of his inauguration, Harrison fell ill; he died of pneumonia on April 4, 1841, less than a month in office, followed by John Tyler, who thus became the first man to enter the White House on the death of his predecessor.

When Tyler took office, the Whigs' plans for a national bank of issue ground to a final halt. Harrison had stood for "soft" money *and* government intervention in the economy. Tyler, in contrast, was a long-time advocate of states' rights and national expansion, and once established in office he opposed nearly everything that the majority of Whigs sought. As befits the subject of this book, the first clash between Tyler, a "Republican Whig" like Tennessee Judge Hugh Lawson White, and the Clay faction, or "National Whigs," involved monetary policy. Tyler's veto, in 1841, of the Fiscal Bank Act that Henry Clay had pushed through Congress, not only caused an uproar among Clay's supporters, but also brought back the Bank War, and with a vengeance. In this regard, it is truly ironic that at the December 1839, national convention the victorious Harrisonians had originally offered the vice-presidential nomination to Clay, who, piqued because he lost the nomination for president, did not reply. It was only after much searching that the Harrisonians turned to Tyler, who did accept.[88]

The Whigs, thanks to their congressional majority, managed to have Van Buren's Independent Treasury Act repealed. They then went on to draw up legislation to charter a third Bank of the United States, this time in Washington, DC. The plan included the states' right to refuse establishment of the bank's branches. Still, Tyler vetoed the bill, on the grounds that the bank was unconstitutional. The Whigs, who did not have the two-thirds majority to override the president's veto, passed another bank bill, which this time prohibited the establishment of any branches in the states without their consent. Tyler vetoed this bill also. The professed views of this president have been stated in Chapter 3: Tyler was uncommitted to any nationalist program, and had turned Whig chiefly for his aversion to Andrew Jackson. Yet like Jackson, Tyler considered the charter of a national bank of issue an unconstitutional extension of federal power. And again like Jackson, Tyler seemed dead set against any money that was not fully convertible into gold or silver.[89] There was as well a hidden agenda: Tyler had no interest in reaching an accommodation with Henry Clay. "If a compromise bank bill passed," Daniel Howe notes, "Clay would have remained leader of the Whig Party and its next presidential nominee."[90] As a result of Whig infighting, the government possessed neither an Independent Treasury nor a reconstituted Bank of the United States, and so had to once again place its funds in commercial banks. "Soft" money thus prevailed, both over "hard" money and over the Whig idea of a national bank of issue. Tyler, once he was expelled from the Whig Party, tried to form a party of his own, with a bid for reelection in mind. To achieve this goal, he set to purging Whig appointees from federal offices, replacing them with states' rights men, most of them Democrats. Poe, we have seen, also sought office, though his quest was in vain.

Two years later Poe, seemingly against all odds, professed to have retained an "earnest desire for the future."[91] He never explicitly stated, however, whether this was to be a Whig or a Democratic future. Explicitness would have mattered, as it was in their conception of the future that Whigs and Democrats differed markedly. The Democrats were basically content with the way America was — an essentially agrarian country, where "popular sovereignty" would ensure cultural diversity as well as the equal rights of the common white man. The notion of "popular sovereignty" likewise made them oppose a national bank of issue, as they suspected government favors to privileged elites. The Whig version of America's future was strikingly different. Their ideal America was an economically developed nation, in which industry and commerce would take their place alongside agriculture. Economic diversification had its price, though, in the form of cultural uniformity. The Whigs, after all, feared nothing more than lawlessness, mob rule, and demagoguery. In order to achieve their goal, the Whigs deemed it necessary to rely on economic planning, a strong federal government, and, not to forget, a national bank of issue. Yet the Whig Party, despite its strength in the electorate, its gifted leadership, and the soundness of its program, was deprived by a cruel fate and a hair-raising blunder (the death of Harrison and the selection of Tyler as his running mate) of the chance to carry out the mandate it received in the election of 1840. As a result, Clay's plan for a comprehensive American System was not enacted, nor was a national bank reconstituted. And never again did the party control the presidency and both houses of congress at the same time. When Zachary Taylor was elected president, in 1848, the issue of currency and banking, which had been associated with the Whig Party for so long, had become a thing of the past.[92]

For a time, the lone exception in defending the idea of a national bank remained the reformer and editor of the New York *Tribune*, Horace Greeley. Greeley's defense of a national bank rested on the Whiggish belief that there must be some regulating authority with the power to maintain order. "*A Currency of Bank Paper without any National regulation or central energy is not a WHIG Currency*," Greely insisted in his campaign paper *The Log Cabin*.[93] Some control, the Whigs believed, was imperative for commercial banks to act responsibly and to coordinate their efforts with an understanding that other banks would do likewise. For a number of Whigs, however, this amount of control was not nearly enough. For them, it was self-evident that the government not only regulate private banking, but also issue the money and control its supply. Charles Francis Adams, mindful of inflation and the suspension of specie payment in the wake of 1837, asserted that "the power to issue bank notes as money cannot, in any manner, be made safe in private hands, and should remain exclusively with the sovereign authority of the state."[94] Adams's views at the time were not those of a majority, though he had a prominent ally, George Tucker, the political economist and former representative for Virginia, whose book *Theory of Money and Banks Investigated* Adams reviewed for *Hunt's*, with Poe as a likely reader.[95]

On the level of politics, Jackson had won the war over the Second Bank, though his victory had done nothing to alleviate people's sufferings from the uncertainties of paper money. On the contrary, the destruction of the Bank of the United States removed all restraints from the commercial banks, enabling them to behave more waywardly than ever. Not that a reestablished BUS would have been the only possible source of a national paper currency. Since a national bank always would be plagued by questions of its constitutionality, a national paper currency might simply be issued by the federal government, the notes' value backed by proceeds from the sale of public lands and their amount fixed by law. The notes, which would be fully redeemable, would serve both as a medium of exchange and be acceptable in payment to the federal government. Although serious proposals existed for such a general circulating medium, that is, for a "paper money of equal value throughout all the states," America's lawmakers duly ignored them.[96] Eliminating the Bank of the United States, whose notes had constituted the most reliable form of paper money in the antebellum period, thus only made worse the difficulties that continued to plague America's money until the Civil War.

The Bank's destruction also foreclosed further analysis of the theoretical problem that even a fully exchangeable paper money is not valuable in and of itself. Since such money is only "representative of value," it may serve as a "measure" of value, that is, as a medium of exchange, though it cannot be a "standard" of value. This is not a problem in itself, though in a situation in which commercial banks may increase note issue at their "pleasure," bank bills over the years tend to become worth less. This is fatal to creditors, much as it undermines "confidence" among the public at large. The result is financial panics.[97] During Poe's lifetime, panics occurred in 1809, 1814, 1820, 1825, 1837, and 1839. Another panic occurred in 1857, with several more panics hitting the nation through the end of the century, most notably in 1861, 1873, 1881, and 1893. (On average, periodic economic crises occurred about every eleven years.) Each of these economic collapses resulted from the piling up of credit, the creation and eventual melting into thin air of huge fortunes on paper only. When wary or frightened depositors in the antebellum period began withdrawing their money, banks suspended the payment of specie. Although in most cases they were allowed to do so up to a year under state laws, by suspending specie payment they refused to fulfill the obligations or promises to pay that were implied or expressed on a bill's face. At worst, the banks were forced to close. In any case, suspensions of specie payment were followed by more inflation. Prices for goods and services always rose in terms of *paper* money, though when coin payments were resumed, prices did not necessarily return to their former lower level.[98]

Overall, then, a deep malaise had gripped American culture by the 1840s, though it was not then politically practicable to face it. Because of the refusal to deal with the malaise, let alone to confront it, "omens of public bankruptcy," to borrow from Madison, accompanied America's financial and monetary history until the introduction of federal paper money in the first years of the Civil War.[99] Eventually, this type of money ceased to be backed by tangible assets such as gold or silver, coming to rest solely on the faith that citizens have in their government. A currency whose value is guaranteed by an institution of power that people would trust clearly constitutes the type of credit money that politicians like the former Treasury Secretary Albert Gallatin or Whig leader Henry Clay had advocated and that commentators had envisioned in *Hunt's Merchants' Magazine*, though one wonders what Poe would have said about its introduction. The transition from paper money issued by commercial banks to a federal paper money based on a more reliable authority certainly formed an immediate resolution to the problem Poe had named and rehearsed in "The Gold-Bug." Yet the author of that resolution was the "Yankee Leviathan," as the victorious North came to be called, and so it is anybody's guess whether Poe would have applauded or not.[100]

From a modern point of view, the introduction of federal paper money shows, above all, that Andrew Jackson may have won the battles of the day against Henry Clay and his fellow Whigs, though the Whigs would win the larger contest. "America's future," Daniel Walker Howe concludes, "lay predominantly within the Whig vision of economic development and a stronger central government."[101] But had not Poe declared, in 1841, that his "political principles" were with the existing Whig administration? Moreover, had he not claimed to have "battled with right good will for Harrison"?[102] Critics have pointed out that there is no evidence that Poe participated in any way in the campaign of 1840, and that his claim may refer at best to his various political satires. At worst, Poe's claim may have been a blatant lie, placed strategically in order to land a government job.[103] Yet what if in this instance professed and real conditions of existence converged in a deep-felt desire? In such a case, Poe's claim would be very close to wishful thinking, mindful of the fact that, if Harrison had lived, there would have been a national bank of issue. William Henry Harrison rarely revealed his views, though he did make a significant admission at Dayton, Ohio, during the election campaign: "Methinks I hear a soft voice asking, Are you in favor of paper money? I AM." Harrison's words excited shouts of applause among the "acres of Whigs" present at the convention. Professing to be a "democrat," Harrison also admitted, again to great applause and tremendous cheering, that he had no hopes for the country to prosper under a hard money currency. Such a currency "but makes the poor poorer, and the rich richer. A properly devised banking system alone, possesses the capability of bringing the poor to a level with the rich."[104] Such a message, which Harrison repeated almost verbatim in his inaugural address, must have rung sweetly in Poe's ears, given his poverty. More importantly, perhaps, a paper currency coming from a national bank and regulated by a strong central government also would have been the fulfillment of one of Poe's much deeper desires, a desire for permanence and continuity, what the philosopher Arnold Gehlen calls "*dauer.*"[105]

Permanence and continuity were Poe's life theme and his condition of existence, and they may well find a symbolic expression in gold. In real life, however, gold guarantees neither permanence nor continuity, as the price of gold is subject to fluctuations on the market. What may guarantee permanence and continuity is, for instance, a trustworthy authority represented by the nation state. In the German language that ideal institution, powerful but beneficent and self-controlled, is often expressed through the phrase "*Vater Staat.*" With a view on Poe's life and work, the phrase registers, on a deep psychological level, this author's yearning for a father in his archetypal fashion, for a powerful yet beneficent instance to lean on, providing security, support and mainstay, and stabilizing his actions from the outside.[106] "I have no father — nor mother," Poe is quoted as saying as early as 1829. Six years later, Poe writes to Beverley Tucker, bemoaning the fact that he has never known parental love: "I [...] never knew [my mother] — and never knew the affection of a father."[107] The early death of Poe's mother, we have seen, may well have produced a psychological symptom like autism, to be compensated for by all kinds of repetitive behavior, including the repetition of ciphers. The absence of a father likewise left traces in Poe's psyche, much as it impacted on his writings. There are, that is to say, no fathers in Poe's major works; nor are there mothers, or parents. Such figures are conspicuously absent, expunged, perhaps denied. It is tempting, therefore, to construe the central character's name in "The Gold-Bug," William Legrand, as an echo, perhaps even an oblique homage, to General William Henry Harrison, the pro-slavery governor of the Indiana Territory who in 1809 negotiated the Treaty of Fort Wayne and who in 1840 was elected President of the United States. Poe's political sympathies for the Whigs at the time have been mentioned, together with his anti-abolitionist bias. Poe also knew a long poem, by the title of "The Mighty Dead," his friend Thomas Chivers wrote on the occasion of Harrison's death. Poe was impressed by the poem, though he considered it perfectly "unsaleable" under the circumstances.[108] As regards "The Gold-Bug," the possibility of Poe commemorating President Harrison in the hero of the tale certainly adds the weight of autobiography to reading the story as a parable of finance. And, not to forget, there is the etymological link to the French "le grand" as an epithet for a great or famous person — as in "William Harrison the Great."

To posit President Harrison as a kind of "key signifier," the one signifier that holds the whole thing together and functions as the ground of the reading process is not without its dangers, though, and I can easily foresee a possible objection. For, in Poe's writings a supposed "key signifier" often returns, in uncanny or unpleasant fashion, as the reader's own reading.[109] To any such objection one would have to respond that, ultimately, it does not really matter whether Poe really "battled" for Harrison or not. There was one man who certainly did — Abraham Lincoln. As a Whig state legislator in Illinois, Lincoln, though he was an admirer of Henry Clay, backed Harrison before the party convention. Tellingly, Lincoln tied his support to the question of a national bank of issue. Lincoln had demanded such a bank already in a speech he made in 1832 while campaigning for office himself. Now, he made a number of campaign speeches in behalf of Harrison, in which he denounced Van Buren's Independent Treasury system as a threat to the country's currency. Concerned about the deflationary momentum in Van Buren's system, Lincoln explained that the former Bank of the United States had "established and maintained" a sound and uniform circulating medium and that it "can do so again, by the *aid* of [the national] government," whose most "imperative" duty to the people is that of "furnishing them a sound and uniform currency."[110] Lincoln's defense of the Bank of the United States notwithstanding, Illinois went to Van Buren, though in Lincoln's hometown of Springfield, voters delivered a majority to the Whigs.

Lincoln continued to battle for a central bank of issue, arguing that the agrarian state of Illinois needed more not less government. Illinois, Lincoln saw clearly, depended on safe and easy credit. With a *national* bank of issue out of reach, he defended the Illinois state bank against the Democrats.[111] The bank also was an important element in Lincoln's program of modernization and internal improvement paid for by public money — the "Illinois System," in analogy to the "American System" of Adams and Clay, called into existence since federal money was not forthcoming. Lincoln remained an active and loyal Whig until the newly organized Republican Party absorbed most northern Whigs in the 1850s. The "Illinois System" may have failed, yet it initiated a nationalizing trend that bore fruit in 1861, when the economy became a central element in Lincoln's patriotic nationalism. As regards a new Bank of the United States, Lincoln's private notes of March 1848 indicate that, were he president, he would "*not* urge it's [sic!] reagitation upon Congress," though should Congress see fit to establish such an institution, he certainly would "*not* arrest it by veto."[112]

Neither a policy of economic nationalism nor a national bank of issue was on the horizon during Poe's later years. John Quincy Adams was now dead, Henry Clay had lost his last bid for the presidency, and Abraham Lincoln's campaign biography, in which Poe appears to have found at long last his true "capital" reader, had not yet been written.[113] Poe's professed "scorn of all things present"[114] remained an empty threat and so political and economic circumstances gave rise to any number of intellectual incongruities, not only *between* Poe's "art" and "politics," but also *within* each of these realms. This is evident, for instance, from Poe's magazine projects. In the prospectus for *The Stylus*, which the Philadelphia *Saturday Museum* printed on March 4, 1843, Poe described the absence of an international copyright as "but an index of the universal *disgust* excited by what is quaintly termed the cheap literature of the day." This passage, as well as the promise to include, in each issue of the proposed magazine, "a Retrospect of our Political History," disappeared in the final version of the prospectus, dated April 1848.[115] Poe's art is equally incongruous, destabilized by images of deception that undermine the very real issues Poe thematizes. If his writings are so difficult to be trusted, a major reason is that the actors usually play the characters of their own invention. Thus, the intellectuals in Poe's tales are often misfits whose estrangement — what Rufus Griswold, in referring to Poe himself, called bizarre if not "perverse"[116] behavior — takes many forms. Legrand is no exception here. Described in the tale as coming from "an ancient Huguenot family" that had "once been wealthy" but through a "series of misfortunes" had been "reduced to want," his scheme to escape from poverty is truly vengeful. As befits his temper ("infected with misanthropy"), he not only solves the riddle with a bitter and vengeful intensity but also vengefully plots to "punish" the narrator "quietly, with a little bit of sober mystification."[117]

For Poe, the prospect of defeating or humiliating a rival was a recurrent fantasy, much as the unfolding of the mystery of the stories is a key to all of Poe. In the case of "The Gold-Bug," however, both the morally ambiguous finding of the treasure and the compensatory ratiocination concerning it confront a signifying environment where knowledge about money is not so much contested as it is imperiled by overproduction. Overproduction drives prices down to zero, of commodities, bank bills, literary works, and of knowledge. A fall in exchange value is accompanied by a corresponding decline in use-vale or utility. Put differently, Poe was acutely aware of the fact that he could not or could no longer speak usefully to "the nation," let alone articulate a single ideology uniting gold bugs and paper money men. A monetary discourse can perform its differential function only by positing some larger social unity. Such a unity may take many forms, from of a modern democracy depending on differences between political factions, principles, and programs to a post-partisan utopia. Poe, David Long has shown, turned his dissent from the American status quo into a desperate search for reviving (if not reinventing) an American vocabulary of dissent. Yet Poe did not find such a vocabulary either in the present or in the past, and so was compelled to restricting his search to a community of one. In taking this step, Poe not only suppressed any communal pulse but also abused his own "autorial power," that is, the "commenting power" in his criticism, displayed by a writer when weaving his own opinions into a narrative.[118] By restricting this power to himself— by placing radical individualism over community, an uncompromising antagonism over cooperation, total annihilation over salvation — Poe in the end was no longer able to see a whole body politic but only a fragmented, exploded one, a "Nothingness" in which Whigs and Democrats, the "commonwealth" and the "mob" had become indistinguishable.[119]

If there was any strain in Poe's view of himself with respect to political sympathies, this is perhaps less important than the recognition that he was a commercial writer in a capitalist society torn apart by its own cultural contradictions and that he knew it. It was knowledge of this kind that compelled Poe, towards the end of his life, to suppress collective thought, which to him had come to represent a mere threat. To Emerson, America in 1844 appeared as "the country of the Future [...] of beginnings, of projects, of vast designs, and expectations."[120] Poe, in contrast, often professed a rather dim vision of the future. Already at the time he was preparing to enter West Point he compared progress and modernization to a "Vulture, whose wings are dull realities."[121] Often enough, such pronouncements resulted from Poe's romantic posing, and they most certainly contradict his glowing description, in 1836, of the country as "holding [...] a high rank in the scale of nations [...] unencumbered by the oppression of a national debt, and free from many other drawbacks which fetter and control the measures of the trans–Atlantic governments."[122] Yet Poe's exposure, for years on end, both to the shifting political commitments of paper-money men and gold bugs, and to a cultural regime of deception that was at once indulged in and denied, ultimately made him unable or unwilling to conceive of alternative views to the unstable currency of his time. Accordingly, he counterbalanced such views by images of mere chance, if not of dissolution. Poe's professed sense of futility — famously captured in the raven's ominous "Nevermore"[123] — culminated in his diatribe that American democracy can no more be improved than a national literature that was dominated by writers who — in his eyes — were merely pandering to popular taste. Poe, too, pandered to popular taste, at the same time as he assaulted the very idea of a popular audience. Even his most celebrated tale is a kind of hoax. Like paper money from the commercial banks, it promises value even as it flaunts its worthlessness. Like the beetle of its title, "The Gold-Bug," the story, is "no tin," too.

For the critic, this marks the final word in an attempt to explain a literary output that simply defies easy categorization. For Poe, uncertainty marked the final horizon beyond which the nation's money ceased to signify. But as the debates from the Civil War through the end of the nineteenth century demonstrate, fundamental political and ideological contradictions continued to keep the money question boiling. And it is these contradictions we now move on to consider.

Epilogue

The National Currency and
Methods in Madness

In this book I have tried to show that the writings and career of Edgar Allan Poe cannot be separated from the world of banking and finance in antebellum America; indeed, that to talk about Poe's genius as producing nothing but unearthly visions is to diminish his hold of the language of banking and finance, which he raised to a higher pitch of intensity and imaginative power. By tracing how Poe entered into and historicized the world of banking and finance, I have attempted to revive a Poe we no longer know, a historical figure largely lost from sight in our continuing contest to identify ever greater complexities, ever more nuanced meanings in his writings. To revive Poe as a historical figure of course meant to consider the material conditions of the writer's existence. Poe's world was Andrew Jackson's America, a world of banking collapse, financial panics and bankruptcies, and grinding depression. Poe, who was without independent means, was especially vulnerable to market forces, not least to those working on the literary market. Shaped by a capitalist publishing industry from the beginning of his writing career, Poe came to produce texts for a largely anonymous mass of readers. These readers constituted a national rather than a regional or sectional audience; moreover, they were caught up in a cultural logic of deception and lack of seriousness that inevitably led to a lived experience disconnected from a reflective view of it. Poe, who could not extricate himself from either of these constraints, increasingly produced writings that worked against injunctions to stabilization, thus expelling anything outside the fiction that would reflect on the action inside it, including, of course, politics. A depoliticized Poe makes any attempt to read politics back into Poe's work a truly purgatorial task for the critic; for Poe himself, it meant that ultimately he was unable to find a practical way to articulate a solution to the monetary uncertainties he experienced — a "sound and uniform currency."

A "sound and uniform currency" was finally furnished by Abraham Lincoln. Lincoln, unlike Poe, was in a position to exert "the power of regulation" and thus saved the Union not just militarily but also economically.[1] Under Lincoln, the United States government turned worthless paper into legal tender, simply by putting its stamp on it. Yet it did so, not in an illogical or unnatural way, as critics of paper money had feared, but in a thoroughly *political* way. When the transition was completed, the promise of specie money or specie-backed money had been superseded by one that rested on a far more abstract and transcendent notion — the credit of the nation. At first, this meant little more than a confidence that the federal government would be able to pay its bills. However, with the war effort being represented as a struggle for the preservation of the union, these obligations assumed a deeper significance.

Already the $5 Demand notes of 1861 offered nothing less than an "object lesson in economic and political nationalism."[2] The federal legislation on which the issue was based — the "ACT OF JULY 17, 1861" — is set above a portrait of Alexander Hamilton, who was one of the earliest (and strongest) believers in a federal currency as a tangible manifestation of government regulation. The oversize obligation on the face — "THE UNITED STATES PROMISE TO PAY TO THE BEARER ON DEMAND" — was one that Hamilton clearly would have endorsed.[3] Hamilton also would have agreed with the symbolism of Thomas Crawford's statue *Freedom in War and Peace*, which appears at left. Originally designed in the 1850s and moved to the top of the U.S. Capitol in 1863, Liberty here serves as a symbol of national unity. A brooch marked "US" holds her robes in place; the shield in her left hand contains the Seal of the U.S.; and the famous motto *E Pluribus Unum* ("Out of Many, One") is wrapped around the statue's base. As pieces of propaganda, the notes conveyed a message of *national* unity directed not just to the financiers in the North who were to underwrite the war, but also to the Southern states whose secession had precipitated the violence.[4]

The first of the Demand notes were put into circulation as of August 10, 1861, in denominations of $5 or more. They were the product of a borrowing program authorized by Congress, which allowed for a portion of those funds to be turned into federal paper money. The bills were issued to the extent of $60 million, which was about twice the amount of gold and silver coins then struck in one year. They promised payment in specie "on demand," hence their name. Yet from the beginning, it was difficult to imagine that convertibility could be safely maintained for an extended period of time. Intimations of a pending crisis came when in December 1861 Treasury Secretary Salmon P. Chase reported that the costs of the war were increasing dramatically, while federal revenues were decreasing at an equally dramatic rate. As a result, the government's ability to redeem the notes was seri-

United States Five-dollar Demand note, 1861, face, with "Patented 30 June 1857," for the "Canada Green" tint, below "Boston" (American Numismatic Association Money Museum).

ously jeopardized. By the end of the month, commercial banks, which had been lending money to the government by buying bonds with gold, suspended specie payment on their notes, creating in turn an unexpected run on government offices. In early January 1862, the United States government also suspended. Both the nation's banks and the government thus were forced off the gold standard. A month later, Congress passed and President Lincoln approved the Legal Tender Act. The bill brought about both a solution and a significant change. The notes authorized by the bill — originally set at a limit of $150,000,000, but eventually raised to $450,000,000 — were no longer backed by specie but had to be accepted solely upon trust: they now constituted a true *fiat* or *fiduciary* currency, one that was based at the same time on the faith of citizens in their government as an institution of power and on people's relationship to one another.[5]

The North's greenbacks, it has been suggested, were issued "by the nation, for the nation, in order to pay for the preservation of the nation."[6] The sentiment was being articulated in similar terms in the Northern press of the postbellum period. In a typical dispatch, the *New York Herald* spoke of the "general joy and satisfaction" with which people hailed a currency standing on the good faith of the nation. The greenbacks accordingly were showcased as "a currency as secure as the nation itself" and thus as a proxy for the "patriotism of the people, who, under no circumstances, will depreciate them."[7] Throughout the post-Civil War period, insistence on the inherent patriotism of federal paper money even spawned suggestions for the abolition of the national bank system and a concomitant replacement of its notes with greenbacks. The most radical proposal came in 1866, when Representative Lewis W. Ross directed a resolution to the Committee on Banking and Currency in which he suggested that the committee "inquire into the expediency of withdrawing the national currency and winding up the national banks and furnishing the country in lieu of said national currency with greenbacks or other currency of similar character." Politically this measure, as did others before and after, neatly combined western agrarian hostility to the bank system with a general predilection for an inflationary expansion of greenbacks.[8]

Financiers had a different view of the matter. Convinced that the British political system was more stable and sophisticated than the American one, they favored an international (cosmopolitan) monetary order based on the gold standard. Resumption of course would transfer a measure of power from the United States to the United Kingdom, but finance capitalists expected better returns from the orderly conducted Bank of England than from what they saw as the haphazard policies of the U.S. Treasury. Both Irwin Unger in *The Greenback Era* and Robert Sharkey in *Money, Class, and Party* describe the politics of resumption as primarily a struggle between debtors and creditors in which neither financial stability nor economic nationalism was ever an issue. Representative Lewis W. Ross's resolution of course was not patriotic per se, but it fit nicely into the rhetoric of a *national* currency. The finance capitalists, in their efforts to maximize profits, also were not per se concerned with the nation; it was nevertheless possible to interpret their rejection of governmental control of their pecuniary interests in terms of "cosmopolitanism."[9]

At the time, the rhetorical strategy of relating the form of money to the mutually exclusive notions of "cosmopolitanism" versus "patriotism" muffled, if only barely, the racial marking of "Jewishness" in the descriptor "cosmopolitan." Ironically, it also resurrected the political commitments of paper-money men and bullionists of the pre-Revolutionary era. Then, hard-money had been on the agenda of the loyalist Tories, whereas paper-money advocacy had been linked with anti-royalist protest and the push towards political sovereignty. When Republican administrations, in their pursuit of a national economy dusted off these political commitments at mid-century, what also came to the fore was the plain truth that the United States was not an island, separate and distinct from the rest of the world, but was in fact a nation among nations. There were, however, insecurities about the country's role among other nations. Not only was the United States a debtor nation at the time. Altogether, America's money then was a rather "subordinate, derivative currency, one that took its cue — and was overwhelmed by — the currencies of other countries and empires."[10] Contemporaries were aware of this situation, though they looked upon the matter in terms of their political allegiances. Senator Benton, in attempting to justify the hard-money policies of Presidents Jackson and Van Buren, claimed that "gold goes where it finds value, and that value is what the laws of the great nations give it [...] we must place the same value upon gold that other nations do, if we wish to gain any part of theirs, or regain any part of our own."[11] A. K. Shepard, in contrast, was a loyal follower of Lincoln's economic nationalism and thus fully in favor of eliminating, by means of taxation, the paper bills from state-chartered commercial banks. These bills, Shepard noted in 1864, are "an intolerable nuisance, unworthy the genius of a people making as high pretensions as Americans."[12]

Banks and other institutions issuing notes for circulation had been taxed since 1863; on March 3, 1865, Congress adopted a ten percent "death tax" on the circulation of notes issued by commercial banks, ten times the rate charged to national banks. The measure effectively outlawed all notes except those issued by national banks and the federal government. In the long run, the new system made banking both profitable and, compared to the previous state-chartered organization, very secure. At the same time, the "imagined" value of token or fiduciary money in encouraging recognition of one's membership in the nation assumed an ever more significant role. The reverence with which the political economist William Graham Sumner later spoke of the rise of a national banking system is merely a belated echo of this role. The system's "first great feature," Sumner wrote in his *History of Banking*, "was that it was national and federal;–a thing which in the days of misery under the local bank system people had sighed for again and again as an unattainable hope." Sumner then went on to extol the system's many virtues — its uniformity, stability, and the fact that it operated under what he termed "federal control."[13]

Altogether, what was happening from the 1860s onward was the precise opposite to what had taken place in the early years of the republic. During the 1770s and 1780s, people were disillusioned with public currency, thus forcing the emergence of private currency that held sway until the mid-nineteenth century. Now that another war was raging, people became disillusioned with private currency; this led to the re-introduction of public currency, and to the ultimate demise of private currency. Still it took time for people to realize that a modern economy rested on credit and that credit depended fundamentally on trust between creditor and debtor. Such confidence could be hard to come by, and supporters of a "hard" currency took refuge in notions of genuine or "intrinsic" value; for them, this kind of value was located also in "oil paintings, wood paneling, and old family gentility."[14] For Greenbackers, such ideas only proved that these people were living in the past. The future, they maintained, belonged to the people who would control the monetary system through a democratically elected government. But a democratically elected government also could have in its fold a Treasury Secretary Hugh McCulloch, for whom money was effectual only when it represented "real" money, that is, when it was convertible into gold, the uncontested general equivalent of all products and thus "the only true measure of value." Truthfulness, the Secretary added, came from God and nature: "I myself have no more doubt that [gold and silver] were prepared by the Almighty for this purpose, than I have that iron and coal were prepared for the purposes for which they are being used."[15] In the eyes of bullionists like McCulloch only God and nature, not government or society, could create value and identity. Specie-based currencies, moreover, had been tried; their historical importance was taken as proof of the superiority of gold. Ultimately, a freely convertible currency could be taken as a sign of "the possession of that first of Christian virtues, upright and downright honesty."[16] Thus, only a return to the gold standard would ensure the return of the United States to the ranks of civilized Christian nations.

Specie convertibility was resumed in 1879 when, in the aftermath of the economic crisis of 1873–74, a Republican-dominated Congress adopted the gold standard. Two years later, the Republican Party platform included the following plank in favor of a fully convertible currency: "Commercial prosperity, public morals, and the national credit demand that [the promise to redeem the United States notes in coin] be fulfilled by a continuous and steady progress to specie payment." In 1880, the Democratic Party came around too, pledging itself to "honest money — the strict maintainance [sic!] of gold and silver, and paper convertible into coin on demand."[17] Henceforth, the dollar was to be a gold dollar, and to further highlight this policy a type of currency called "Gold Certificates" was revived.[18] The Gold Standard Act of 1900 finally established the gold dollar as the standard unit of value, though gold did not fulfill the grandiose expectations vested in it by the powerful. Already by the end of the nineteenth century the demand for gold had increased dramatically because a large number of nations worldwide accepted gold as their monetary standard. Consequently, the gold price rose; at the same time, product prices fell. The political discontent following from this, as well as the fluctuations of the value of gold on the international market ultimately led to the abandonment of the gold standard in 1933 under the administration of Franklin D. Roosevelt. In the same year, the paper dollar was devalued in order to attract more money from abroad. When Congress formally declared all United States coins and currencies as equal legal tender, this was merely an afterthought to the standardization of the currency that the American state had achieved within some four decades.

The final chapter was opened in August 1971, when President Richard Nixon decreed that redemption, the convertibility of paper to gold, be stopped altogether. With the "gold window" closed, the dollar was no longer pegged to a specific value in a commodity. Instead, it was let to "float" relative to all other currencies, forever exposed to the whims of traders on Wall Street, in London, Tokyo, and Zurich. Ever since, paper dollars have been intrinsically worthless, with nothing payable to the bearer "on demand." Instead of the obligation there is the inscription "In God We Trust," which was first put on the $1 Silver Certificate in 1957 and has appeared on all currency notes from 1963. The inscription as it were notarizes the completion of the monetary cycle, at which point the paper currency is backed by nothing more — and nothing less — than confidence in the nation state and in people's relationship to one another. Such a currency is by definition a contradictory creature. Since it involves the creation of debt leveraged against limited assets, it not only depends on trust and confidence in an authority of power but also invites the possibility of fraud or, at the very least, serious disappointment.

In some deep, unsettling sense, then, a currency based on credit depends on credulousness. To phrase the matter differently, a currency based on credit depends on promises — and promises, as the saying goes, are also made to be broken. If this is reasonable, such reason at the same time is utterly unreasonable, as is the "madness" in Poe's "The Gold-Bug," which cannot be completely obliterated by "certain indications of method" displayed in this celebrated tale.[19] The "method," in "The Gold-Bug" as well as in other of his writings, directed the full force of censure to the acrimonious debates about America's money, Andrew Jackson's bank war, the panic of 1837 and the ensuing depression, and the nation's inability to furnish a "sound and uniform currency." Yet we also should not overlook the many-sidedness to Poe's response to the world of money and banking. His censure of the world of money and banking is most overt in his early satires; it is more subdued in "The Gold-Bug," almost a judicious probing into the monetary uncertainties of his own time; it takes the form of a soft voice asking in a number of poems and other tales; and it comes back with renewed force in writings that enter into and historicize the discovery of gold in California. This shifting back and forth between negation and affirmation is further compounded by Poe's predilection for hoaxes and other forms of overt manipulation. Caught up as he was in a cultural logic of hoaxes, Poe relentlessly worked against stable understandings of his writings. In fact, the destabilization of understanding is often the point of his writing and its payoff. All this demonstrates the difficulty, not only of establishing a stable authorial intent but also of establishing a stable author. Poe certainly did not fashion an ideological position on the money question. Yet he also did not just shrug his shoulders and turn to unearthly visions. What Poe fashioned, I would suggest, was an intellectual position that registers, not only the cultural contradictions of his time but also the complexities and paradoxes of the world of money and banking and thus assigns contrasting and shifting meanings to it. From a modern perspective, it would of course be easy to take Poe to task for a political agenda that was so elusive that it requires painstaking efforts at decryption. That was not my intention in this book. I rather hope to suggest that we deepen, and in some respects usefully complicate, our understanding of Poe by seeing that necessarily a career such as his at once conceals and reveals — in this instance, a deeply felt desire for an authority guaranteeing a measure of permanence and continuity also to the currency. Call this desire "madness" if you will.

Chapter Notes

Prologue

1. Sun Ra, quoted in John F. Szwed, *Space Is the Place: The Lives and Times of Sun Ra* (New York: Pantheon, 1997), 130. I am grateful to Gerwin Gallob (University of California at Santa Cruz) for pointing out to me Sun Ra's familiarity with and enthusiasm for Poe's writings.

2. Richard F. Teichgraeber III, *Sublime Thoughts/Penny Wisdom: Situating Emerson and Thoreau in the American Market* (Baltimore: Johns Hopkins University Press, 1995), xxii.

3. F. R. Ankersmit, *Sublime Historical Experience* (Stanford: Stanford University Press, 2005), 9.

4. Stephen Mihm, *A Nation of Counterfeiters: Capitalists, Con Men, and the Making of the United States* (Cambridge: Harvard University Press, 2007), 319.

5. Richard Wilbur, "The House of Poe," in *Poe: A Collection of Critical Essays*, ed. Robert Reagan (Englewood Cliffs, NJ: Prentice-Hall, 1967), 98–120, quotation 99.

6. Thomas Ollive Mabbott, Introduction, *The Collected Works of Edgar Allan Poe*, vols. 2 and 3, *Tales and Sketches*, ed. Thomas Ollive Mabbott with the assistance of Eleanor D. Kewer and Maureen C. Mabbott (Cambridge: Belknap Press of Harvard University Press, 1978), 2: xxvi.

7. In the mid–1830s, Poe asked each of his relatives for financial assistance for his aunt, Mrs. Clemm, well knowing that they had the resources to provide the aid he sought. In 1840, Poe solicited William's support for his proposed *Penn* magazine; in November 1845, he asked George Jr. for a loan of $200 to keep the *Broadway Journal* afloat. *The Collected Letters of Edgar Allan Poe*, 2 vols., originally ed. by John Ward Ostrom, 3d ed., rev., corr., and exp. by Burton R. Pollin and Jeffrey A. Savoye (Staten Island: Gordian Press, 2008), 1:98–101, 117–19, 130–31; 236, 537.

8. Poe, letter to John Pendleton Kennedy, June 21, 1841, in *Letters* 1:277. This is only one of a whole series of similar letters Poe wrote at the time, including to Irving, Longfellow, Fitz-Greene Halleck, and Cooper. Ibid., 1:274, 280, 283, and 289. A few years later, Poe repeated his insight into the commercialization of meaning, writing that writers and readers were forced University Presson "the curt, the condensed, the well-digested in place of the voluminous — in a word, upon journalism in lieu of dissertation." Poe, "Marginal Note," *Godey's Lady's Book*, September 1845, in *Essays and Reviews*, ed. G. R. Thompson (New York: Library of America, 1984), 1377.

9. Poe, letter to John Pendleton Kennedy, June 21, 1841, in *Letters*, 1:278.

10. Poe, review of Thomas Moore, *Burton's Gentleman's Magazine*, January 1840, in *Essays and Reviews*, 334.

11. Poe, "The Philosophy of Furniture," in *Poetry and Tales*, ed. Patrick Quinn (New York: Library of America, 1984), 382.

12. Reference is to Poe's essay "Some Secrets of the Magazine Prison-House," *The Broadway Journal*, February 15, 1845, in *Essays and Reviews*, 1036–38.

13. Lucian Minor, "The New Year," *Southern Literary Messenger*, 1 (April 1835) 1, quoted in Terence Whalen, *Edgar Allan Poe and the Masses: The Political Economy of Literature in Antebellum America* (Princeton, NJ: Princeton University Press, 1999), 5.

14. Whalen, *Poe and the Masses*, 6. Reference to "fat" editors and proprietors is to "Some Secrets of the Magazine Prison-House," in *Essays and Reviews*, 1038.

15. In Ian Walker's estimation, Poe's total income from books in more than twenty years was some $300. *Edgar Allan Poe: The Critical Heritage*, ed. Ian Walker (London: Routledge, 1986; repr. 1997), 8. Poe's income from magazine publications was equally meager, at an average of $4 per printed page. Poe received a total of some $121 for all his writings for *Graham's Magazine*, which by 1842 had been the most successful magazine in the United States, with a circulation approaching 40,000 copies. Ibid., 13–17, and Jeffrey Meyers, *Edgar Allan Poe: His Life and Legacy* (New York: Scribner's, 1992; repr. New York: Cooper Square Press, 2000), 121–124, 138–140.

16. Whalen, *Poe and the Masses,* 6.

17. Poe to Charles Anthon, late October 1844, in *Letters*, 1:470.

18. Poe, in *Essays and Reviews*, 349.

19. Copyrighting a single story was quite an unusual step at the time. A copyright for "The Gold-Bug" was entered on June 23, 1843, but many newspapers disregarded it and reprinted the story without permission. Mabbott, in *Collected Works*, 3:804.

20. Poe, in *Letters*, 1:441.

21. Poe, letter to Frederick William Thomas, May 4, 1845, in *Letters,* 1:505.

22. Terence Whalen, who also solved the cipher, explores the issue in great detail in chap. 7 of his *Poe and the Masses*.

23. Bray Hammond, *Banks and Politics in America from the Revolution to the Civil War* (1957; repr. Princeton, NJ: Princeton University Press, 1991), 273.

24. Q. David Bowers, *Obsolete Paper Money Issued by Banks in the United States, 1782–1866* (Atlanta: Whitman, 2006), 34–39, 518–19.

25. For "sound and uniform currency," see Abraham Lincoln, "Speech

on the Subtreasury," Springfield, Illinois, December 1839, in *The Collected Works of Abraham Lincoln*, ed. Roy P. Basler (New Brunswick, NJ: Rutgers University Press, 1953–1955), 1:159–79, here 164. For "power of regulation" see Charles Francis Adams, "The State of the Currency II," *Hunt's Merchants' Magazine*, December 1839, 505–517, here 506. On Lincoln as a reader of Poe, see William Dean Howells, *Life of Abraham Lincoln* (Columbus, OH, 1860; repr. Bloomington: Indiana University Press, 1960), 31–32.

26. Michel Foucault, *The Order of Things: An Archaeology of the Human Sciences* (New York: Pantheon, 1970), 175–76.

27. Ward Hill Lamon, *Recollections of Abraham Lincoln*, ed. Dorothy Lamon (Chicago: A. C. McClurg, 1895), 215. For the myth that Lincoln had originated the greenbacks, see Gabor S. Boritt, *Lincoln and the Economics of the American Dream* (1978; Urbana: University of Illinois Press, 1994), 346n35.

28. George Wood, "The Currency," *Hunt's Merchants' Magazine*, April 1841, 317–33, here 329. For a similar vision of a "paper money of equal value throughout all the states," see J. Louis Tellkampf, "The Currency," *Hunt's*, January 1842, 65–71, quotation 67. See chapter 5, 159n96.

29. Reginald Charles McGrane, *The Panic of 1837: Some Financial Problems of the Jacksonian Era* (Chicago: University of Chicago Press, 1924; repr. 1965), 1.

30. John Tyler, a Virginian, had been nominated as Vice President to placate the South. On his nomination, see Oliver Perry Chitwood, *John Tyler, Champion of the Old South* (1939; rpt. New York: Russell & Russell, 1964). William M. Gouge, a contemporary observer, noted that following Tyler's first veto, a "mob of paper money men assembled in front of [Tyler's] dwelling, and [...] also burned the effigy of the president." Gouge, *Journal of Banking* (Philadelphia, July 1841–July 1842; repr. London: Routledge/Thoemmes Press, 1996), 75.

31. Poe, "King Pest. A Tale Containing an Allegory," in *Poetry and Tales*, 240–252. "King Pest" was first published in the *Southern Literary Messenger* in 1835; it was republished in *Tales of the Grotesque and Arabesque* in 1840 and again in the *Broadway Journal* of 1845. Its title probably recalls a cholera epidemic that raged in Baltimore in September 1831. Poe like other commentators at the time may have linked the epidemic with politics. See Arthur Hobson Quinn, *Edgar Allan Poe: A Critical Biography* (New

York: Appleton-Century-Crofts, 1941; repr. Baltimore: Johns Hopkins University Press, 1998), 187, 214.

32. See H. Allan Greer, "Poe's 'Hans Pfaall' [sic] and the Political Scene," [Poe] supplement, pt. 2, *ESQ (Emerson Society Quarterly)* 60 (1970): 67–73. Poe first published "Hans Phaall — A Tale" in the *Southern Literary Messenger* of June 1835; it was particularly well received and reappeared in 1840 in his *Tales of the Grotesque and Arabesque* as "The Unparalleled Adventure of One Hans Pfaall." Poe, in *The Collected Writings of Edgar Allan Poe*, ed. Burton Pollin, 5 vols. (Boston: Twayne, 1981; New York: Gordian Press, 1985), 2:25–95.

33. William Whipple, "Poe's Political Satire," *Texas Studies in English*, 35 (1956), 81–95, here 81; 88–91. "Vanny Buren" is from "How to Write a Blackwood Article," *The Broadway Journal*, July 12, 1845, in *Poetry and Tales*, 278–97, quotation 294.

34. Thomas Ollive Mabbott does not believe that Poe created a political satire through the references, though it may be well to reconsider this in light of Whipple's claim that the used-up man is a satirical portrait of Colonel Richard M. Johnson, the hero of the Battle of the Thames in October 1813, who was Van Buren's running mate in the Presidential elections of 1836 and 1840. Mabbott, in *Collected Works*, 2:376; Whipple, "Poe's Political Satire," 91–94.

35. Russell Rulau, *Standard Catalog of United States Tokens, 1700–1900*, 4th ed. (Iola, WI: Krause, 1997), 5. For images of this and other political tokens, see ibid., 70, 75–81. Ernie Nagy recently has retold the story of the rhetorical battle fought through hard times tokens: "Artifacts of Andrew Jackson's Bank War," *The Numismatist*, 23, no. 9, September 2010, 51–56.

36. See, for instance, William Charvat, "American Romanticism and the Depression of 1837," *The Profession of Authorship in America, 1800–1870*, ed. Matthew J. Bruccoli (New York: Columbia University Press, 1992), 49–67, here 61.

37. The purpose of the subtreasuries was to discourage speculation and protect government funds by removing these funds and revenues from commercial banks and placing them in various sub-treasuries throughout the country. By doing so, the amount of specie on which banks could issue paper was reduced, keeping the economy from overheating. The sub-treasuries were finally established by James Polk in 1846 and were kept in function until the

creation of the Federal Reserve System in 1913. The original Sub-Treasury Bill, which also contained a specie clause stipulating that only coins or Treasury paper be used in payments both to the government and in demands against it, had been rejected in 1837. This was owed largely to the efforts of Daniel Webster, whose speech in the United States Senate in September of that year is generally considered one of the most effective of his arguments on the subjects of money and finance. On Van Buren's Sub-Treasuries and other "experiments" in the plan to completely divorce the affairs of the federal government from banks, see David Kinley, *The Independent Treasury of the United States and Its Relations to the Banks of the Country* (Washington, DC: U.S. Government Printing Office, 1910; repr. New York: A. M. Kelley, 1970).

38. Jeffrey A. Savoye, "Reconstructing Poe's 'The Gold-Bug': An Examination of the Composition and First Printing(s)," *The Edgar Allan Poe Review* 8, no. 2 (2007): 34–48, here 39.

39. The contest had been announced in several papers at the time, with the specification of an "*American*" subject appearing in the Baltimore *Sun*. Savoye, "Reconstructing Poe's 'The Gold-Bug,'" 36, emphasis added. The prize was not Poe's first cash award; on October 12, 1833, the Baltimore *Saturday Visiter* announced that Poe had won its contest with tale "Manuscript Found in a Bottle." The premium then paid was $50. The tale was published in the *Visiter's* October 19 issue. Dwight R. Thomas and David K. Jackson, *The Poe Log: A Documentary Life of Edgar Allan Poe, 1809–1849* (Boston: G. K. Hall, 1987), 132–133.

40. The liquidation of the bank was a major cause for the shift of financial leadership from Philadelphia to New York. Also affected by the crisis was the nation's gross domestic product. From a peak at $1.84 billion in 1836, it dropped 12.5 percent to $1.61 billion by 1843. Moreover, since the nation's population was growing quickly in those years, the decrease in per capita GDP was even more dramatic, from $119 in 1836 to $85 in 1843, a decrease of over 28 percent. Robert E., Wright and David J. Cowen, *Financial Founding Fathers: The Men Who Made America Rich* (Chicago: University of Chicago Press, 2006), 182.

41. See, for instance, Richard Caton Woodville, *Politics in an Oysterhouse* (1848), oil on fabric; original size 16 x 13 in.; Walters Art Museum,

Baltimore, www.walters.org. The Prints & Photographs Division of the Library of Congress holds an image of a lithograph of the Oysterhouse painting, done by Fanoli and printed by Lemercier, in Paris, ca. 1851. Library of Congress, http://www.loc.gov/pictures/item/96509643/.

42. For this, the Whigs would claim the glory, though in truth it was also due to President Van Buren's "experiments" involving the Sub-Treasuries, which the Whigs denounced as a vast conspiracy against private property and a movement towards despotism. But these were political and social arguments, whereas economic objections were rarely raised.

43. Fredric Jameson, *The Political Unconscious: Narrative as a Socially Symbolic Act* (Ithaca: Cornell University Press, 1981; repr. London: Routledge, 2002), 20.

44. On this issue, see Martin Jay, "Historical Explanation and the Event: Reflections on the Limits of Contextualization," *New Literary History* 42, no. 4 (2011), 557–71, here 562.

45. Claude Romano, *Event and World*, trans. Shane Mackinlay (New York: Fordham University Press, 2008), 152.

46. Poe, "Marginalia," *Democratic Review*, November 1844, in *Essays and Reviews*, 1318.

47. Whalen, *Poe and the Masses*, 220.

48. Poe, "The Gold-Bug," in *Poetry and Tales*, 586.

Chapter 1

1. Poe, "The Gold-Bug," in *Poetry and Tales*, ed. Patrick F. Quinn (New York: Library of America, 1984), 566, 578, 579, 580, 568.

2. Mary McCarthy, *On the Contrary* (New York: Farrar, Straus, and Cudahy, 1961), 255.

3. *Poetry and Tales*, 561, 560.

4. John Allan's troubles began in early 1819, when tobacco prices began to fall; remittances from Virginia failed to arrive as state banks had begun failing, taking with them merchants and farmers. By October, Allan's firm was almost $223,000 in debt, though thanks to his creditors' patience, Allan eventually was able to clear himself. In July 1820, he and his family arrived back in New York. Kenneth Silverman, *Edgar A. Poe: Mournful and Never-Ending Remembrance* (New York: Harper Perennial, 1991; 2009), 20–22, 27–28.

5. For a discussion of the mon-etary debates and practices in nineteenth-century America, see Heinz Tschachler, *The Greenback: Paper Money and American Culture* (Jefferson, NC: McFarland, 2010), 166–177.

6. Ralph Waldo Emerson, "Nature," in *The Collected Works of Ralph Waldo Emerson*, ed. Alfred A. Ferguson (Cambridge: Belknap Press of Harvard University Press, 1971), 1–45, here 20.

7. In all likelihood, the saying originated from *Niles' Weekly Register*, which reported that American eagles, "being worth ten dollars and eighty five cents in silver, for the British Mint, have nearly all taken wings and flown away." *Niles' Weekly Register*, March 9, 1822, 23. A few years earlier, *Niles'* had carried a report about two ships sailing from Boston to England, carrying away $500,000 in specie, expected to fetch from 28 to 34 percent advance, compared with Bank of England notes. As a result of such shipments, *Niles'* notes, "money is scarcer in Boston than in any other part of the United States." *Niles' Weekly Register*, July 15, 1815, 352. Poe uses the idiom in "Ligeia" of 1838, though there it is not the eagle flying away, but the narrator's expectations. Poe, in *Poetry and Tales*, 262–77, here 266.

8. "Foreign bank notes" here means paper bills from another state, which until the Civil War were considered as *foreign*, including in bank records, statements, and other accounts. Such currency usually sold at a discount, which reflected not only a bank's perceived standing but also the cost of sending messengers to the outlying banks to attempt redemption. Bills from the Bank of the United States and its branches, in contrast, were traded at par. Q. David Bowers, *Obsolete Paper Money Issued by Banks in the United States, 1782–1866* (Atlanta: Whitman, 2006), 138, 220.

9. *Niles' Weekly Register*, February 24, 1821, 417. In its issue of October 5, 1816, *Niles'* had denounced small-denomination paper notes as "trash in circulation" (81). There were many other colloquialisms for paper bills, such as "rag-money," "wildcats," "red dog," "blue pup," or "owl." Thomas Hart Benton used nearly all of these terms in a Senate speech on January 13, 1842. Benton, "Remarks on the Plan for a Federal Board of Exchequer," in *The Congressional Globe* (Washington, DC: Globe Office, January 1842), Appendix of the Second Session of the Twenty-Seventh Congress, 62–72, here 65. William H. Dillistin cites the speech in *Bank Note Reporters and Counterfeit Detectors,* *1826–1866* (New York: American Numismatic Society, 1949), 71, as does Bowers in *Obsolete Paper Money*, 114. For "rag-money," see Richard Doty, *America's Money—America's Story*, 2d ed. (Atlanta: Whitman, 2008), 91.

10. In this context, Emerson's 1842 journal entry on the "superficial" nature of urban life is particularly enlightening: "In New York city lately, as in cities generally, one seems to lose all substance, & become surface in a world of surfaces. Everything is external, and I remember my hat & coat, and all my other surfaces, and nothing else." Ralph Waldo Emerson, in *The Journals and Miscellaneous Notebooks of Ralph Waldo Emerson*, ed. William H. Gilman (Cambridge: Belknap Press of Harvard University Press, 1970), 204.

11. Andrew Jackson, Farewell Address, March 4, 1837, in *Presidential Messages and State Papers ... from George Washington to Woodrow Wilson*, ed. Julius W. Muller (New York: Review of Reviews, 1917), 4:1232–48, here 1242.

12. William Dodge, "Recollections, 1818–1880," in Carlos Martyn, *William E. Dodge: The Christian Merchant* (New York: Funk & Wagnalls, 1890), 112.

13. Eric Helleiner, "National Currencies and National Identities," *American Behavioral Scientist* 41, no. 10 (1998): 1409–36, here 1414.

14. These institutions generally came by the name "private banks." Mostly these banks for political or other reasons could not obtain a state charter but went into business nevertheless, such as the Bank of New York in 1784, which was caught up in political wrangling between the city's Federalists and Democrats. All these banks usually were accepted as legitimate in their own time, though. Bowers, *Obsolete Paper Money*, 30–31, 46–48, 493.

15. Edward Pessen, *Jacksonian America: Society, Personality, and Politics*, rev. ed. (Urbana: University of Illinois Press, 1985), 103. Under Free Banking laws, which were passed mostly by Democratic state legislatures reasoning that more banks meant more prosperity, banks could be incorporated by ten or more persons, usually with a capital of $50,000 to $200,000. They were permitted to issue bills against securities deposited with the state. The states thus had charge of the currency, delegating officials to countersign bills issued by the banks, and thus adding a measure of protection for the holders of currency. Bowers, *Obsolete Paper Money*, 240–45, 534–37.

16. Quotations respectively from Howard Bodenhorn, *A History of State Banking in Antebellum America* (New York: Cambridge University Press, 2000), 215, and Joyce Appleby, *Inheriting the Revolution: The First Generation of Americans* (Cambridge: Belknap University Press, 2000), 86.

17. Daniel Walker Howe, *What Hath God Wrought: The Transformation of America, 1815–1848*, Oxford History of the United States, vol. 5 (New York: Oxford University Press, 2007), 561.

18. By contrast, the amount of specie in circulation was never more than roughly two thirds the denominational value of notes. Treasury Reports, in *Documentary History of Banking and Currency in the United States*, ed. Herman E. Krooss, 4 vols. (1969; New York: Chelsea House, 1983), 1:266, 2:130.

19. John Jay Knox, *A History of Banking in the United States* (New York: Bradford Rhodes, 1900), 702, 703.

20. Quoted in Goodwin, *Greenback: The Almighty Dollar and the Invention of America* (New York: Henry Holt, 2003), 150.

21. Charles Francis Adams, "The State of the Currency I," *Hunt's Merchants' Magazine*, July 1839, 44–50, here 48.

22. Charles Francis Adams, "The State of the Currency II," *Hunt's Merchants' Magazine*, December 1839, 505–17, here 506.

23. Murray Teigh Bloom, *Money Of Their Own: The Great Counterfeiters* (New York: Scribner's, 1957), 97.

24. Karl Marx, *A Contribution to the Critique of Political Economy*, trans. W.I. Stone (1859; Chicago: Charles H. Kerr, 1904), 141.

25. Poe, "King Pest," in *Poetry and Tales*, 240–52, here 241.

26. Alexander Del Mar, *Gold Money and Paper Money* (New York: Anson D. F. Randolph, 1863), 32.

27. *The Haunted Merchant* (New York: John Allen, 1843) became the first and only number of a projected series of *Bankrupt Stories*. Briggs had already published and become popular, in 1839, with another novel, *The Adventures of Henry Franco: A Tale of the Great Panic*. The novel, which describes the speculative fever in New York, tells the story of a boy from University Pressstate New York who arrives at the City Hotel and is fleeced by real-estate operators and auctioneers. Silverman, *Edgar A. Poe*, 243–45; for a brief citation of *The Haunted Merchant*, see *Hunt's Merchant's Magazine*, July 1843, 104.

28. *Poetry and Tales*, 580, 579. For

Solomon's household, see 1 Kings 10:21: "And all king Solomon's drinking vessels were of gold [...] none were of silver." The "specie requirement," which prohibited *all* paper notes in payment to the government, was a part of the Independent Treasury Act. It was only the last in a series of circulars that began in 1835, when notes under $5 were banned. Both the Act and the various circulars effectively reversed a joint congressional resolution of 1816 that had made all notes from note-issuing banks acceptable in tax payments. James Willard Hurst, *A Legal History of Money in the United States, 1794–1970* (1973; Frederick, MD: Beard Books, 2001), 80.

29. Senate Select Committee, *The New American State Papers: Public Finance*, ed. Sidney Ratner (Wilmington, DE: Scholarly Resources, 1972), 27:292.

30. In October 1833, there had only been thirty million dollars of specie in the country, of which twenty-six million was in bank vaults. By the time of the report, in December 1836, specie had risen to seventy-three million dollars, of which only forty-five million was in the banks. Levi Woodbury, "Report on the Finances, December, 1836," in *Reports of the Secretary of the Treasury of the United States*, vol. 3 (Washington, DC: Blair & Rives, 1837), 679–744, here 694–96.

31. Reference to the respective Acts of Congress is to Del Mar, *Gold Money and Paper Money*, 14. For Poe's commentary on the $1 gold dollar, see chapter 4, 128.

32. Poe, in *Poetry and Tales*, 573.

33. Bowers, *Obsolete Paper Money*, 78.

34. Alpheus Felch, "Early Banks and Banking in Michigan" [1838], in *Senate Executive Documents*, Number 38, 52nd Congress, 2nd session, 79–82.

35. Levi Woodbury, "Report on the Finances," 694–96.

36. Bowers, *Obsolete Paper Money*, 230.

37. There were very few exceptions at the time, one being the notes issued by the Bank of the State of Missouri, which according to Bowers were "as solid as gold." Ibid., 527.

38. John Tomlin, letter to Poe, in *The Complete Works of Edgar Allan Poe*, ed. James A. Harrison, The Virginia Edition, 17 vols. (New York: T. Y. Crowell, 1902; repr. New York: AMS Press, 1965, 1979), 17:61. At the time, Tennessee notes sold at Philadelphia at a discount of 5½ to 10 percent; Virginia notes traded at par to a discount of 2 per cent; North Carolina

notes at ¾ to 3 percent discount; and South Carolina notes from 2 per cent discount to 3 per cent premium. William Gouge, "Bank Statistics," *Hunt's Merchants' Magazine*, July 1842, 94.

39. Examples of the pervasive mix of banking and politics are documented in Bowers, *Obsolete Paper Money*, 38–40. *Hunt's Merchants' Magazine* offers a detailed list of the banks, altogether some 112, formed within a year under the General Banking Law. *Hunt's*, July 1839, 81–83.

40. Hurst, *A Legal History*, 136–37. Treasury Notes, which were backed by specie deposits and fully redeemable, were receivable in payment for duties; they superseded the necessity of using specie in settling debts with the government. The Committee report in fact responded to an initiative that had originally come from President Tyler, who in his Annual Messages of 1841 and 1842 proposed a government bank of issue, to consist of Treasury notes to the amount of $15 million. A Senate report, perhaps as a conciliatory gesture, in early 1842 recommended similar types of notes as a remedy against the lack of a "uniform currency." John Tyler, in *Presidential Messages and State Papers*, 4:1417–19, 1461–62; Senate report on the currency, in *Niles' National Register*, March 5, 1842, 9, 10.

41. Chief Justice John Marshall upheld the Bank's constitutionality, also in 1816. Howe, *What Hath God Wrought*, 144–46. For the charter proposal of 1816, see Bowers, *Obsolete Paper Money*, 141. For the "general welfare" clause, see United States Constitution, Art. 1, Section 8, §1: "The Congress shall have Power To lay and collect Taxes, Duties, Imposts and Excises, to pay the Debts and provide for the common Defence and general Welfare of the United States; but all Duties, Imposts and Excises shall be uniform throughout the United States."

42. *Niles' Weekly Register*, May 12, 1832, 198.

43. Poe, in *Essays and Reviews*, ed. G. R. Thompson (New York: Library of America, 1984), 1318.

44. Terence Whalen, *Edgar Allan Poe and the Masses: The Political Economy of Literature in Antebellum America* (Princeton, NJ: Princeton University Press, 1999), 277n26. For Poe's familiarity with commerce and economics, see ibid., 48–50.

45. Henry C. Carey, "Causes of the Unsteadiness of the Currency, and the Remedy Therefore — I," *Hunt's Merchants' Magazine*, May 1840, 372–79, here 378. As regards the importance

of political economy in the antebellum South, Michael O'Brien notes that Adam Smith's *Wealth of Nations* had been used as a college textbook from the 1790s; Thomas Drew lectured on the subject in the 1820s, as did George Tucker at the University of Virginia, where Thomas Jefferson had made political economy fundamental to the curriculum. And, not to forget, there was Henry Clay, whose "American System" essentially was what Southern political economy came to do. Michael O'Brien, *Conjectures of Order: Intellectual Life and the American South, 1810–1860*, 2 vols. (Chapel Hill: University of North Carolina Press, 2003), 2:877–937.

46. Poe, *Poetry and Tales,* 580, 579. For "millionaire," see Christopher Clark, *Social Change in America: From the Revolution Through the Civil War* (Chicago: Ivan R. Dee, 2006), 196; George Tucker, "The Increase of Wealth [in the U.S.]," *Hunt's Merchants' Magazine*, December 1843, 509–16. Poe uses "millionaire" at least twice, in an editorial miscellany for the *Broadway Journal* of October 11, 1845, and at the beginning of "The Cask of Amontillado" (1846). *Essays and Reviews*, 1081; *Poetry and Tales*, 848.

47. *Poetry and Tales*, 580, 568.

48. "The materials of which 'The Gold-Bug' is constructed are, apparently, of the simplest kind. It is the mode of grouping them around the main idea, and their absolute necessity of each to the whole [...] in which the perfection of their use consists. The solution to the whole is the most curious part of the whole, and for this, which is a splendid specimen of analysis, we refer the reader to the book." Review of *Tales*, 1845, in *Essays and Reviews*, 869–70.

49. Monika Elbert, "Poe's Gothic Mother and the Incubation of Language," *Poe Studies* 26 (1993), 23–34, quotation 26. Kenneth Silverman has used the psychoanalytic prototype of the bereaved child that is unable to mourn the loss of a parent as a heuristic model for his narrative of Poe's life: *Edgar A. Poe*, 78.

50. Marie Bonaparte, *The Life and Works of Edgar Allan Poe: A Psycho-Analytic Interpretation*, trans. John Rodker (London: Imago, 1949), 639–68. For Poe's fixation on his dead mother, see ibid., 83. It is also worth noting that "treasure" for Poe meant any precious hidden or buried things that in quite of few of his stories come back or are reclaimed — not merely in "The Gold-Bug," but also in "The Purloined Letter," "The Oblong Box," or in "Thou Art the Man," where the corpse of a murder's victim is made to

spring up from a crate, "bruised, bloody and nearly putrid." Poe, in *Poetry and Tales*, 740.

51. Nikolaus Ruhe, "'Kidding the Reader': Ein Beitrag zur Entomologie von 'The Gold-Bug,'" *Amerikastudien/American Studies* 40 (1995), 593–617.

52. Poe also avoided any semblance of the local or regional. When in 1843 he changed the title of his proposed magazine from *The Penn Magazine* to *The Stylus*, his explanation for the modification was that *Penn Magazine* "was a name somewhat too local in its suggestions." Poe, "Prospectus of *The Stylus*," in *Essays and Reviews*, 1033.

53. Reference to "potential capital" is to Whalen's discussion of Poe's "Murder in the Rue Morgue," in *Poe and the Masses*, 240.

54. *Poetry and Tales*, 560–61. Reference to the "worshippers of Mammon" is to "The Philosophy of Furniture," ibid., 384.

55. Ibid., 560. Thomas Ollive Mabbott has found that "Le Grand is the name of a Huguenot family once represented in Charleston. Poe may have known of a Baltimore orator, John C. Legrand, who became a judge, and there was a seventeenth-century French natural historian named Antoine Legrand," Mabbott, in *The Collected Works of Edgar Allan Poe*, vol. 3, *Tales and Sketches*, ed. Thomas Ollive Mabbott with the assistance of Eleanor D. Kewer and Maureen C. Mabbott (Cambridge:: Belknap Press of Harvard University Press, 1978), 854n1.

56. Doty, *America's Money*, 115; Veronika Timpe, "Beyond Face Value: Images of Slaves on Nineteenth-Century American Currency," in *Almighty Dollar: Papers and Lectures from the Velden Conference*, ed. Heinz Tschachler, Eugen Banauch, and Simone Puff (Vienna-Münster: LIT Verlag, 2010), 63–79, here 67–77.

57. Poe, review of Joseph Holt Ingraham, *The South-West: By a Yankee*, *Southern Literary Messenger*, January 1836, 122.

58. Whalen, *Poe and the Masses*, 112–46; and see below, chapter 3, 88.

59. Review of *Tales*, 1845, in *Essays and Reviews*, 869.

60. Poe, in *Poetry and Tales*, 561.

61. Indeed, in all of Poe's writings, there are very few references to slavery, and many of these, Terence Whalen points out, "are made in the context of a broader assault on a literary enemy who is 'vulnerable' for having abolitionist tendencies (e.g., Longfellow)." *Poe and the Masses*, 307n62.

62. Ibid., 141–42.

63. John Allan had come to the U.S. in 1795. In 1804 he took the naturalization oath before Chief Justice John Marshall. Arthur Hobson Quinn, *Edgar Allan Poe: A Critical Biography* (New York: Appleton-Century-Crofts, 1941; repr. Baltimore: Johns Hopkins University Press, 1998), 51.

64. Needless to say, these industries also exploited slave labor, on occasion even firing white workers to replace them with slaves. Howe, *What Hath God Wrought*, 550.

65. For the Christian tradition, see 1 Timothy 3:3. For a Freudian reading see Marie Bonaparte, who consequently identifies the gold bug as "*Dukatenscheisser*," *The Life and Works of Edgar Allan Poe*, 353–69.

66. Poe to Frederick William Thomas, July 4, 1841, in *The Collected Letters of Edgar Allan Poe*, 2 vols., originally ed. by John Ward Ostrom, 3d ed., rev., corr., and exp. by Burton R. Pollin and Jeffrey A. Savoye (Staten Island: Gordian Press, 2008), 1:292.

67. Robinson's lithograph was published in July 1837. I have also drawn in this paragraph on Arthur M. Schlesinger, Jr., *The Age of Jackson* (Boston: Little, Brown, 1945), 217–26; Howe, *What Hath God Wrought*, 501–24; and Bowers, *Obsolete Paper Money*, 221–26.

68. Poe, letter to Thomas H. Chivers, September 27, 1842, in *Letters*, 1:364.

69. One of the magazines that were forced to cease payment for contributions was *Burton's Gentleman's Magazine*, with which Poe was closely associated. Dwight R. Thomas, "Poe in Philadelphia, 1838–1844: A Documentary Record," PhD diss., University of Pennsylvania, 1978, 87.

70. Mabbott, "Annals," in *Collected Works*, 1:548, and Poe, in *Letters*, 1:175–77.

71. Poe, "Ligeia," 1838, in *Poetry and Tales*, 262–77, quotations 268–69; Poe later published the poem separately as "The Conqueror Worm." Ibid., 77–79. On the poem's social significance, see below, chapter 3, 93.

72. Poe, "The Fall of the House of Usher," 1839, in *Poetry and Tales*, 317–36, quotations 325, 327, 322; for the poem as a separate piece, see ibid., 76–77, and below, chapter 3, 93; for Poe's intention to imply, in the poem, "a mind haunted by phantoms — a disordered brain," see his letter to Rufus W. Griswold, in *Letters*, 1:272. The notion of the poem representing a disordered mind has been adopted by Richard Wilbur, "Introduction," *Poe*, ed. Richard Wilbur (New York:

Dell, 1959), 7–39; generally on Poe's interest in the metaphysics of mental disturbances, see Elizabeth Phillips, *Edgar Allan Poe: An American Imagination. Three Essays* (Pt. Washington, NY: Kennikat Press, 1979), 140.

73. Poe, "The Colloquy of Monos and Una," in *Poetry and Tales*, 449–57, quotation 453. Already in "The Conversation of Eiros and Charmion," which dates from 1839, the world comes to an end in a conflagration, though Poe does not in that tale make a connection to politics. Ibid., 363. See below, chapter 5, 152–53.

74. Poe, "Mellonta Tauta," in *Poetry and Tales*, 871–85, quotation 880; and see below, chapter 3, 84–87; for "Mellonta Tauta" and for "Some Words with a Mummy," see below, chapter 5, 153.

75. Poe, "A Descent into the Maelström," in *Poetry and Tales*, 432–48, quotations 438, 445, emphases added. For a reading of the tale as an archetypal sea voyage that leaves the survivor a prophet, whose task is "ever to lead others to the truth revealed to them," see Margaret J. Yonce, "The Spiritual Descent into the Maelström: A Debt to 'The Rime of the Ancient Mariner,'" *Poe Newsletter* 2, no. 2 (April 1969), 26–29, http://www.eapoe.org/pstudies/ps1960/p1969202.htm, quotation 26.

76. Poe, "Eleonora," in *Poetry and Tales*, 468–73, quotation 473. For the publication of the piece in the *Madisonian*, see below, chapter 3, 100 and 108.

77. Poe, letter to Joseph Evans Snodgrass, April 1, 1841, in *Letters*, 1:264. The letter continues with Poe's mentioning that he had accepted an offer at *Graham's Magazine* and, on a note of optimism, that the "*Penn* project will unquestionably be resumed hereafter." A similar letter, also dated April 1, 1841, went to Thomas Wyatt; Poe also blames the ill fate of the *Penn* magazine on the "breaking up of the banks" in his letter to John P. Kennedy of June 21, 1841. Ibid., 1:266–67; 277–79. Other references in this paragraph are to Thomas, "Poe in Philadelphia," 134–77 (passim), 183–184, 195–196.

78. Robert Remini, *Andrew Jackson and the Bank War* (New York: W. W. Norton, 1967), 123.

79. Bowers, *Obsolete Paper Money*, 155–56.

80. Ibid., 45. For the "Anti-Chartered Monopoly Association," see William M. Gouge, *Journal of Banking* (Philadelphia, July 1841–July 1842; repr. London: Routledge/Thoemmes Press, 1996), 106.

81. Silverman, *Edgar A. Poe*, 185; Thomas, "Poe in Philadelphia," 193. Poe expresses his wish to declare himself bankrupt in a letter to James Herron in early June 1842: "My only hope is the 'Bankrupt Act,' of which I shall avail myself as soon as possible." Poe, in *Letters*, 1:336. Poe filed for bankruptcy on December 19, 1842, and it was granted on January 13, 1843.

82. Poe, in *Poetry and Tales*, 570.

83. Poe, "The Philosophy of Composition," in *Essays and Reviews*, 21; originally in *Graham's Magazine* of April 1846.

84. Elizabeth Phillips, *Edgar Allan Poe: An American Imagination. Three Essays* (Pt. Washington, NY: Kennikat Press, 1979), 60. In a review of Poe's *Works*, published in the *American Whig Review* of March 1850, George Washington Peck describes the passages from "The Gold-Bug" as "a Salvator Rosa-like landscape." Peck, in *Edgar Allan Poe: The Critical Heritage*, ed. Ian Walker (London: Routledge, 1986; repr. 1997), 345. William Gilmore Simms, in an editorial review of the *Tales*, in the *Southern and Western Magazine and Review* of December 22, 1845, commented that every Charlestonian who reads "The Gold-Bug" for "geographical peculiarities" must be "revolted when required to believe in the rocks and highlands in and about Sullivan's Island." Simms, in *The Critical Heritage*, 201.

85. Poe, unfinished notes for the Introduction to the planned book, in *Collected Works*, 1:189; the quotation according to Mabbott is from the original manuscript of 1846 to 1848, now in the Pierpont Morgan library in New York.

86. Bonaparte, *The Life and Works of Edgar Allan Poe*, 639–68.

87. Poe, in *Poetry and Tales*, 578.

88. William James, *The Principles of Psychology*, 1890; repr. with an Introduction by George A. Miller (Cambridge: Harvard University Press, 1983), 1271.

89. Poe, in *Poetry and Tales*, 578.

90. Charles Baudelaire in 1856 pointed out that all of the coins are being catalogued, which the happy finders undertake with almost scientific rigor. Baudelaire, "Edgar Allan Poe: His Life and Works," in *Edgar Allan Poe: The Critical Heritage*, ed. Ian Walker (London: Routledge, 1986; repr. 1997), 403–12, here 407. References to "The Gold-Bug" are to *Poetry and Tales*, 579, 586. A further development of the unused treasure motif can be seen in "The Cask of Amontillado" (1846): as Daniel Hoffman has pointed out, when Montresor leads his victim, Fortunato into the farthest

vaults of the family's wine-cellar, he as it were conducts his own treasure, his own fortune back down into the bowels of the earth, the maternal womb. Hoffman, *Poe, Poe, Poe, Poe, Poe, Poe, Poe* (Garden City, NY: Doubleday-Anchor Press, 1973), 218–21.

91. Poe, letter to Charles W. Thomson, June 28, 1840, in *Letters*, 1:232.

92. William Whipple, "Poe's Political Satire," *Texas Studies in English* 35 (1956), 81–95; Christopher J. Forbes, "Satire of Irving's *A History of New York* in Poe's 'The Devil in the Belfry,'" *Studies in American Fiction* 10 (1982): 93–100; J. A. Leo Lemay, "Poe's 'The Business Man': Its Contexts and Satire of Franklin's *Autobiography*," *Poe Studies* 15 (1982): 29–37.

93. Yonce, "The Spiritual Descent into the Maelström"; Richard D. Finbolt, "The Vision at the Brink of the Abyss: 'A Descent into the Maelstrom' in the Light of Poe's Cosmology," *Georgia Review* 27 (1973): 356–366; Robert E. Seaman, "Lacan, Poe, and the Descent of the Self," *Texas Studies in Language and Literature* 31 (1989): 196–214.

94. Kent P. Ljungquist, *The Grand and the Fair: Poe's Landscape Aesthetics and Pictorial Techniques* (Potomac, MD: Scripta Humanistica, 1984), especially 17–52; Jochen Achilles, "Edgar Allan Poe's Dreamscapes and the Transcendentalist View of Nature," *Amerikastudien/American Studies* 40 (1995): 553–573.

95. Poe, "The Rationale of Verse," *Southern Literary* Messenger, October–November 1848, in *Essays and Reviews*, 27; reference to "palpable places" and "huge abysses" is to *Poetry and Tales*, 13.

96. Whipple, "Poe's Political Satire"; Burton R. Pollin, "Politics and History in Poe's 'Mellonta Tauta': Two Allusions Explained," *Studies in Short Fiction* 8 (1971): 627–31.

97. D. H. Lawrence, *Studies in Classic American Literature* (1923; New York: Penguin, 1977), 86. Reference to "one of the most popular stories in the world" is to *Collected Works*, 3:799.

98. W. K. Wimsatt, Jr., "What Poe Knew about Cryptography," *PMLA* 58 (September 1943): 754–79, here 778–79.

99. *Graham's Magazine*, September 1845, in *The Critical Heritage*, 191.

100. The London *Literary Gazette*, January 31, 1846, ibid., 203.

101. *The Critic*, September 6, 1845, ibid., 184.

102. Griswold, in *Poe in His Own*

Time: A Biographical Chronicle of His Life, Drawn from Recollections, Interviews, and Memoirs by Family, Friends, and Associates, ed. Benjamin F. Fisher (Iowa City: University of Iowa Press, 2010), 122.

103. "I have solved others of an abstruseness ten thousand times greater." Poe, in *Poetry and Tales*, 587.

104. Richard Hull, "Puns in 'The Gold-Bug': You Gotta be Kidding," *Arizona Quarterly* 58, no. 2 (Summer 2002): 1–18, here 4.

105. *Poetry and Tales*, 568.

106. On the distinction of accidental from necessary relationships as a major theoretical problem in "The Gold-Bug," as in most detective fiction, see Marc Shell, "The Gold-Bug: Introduction to 'The Industry of Letters' in America," in *Money, Language, and Thought: Literary and Philosophic Economies from the Medieval to the Modern Era* (Baltimore: Johns Hopkins University Press, 1982), 5–23, here 17.

107. J. O. Bailey, quoted in J. Woodrow Hassell, Jr., "The Problem of Realism in 'The Gold-Bug,'" *American Literature* 25 (May 1953): 179–92, here 192.

108. Barton Levi St. Armand, "Poe's 'Sober Mystification': The Uses of Alchemy in 'The Gold-Bug,'" *Poe Studies* 4, no. 1 (June 1971): 1–7, here 4, col. 2; 2, cols. 1 and 2.

109. Ibid., 3, cols. 1 and 2.

110. Ibid., col. 2; 5, col. 1.

111. Jean Ricardou, "Gold in the Bug," *Poe Studies* 9, no. 2 (June 1976): 33–39. Similar points have been made respectively by Mark M. Hennelley, Jr., and Michael Williams. Hennelley argues that Legrand, "a mask for Poe, assumes his rightful role as Narrator" only in the second part of the tale, teaching the reader, and the first narrator, too, how to best analyze the apparent mystery. "Le Grand Captain Kidder and His Bogus Bug," *Studies in Short Fiction* 17 (1980): 77–79, here 77. Quite similarly, Williams sees Legrand as the only one who "can make accommodations that new circumstances require, an ability that is tested to the full by the cipher." "'The *language* of the cipher': Interpretation in 'The Gold-Bug," *American Literature* 53, no. 4 (January 1982): 646–60, here 653.

112. James W. Mathews, "Legrand's Golden Vision: Meaning in 'The Gold Bug,'" *CEA Critic: An Official Journal of the College English Association* 53 (College Station, TX, 1991): 23–29, here 24.

113. Ibid., 25; reference to Scripture is to Matthew 13:44.

114. Mathews, "Legrand's Golden Vision," 27, 28; reference to the narrator as the only one to be trusted is to *Poetry and Tales*, 569.

115. Hoffman, *Poe, Poe, Poe, Poe, Poe, Poe, Poe*, 123, 124.

116. Daniel Kempton, "The Gold/Goole/Ghoul Bug," *ESQ* (*Emerson Society Quarterly*), 33, no. 1 (1987): 1–19, here 3, 6–7.

117. See, *inter alia*, Jeffrey Meyers, *Edgar Allan Poe: His Life and Legacy* (New York: Scribner's, 1992; repr. New York: Cooper Square Press, 2000), 135–37, and, most recently, Richard Kopley, who relates the form of "The Gold-Bug" to that of the Dupin tales: "'Scrutinizing the Parchment More Closely': The Form of 'The Gold-Bug' and Its Relation to That of the Dupin Tales," paper given to the 126th MLA Convention, Los Angeles, January 7, 2011.

118. Poe, "Ligeia," in *Poetry and Tales*, 268. For a more recent example of the "Madness and more of Sin, and Horror" school of critical thought, see *El Genio de lo Perverso: Ensayos del Coloquio en Conmemoración del Bicentenario del Nacimiento de Edgar Allan Poe*, compilación de Ana Elena González Treviño (México DF: Samsara Editorial, 2011).

119. Larzer Ziff, *Literary Democracy: The Declaration of Cultural Independence in America* (New York: Viking, 1981), 67, emphasis added.

120. Poe, "Loss of Breath," in *Collected Works*, 2:69.

121. Poe, in *Letters*, 1:364.

122. Whalen, *Poe and the Masses*, 9.

123. Eric P. Newman, *The Early Paper Money of America*, 4th ed. (Iola, WI: Krause, 1997), 139–49; for illustrations of rattlesnake bills, see 40 and 145, and Bowers, *Obsolete Paper Money*, 17.

124. Poe, letter to William E. Burton, June 1, 1840, in *Letters*, 1:218. On John Allan as a possible source, see Eric W. Carlson, *Introduction to Poe: A Thematic Reader* (Glenview, IL: Scott, Foresman, 1967), 573; assuming that Poe indeed had the motto from Allan, the allusion would constitute a final personal element of the story in its revenge aspect. Edward Craney Jacobs, in contrast, claims that Poe borrowed the motto from John Fenimore Cooper, who used it in chapter 16 of *The Last of the Mohicans*: "Marginalia — A Possible Debt to Cooper," *Poe Studies*, 8, no. 1 (June 1976), 23. On the historic origin of the motto, see Ian J. Gentles, "The Iconography of Revolution: England 1642–1649," in *Soldiers, Writers and Statesmen of the English Revolution*, ed. Ian J. Gentles, John Stephen Morrill, and Blair Worden (Cambridge: Cambridge University Press, 1998), 91–113, here 100.

125. Whalen, *Poe and the Masses*, 22–23. One of Poe's earliest poems, written probably around 1825, portrays a young clerk in a dry-goods store. The poem, which is after Cicero, is titled "Oh, Tempora! Oh, Mores!" In *Poetry and Tales*, 21–23. The earliest known lines of poetry by Poe, probably from 1819, were written on a sheet of paper covered by John Allan's figures dealing with his precarious financial situation. Hervey Allen, *Israfel: The Life and Times of Edgar Allan Poe* (New York: Rinehart, 1949), 83–85; for an illustration, see ibid., between 44 and 45.

126. Whalen, *Poe and the Masses*, 23.

127. Poe, "The Business Man," in *Poetry and Tales*, 373. For the view that Poe with this tale took his revenge on Allan, who was long dead at the time, see Hervey Allen, *Israfel*, 159–60.

128. Poe, "How to Write a Blackwood Article," in *Poetry and Tales*, 278–97, quotations 280, 283, 284. The piece is not merely a bitter satire of magazine publishing. The fact that the editor offers merely a most "paltry" sum for Signora Zenobia's contribution (ibid., 280) also points to the general devaluation of writing in the aftermath of the panic of 1837. Not only did poetry become "unsaleable," but magazine publishers also discontinued paying for contributions. Poe himself became desperate, writing to James Kirke Paulding that he "could not possibly live by literary labor" alone. *Letters*, 1:364 and 175–77. See above, 61.

129. The table is reprinted in *The Collected Writings of Edgar Allan Poe*, ed. Burton Pollin, 5 vols. (Boston: Twayne, 1981; New York: Gordian Press, 1985), 3:353. Poe's remarks on Freeman Hunt and his journal, which receives praise for its "subscribers and regular contributors" being "among the most intelligent and influential in America," appeared in *Godey's Lady's Book* in June 1846. Poe, in *Essays and Reviews*, 1147–49, quotation 1148. The year before, Hunt had favorably reviewed Poe's *Tales* in the August issue of his magazine, writing that the volume contains "fine specimens of the genius of that author, who takes so high a stand among our American fiction writers and poets. A glance at some of the tales convinces us that Mr. Poe's exuberance of fancy displays itself in these, as in his previous writings." *Hunt's Merchants' Magazine*, August 1845, 205.

130. This cursory list covers the period from the first issue of July 1839 through December 1845. Reference to the "party-ridden house of Congress" is to Adams's review, *Hunt's Merchant Magazine*, August 1839, 124; reference to Tucker is to "The Currency," May 1842, 433–39; reference to Webster is to "Banking in the United States," November 1844, 437; reference to "national paper currency" is to J. Louis Tellkampf, "The Currency [I]," January 1842, 65–71; reference to "convenient national currency" is to John C. Crocheron, "The Currency," January 1844, 63.

131. Reference to the "kernel of an idea" is to Jeffrey A. Savoye, "Reconstructing Poe's 'The Gold-Bug': An Examination of the Composition and First Printing(s)," *The Edgar Allan Poe Review* 8, no. 2 (2007): 34–48, here 39.

132. John Allan, letter to General John H. Cocke, February 3, 1817, quoted in Whalen, *Poe and the Masses*, 22.

133. Shell, *Money, Language, and Thought*, 10.

134. Legrand's classifications extend beyond entomology to conchology, botany, and even numismatics, as when the narrator calls coins "specimens" hitherto unseen. *Poetry and Tales*, 579.

135. *Poetry and Tales*, 595.

136. *OED*, s.v. "humbug"; Shell, *Money, Language, and Thought*, 10–11.

137. For the idea that Legrand, bitten by the gold bug, *is* insane, see Hull, "Puns in 'The Gold-Bug,'" 14–15. Armand considers Legrand's "madness" as typical of all "alchemists in their quest for riches, whether sacred or profane." "Poe's 'Sober Mystification,'" 3. On the usage of the noun "bug" as a slang term for "madman," see ibid., 6, col. 1.

138. Shell, *Money, Language, and Thought*, 12.

139. "D," quoted ibid., 12–13. "D" was Francis H. Duffee, a minor Philadelphia journalist and playwright, who may have had his own axe to grind when he produced this utterly caustic innuendo. Duffee's action, which accused Poe of colluding with *Dollar Newspaper* in the prize contest, led Poe to initiate legal proceedings against Duffee, who eventually published a retraction. Thomas, "Poe in Philadelphia," 577–79, 582–83.

140. Shell, *Money, Language, and Thought*, 13; below, chapter 3, 86.

141. The earliest known date of Poe's being in Philadelphia is July 19, 1838, in *Letters*, 1:175.

142. Silverman, *Edgar A. Poe*, 130–

32. Silverman describes *Pym* as "a book largely about hunger," reflective of Poe's long familiarity with pecuniary want, which remained a fact of his life even after Poe had published the novella. Ibid., 136, 137. Reference to *The Narrative of Arthur Gordon Pym* is to *Poetry and Tales*, 1009.

143. Silverman, *Edgar A. Poe*, 140.

144. Shell, *Money, Language, and Thought*, 13. Poe had used the term in this sense as early as 1831, in "The Cat's Tail," as see *OED*, s.v. "humbug."

145. George Wood, "The Currency," *Hunt's Merchants' Magazine*, April 1841, 317–33, here 320, 317, 319, 322.

146. Shell, *Money, Language, and Thought*, 14.

147. Wood, "The Currency," 317.

148. Shell, *Money, Language, and Thought*, 10, emphasis added.

149. *Poetry and Tales*, 579.

Chapter 2

1. Review of *Tales*, in *Essays and Reviews*, ed. G. R. Thompson (New York: Library of America, 1984), 869. Thompson notes that the review "was almost certainly written by Poe" (ibid., 1502n). Thompson's view is shared, *inter alia*, by Terence Whalen and Ian Walker. *Edgar Allan Poe and the Masses: The Political Economy of Literature in Antebellum America* (Princeton, NJ: Princeton University Press, 1999), 197; *Edgar Allan Poe: The Critical Heritage*, ed. Ian Walker (London: Routledge, 1986; repr. 1997), 192. I am here following Thomas Ollive Mabbott, who attributes the review to Thomas Dunn English, the editor of the *Aristidean*. *The Collected Works of Edgar Allan Poe*, vols. 2 and 3, *Tales and Sketches*, ed. Thomas Ollive Mabbott with the assistance of Eleanor D. Kewer and Maureen C. Mabbott (Cambridge: Belknap Press of Harvard University Press, 1978), 2:395.

2. Poe, in *Essays and Reviews*, 349. Poe's review article originally appeared in *Graham's Magazine* for November 1841.

3. The reply is presumed to be by the paper's editor, Joseph Sailer, in *The Collected Works of Edgar Allan Poe*, 3:802. Reference to Baudelaire is to *The Critical Heritage*, 407. Reference to "money-seekers" is to "The Gold-Bug," in *Poetry and Tales*, ed. Patrick Quinn (New York: Library of America, 1984), 585–86.

4. English, in *Essays and Reviews*, 869.

5. J. Gerald Kennedy, who reads Poe back into the fascination with death that evolved during the early nineteenth century, thus argues that the communication of the buried secret is possible only through death. *Poe, Death, and the Life of Writing* (New Haven: Yale University Press, 1987), 195–97.

6. Barton Levi St. Armand, "Poe's 'Sober Mystification': The Uses of Alchemy in 'The Gold-Bug,'" *Poe Studies* 4, no. 1 (June 1971): 1–7, here 3, col. 2; 7n15.

7. Poe, "The Gold-Bug," in *Poetry and Tales*, 579.

8. In terms of economics, a store of value may be useful for the individual, though its problems are instantly evident if we assume that every member of a society stores up their money and retires to an island. In such a case, the amount of the currency is diminished, and prices in general will fall. Everybody will starve for lack of current production. Henry C. Carey, discussing the causes of the unsteadiness of the currency, in 1840 put the matter as follows: "the smaller the tendency to hoarding money [...] the less will be the tendency to variation in the amount of the currency from diminution that is liable to be followed by expansion." Carey, "Causes of the Unsteadiness of the Currency, and the Remedy Therefore — II," *Hunt's Merchants' Magazine*, June 1840, 450–64, here 453. As regards the Never-Never Land, Poe seems to have perfected what Washington Irving invented in "Rip van Winkle" and what Michael Warner aptly calls "pirate time": "Pirates in their fictional modality are permanently Jacobean, hoarding doubloons that never seem to circulate, in a temporality so alien to history that it eventually had to be declared a separate place: Never-Never Land." Michael Warner, "Irving's Posterity," *ELH* 67 (2000), 773–99, here 798n46.

9. Carey, "Causes of the Unsteadiness of the Currency — II," 450.

10. Ralph Waldo Emerson, "Wealth," in *The Collected Works of Ralph Waldo Emerson*, ed. Alfred A. Ferguson (Cambridge: Belknap Press of Harvard University Press, 1971), 6:54, 55. "Wealth" originally was part of a series of lectures Emerson gave in March 1851 to the Young Men's Mercantile Library Association in Pittsburgh. He included it in *The Conduct of Life* of 1860.

11. As William Gouge wrote in July 1841, specie money is not "merely the representative of property [...] Money of gold and silver *is* property — is *wealth*." *Journal of Banking*

(Philadelphia, July 1841–July 1842; repr. London: Routledge/Thoemmes Press, 1996), 29.

12. Sir Philip Sidney, *A Defence of Poetry*, ed. Jan van Dorsten (Oxford: Oxford University Press, 1966; 1975), 23.

13. Poe, "The Poetic Principle," in *Essays and Reviews*, 92; often delivered as a lecture during the last years of his life, "The Poetic Principle" was published after Poe's death in the *Home Journal* of August 31, 1850, and in *Sartain's Union Magazine* of October 1850.

14. Armand, "Poe's 'Sober Mystification,'" 5. References to Poe as a dreamer respectively are to Francis Gerry Fairfield and "Ludwig" [Rufus Wilmot Griswold], in *Poe in His Own Time: A Biographical Chronicle of His Life, Drawn from Recollections, Interviews, and Memoirs by Family, Friends, and Associates*, ed. Benjamin F. Fisher (Iowa City: University of Iowa Press, 2010), 277, 77. Reference to Poe's reckless and wild imagination is to Nathaniel Parker Willis's estimate of Poe from March 1850 regarding "Eureka," ibid., 170.

15. Marc Shell, "The Gold-Bug: Introduction to 'The Industry of Letters' in America," in *Money, Language, and Thought: Literary and Philosophic Economies from the Medieval to the Modern Era* (Baltimore: Johns Hopkins University Press, 1982), 5–23, here 14. Reference to the intellectual glow-worm is to a passage in which Legrand is made to say, "there seemed to glimmer, faintly within the most remote and secret chambers of my intellect, a glow-worm-like conception of that truth which [the unearthing of gold] brought so magnificent a demonstration." Poe, "The Gold-Bug," in *Poetry and Tales*, 582.

16. Johann Wolfgang von Goethe, *Faust. Part Two*, First Act, "Pleasure Garden. Morning Sun," trans. Walter Arndt, ed. Cyrus Hamlin, Norton Critical Edition, 2d ed. (New York: W. W. Norton, 2000), 177. As regards the *Scarabaeus* beetle, Thomas Ollive Mabbott claims that Poe "undoubtedly knew of them as symbols of life." Poe, in *Collected Works*, 3:845.

17. Gouge, *Journal of Banking*, 181. The poem, which is titled "The Wall Street Chorus," originally appeared in the *New York Era*.

18. In *Politics*, Aristotle contrasts *oikos* (household management), in which everything is directed towards keeping self and family alive and healthy, with *chrematistos*, that is to say, with the accumulation of money for its own sake: "There are two sorts of wealth-getting, as I have said; one is a part of household management, the other is retail trade: the former necessary and honorable, while that which exists in exchange is justly censured; for it is unnatural, and a mode by which men gain from one another. The most hated sort, and with the greatest reason, is usury, which makes a gain out of money itself, and not from the natural object of it. For money was intended to be used in exchange, but not to increase at interest. And this term interest, which means the birth of money from money, is applied to the breeding of money because the offspring resembles the parent. Wherefore of all modes of getting wealth this is the most unnatural." Aristotle, *Politics*, trans. Benjamin Jowett (New York: Modern Library, 1943), 71.

19. Daniel Defoe, *The Chimera; or, The French Way of Paying National Debts Laid Open* (London: T. Warner, 1720), 5–6. John Kenneth Galbraith discusses Law's paper money scheme in *Money: Whence It Came, Where It Went* (Boston: Houghton Mifflin, 1975), 22–27. Law's scheme has been famously retold in Washington Irving's sketch "The Great Mississippi Bubble," written at the height of the financial depression following the panic of 1837; it also caught the attention of Francis Wharton, who published a lengthy article on "The Mississippi Scheme" in *Hunt's Merchants' Magazine*, July 1841, 9–26.

20. Alexander Pope, *Epistle to Allen, Lord Bathurst. Epistles to Several Persons (Moral Essays)*, ed. F. W. Bateson, The Twickenham Edition (London: Methuen, 1951), 144.

21. Ebenezer Cooke, *Sot-Weed Redivivus: or, the Planter's Looking-Glass*, in *Early Maryland Poetry: The Works of Ebenezer Cooke, Gent.* (Baltimore: Maryland Historical Society-John Murphy, 1900), 33–50, here 37, 39. Kevin McLaughlin, "Just Fooling: Paper, Money, Poe," *Differences: A Journal of Feminist Cultural Studies* 11, no. 1 (Spring 1999): 38–67, here 47.

22. John Wise, "Massachusetts-Bay in New England," in *Colonial Currency Reprints, 1680–1751*, ed. Andrew McFarland Davis, 4 vols. (Boston: Prince Society, 1911; repr. New York: Augustus M. Kelley, 1964), 1:162–223, here 209.

23. Franklin, "A Modest Enquiry," in *Documentary History of Banking and Currency in the United States*, ed. Herman E. Krooss, 4 vols. (1969; New York: Chelsea House, 1983), 1:11–22.

24. Franklin, "Remarks on the Report published in our last [*Pennsylvania*] *Chronicle*," London, March 11, 1767, *The Papers of Benjamin Franklin*, http://franklinpapers.org/franklin/framedVolumes.jsp?vol=14&page=076a. What Franklin did not say was that the development of paper money alongside credit took place in an inherently unstable signifying structure. The principal reason was that the main investment outlet was not land so much as land *speculation*. This, John M. Kleeberg found, "meant high indebtedness, meager cash flow, and frequent financial catastrophes." "Introduction," *Money of Pre-Federal America*, ed. John M. Kleeberg, Coinage of the Americas Conference Proceedings, Number 7 (New York: American Numismatic Society, 1992), ix–xi, here ix. Harvests in particular were a problem, as they "always put unusual strains on the financial system, often leading to collapse: this is why stock market crashes occur in October" (ibid.).

25. On the legality of the Continentals, see James Willard Hurst, *A Legal History of Money in the United States, 1794–1970* (1973; Frederick, MD: Beard Books, 2001), 5–6. For a detailed schedule of their depreciation, see Q. David Bowers, *Obsolete Paper Money Issued by Banks in the United States, 1782–1866* (Atlanta: Whitman, 2006), 20. Notes issued by individual states likewise were caught up in a downward spiral, though apparently this was noticed less than the fate of the Continentals.

26. The "*Bank mania*," Jefferson warned, was "one of the most threatening of these imitations: it is raising up a moneyed aristocracy in our country which has already set the government at defiance [...]." Thomas Jefferson, in Gouge, *Journal of Banking*, 14.

27. Charles Francis Adams, "The Theory of Money and Banks," *Hunt's Merchants' Magazine*, August 1839, 109–24, here 110.

28. Gouge, *Journal of Banking*, 294.

29. William Leggett, commentary in the *Evening Post*, August 6, 1834, in *A Collection of the Political Writings of William Leggett*, ed. and intro. Theodore Sedgwick, Jr., 2 vols. (New York: Taylor & Dodd, 1840), 1:45.

30. Bowers, *Obsolete Paper Money*, 270. William Gouge, in his *Journal of Banking* likewise took note, adding reports of riots in Louisville, Kentucky, and New Orleans (232, 248, 390–391, 403). Other references to fraudulent banking practices in this paragraph and the following two paragraphs are to Bowers, *Obsolete Paper Money*, 229, 246, 558, 226–27, 242, 344–47, 363–64; for a compre-

hensive account of such practices, see ibid., chapter 13, "Wildcats and Quasi-Banks," 227–61.

31. Alpheus Felch, "Early Banks and Banking in Michigan" [1838], in *Senate Executive Documents*, Number 38, 52nd Congress, 2nd session, 79–82.

32. For the origin of the term "carpetbagger" from the realm of banking, see Dillistin, *Bank Note Reporters and Counterfeit Detectors*, 63–65, and Bowers, *Obsolete Paper Money*, 226.

33. *Niles' Weekly Register*, October 1, 1836, 80. For contemporaries at least, Niles's allusion to the Bible would not have been lost: "For the love of money is the root of all evil: which while some coveted after, they have erred from the faith, and pierced themselves through with many sorrows" (1 Timothy 6). The passage, which in the Latin original reads as *Radix malorum est cupiditas*, is often misquoted as "*money* is the root of all evil," though this is rather to take the neutral instrument for the devil himself.

34. Poe, "Fifty Suggestions," no. 21, *Graham's Magazine*, May–June 1849, in *Essays and Reviews*, 1300. Reference is to "The Cock" (sometimes called "The Dream") by the Greek satiric writer Lucian of Samosata, in which the cock, speaking to himself as a sovereign, says, "I was like those colossal statues [...] they too look extremely well from outside [...] but take a peep inside, and what have we? [...] everything unsightly ..." *The Works of Lucian of Samosata*, trans. H. W. Fowler and F. G. Fowler, 4 vols. (Oxford: Clarendon Press, 1905), 3:105–26, quotation 121.

35. Bowers, *Obsolete Paper Money*, 85.

36. George Wood, "The Currency," *Hunt's Merchants' Magazine*, April 1841, 317–33, here 321.

37. Raguet had begun as a merchant; ruined by the panic of 1819, he turned into one of the fiercest critics of the paper money system. His death, in March 1842, was duly noted by William Gouge in the *Journal of Banking*, 309–10.

38. *Poetry and Tales*, 580. The question is quite explicit in Hawthorne's "The Seven Vagabonds" when the narrator gives a beggar a five-dollar bill, saying that "it is a bill from the Suffolk Bank ... and better than the specie." Nathaniel Hawthorne, *Tales and Sketches*, ed. Roy Harvey Pearce (New York: Library of America, 1982), 147. In the narrative, which was written in 1832 and included in *Twice-Told Tales* in 1837, the beggar deposits the bill in his

leather bag. To the narrator's astonishment the bag contains "a very comfortable treasure of silver coins, of all sorts and sizes, and I even fancied that I saw, gleaming among them, the golden plumage of that rare bird in our currency, the American Eagle. In this precious heap was my bank note deposited, the rate of exchange being considerably against me" (Ibid.).

39. Poe, review of Rufus Wilmot Griswold's *The Poets and Poetry of America*, *The Boston Miscellany*, November 1842, 218–221, in *Essays and Reviews*, 549.

40. Poe uses "foolscap" in the sense of writing-paper in his review of Augustus Baldwin Longstreet's *Georgia Scenes, Southern Literary Messenger*, August 1836, in *Essays and Reviews*, 778–96, here 787.

41. For instance, the eponymous protagonist in Hawthorne's "Peter Goldthwaite's Treasure" (1838) at the end of his treasure hunt finds a hoard of "parchment pennies" from the colonial era. Another of Hawthorne's paper-money fables, "My Kinsman, Major Molineux" (1832), contains several references to a "parchment three-penny." *Tales and Sketches*, 541, 69, 71, 73. For a reading of Hawthorne's tales as attempts to enter into and historicize the debates over America's money, see Andrew Loman, "'More Than a Parchment Three-Pence': Crises of Value in Hawthorne's 'My Kinsman, Major Molineux,'" *PMLA* 126, no. 2 (2011): 345–62. In "The Gold-Bug," Legrand's servant, Jupiter, unwittingly adds to the deception by referring to the parchment as "paper" upon his visit to Charleston. *Poetry and Tales*, 565. Other references to "The Gold-Bug" in this paragraph to are to *Poetry and Tales*, 562, 581, 583, 584. In my attempt to identify words and phrases suggestive of the world of paper or paper money, I have also drawn on McLaughlin, "Just Fooling."

42. *Poetry and Tales*, 583, 564.

43. Ibid., 584. Parchment is the skin of a goat or sheep, prepared as a surface for writing. Vellum is of a finer kind, made from calfskin, lambskin, or kidskin. It is only when Legrand has reconceived the design of the goat on the parchment as a kid that he describes the paper as "vellum."

44. On many notes the back was blank through the middle of the nineteenth century, when back printing began to be widely used to deter counterfeits, a measure that could hardly have escaped Poe's attention.

45. *Poetry and Tales*, 595. Reference to the dollar sign is to Eric P. Newman, "The Dollar $ign: Its

Written and Printed Origins," *America's Silver Dollars*, ed. John M. Kleeberg, Coinage of the Americas Conference, Proceedings No. 9 (New York: American Numismatic Society, 1995), 1–49, here 36.

46. Shell, *Money, Language, and Thought*, 18. On purposefully incorporated "errors" as well as other anti-counterfeiting methods on paper money, see Eric P. Newman, *The Early Paper Money of America*, 4th ed. (Iola, WI: Krause, 1997), 93, and "Unusual Printing Features on Early American Paper Money," *Money of Pre-Federal America*, ed. John M. Kleeberg, Coinage of the Americas Conference, Proceedings No. 7 (New York: American Numismatic Society, 1992), 59–83.

47. *Poetry and Tales*, 584.

48. *Collected Works*, 3:832, 847n28. I thank my student Isabell Koinig for drawing my attention to this important textual variant.

49. *Poetry and Tales*, 587, emphasis added. For the 1843 version, see *Collected Works*, 3:835.

50. Rees's *Cyclopaedia* or *Universal Dictionary of the Arts, Sciences, and Literature* was edited by Abraham Rees and published by Longman, Hurst, Rees, Orme and Brown in London between 1802 and 1820. Samuel Bradford of Philadelphia published an American edition between 1806 and 1822. John Allan was a subscriber.

51. On Poe's lack of experience with invisible inks, see W.K. Wimsatt, Jr., "What Poe Knew about Cryptography," *PMLA* 58 (September 1943): 754–79, here 775n98; and J. Woodrow Hassell, Jr., "The Problem of Realism in 'The Gold-Bug,'" *American Literature* 25 (May 1953): 179–92, here 181. The *Oxford English Dictionary* defines "zaffre" (a. spelt zaffer) as an impure oxide of cobalt, obtained by roasting cobalt-ore, and used in the preparation of smalt (a species of glass, usually of a deep blue) and as a blue coloring-matter (cobalt blue) for pottery, glass, etc. The word was adopted into the English language in the late seventeenth century. "Regulus" is a chemical term referring either to the purer or metallic part of a mineral (in this case, cobalt) or, in a later sense, to a product of the smelting of various ores (thus to metal in a still impure state). *Aqua regia* is a mixture of nitric and hydrochloric acids. Geber (Abu Musa Jabir in Arabic) first isolated it in the eighth century in present-day Iraq; see Georges C. Anawati, "Arabic Alchemy," in *The Encyclopaedia of the History of Arabic Science*, ed. Roshdi Rashed (London:

Routlegde, 1996), 1:853–902, here 868. *Aqua regia*, it is important to notice, dissolves gold. Already Paracelsus knew this, writing about the phenomenon in his early sixteenth-century treatise *Of the Nature of Things*, in which he also muses on a process that makes gold "grow in a glasse like a tree, with many wonderful boughs, and leaves." Paracelsus, quoted in Cottie Arthur Burland, *The Arts of the Alchemists* (London: Weidenfeld & Nicolson, 1967; repr. Brooklyn: AMS Press, 1989), 183.

52. For a tabulation of color words in Poe, together with a tentative psychology of color, see Wilson O. Clough, "The Use of Color Words by Edgar Allan Poe," *PMLA* 45 (1930), 598–613.

53. Susan Sontag, *On Photography* (New York: Farrar, Straus and Giroux, 1977), 3.

54. *Niles' National Register*, vol. 57, September 21, 1839, 64; vol. 64, September 9, 1843, 32; see ibid., May 20, 181–83, for an article on "Inventions, Improvements, &c.," which describes the daguerreotype process in great detail; ibid., June 24, 272, for a report on fixing colors "with all the strength and vividness of nature [and rivaling] in tint the most finished efforts of [painters]"; on Cantar, see *National Police Gazette*, June 13, 1846, 340, and *Van Court's Counterfeit Detector*, December 1854, 3, both quoted in Mihm, *A Nation of Counterfeiters*, 286n33. A random search for "daguerreotype" in the digital collections of the Library of Congress led to almost eight hundred results in newspapers across the nation; most of these results referred to advertisements for daguerreotype portraits: see, for instance, the *New-York Daily Tribune*, April 11, 1844, 1, and October 1, 1845, 3.

55. *Bankers' Magazine and Statistical Register*, March 1855, 738–39; April 1855, 812–13; *Reports of the Board of Managers of the Association for the Suppression of Counterfeiting* (Boston: William A. Hall, 1855, 1857), quoted in Mihm, *A Nation of Counterfeiters*, 301n53; *Encyclopedia of Nineteenth-Century Photography*, ed. John Hannavy (New York: Routledge, 2007), s.v. "daguerreotype," "calotype," "collodio-type;" Robert Taft, *Photography and the American Scene: A Social History, 1839–1889* (New York,: Macmillan, 1938; repr. 1942), 3–15, 32–40; 106–18; 118–20.

56. A. H. Guernsey, "Making Money III — The American Bank Note Company," *Harper's New Monthly Magazine*, February 1862, 315.

57. Heinz Tschachler, *The Greenback: Paper Money and American Culture* (Jefferson, NC: McFarland, 2010), 60; "Photographic Counterfeiting," *Bankers' Magazine and Statistical Register*, September 1856, 188–90; Richard Doty, who is one of America's most eminent numismatists, knows of "no use of green color before about 1848," though he knows of "a New Jersey note with red ink" from 1841. Email to author, March 23, 2010.

58. A. H. Guernsey, "Making Money III: The American Bank Note Company," *Harper's New Monthly Magazine*, February 1862, 306–25, here 315. An additional process also was rendered necessary for the production of legitimate notes. Thus, there was the main plate, which was printed in black; separate plates were used to have the back and parts of the face printed in colors, though it had to be done "in such a way that they cannot be effaced without injuring the designs or letters printed in black, or damaging the texture of the paper." *Bankers' Magazine and Statistical Register*, April 1855, 813.

59. Guernsey, "The ABNCo," 315. Thus in the late 1840s, experiments were made to produce a paper from which the ink could not be removed. "Improved Bank Note Paper," *Bankers' Magazine and State Financial Register*, 3 (1848/49), 577–82.

60. Bowers, *Obsolete Paper Money*, 329.

61. Guernsey, "The ABNCo," 315.

62. The very first note to have a green back was the $500 interest-bearing Treasury note authorized by the Act of December 23, 1857. These notes were not intended as general currency, even though they did at times pass from hand to hand. Thus it is entirely correct to say that the very first "greenbacks" were the Demand notes of 1861, though the term was more widely applied to the later Legal Tender Notes, which were issued in far greater quantities. Gene Hessler, "The United States' First Dollar Note," *The Numismatist*, August 1992, 1106–7, here 1106.

63. Bowers, *Obsolete Paper Money*, 76, 176.

64. Ibid., 75–76, 197, 377–385; Gene Hessler, *The Engraver's Line: An Encyclopedia of Paper Money and Postage Stamp Art* (Port Clinton, OH: BNR Press, 1993), 71–75.

65. Poe, January 15, 1840, in *Edgar Allan Poe's Contributions to "Alexander's Weekly Messenger,"* ed. Clarence Saunders Brigham (Worcester, MA: American Antiquarian Society, 1943; repr. Folcroft, PA: Folcroft Library Editions, 1973), 21–22; a second part, in

which Poe predicts that "the production of the Daguerreotype effects on paper is likely to be soon accomplished," appeared on May 6, 1840. Ibid., 82. Poe also wrote a brief comment on the daguerreotype process for *Burton's Gentleman's Magazine* for April 1840, as the second installment of the series "A Chapter on Science and Art" (193–94). In "The Thousand-and-Second Tale of Scheherazade," first published in the *Tales* of 1845, he once again refers to the daguerreotype, writing, "Another of these magicians [inventors] directed the sun to paint his portrait, and the sun did." *Poetry and Tales*, 787–804, quotation 802–3.

66. Poe, *Collected Works*, 3:1365n7. Poe eventually came to view Draper with antipathy. In "Von Kempelen and His Discovery" he mentions slightingly "so eminent a chemist as Professor Draper," who demonstrates "how very easily men of science are *mystified*, on points outside their usual range of inquiry." Ibid., 3:1243n3. In *Eureka*, Poe explains that his scorn derives from Draper's (and other "Hogites") habit of debasing science by churning out endless quantities of dull "facts" for the marketplace. In a letter to George Eveleth of June 26, 1849, Poe makes it clear that Draper was one of his principal targets in *Eureka*, though the reasons for Poe's dislike are not entirely clear. *Letters*, 2:813–16; Whalen, *Poe and the Masses*, 285n69. For a less biased treatment of Draper, see Taft, *Photography and the American Scene*, 17–32. Improvements in the daguerreotype process are described in great detail in *Niles' National Register*, vol. 64, May 20, 1843, 181–83, as well as in the *New-York Daily Tribune*, March 22, 1844, 1. Also in 1843, Draper revised and arranged the American ed. of Robert Kane's *Elements of Chemistry* (New York: Harper & Brothers), which was duly noted in *Hunt's Merchants' Magazine*, October 1843, 396. His own book *Human Physiology* (New York: Harper & Brothers, 1856) became the first American book to use photographs as illustrations. See "On the Application of Photography to Printing," *Harper's New Monthly Magazine*, September 1856, 433–41.

67. Dwight R. Thomas, "Poe in Philadelphia, 1838–1844: A Documentary Record," PhD diss., University of Pennsylvania, 1978, 718–19. On the "McKee" daguerreotype, see Michael J. Deas, *The Portraits and Daguerreotypes of Edgar Allan Poe* (Charlottesville: University of Virginia Press, 1989), 12–15, ill. 13.

68. See *Poetry and Tales*, 802–3. A

comment in *Alexander's Weekly Messenger* of January 15, 1840, is particularly revealing. Not only does Po refer to the daguerreotype as "sun-painting," he also claims that the method is "infinitely more accurate in its representation than any painting by human hands." Poe, in *Poe's Contributions to "Alexander's Weekly Messenger,"* 21–22. Poe intuitively grasped that Daguerre's invention originated from a visual sensibility that had been shaped by Daguerre's work as a painter and designer in the Parisian theater. See Stephen C. Pinson, *Speculating Daguerre: Art and Enterprise in the Work of L. J. M. Daguerre* (Chicago: University of Chicago Press, 2011).

69. *Poetry and Tales,* 482, 483–84. The version published in *Graham's Magazine* ends in a slightly different way: "The painter then added — But is this indeed Death?" Mary E. Phillips as well as Killis Campbell have said that "Life in Death" (aka "The Oval Portrait") originated from a painting done by the artist Robert M. Sully. Philips, *Edgar Allan Poe: The Man* (Chicago: John C. Winston, 1926), 691; Campbell, *The Mind of Poe and Other Studies* (Cambridge: Harvard University Press, 1933), 170.

70. *Poetry and Tales,* 485.

71. As Kenneth Silverman records, Poe described the incident in terms of Virginia having "'ruptured a blood-vessel.' More accurately, she was hemorrhaging from her lungs, in an early stage of 'death-in-life,' as many people then referred to tuberculosis." Silverman, *Edgar A. Poe: Mournful and Never-Ending Remembrance* (New York: Harper Perennial, 1991; 2009), 179, and see 334; reference to Poe is to a letter to Frederick W. Thomas, February 3, 1842, in *Letters,* 1:324. Virginia's health thus may be seen as another "treasure" to be searched for and found.

72. *Poetry and Tales,* 489, 490.

73. Ibid., 562, 566–67, 569, 575.

74. Jonathan Elmer, *Reading at the Social Limit: Affect, Mass Culture, and Edgar Allan Poe* (Stanford: Stanford University Press, 1995), 211–12.

75. Poe, review of Hawthorne's *Twice-Told Tales, Graham's Magazine,* May 1842, in *Essays and Reviews,* 572.

76. *Poetry and Tales,* 568.

77. William Blackstone, "Of Title by Alienation," in *Commentaries on the Laws of England,* Book II, *The Rights of Things* (1758; Oxford: Clarendon Press, 1770), 2:287–94, here 288. An American edition of the *Commentaries* was published in New York in 1841 (W. E. Dean, and Collins, Keese), and briefly reviewed in *Hunt's Merchants' Magazine,* July 1841, 559.

78. Gunnar Heinsohn and Otto Steiger, "Interest and Money: the Property Explanation," *A Handbook of Alternative Monetary Economics,* ed. Philip Arestis and Malcolm C. Sawyer (Cheltenham, UK, and Northampton, MA: Edward Elgar, 2006), 490–507.

79. As Stuart Banner has demonstrated, ownership of land was quite revolutionary in eighteenth-century America; generally, Americans demolished old British laws concerning property (the common-law tradition) and rebuilt them from the ground up. Bartleby's persistent "I would prefer not to" thus may be seen as Melville's strategy to undermine the contractual ideology that had come to dominate American law by mid-century. Banner, *American Property: A History of How, Why, and What We Own* (Cambridge: Harvard University Press, 2011).

80. Nadja Gernalzick, "Sacrificial or Legal: Money in American Literature — Charles Brockden Brown, James Fenimore Cooper, Frank Norris, Ezra Pound, Don DeLillo," in *Almighty Dollar: Papers and Lectures from the Velden Conference,* ed. Heinz Tschachler, Eugen Banauch, and Simone Puff (Vienna: LIT Verlag, 2010), 137–57, here 141–53.

81. Adam Smith, *Enquiry into the Nature and Causes of the Wealth of Nations,* ed. Edwin Cannan (New York: Modern Library, 1937), 28.

82. One of Thomas Nast's cartoons, for instance, depicted a precious coin casting on the wall a shadow inscribed with the word "GREENBACKS." The cartoon, which is captioned "A Shadow is Not a Substance," first appeared in 1876 in *Robinson Crusoe's Money,* a gold standard fable by David Wells. Marc Shell, *Art and Money* (Chicago: University of Chicago Press, 1995), 79.

83. Thomas Carlyle, *The French Revolution: A History* (Oxford: Oxford University Press, 1989), 31.

84. Thomas Love Peacock, *Melincourt: The Works of Thomas Love Peacock,* ed. H.F.B. Brett-Smith and C.E. Jones, The Halliford Edition, vol. 2 (London: Constable, 1924), 330. William Gouge published an extract of this 1817 novel, titled "The Paper Mill," in the October 13, 1841, issue of his *Journal of Banking,* 120–121.

85. Poe, in *Collected Writings,* 2:196. As regards Carlyle, Poe in one of his "Marginalia" of April 1846 writes that he does not have "the slightest faith" in him and therefore "would blame no man of sense for leaving the works of Carlyle unread." *Essays and Reviews,* 1392.

86. S.v. "gold," 10.a., from the full text of the *New Edition* (in progress, 2000-), http://dictionary.oed.com. For the borrowed-from-Poe's-story-hypothesis, see also Milton Friedman and Anna Jacobson Schwartz, *A Monetary History of the United States, 1867–1960* (Princeton, NJ: Princeton University Press, 1971, 1993), 98; and Armand, who adds that use of the term "may well have been strengthened by the currency of Poe's story, one of the most famous 'detective' tales of the century." "Poe's 'Sober Mystification,'" 7n20.

87. The entry in Funk and Wagnalls's dictionary reads: "gold-bug" (n.) [Slang U.S.] *Politics* 1. An advocate of a single (gold) standard 2. A gold beetle." *Standard Dictionary of the English Language,* ed. Isaac K. Funk (New York: Funk & Wagnalls, 1928).

88. *Webster's Third New International Dictionary of the English Language* (Chicago: Encyclopaedia Britannica, 1981), 1:975.

89. *A Dictionary of American English,* ed. William A. Craigie and James R. Hulbert, 4 vols. (Chicago: University of Chicago Press, 1939, 1940, 1974), 2:1136.

90. *A Dictionary of Americanisms,* ed. Mitford M. Mathews (Chicago: University of Chicago Press, 1951, 1966), 710. Poe scholar Thomas Ollive Mabbott has added an interesting facet, explaining that the word bug in America was used for any beetle, but in England had long meant only a bedbug. Mabbott quotes Nathaniel Parker Willis, a journalist, editor, dramatist, and the author of much sentimental poetry, who in "Letter from London" wrote that the difference in meaning might interfere with sales of *Poe's Tales* in England. In his reply, Thomas Dunn English wrote, "Willis … talks about … the word 'bug.' This is mere affectation … the junction with 'gold' saves it." Still, in a London collection of works by Poe, *Tales of Mystery, Imagination, & Humour; and Poems* (1852), the tale is called "The Gold-Beetle." Nathaniel Parker Willis, "Letter from London," New York *Weekly Mirror,* October 4, 1845; Thomas Dunn English, reply to Willis, *Aristidean,* October 1845, both in *Collected Works,* 3:844. It is possible, though not proven, that Poe's English publisher wanted to avoid confusion with a Suffolk dialect word, "gowden-bug," meaning "lady-bug," in children's rhyme. Burton R. Pollin, "Compound Words Coined by Poe," Edgar Allan Poe Society of Baltimore, 1980, 85, accessed April 27, 2011, http://www.eapoe.org/papers/ps-blctrs/pl19741c.htm.

91. David Wells, in *Dictionary of American English*, 2:1136.

92. For the "silver menace," see Tschachler, *The Greenback* 174–75. For Bryan's "Crown of Thorns" speech, see *Speeches of William Jennings Bryan*, 2 vols. (New York: Funk & Wagnalls, 1911), 1:238–51, quotation 251. For a study of the political culture of the time, see Paul Glad, *McKinley, Bryan, and the People* (1964; Chicago: Ivan R. Dee, 1991).

93. George W. Warder, *Conflict Between Man and Mammon; or, Gold Slavery the Curse of the World* (Kansas City: The League Pub. Co., 1896), 42, quoted in Louis Kern, "In the Land of the Dollar, But Which Dollar? The 'Crime of '73,' the Free Silver Crusade, and the Populist Dollar," in *Almighty Dollar: Papers and Essays from the Velden Conference*, ed. Heinz Tschachler, Eugen Banauch, and Simone Puff (Vienna: LIT Verlag, 2010), 45–62, here 51.

94. Warder, *Man and Mammon* 99, quoted ibid., 52.

95. David A. Wells, *Robinson Crusoe's Money; or, the Remarkable Financial Fortunes and Misfortunes of a Remote Island Community* (New York: Harper & Brothers, 1876), 57.

96. The analogy probably originated with the French Encyclopedists, who described linguistic signs as a means to secure for humanity the possession of its ideas and to pass them on, with interest, to posterity as a kind of cultural heritage — just like the purpose of money is to secure possessions as property. Anne-Robert-Jacques Turgot, *Réflexions sur la formation des richesses* [1766], *Valeur et monnaie*, and *Tableau des progrès successifs de l'esprit humain* (1750), in Michel Foucault, *The Order of Things: An Archaeology of the Human Sciences* (New York: Pantheon, 1970), 112, 156. On the distinctions respectively between substance and sign in monetary theory and between the understanding of symbolization and linguistic representation, see Shell, *Money, Language, and Thought*, 18, and "The Issue of Representation," in *The New Economic Criticism: Studies at the Intersection of Literature and Economics*, ed. Martha Woodmansee and Mark Osteen (London: Routledge, 1999), 53–74, here 57–61.

97. Ralph Waldo Emerson, "Nature," *The Collected Works of Ralph Waldo Emerson*, ed. Alfred A. Ferguson, vol. 1, *Nature, Addresses, and Lectures* (Cambridge: Belknap Press of Harvard University Press, 1971), 1–45, here 20.

98. Washington Irving, "'A Time of Unexampled Prosperity.' The Great

Mississippi Bubble, [1840], in *Wolfert's Roost*, ed. Roberta Rosenberg, *The Complete Works of Washington Irving*, ed. Richard Dilworth Rust, vol. 27 (Boston: Twayne, 1979), 95–119, here 95.

99. Shell, *Money, Language, and Thought*, 20–22.

100. Ibid., 20.

101. *Poetry and Tales*, 562. See also Shell's remark that "*an*" in Greek means "no" in English, so that "*antennae* may be understood as 'no tin in.'" *Money, Language, and Thought*, 21n46.

102. *Poetry and Tales*, 567, 586.

103. In the post–Civil War era, for instance, the irredeemability of the greenbacks was held to be the sign of the paper money *diabolus*, the sign impressed on Cain's forehead. Shell, *Art and Money*, 165–66.

104. Shell, *Money, Language, and Thought*, 21. Other references to "The Gold-Bug" in this paragraph are respectively are to *Poetry and Tales*, 576, 573, 562, 576, 567, 568, 584, and 569.

105. Joseph Jacobs, "The Goose with the Golden Eggs," in *The Fables of Aesop*, with illustrations by Richard Heighway (1894; repr. London: Dover, 2002), 57. Reference to Jupiter's "gose" is to *Poetry and Tales*, 565.

106. Herman Melville, *The Confidence-Man: His Masquerade*, ed. Hershel Parker (New York: W. W. Norton, 1971), 214; Shell, *Money, Language, and Thought*, 21.

107. Poe, review of Willis's play, which he probably attended at Philadelphia's Walnut Street Theatre on June 20, 1839, both in *The Examiner* of July and in *Burton's Gentleman's Magazine* of August 1839; an expanded version, for Poe's "The American Drama," was republished in *The American Whig Review* of August 1845; another in *Godey's Lady's Book* for May 1846, as part of "The Literati of New York City," *Essays and Reviews*, 360–72; 1123–30, quotation 1129; Arthur Hobson Quinn, *Representative American Plays from 1776 to the Present Day* (New York: Appleton-Century, 1938), 237–43. Reference to usury is to act 1, scene 1, as is the reference to the phrase "omnipotence of money," expressing Tortesa's hope that his wealth will get him the daughter of Count Falcone.

108. Aristotle's argument that of all forms of generation usury is the most unnatural, since the Middle Ages has been extended by the idea that punning is usury's linguistic counterpart, since punning makes an unnatural, even a diabolical supplement of meaning from a sound that is properly attached to only one (if any) meaning.

109. "It would have been impossi-

ble," the narrator remarks, "to force our way but for [Jupiter and his] scythe." *Poetry and Tales*, 570; Shell, *Money, Language, and Thought*, 22.

110. Whalen, *Poe and the Masses*, 217. The prospect that something can be created out of nothing perhaps applies best to Poe's "The Purloined Letter," whose inversion of the productive logic is inherent to the comment in the review of *Tales*, that there is "much made of nothing." *Essays and Reviews*, 872.

111. Poe, "The Gold-Bug," in *Poetry and Tales*, 593, 594; other references in this paragraph to the tale are ibid., 595, 570.

112. Daniel Kempton, "The Gold/Goole/Ghoul Bug," *ESQ (Emerson Society Quarterly)* 33, no. 1 (1987): 1–19, here 9.

113. Tschachler, *The Greenback*, 16–20; reference to "properties of representation" is to Foucault, *The Order of Things*, 175.

114. *Poetry and Tales*, 585.

115. "What began at a bank also ends at one," Shell writes. "It is [...] paper to paper. The treasure itself returns to the bank where, so to speak, it originated." *Money, Language, and Thought*, 23. For the claim that the relationship is "absurd," see ibid., 17.

116. Poe, *Poetry and Tales*, 581, 586. As Michael Williams points out, Legrand's labor is "doubly difficult" insofar as he "has not only to cope with the unreliability of language but also to discover meaning in a text which human ingenuity has deliberately rendered obscure." "'The *language* of the cipher': Interpretation in 'The Gold-Bug,'" *American Literature* 53, no. 4 (January 1982): 646–60, here 653.

117. *Poetry and Tales*, 563. For the Queen of Sheba's words, see 1 Kings, 10:7: "Howbeit I believed not the words, until I came, and mine eyes had seen it."

118. McLaughlin, "Just Fooling," 54, emphasis added.

119. Dwight R. Thomas and David K. Jackson, *The Poe Log: A Documentary Life of Edgar Allan Poe, 1809–1849* (Boston: G. K. Hall, 1987), 414. The reference to "The Gold-Bug" as a "capital story" was repeated both in the Baltimore *Sun* and in the Philadelphia *Public Ledger*; see ibid., 419.

120. Elmer, *Reading at the Social Limit*, 211–12.

121. Charles Francis Adams, "The State of the Currency I," *Hunt's Merchants' Magazine*, July 1839, 44–50, here 45.

122. Aaron White, in Bowers, *Obsolete Paper Money*, 471.

123. Jason Goodwin, *Greenback:*

The Almighty Dollar and the Invention of America (New York: Henry Holt, 2003), 186.

124. Charles Francis Adams, "The State of the Currency II," *Hunt's Merchants' Magazine*, December 1839, 505–17, quotation 515; "The Theory of Banking, by a Merchant of Boston," *Hunt's Merchants' Magazine*, July 1841, 27–37; Nathan Appleton, *Remarks on Currency and Banking; Having Reference to the Present Derangement of the Circulating Medium in the United States* (Boston: Little, Brown, 1841), 28, 42; Gouge, *Journal of Banking*, 96. Jacksonians generally advocated free banking only in states where banks were too firmly established to be destroyed. Wherever banks were vulnerable, Jacksonians sought to do away with them entirely. James Roger Sharp, *The Jacksonians versus the Banks: Politics in the States after the Panic of 1837* (New York: Columbia University Press, 1970), 321–25; William G. Shade, *Banks or No Banks: The Money Issue in Western Politics, 1832–1865* (Detroit: Wayne State University Press, 1972). Detailed empirical analyses of the records of the private banks have shown that, notwithstanding contemporary observations about the system of "free banking" being the "principal cause of social evil in the United States," most private banks managed the business of paper money quite responsibly. The final stripping of these banks of their power to issue money came, not because the freedom they enjoyed had degenerated into lawlessness but because of political movements to centralize power in Washington. The research is listed in Jack Weatherford, *The History of Money: From Sandstone to Cyberspace* (New York: Crown, 1997), 272. For the observation about private banks as the "cause of social evil," see Arthur Nussbaum, *A History of the Dollar* (New York: Columbia University Press, 1957), 67.

125. Bowers, *Obsolete Paper Money*, 224.

126. Poe, *Poetry and Tales*, 380. The sham-post incident itself seems to have been suggested by a story in the *Saturday Evening Post*, November 12, 1842, as see *Collected Works*, 2:492.

127. Poe, "Diddling Considered as One of the Exact Sciences," in *Poetry and Tales*, 607–17, quotations 607, 608.

128. Claude Richard, "Poe and the Yankee Hero: An Interpretation of 'Diddling Considered as One of the Exact Sciences,'" *Mississippi Quarterly* 21 (Spring 1968), 93–109.

129. Melville, *The Confidence-Man*, 213–14. For contemporary scholarship addressing the theme of confidence and authority in Melville, see David S. Reynolds, *Beneath the American Renaissance: The Subversive Imagination in the Age of Emerson and Melville* (Cambridge: Harvard University Press, 1988), 300–4. "Counterfeit detectors" were state-by-state listings of banks as well as of genuine and fraudulent notes. The fact that they included detailed descriptions of denominations and types ultimately made them a delight for counterfeiters, who turned them to their own advantage, for instance by altering their plates so that they did not correspond to the descriptions given. It is also a matter of record that certain wayward banks paid large sums to publishers of counterfeit detectors to "quote" their fraudulent money "right." Richard Doty, *America's Money—America's Story*, 2d ed. (Atlanta: Whitman, 2008), 110. For a detailed treatment of these reporters and detectors, see William H. Dillistin's remarkable monograph, *Bank Note Reporters and Counterfeit Detectors, 1826–1866* (New York: American Numismatic Society, 1949).

130. Walter Benn Michaels, *The Gold Standard and the Logic of Naturalism: American Literature at the Turn of the Century* (Berkeley: University of California Press, 1987), 93, 92. Indeed, Michaels argues, aristocracy's claim to land is in a certain sense strengthened, or at least purified, since the assertion of what Blackstone calls the "mere right of property," a right that stands independent of any right of possession, is the assertion of a right that is truly inalienable: it cannot be exchanged for anything else, it cannot be taken from you, it cannot even be given away.

131. Hawthorne, *The House of Seven Gables*, ed. Seymour L. Gross (New York: W. W. Norton, 1987), 38.

132. Reference to Fuller is to "About Critics and Criticism," *Graham's Magazine*, January 1850, in *Essays and Reviews*, 1040. Reference to "busy-bodies, toadies, quacks" is to "The Literati of New York City," ibid., 1118.

133. Reference to "stupidity" is to the Drake-Halleck review of April 1836, in *Essays and Reviews*, 506. Reference to "self-bepuffed" is to Poe's review, in Philadelphia's *Saturday Museum* of January 1843, of Lowell's *Pioneer* magazine. Thomas Ollive Mabott, "A Review of Lowell's Magazine," *Notes and Queries* 178 (June 29, 1940): 457–58; and Poe, letter to Lowell, March 27, 1843, in *Letters*, 1:393–95.

134. Jill Lepore, "The Humbug: Edgar Allan Poe and the Economy of Horror," *The New Yorker*, April 27, 2009, 8, http://www.newyorker.com/arts/critics/atlarge.

135. "Credit or belief," Marc Shell notes, "involves the very ground of aesthetic experience, and the same medium that seems to confer belief in fiduciary money (bank notes) and in scriptural money (created by the process of bookkeeping) also seems to confer it in literature." *Money, Language, and Thought*, 8.

Chapter 3

1. Poe, "The Gold-Bug," in *Poetry and Tales*, ed. Patrick Quinn (New York: Library of America, 1984), 560–596, here 586.

2. For instance, Nathaniel Hawthorne's "Peter Goldthwaite's Treasure" (1838) is about a treasure hunt that goes awry. In this little-known and unappreciated tale, the eponymous protagonist destroys the hereditary mansion in search of hidden wealth, only to discover a concealed chest filled with his ancestor's "hoard of old rags," that is, with old provincial bills of credit and other worthless paper notes. For a reading of this tale as well as of "My Kinsman, Major Molineux" in the context of America's monetary history, see Andrew Loman, "'More Than a Parchment Three-Pence': Crises of Value in Hawthorne's 'My Kinsman, Major Molineux,'" *PMLA* 126, no. 2 (2011): 345–357.

3. *Poetry and Tales*, 561.

4. David Galloway, "Introduction," *Selected Writings of Edgar Allan Poe: Poems, Tales, Essays and Reviews*, ed. David Galloway (Harmondsworth, UK: Penguin, 1967, 1976), 41. Reference to "Parian marble" is to "Fifty Suggestions," no. 21, *Graham's Magazine*, May-June 1849, in *Essays and Reviews*, ed. G. R. Thompson (New York: Library of America, 1984),1300. See above, chapter 2, 57.

5. Kenneth Silverman, *Edgar A. Poe: Mournful and Never-Ending Remembrance* (New York: Harper Perennial, 1991; 2009), 376.

6. Georg Simmel, *The Philosophy of Money*, trans. Tom Bottomore and David Frisby (1978; London: Routledge, 2004), 171. This, Walter Benn Michaels argues, is "to admit the possibility of money and a money economy." *The Gold Standard and the Logic of Naturalism: American Literature at the Turn of the Century* (Berkeley: University of California Press, 1987), 157.

7. Poe, review of R. H. Horne, *Orion: an Epic Poem in Three Books*, *Graham's Magazine*, March 1844, in *Essays and Reviews*, 289–310, quotation 302.

8. See chapter 1, 31.

9. Charles Ellis and John Allan to Robert Gwathmey, January 25, 1811, the Ellis-Allan Papers, Library of Congress, quoted in Terence Whalen, *Edgar Allan Poe and the Masses: The Political Economy of Literature in Antebellum America* (Princeton, NJ: Princeton University Press, 1999), 196.

10. *Richmond Compiler*, January 5, 1825, in Dwight R. Thomas and David K. Jackson, *The Poe Log: A Documentary Life of Edgar Allan Poe, 1809–1849* (Boston: G. K. Hall, 1987), 63. Branches of the Bank of Virginia were operated in Buchanan, Charleston, Danville, Fredericksburg, Jeffersonville, Lynchburg, Norfolk, Petersburg, Portsmouth, and Union. On Poe's conflicted relation with John Allan, which got much worse when Edgar in February 1826 enrolled at the University of Virginia, see Silverman, *Edgar A. Poe*, 26–38.

11. Q. David Bowers, *Obsolete Currency Issued by Banks in the United States, 1782–1866* (Atlanta: Whitman, 2006), 557–58.

12. Ibid., 558. Bowers also notes that a law enacted on April 2, 1842, mandated resumption of specie payment as of November 1 and to continue issuance of low-denomination currency until January 1, 1843.

13. "Mob in Cincinnati," *Niles's National Register* (formerly *Niles' Weekly Register*), January 22, 1842, 336; the Cincinnati incident is also reported in Gouge's *Journal of Banking*, together with similar incidents from across the nation (Philadelphia, July 1841-July 1842; repr. London: Routledge/Thoemmes Press, 1996), 232–33, 248, 390–91, 403.

14. On the financial collapse of the Bank of Maryland, see *Memorial to the Legislature of Maryland* (Baltimore: Lucas and Deaver, 1836), by John B. Morris, a successful lawyer and businessman, president of the Mechanics Bank and director of the Baltimore and Ohio Railroad; concerning Poe's relation to Morris, see *The Collected Letters of Edgar Allan Poe*, 2 vols., originally ed. by John Ward Ostrom, 3d ed., rev., corr., and exp. by Burton R. Pollin and Jeffrey A. Savoye (Staten Island: Gordian Press, 2008), 1:410 and 541. For a comprehensive account of the Baltimore riots, see J. Thomas Scharf's *The Chronicles of Baltimore* (Baltimore: Turnbull Brothers, 1874). There were other bank failures in the state of Maryland, including the Susquehanna Bank, which failed to the extent that it had almost $330,000 in bills in circulation, but a mere 97¢ in specie. Bowers, *Obsolete Currency*, 515.

15. Poe sent the letter, which is dated May 4, 1833, with the manuscript of "Epimanes," which he called "an original tale." *Letters*, 1:77.

16. Reprinted in Rufus Wilmot Griswold, "Memoir of the Author," *The Literati ... By Edgar A. Poe* (New York: J. S. Redfield, 1850), xiii, in Thomas and Jackson, *The Poe Log*, 149. In his diary, Kennedy noted that he had discovered Poe in a "state of starvation" and "brought him up from the very verge of despair." Ibid., 148–49.

17. Graham offered eight hundred dollars a year for the position, an amount that Poe, who desperately needed employment following eight months without a salary, considered "liberal" and accepted "with great pleasure." Letter to Joseph Evans Snodgrass of April 1, 1841, in *Letters*, 1:264.

18. Poe, letter to Joseph Snodgrass, November 11, 1839, in *Letters*, 1:202; reference to Poe's "want of capital" is to his letter to Charles W. Thomson, June 28, 1840, ibid., 1:232.

19. Poe, "The Business Man," in *Poetry and Tales*, 379.

20. Poe, "King Pest," in *Poetry and Tales*, 240–52, quotations 240, 242, 244; the stairway of Jackson's home near Nashville, Tennessee, was named "St. Andrew's Stair." William Whipple also identifies further members of Jackson's kitchen cabinet, encountered by two drunken sailors at a banquet held at an undertaker's parlor. "Poe's Political Satire," *Texas Studies in English* 35 (1956): 81–95, here 83–86.

21. For "Old Bullion," see Robert Remini, *Andrew Jackson and the Bank War* (New York: W.W. Norton, 1967), 134; for "Benton mint drops," which were also called "Bentonian currency" in order to emphasize hard money as opposed to paper money, see ibid., 135. Reference is to the $2.50 and $5 gold coins that were minted beginning August 1, 1834. Although the coins were of a lighter standard weight than earlier issues, they nevertheless sold at a premium over paper money; many of them disappeared from circulation, as in earlier times.

22. Poe, "A Chapter on Autobiography (Part III)," *Graham's Magazine*, January 1842, 44–49, here 48. On Locke's position in the debates about America's money, see Arthur M. Schlesinger, Jr., *The Age of Jackson* (Boston: Little, Brown, 1945), 232–33.

23. Sean Wilentz, "The Mirage: The Long and Tragical History of Post-Partisanship, from Washington to Obama," *The New Republic*, November 17, 2011, 25–33.

24. George Washington, "Farewell Address of 1796," The Avalon Project at Yale Law School, 1996, http://avalon.law.yale.edu/18th_century/washing.asp.

25. Thomas Jefferson, "Inaugural Address of 1801," The Avalon Project at Yale Law School, 1996, http://avalon.law.yale.edu/19th_century/jefinaul.asp.

26. Burton Pollin, *Discoveries in Poe* (Notre Dame: University of Notre Dame Press, 1970), 220.

27. Poe, letter to Thomas H. Chivers, September 27, 1842, in *Letters*, 1:363. At the time of his correspondence with Poe, Chivers was a doctor living in Oak Grove, Georgia, but making frequent visits to the North. He also wrote poetry, to some reputation, but also claimed that Poe had borrowed ideas and metrical effects from him.

28. George Washington to the Secretary of War, July 27, 1795, in *The Writings of George Washington, from the Original Manuscript Sources, 1745–1799*, ed. John C. Fitzpatrick, 39 vols. (Washington, DC: Government Printing Office, 1931–1944), 34: 251, italics added.

29. Poe, letter to Frederick William Thomas, June 26, 1841, in *Letters*, 1:287.

30. *The Broadway Journal*, September 6 and December 27, 1845, in *The Collected Writings of Edgar Allan Poe*, ed. Burton Pollin, 5 vols. (Boston: Twayne, 1981; New York: Gordian Press, 1985), 3:242, 353. Poe also included Freeman Hunt among *The Literati of New York City*, which he published serially in *Godey's Lady's Book* between May and October 1846: *Essays and Reviews*, 1147–49. For a fuller account of Hunt's friendship with Poe, see Burton R. Pollin, "Poe, Freeman Hunt, and Four Unrecorded Reviews of Poe," *Texas Studies in Literature and Language* 16, no. 2 (Summer 1974): 305–13, here 306–9.

31. Both the prospectus for the *Messenger* and Charles F. Briggs's warning are quoted in Whalen, *Poe and the Masses*, 31. Briggs's warning seemingly refers to abolitionist writings of the time.

32. Thomas and Jackson, *The Poe Log*, 33. Originally from the William R. Perkins Library, Duke University, Durham, NC, William Galt, Jr., Papers.

33. Whalen, *Poe and the Masses*, 145.

34. Vernon Lee Parrington, *Main Currents in American Thought: An Interpretation of American Literature from the Beginnings to 1920*, 4 vols. (New York: Harcourt, Brace & World, 1927–1930; repr. Norman: University of Oklahoma Press, 1987), 2:55–56.

35. Evert A. Duyckinck, ms. diary, November 1, 1875, in *Edgar Allan Poe: The Critical Heritage*, ed. Ian Walker (London: Routledge, 1986; repr. 1997), vi.

36. Poe, "Ms. Found in a Bottle," in *Poetry and Tales*, 189–99, quotations 193, 199.

37. Thomas Ollive Mabbott, in *The Collected Works of Edgar Allan Poe*, vols. 2 and 3, *Tales and Sketches*, ed. Thomas Ollive Mabbott with the assistance of Eleanor D. Kewer and Maureen C. Mabbott (Cambridge: Belknap Press of Harvard University Press, 1978), 2: xxvi.

38. Van Buren's Whig opponents criticized the policy as "executive experiment." See above, Prologue, 16–17. On the persistence of subtext in Poe's writings, see Louis Renza, "Poe's Secret Autobiography," in *The American Renaissance Reconsidered: Selected Papers from the English Institute*, ed. Walter Benn Michaels and Donald E. Pease (Baltimore: Johns Hopkins University Press, 1985), 58–89, here 65.

39. Poe, "Shadow — A Parable," in *Poetry and Tales*, 218–20, quotations 218.

40. Poe, "Silence — A Fable," in *Poetry and Tales*, 221–24, quotation 222.

41. Ibid.; on Tyler, see below, 96–98; on the election of 1832, in Howe, *What Hath God Wrought*, 386; on the importance of the Roman republic for the symbolic constitution of the United States, see Bernard Bailyn, *The Ideological Origins of the American Revolution* (Cambridge: Harvard University Press, 1967), especially chapter 2, "Sources and Traditions," 22–54; and Meyer Reinhold, *Classica Americana: The Greek and Roman Heritage of the United States* (Detroit: Wayne State University Press, 1984).

42. Poe, "The Philosophy of Furniture," in *Poetry and Tales*, 382.

43. Ibid., 385–86.

44. A poem titled "The Wall Street Chorus" and republished in Gouge's *Journal of Banking* of December 8, 1841, 181, testifies to this. For the text of the poem, which originally appeared in the *New York Era*, see above, chapter 2, 52.

45. Poe, "Mellonta Tauta," originally published in *Godey's Lady's Book*, February 1849, 133–38, in *Poetry and Tales*, 871–85, quotations 876, 883.

46. Ibid., 883, 879, 880. Reference to "The Sphinx" is to ibid., 846.

47. Silverman, *Edgar A. Poe*, 395–96.

48. Daniel Walker Howe, *What Hath God Wrought: The Transformation of America, 1815–1848*, Oxford History of the United States, vol. 5 (New York: Oxford University Press, 2007), 793–94.

49. Poe, "Mellonta Tauta," in *Poetry and Tales*, 871. The "Nubian geographer" is the mysterious Ptolemy Hephestion aka Al-Idrisi, whom Poe also used in "Descent into the Maelström" and *Eureka*, as well as in "Eleonora" and "Berenice." Ibid., 1394.

50. Ibid., 883.

51. Ibid., 1397, and Burton R. Pollin, "Politics and History in Poe's 'Mellonta Tauta': Two Allusions Explained," *Studies in Short Fiction* 8 (1971), 627–31, here 630. Reference to "Mellonta Tauta" is to *Poetry and Tales*, 884.

52. Ibid. Pollin, "Politics and History in Poe's 'Mellonta Tauta,'" 628–29. The cornerstone for the Washington, D.C., monument in fact was laid on July 4, 1848, thus much closer to Poe's writing the story. The date is part of the inscription on the west face of the Washington Monument apex. National Park Service, http://www.nps.gov/nr/travel/wash/dc72.htm.

53. Poe, "Mellonta Tauta," in *Poetry and Tales*, 885.

54. Hervey Allen, *Israfel: The Life and Times of Edgar Allan Poe* (New York: Rinehart, 1949), 537. In 1855 John Smith became the fifth Presiding Patriarch of the Church, staying in office until his death in 1911.

55. Zachary Taylor, letter to Robert C. Wood, September 27, 1847, in William K. Bixby, *Letters of Zachary Taylor from the Battle-Fields of the Mexican War* (Rochester: Genesee Press, 1908), 133, 134. Poe to Mrs. Sarah H. Whitman, ca. November 3, 1848, *Letters*, 2:717n.

56. Poe, "Mellonta Tauta," in *Poetry and Tales*, 873; reference to "These things are in the future" are ibid., 1396. Poe had previously used the phrase as a motto for "The Colloquy of Monos and Una," ibid. 449.

57. On the Whig world, see Lawrence Frederick Kohl, *The Politics of Individualism: Parties and the American Character in the Jacksonian Era* (New York: Oxford University Press, 1989), 63–99, 145–85. John Adams captures the "perversity" of human nature in his screed on "the idle, vicious, and abandoned" living on the spoils of "the industrious, virtuous, and deserving." John Adams, *A Defence of the Constitution of Government*

46. *of the United States*, 3 vols. (London: Stockdale, 1794), 3:90.

58. References in this paragraph are to Arthur Hobson Quinn, *Edgar Allan Poe: A Critical Biography* (New York: Appleton-Century-Crofts, 1941; repr. Baltimore: Johns Hopkins University Press, 1998), 199–202, and Whipple, "Poe's Political Satire," 83–84. The screed about "King 'Mob'" is by Joseph Story, a Supreme Court Justice and close friend and disciple of John Marshall's, and is quoted in Sean Wilentz, *The Rise of American Democracy: Jefferson to Lincoln* (New York-London: Norton, 2005), 312.

59. Review of Paulding, *Slavery in the United States* and *The South Vindicated*, *Southern Literary Messenger*, April 1836, in *The Complete Works of Edgar Allan Poe*, ed. James A. Harrison, The Virginia Edition, 17 vols. (New York: T. Y. Crowell, 1902; repr. New York: AMS Press, 1965, 1979), 8:265–75, quotations 267–68. Other references in this paragraph are to Whipple, "Poe's Political Satire," 83–84. For the text of "Four Beasts in One," see *Poetry and Tales*, 181–88, quotations 186, 187.

60. Joan Dayan, "Amorous Bondage: Poe, Ladies, and Slaves," in *The American Face of Edgar Allan Poe*, ed. Shawn Rosenheim and Stephen Rachman (Baltimore: Johns Hopkins University Press, 1995), 179–209, here 179. For a full discussion of the dispute over Poe's alleged authorship, see Whalen, *Poe and the Masses*, 112–46.

61. Ernest Marchand, "Poe as Social Critic," *American Literature* 6 (March 1934-January 1935): 28–43, here 37, 42–43.

62. "Slavery," in *Complete Works*, 267–68.

63. David A. Long, "Poe's Political Identity: A Mummy Unswathed," *Poe Studies* 23 (June 1990): 1–22, here 17–18.

64. Poe, "Some Secrets of the Magazine Prison-House," *The Broadway Journal*, February 15, 1845, in *Essays and Reviews*, 1036–38, quotation 1037. Reference to the "class proverbial for conservatism" is to "The Living Writers of America," manuscript, Pierpont Morgan Library, in Silverman, *Edgar A. Poe*, 249.

65. Alexis de Tocqueville, *Democracy in America*, abridged and intro. by Thomas Bender (1945; New York: Random House/Modern Library, 1981), 367.

66. Poe, "Marginalia," *Southern Literary Messenger*, May 1849, in *Essays and Reviews*, 1449.

67. Ugo Rubio, in conversation with this author, "International Edgar Allan Poe Bicentennial Conference: The Long

Shadow of a Tormented Genius," University of Extremadura, Cáceres, Spain, November 19–21, 2009.

68. Poe to Thomas, February 3, 1842, in *Letters*, 1:325.

69. Samuel L. Young, "Oration Delivered at the Democratic Republican Celebration of the 64th Anniversary of the Independence of the United States, Delivered at the Methodist Episcopal Church Greene St, New York, July 4, 1840" (New York: Jared W. Bell, 1840), 21, in *The American Party Battle: Election Campaign Pamphlets, 1828–1876*, 2 vols., ed. Joel H. Silbey (Cambridge: Harvard University Press, 1999), 1:17. Poe's description of himself as a "poor-devil author" is from his letter to E. H. N. Patterson of May 23, 1849, concerning a new revival of the *Stylus* magazine, in *Letters*, 2:803–5; quotation 804.

70. Robert Rantoul, "An Oration Delivered before the Democratic Citizens of the County of Worcester," in *The American Party Battle*, 1:17; "To the Electors of Massachusetts," ibid., 149–50.

71. "Introductory," *The American Review*, January 1845, 1–4, quotations 2 and 3.

72. Charles Francis Adams, "The Theory of Money and Banks," *Hunt's Merchants' Magazine*, August 1839, 109–24, here 122, 123. Adams expands his defense of a national bank of issue in "Banks and the Currency," published in *Hunt's*, September 1839, 214–27. Quite similar views were expressed by a "Merchant of Boston" (presumed to be Henry Williams), who suggested that a re-established national bank receive notes from the commercial bank, returning them for redemption: "The Theory of Banking," *Hunt's Merchants' Magazine*, July 1841, 27–37; Nathan Appleton, a former member of Congress who in 1832 had tried to stem Jackson's bank veto, suggested that, with a national bank re-established, the right of commercial banks to issue notes could be curtailed. *Remarks on Currency and Banking; Having Reference to the Present Derangement of the Circulating Medium in the United States* (Boston: Little, Brown, 1841), 28, 42.

73. See, for example, Adams's suggestion that control over the currency should be exerted neither by "the commercial interest," nor by "politicians" of any "denomination." If the former, through their greed, had made the currency unsafe, the latter had discredited themselves through their forsaking the legacy of the founders — "virtue" and "the very highest grade of personal integrity." Adams, "Theory of Money and Banks," 124.

74. Rantoul, "Oration," 68, in *The American Party Battle*, 1:18.

75. "The Answer of Continental Currency to the Representation and Remonstrance of Hard Money," by Hortensius, *United States Magazine*, March 20, 1779, in H. H. Brackenridge, *Gazette Publications* (Carlisle, PA: Alexander & Phillips, 1806), 139–55, here 139, 143, 146.

76. *Poetry and Tales*, 821. "Some Words with a Mummy" was first published in the *American Whig Review* of April 1, 1845. Burton Pollin, "Poe's 'Some Words With a Mummy' Reconsidered," supplement, *ESQ: Emerson Studies Quarterly* 60 (Fall 1970), 60–67.

77. *Letters*, 1:449.

78. Ibid., 448.

79. Whalen, *Poe and the Masses*, 30.

80. "My whole existence has been the merest Romance — in the sense of the most utter unworldliness." Poe, letter to Jane Ermine Locke, May 19, 1848, in *Letters*, 2:665–67; reference to Byron is to Poe's letter to James Russell Lowell, July 2, 1844, in *Letters*, 1:448.

81. Poe, "Berenice," in *Poetry and Tales*, 225–33, quotations 226, 225. Poe composed or first published "Berenice" in 1835; he also published it in the *Broadway Journal* of April 5, 1845; review of Nathaniel Hawthorne's *Twice-Told Tales*, *Graham's Magazine*, May 1842, *Essays and Reviews*, 573.

82. Poe, "The Haunted Palace," in *Poetry and Tales*, 76–77; in 1839, Poe inserted the poem into "The Fall of the House of Usher," ibid., 325–27. Reference to the "legitimate" terrors of Jackson's America is to Poe's preface to *Tales of the Grotesque and Arabesque*, in which "Usher" originally appeared. Ibid., 129. See above, chapter 1, 35. Political allegory is, of course, only one possible reading, and David Leverenz has suggested three more — psychological, social, and philosophical. "Spanking the Master: Mind-Body Crossings in Poe's Sensationalism," in *A Historical Guide to Edgar Allan Poe*, ed. J. Gerald Kennedy (New York: Oxford University Press, 2001), 95–127, here 113–14.

83. Poe, "The Conqueror Worm," in *Poetry and Tales*, 77–79, quotations 78, 79; ibid., 268–69, 1375. See above, chapter 1, 35. For a commentary on the "improvement" of "Ligeia," chiefly through inserting "The Conqueror Worm," see Mabbott, *Collected Works*, 2:307–10; on the poem as the most nihilistic of Poe's poems, see Floyd Stovall, *Edgar Poe the Poet* (Charlottesville: University Press of Virginia, 1969), 219.

84. Poe, "The Dream-Land," in *Poetry and Tales*, 79, 80; reference to "my best poems" is to Poe's letter to James Russell Lowell of July 2, 1844, in *Letters*, 1:450.

85. Poe, review of Coleridge's *Letters, Conversations and Recollections*, *Southern Literary Messenger*, June 1836, in *Essays and Reviews*, 181–88, quotation 188. On Poe's debt to Coleridge, see Floyd Stovall, "Poe's Debt to Coleridge," *University of Texas Studies in English* 10 (July 1930), 70–127; Alexander Schlutz, "Purloined Voices: Edgar Allan Poe Reading Samuel Taylor Coleridge," *Studies in Romanticism* 47, no. 2 (Summer 2008), 195–224.

86. Poe, Preface to "Eureka," in *Poetry and Tales*, 1259.

87. Poe, letter to Thomas H. Chivers, September 27, 1842, in *Letters*, 1:364.

88. Long, 8–9; Poe, "Some Words with a Mummy" in *Poetry and Tales*, 821.

89. Michael F. Holt, *The Rise and Fall of the American Whig Party: Jacksonian Politics and the Onset of the Civil War* (New York: Oxford University Press, 1999), 27–28.

90. Whalen, *Poe and the Masses*, 87. Reference to Poe is to "The Literati of New York," in *Essays and Reviews*, 1134. Poe's description of himself as a "poor-devil author" is from his letter to E. H. N. Patterson of May 23, 1849, concerning a new revival of the *Stylus* magazine, in *Letters*, 2:803–5; quotation 804.

91. Daniel Webster, *Speeches and Forensic Arguments*, 3 vols. (Boston: Perkins & Marvin, 1839), 1:204, 205.

92. On the decisive role for American democracy of the election of 1828, see Lynn Parsons, *The Birth of Modern Politics: Andrew Jackson, John Quincy Adams, and the Election of 1828* (New York: Oxford University Press, 2009).

93. Holt, *The Rise and Fall of the American Whig Party*, 979–80.

94. Poe, letter to Dr. Thomas H. Chivers, September 27, 1842, in *Letters*, 1:363.

95. On Tyler's vetoes, as well as on the dissension in the Whig party that this action created, see Oliver Perry Chitwood, *John Tyler, Champion of the Old South* (1939; rpt. New York: Russell & Russell, 1964), 226–44. David Long too cites such Whigs' characterizations of Tyler as "an unfaithful servant" and of his administration as "an Olympiad of guilt and folly," "Poe's Political Identity," 9. This particular excoriation of Tyler for betraying his party to the Democrats appeared in the same number of the *American*

Whig Review with Poe's "Some Words with a Mummy."

96. *Niles' National Register*, August 21, 1841, 391; the Democratic paper cited is the *Baltimore Republican*.

97. Ibid., 392.

98. "What Is Money?" The *Madisonian*, December 14, 1841, 3. The *Madisonian*, which was established in 1837, generally followed a "soft-money" policy. Publication was suspended in the spring of 1841, but in September of that year President John Tyler revived it. Tyler made it his official press organ at a time when most newspapers — Whig and Democrat alike — were hostile to his cabinet. *The Correspondence of James K. Polk*, ed. Wayne Cutler, vol. 7, *January–August 1844* (Knoxville: University of Tennessee Press, 1989), 40n5.

99. "What Is Money?" 3.

100. Ibid.

101. Tyler, First Annual Message to Congress, December 7, 1841, *Presidential Messages and State Papers ... from George Washington to Woodrow Wilson*, ed. Julius W. Muller, 10 vols. (New York: Review of Reviews Co., 1917), 4:1417.

102. Ibid., 1419. Tyler repeats some of the arguments in his Second Annual Message of December 6, 1842, ibid., 1461–62.

103. Ibid., 1419; Nathan Appleton, *Remarks on Currency and Banking; Having Reference to the Present Derangement of the Circulating Medium in the United States* (Boston: Little, Brown, 1841), 28, 42. George Tucker, political economist and professor at the University of Virginia, suggested a plan for a uniform currency that in many ways resembled Tyler's treasury notes: according to Tucker, the federal government should borrow specie, which would become the basis for paper notes "payable to the bearer" and "receivable and redeemable by the government;" the notes would be lent to the states, which would distribute them to the state banks, from where they would be issued. Tucker, "The Currency," *Hunt's Merchants' Magazine*, May 1842, 433–39, quotations 438. It is also worth noting that as early as 1819 Tyler, speaking in the Senate, had denounced commercial banking as "a system which has done more to corrupt the morals of society than any thing else." John Tyler, in Gouge, *Journal of Banking*, 120. The Jacksonians' objections to Tyler's Treasury notes scheme are summarized in ibid.,130–31.

104. Congressional report on the currency, in *Niles' National Register*, February 26, 1842, 404–9; the Jacksonians' objections to Tyler's Treasury

notes scheme are summarized in Gouge, *Journal of Banking*, 130–31.

105. Reference to Tyler as Poe's "closest counterpart" is to Long, "Poe's Political Identity," 9. Following Terence Whalen's terminology, Tyler was neither Poe's "feared" reader, part of an anonymous and fickle mass audience, whose unpredictable taste must be feared, nor quite his "ideal" reader, that is, a reader of taste with whom an author could form a bond of sympathy; above all, Tyler was a person wielding real power and thus important for the advancement of Poe's magazine schemes and job prospects. Whalen, *Poe and the Masses*, 8–11.

106. *Letters*, 1:333. Poe's decision to leave *Graham's* only repeats the one of June 1840, when he left *Burton's Gentleman's Magazine* after just one year at the job. Silverman, *Edgar A. Poe*, 155.

107. *Letters*, 1:253–54; on the incident, see also Whalen, *Poe and the Masses*, 199; and Dwight R. Thomas, "Poe in Philadelphia, 1838–1844: A Documentary Record," PhD diss., University of Pennsylvania, 1978, 187–88, 714–15.

108. Thomas, "Poe in Philadelphia," 89, 122–25.

109. Frederick William Thomas's position was that of a clerk in the General Land Office. Beginning in 1844, Thomas served as press agent for the president's second wife, Julia Gardiner Tyler. Thomas, "Poe in Philadelphia," 199, 501.

110. Poe, letter to James K. Paulding of July 19, 1838: "Could I obtain the most unimportant Clerkship in your gift —*any thing, by sea or land*— to relieve me from the miserable life of literary drudgery to which I now, with a breaking heart, submit, and for which neither my temper nor my abilities have fitted me, I would never again repine at any dispensation of God. I feel that I could then, (having something beyond mere literature as a profession) quickly elevate myself to the station in society which is my due." *Letters*, 1:175.

111. Poe, letter to Frederick W. Thomas, June 26, 1841, in *Letters*, 1:287.

112. Thomas and Jackson, *The Poe Log*, 295.

113. Whalen, *Poe and the Masses*, 201–2.

114. Poe, in *Essays and Reviews*, 1284.

115. John Tyler, "To the House of Representatives of the United States, September 9, 1841," in *A Compilation of the Messages and Papers of the Presidents*, ed. James D. Richardson, vol. 4, part 2, *John Tyler* (Washington, DC: Bureau of National Literature and Art, 1904), 292.

116. Whalen, *Poe and the Masses*, 204–6.

117. Poe, "Secret Writing," in *Complete Works*, 14:143.

118. Whalen, *Poe and the Masses*, 212. The possibility that W. B. Tyler was none other than Poe himself was first proposed by Louis Renza in 1985. "Poe's Secret Autobiography," *The American Renaissance Reconsidered: Selected Papers from the English Institute, 1982–1983*, ed. Walter B. Michaels and Donald E. Pease (Baltimore: Johns Hopkins University Press, 1985), 58–89. The notion has been adopted and enhanced by several other scholars, most notably Terence Whalen (*Poe and the Masses*, 208–16) and Shawn Rosenheim, *The Cryptographic Imagination: Secret Writing from Edgar Poe to the Internet* (Baltimore: Johns Hopkins University Press, 1997), 34–41. The issue is still controversial. Both Stephen Rachman and the editors of *The Collected Letters of Edgar Allan Poe* seem convinced that the case is entirely conjectural and that neither cryptogram reveals Poe as author. Rachman, "Cipher Solved, But Mystery Remains," *Edgar Allan Poe Review* 3 (Fall 2000), 77–79; editorial note, in *Letters* 1:320. Following is the text of the decoded message: "The soul secure in her existence smiles at the drawn dagger and defies its point. The stars shall fade away, the sun himself grow dim with age and nature sink in years, but thou shalt flourish in immortal youth, unhurt amid the war of elements, the wreck of matter and the crush of worlds." Ibid., 210.

119. "Eleonora" was first published in the *Gift* on September 1, 1841, and was subsequently reprinted in a number of newspapers and magazines. For Jesse E. Dow, see Poe's "A Chapter on Autobiography," in *Complete Works*, 15:228.

120. Poe, letter to Frederick W. Thomas, June 26, 1841, in *Letters*, 1:287. Poe added that he had even fought, "with right good will," for Tyler's predecessor in office, William Harrison (ibid.). There is no evidence that Poe participated in any way in the campaign of 1840, be it stump speaking, composing campaign songs, or writing political essays. At best, his claim that he had "battled with right good will for Harrison" may refer to his satires of Van Buren and his Vice-President Colonel Richard M. Johnson in such stories as "The Devil in the Belfry" and "The Man That Was Used University Press." Whipple, "Poe's Political Satire," 91–94; Whipple also dismisses Campbell's crediting Poe with a stanza titled "Fragment of

a Campaign Song," as this text was written only during the winter of 1843–1844 and was not printed until after Poe's death (ibid., 81). As regards the "Mr. Tyler" with whom Poe claims to have had "some slight personal acquaintance," it is not clear whether this was President John Tyler or his first son Robert, who was a minor poet and a friend of Frederick William Thomas. Thomas, "Poe in Philadelphia," 239.

121. Poe, letter to Frederick W. Thomas, July 4, 1841, in *Letters*, 1:292.

122. Frederick William Thomas, letter to Poe, July 7, 1841, Edgar Allan Poe Society of Baltimore, RCL309, accessed April 27, 2011, http://www.eapoe.org/misc/letters/t4507100.htm.

123. Thomas, "Poe in Philadelphia," 363–64, 366–67, 371–75, 379–80.

124. Ibid., 366–67, 440, 453, 455–58, 462–64, 465–67; Chitwood, *John Tyler*, 367–85; Howe, *What Hath God Wrought*, 572–612. Years later, Poe vengefully compares the ones who "spoke up so boldly for President Tyler" to "a shoal of Preserved Fish." "Marginalia," *Southern Literary Messenger*, July 1849, in *Essays and Reviews*, 1463.

125. Poe, letter to Frederick W. Thomas, May 25, 1842, in *Letters*, 1:333.

126. *Letters*, 1:336.

127. Poe, letter to Thomas H. Chivers, September 27, 1842, in *Letters*, 1:363. Reference to *"desperately pushed for money"* is to Poe's letter to J. and H. G. Langley, publishers of the *Democratic Review*, July 18, 1842, in *Letters*, 1:353.

128. Poe, letter to Frederick William Thomas, in *Letters*, 1:370. For notes of optimism, see Poe's letters to Thomas, Thomas H. Chivers, and John Tomlin, respectively of September 12, September 27, and October 5, in *Letters*, 1:358, 363, and 367.

129. Poe, letter to James Kirke Paulding, July 19, 1838, in *Letters*, 1:175.

130. The prospectus for *The Stylus*, which had first appeared towards the end of February 1843, is reprinted in Thomas, "Poe in Philadelphia," 519–22. Reference to Poe's "sad need of means" and "great haste" is to ibid., 524–25. On the planned appearance of "The Gold-Bug," see below, chapter 4, 110.

131. Thomas Ollive Mabbott, "Annals," in *The Collected Works of Edgar Allan Poe*, vol. 1, *Poems*, ed. Thomas Ollive Mabbott with the assistance of Eleanor D. Kewer and Maureen C. Mabbott (Cambridge: Belknap Press of Harvard University

Press, 1969), 553. For a full chronology of Poe's visit to Washington, see Thomas, "Poe in Philadelphia," 525–37, and W. H. Gravely, "Poe and Thomas Dunn English," *Papers on Poe*, ed. R. P. Veler (Springfield, OH: Chantry Music Press, 1971), 165–205.

132. Letter to Frederick William Thomas and Jesse E. Dow, March 16, 1843, in *Letters*, 1:389.

133. In Thomas, "Poe in Philadelphia," 537.

134. Robert Tyler to Edgar Allan Poe, in *Complete Works*, 17:141; Tyler cites Poe's letter to him. See Thomas, "Poe in Philadelphia," 541–42, 545. Poe's faith in Robert Tyler remained unshaken. More than a year later Poe expressed his conviction that the president's son "really wished" to give him the post in the Philadelphia custom house, the only obstacle being that he "could not, at all times, do as he wished in such matters." Poe to Frederick W. Thomas, September 8, 1844, in *Letters*, 1:458.

135. The Baltimore *Sun*, March 31, 1843, in Thomas, "Poe in Philadelphia," 545.

136. See Poe's undated letter to Graham, September-October 1843, in *Letters*, 1:415; although it seems clear that Poe retrieved "The Gold-Bug" from Graham because he expected to receive a higher remuneration from the *Dollar Newspaper*, in 1848 Poe suggested that Graham was not entirely pleased with the story: "'The Gold-Bug' was originally sent to Graham, but he not liking it, I got him to take some critical papers instead, and sent it to the Dollar Newspaper which had offered $100 for the best story." Letter to George W. Eveleth of January 4, 1848, in *Letters*, 2:641.

137. Thomas, "Poe in Philadelphia," 544, 723.

138. Woodberry, *Life*, 2:2–3, in "'The Gold-Bug,' Manuscripts and Authorized Printings," The Edgar Allan Poe Society of Baltimore, accessed September 30, 2010, http://www.eapoe.org/works/info/pt042.htm.

139. Thomas, "Poe in Philadelphia," 564, 566–68.

140. Ibid., 855, 570. Web versions of "The Banker's Daughter" and "Marrying for Money" are available respectively at http://www.eapoe.org/misc/other/dlr43002.htm and http://www.eapoe.org/misc/other-/dlr43003.htm.

141. Darley's designs for the *Dollar Newspaper*, which were engraved by R. S. Gilbert, SC, were reproduced in the *Saturday Courier*. They may be seen in Mary E. Phillips, *Edgar Allan*

Poe: The Man (Chicago: John C. Winston, 1926), 1:790–91; Hervey Allen, *Israfel: The Life and Times of Edgar Allan Poe* (New York: Rinehart, 1949), between 172 and 173; and http://www.eapoe.org/works/tales/goldbga2.htm. "The Gold-Bug" also was not the first story by Poe that the *Dollar Newspaper* published; on January 25, 1843, this weekly had reprinted "The Tell-Tale Heart," as see Thomas, "Poe in Philadelphia," 488, 494–95.

142. Joseph Evans Snodgrass, in Thomas, "Poe in Philadelphia," 593.

143. Poe, letter to James Russell Lowell, May 28, 1844, in *Letters*, 1:441.

144. Poe to Rufus Wilmot Griswold, in *Letters*, 1:487.

145. Poe, *Broadway Journal*, October 11, 1845, in *Essays and Reviews*, 1083.

146. Quoted in *The Collected Works of Edgar Allan Poe*, vols. 2 and 3, *Tales and Sketches*, ed. Thomas Ollive Mabbott with the assistance of Eleanor D. Kewer and Maureen C. Mabbott (Cambridge: Belknap Press of Harvard University Press, 1978), 3:593–94. Not everyone agreed, though; on July 13, 1843, the *Daily Forum* commented that the prize committee had been dead wrong in its decision and that, "with all deference to the Committee who adjudged the prizes, we think they were exactly reversed in the order of merit; the last should have been first, and the first last." Ibid., 596.

147. Quoted in Thomas, "Poe in Philadelphia," 609.

148. *Collected Works*, 3:804.

149. Ibid., 805, 806.

150. The title in Russian was "Zolotoj zuk." On the early reception of "The Gold-Bug" in Russia, see Joan Delaney Grossman, "Poe's 'The Gold Bug' in Russia: A Note on First Impressions," *American Literature* 42 (1970): 375–79.

151. *Collected Works*, 3:805.

152. Thomas, "Poe in Philadelphia," 577–83, 583–93.

153. Mabbott, in *Collected Works*, 2: xx.

154. Ibid., 3: 800–803.

155. Richard Kopley, "A Tale by Poe," *Edgar Allan Poe's "The Tell-Tale Heart" and Other Stories*, new ed., ed. Harold Bloom (New York: Infobase, 2009), 173–90, here 178.

156. *Collected Works*, 3:803, 847n29.

157. Marc Shell, "The Gold-Bug: Introduction to 'The Industry of Letters' in America," in *Money, Language, and Thought. Literary and Philosophic Economies from the Medieval to the Modern Era* (Baltimore: Johns Hop-

kins University Press, 1982), 5–23, here 21–22.

158. Whalen, *Poe and the Masses*, 217.

159. Ibid., 218; reference to Legrand's "misanthropy" is to *Poetry and Tales*, 560; other references to "The Gold-Bug" in this paragraph are to ibid., 595, 561, 587. F.O.C. Darley chose the discovery of Kidd's murder as his second illustration for the original printing of the tale in *Dollar Newspaper* of June 28, 1843.

160. Whalen, *Poe and the Masses*, 219. The connection between money and language constituted by the word "genus" is also evident from an observation the naturalist Carl Linnaeus made in the 1750s, that "the name of a genus is the solid currency of our botanical republic." *Philosophie botanique*, in Michel Foucault, *The Order of Things: An Archaeology of the Human Sciences* (New York: Pantheon, 1970), 185.

161. *Poetry and Tales*, 581. Other references to "The Gold-Bug" in this paragraph are to ibid., 583.

162. Whalen, *Poe and the Masses*, 222.

163. See above, 76n2.

164. Whalen, *Poe and the Masses*, 219. Reference to "filthy rags" is to *Niles' Weekly Register*, February 24, 1821, 417. For Poe's reviews of *Twice-Told Tales*, which appeared in *Graham's Magazine* respectively of April and May 1842, see *Essays and Reviews*, 568–77; Poe reviewed both *Twice-Told Tales* and *Mosses from an Old Manse* in *Godey's Lady's Book* of November 1847, ibid., 577–88.

165. Poe, *Poetry and Tales*, 580.

166. George Wood, "The Currency," *Hunt's Merchants' Magazine*, April 1841, 317–33, here 319. See chapter 2, 57.

167. See, for instance, William Gouge, *Journal of Banking*, 369–70.

168. Alexander Lovett Stimson, *History of the Express Business; Including the Origin of the Railway System in America* (New York: Baker & Godwin, 1881), 357–60.

169. Benjamin Franklin, *Autobiography and Other Writings*, ed. Osmond Seavey, Oxford World's Classics (New York: Oxford University Press, 1993), 267; John W. Tebbel, *From Rags to Riches: Horatio Alger and the American Dream* (New York: Macmillan, 1963). Reference to "fortune"/ "Fortune" is to "The Gold-Bug," in *Poetry and Tales*, 568.

170. Poe, letter to John Tomlin, August 28, 1843, in *Letters*, 1:404.

171. Tyler, First Annual Message to Congress, December 7, 1841, in *Presidential Messages and State Papers*, 4:1417.

172. *Complete Works*, 14:114.

173. In fact, there are no indications that John Tyler read anything by Poe until 1860, when he quoted (actually, misquoted) a stanza from Poe's "To One in Paradise." Tyler's reading from the poem of "our talented but unfortunate Poe" came at the end of a banquet speech delivered in Richmond, Virginia. In a final irony both of the whole patronage campaign and of the debates about America's money, the banquet was dedicated to the memory of Henry Clay, the "father" of the "American System" of protective tariffs, direct government intervention, and a national bank of issue. Lyon G. Tyler, *Letters and Times of the Tylers* (Richmond: Whittet & Shepperson, 1884–96), 1:467. As for Tyler's misquoting Poe's "To One in Paradise," the president substituted "Alas! Alas for me!/Ambition is all o'er" in place of Poe's "For, alas! Alas! With me/The light of life is o'er!" Whalen, *Poe and the Masses*, 214n47.

Chapter 4

1. "'The Gold-Bug.' Manuscripts and Authorized Printings," accessed September 30, 2010, http://www.eapoe.org/works/info/pt042.htm.

2. Poe, review of Samuel Warren's *Ten Thousand a Year*, in *Essays and Reviews*, ed. G. R. Thompson (New York: Library of America, 1984), 349.

3. Jeffrey A. Savoye, "Reconstructing Poe's 'The Gold-Bug': An Examination of the Composition and First Printing(s)," *The Edgar Allan Poe Review* 8, no. 2 (2007): 34–48, here 39.

4. Both pieces were eventually published in *Godey's Ladies' Book* in October 1842.

5. Savoye, "Reconstructing Poe's 'The Gold-Bug,'" 35.

6. Ibid.

7. Ibid., 39. The review, which Poe wrote at Griswold's request, appeared in the *Boston Miscellany* for November 1842.

8. Ibid., 35. The letter is to Frederick William Thomas, September 12, 1842, in *The Collected Letters of Edgar Allan Poe*, 2 vols., originally ed. by John Ward Ostrom, 3d ed., rev., corr., and exp. by Burton R. Pollin and Jeffrey A. Savoye (Staten Island: Gordian Press, 2008), 1:358–60.

9. Poe, "The Gold-Bug," in *Poetry and Tales*, ed. Patrick Quinn (New York: Library of America, 1984), 560–96, here 561.

10. Savoye, "Reconstructing Poe's 'The Gold-Bug,'" 35.

11. Ibid., 46n.

12. Ibid., 39.

13. Ibid., 35.

14. Poe, in *Letters*, 1:401.

15. Dwight R. Thomas, "Poe in Philadelphia, 1838–1844: A Documentary Record," PhD diss., University of Pennsylvania, 1978, 568–69, 552–53; my calculations of the relative value of the dollar are based on John J. McCusker's *How Much Is That in Real Money? A Historical Price Index for Use as a Deflator of Money Values in the Economy of the United States*, 2d rev. ed. (Worcester, MA: American Antiquarian Society/Newcastle, DE: Oak Knoll, 2001).

16. Poe, letter to John Tomlin, August 28, 1843, in *Letters*, 1:404.

17. Poe, letter to Ezra Holden, August 26, 1843, in *Letters*, 1:402; letter to James Russell Lowell, September 13, 1843, ibid., 1:407. Already in June Poe asked Rufus Wilmot Griswold for money, as see Thomas, "Poe in Philadelphia," 563. Also about this time, poverty and debts (and, possibly, a desire for change or a search for healthier quarters) had made the Poe family seek their fourth house in Philadelphia, a narrow brick cottage on the northern edge of town. Poe often was unable to pay the rent, modest as it was, and partly rented out the house, the writer sleeping under the roof. Jeffrey Meyers, *Edgar Allan Poe: His Life and Legacy* (New York: Scribner's, 1992; repr. New York: Cooper Square Press, 2000), 147.

18. Thomas, "Poe in Philadelphia," 627.

19. See Poe's April 7, 1844, letter to Maria Clemm, in *Letters*, 1:437–38.

20. Poe, letter to Charles Anthon, late October 1844, in *Letters*, 1:470.

21. Poe, letter to Frederick W. Thomas, August 27, 1842, in *Letters*, 1:356; and see Poe's essay "Some Secrets of the Magazine Prison-House," *The Broadway Journal*, February 15, 1845, in *Essays and Reviews*, 1036–38.

22. Thomas, "Poe in Philadelphia," 250, 341–42, 367; Jeffrey Meyers, *Edgar Allan Poe*, 130–33.

23. Reference to the respective positions of Whigs and Democrats on the issue of an international copyright is to Daniel Walker Howe, *What Hath God Wrought: The Transformation of America, 1815–1848*, Oxford History of the United States, vol. 5 (New York: Oxford University Press, 2007), 635. Reference to "pamphleteering" is to Poe, *The Broadway Journal*, July 9, 1845, 27, in *Writings in the Broadway Journal: Nonfictional Prose*, ed. Burton R. Pollin, 2 vols. (New York: Gordian Press, 1986), 1:173. The two realms of writing and finance come together

strikingly in John Moncure Daniel's vituperative review of Poe's *Works* (1850), which this critic for the *Southern Literary Messenger* dismisses as "counterfeit shinplaster, ragged, dirty, ancient, and worn." *Edgar Allan Poe: The Critical Heritage*, ed. Ian Walker (London: Routledge, 1986; repr. 1997), 359.

24. Poe, "Marginalia," *Democratic Review*, December 1844, in *Essays and Reviews*, 1332.

25. Originally from Simms's "Editorial Bureau," *The Southern and Western Magazine and Review* (Charleston, SC), November 1845. Poe copied Simms's editorial for the *Broadway Journal* of December 6, 1845; it is reprinted in *The Critical Heritage*, 13. Reference to "nightmares" is to Poe's prospectus of the *Penn Magazine* of 1840, in *Essays and Reviews*, 1025.

26. Poe, review of Griswold, *The Poets and Poetry of America*, *Boston Miscellany*, November 1842, in *Essays and Reviews*, 554.

27. Poe, "Exordium to Critical Notices," *Graham's Magazine* of January 1842, in *Essays and Reviews*, 1027–32, here 1027. On the issue of Poe and literary nationalism, see also Meredith L. McGill, "Poe, Literary Nationalism, and Authorial Identity," in *The American Face of Edgar Allan Poe*, ed. Shawn Rosenheim and Stephen Rachman (Baltimore: Johns Hopkins University Press, 1995), 271–304.

28. A possible exception is "Morning on the Wissahiccon," a plate article Poe wrote in 1843 and published in *The Opal: A Pure Gift for the Holy Days* in 1844. In this short piece, Poe almost out-Jeffersons Thomas Jefferson in his praise of America's natural scenery as the "Edens of the land." *Poetry and Tales*, 939–44, quotation 939.

29. The *Democratic Review*— or *The United States Magazine and Democratic Review* in full—had been launched in 1837 by John O'Sullivan and his brother-in-law Samuel Langtree. The money for this political-literary magazine came from the Democratic Party, as well as from the "Young America" movement the magazine spearheaded. Established in Washington in order to champion Jacksonian democracy, the *Democratic Review* was moved to New York in April 1840. At the 1844 Democratic National Convention, Sullivan advocated Van Buren's nomination, though this former president was passed over and James Polk was chosen. The *Review* lasted until 1859. See Robert J. Scholnick, "Extermination and Democracy: O'Sullivan, the Democratic Review, and Empire, 1837–1840," *American Periodicals: A Journal of History, Criticism, and Bibliography* 15, no. 2 (2005): 123–41.

30. Poe, *The Broadway Journal*, October 4, 1845, 199–200, in *Essays and Reviews*, 1078.

31. Poe, "Marginal Notes," *Godey's Lady's Book*, September 1845, ibid., 1375, emphasis added.

32. Poe, "The Philosophy of Furniture," in *Poetry and Tales*, 382. This is the slightly revised version of Poe's essay from *Burton's Gentleman's Magazine*.

33. Poe, "The Living Writers of America," manuscript, Pierpont Morgan Library, in Kenneth Silverman, *Edgar A. Poe: Mournful and Never-Ending Remembrance* (New York: Harper Perennial, 1991; 2009), 249.

34. Raymond Williams, *Culture and Society* (1958; London: Hogarth Press, 1990), xviii.

35. *Letters*, 1:432; Poe repeats and somewhat expands these ideas in his letter to Lowell of October 28, 1844, ibid., 462–64.

36. Edward H. N. Patterson, letter to Poe, October 21, 1849, in *The Complete Works of Edgar Allan Poe*, ed. James A. Harrison, The Virginia Edition, 17 vols. (New York: T. Y. Crowell, 1902; repr. New York: AMS Press, 1965, 1979), 17:365–66; for Poe's original proposition, see *Letters*, 2:792–96; for Poe's reply to an earlier letter by Patterson, see ibid., 2:803–805.

37. Poe, letter to Frederick William Thomas, February 25, 1843, in *Letters*, 1:381. As Terence Whalen has demonstrated at great length, Poe at the time even falsified magazine circulation figures in order to secure such a partner. He boasted that, under his editorship, the *Messenger's* circulation grew from 700 to 5,500, whereas in actual fact the magazine had 1,300 subscribers when Poe started, and 1,800 when he left sixteen months later. *Edgar Allan Poe and the Masses: The Political Economy of Literature in Antebellum America* (Princeton, NJ: Princeton University Press, 1999), chapter 2.

38. Poe, "Anastatic Printing," *Broadway Journal*, January 1845, 15, in *Complete Works*, 14:153–59; references in this and the preceding paragraph are to 156, 157, 158. Terence Whalen likewise discusses "Anastatic Printing," in *Poe and the Masses*, 53–54.

39. The religious or spiritualist reading of "anastasis" appeared in Poe's favorable review, published in *Godey's Lady's Book* of May 1846, of *Anastasis*, a book by the Reverend George Bush, a professor of Hebrew in the University of New York and a well-known mesmerist and Swedenborgian. *Essays and Reviews*, 1121–22. For the circular letters made from anastatic printing, see *Letters*, 1:538–42. Poe had come into full possession of the journal on October 24, 1845, though despite his frantic attempts to borrow money from friends and acquaintances it was not making his "fortune" and died in January 1846. See, for instance, Poe's letter to Rufus W. Griswold of October 26, 1845, in *Letters*, 1:529.

40. Poe, letter to James Russell Lowell, October 28, 1844, in *Letters*, 1:463.

41. In an attempt to correct a publisher's miscalculation regarding payment for "Hans Pfaall," Poe in 1835 argued that the thirty-four columns of text had cost him "nearly a fortnight's hard labor" and that he should accordingly receive more for it. Poe, letter to Thomas W. White, July 20, 1835, in *Letters*, 1:96. Poe's argument follows David Ricardo's labor theory of value, which measures value according to the number of hours worked. This was inherently problematic, Samuel Bailey had found, as the implication was that if one worked more slowly, the commodity would be worth more. Bailey proposed instead that a commodity was valued only in relation to others in the marketplace. Samuel Bailey, *A Critical Dissertation on the Nature, Measures, and Causes of Value: Chiefly in Reference to the Writing of Mr. Ricardo and His Followers* (London: Hunter, 1825), 72. Bailey's insight would profoundly influence Karl Marx and his understanding that value does not exist *in* labor but congeals from social relations.

42. Q. David Bowers, *Obsolete Paper Money Issued by Banks in the United States, 1782–1866* (Atlanta: Whitman, 2006), 327–28, 332; Stephen Mihm, *A Nation of Counterfeiters: Capitalists, Con Men, and the Making of the United States* (Cambridge: Harvard University Press, 2007), 301.

43. Heinz Tschachler, *The Greenback: Paper Money and American Culture* (Jefferson, NC: McFarland, 2010), 184–85.

44. The general banking law especially of the state of New York was a great embarrassment for the Jacksonian hard-money men. Drafted by liberal Whigs, who tried to avoid interference with business interests, the law provided only slight restrictions on the issue of paper money. Arthur M. Schlesinger, Jr., *The Age of Jackson* (Boston: Little, Brown, 1945), 286.

45. *Poetry and Tales*, 379.

46. Mabbott, in *The Collected Works of Edgar Allan Poe*, vol. 1, *Poems*, ed. Thomas Ollive Mabbott with the assistance of Eleanor D. Kewer and Maureen C. Mabbott (Cambridge: Belknap Press of Harvard University Press, 1969), 378.

47. Tschachler, *The Greenback*, 177.

48. Poe, in *Letters*, 1:523; Chivers to Poe, September 9, 1845, as quoted in ibid.

49. This is John Woodberry's interpretation. John Sartain, and Poe, refer to it as a fact, though Sartain's explanation is that Poe had forged a check. Sartain, *The Reminiscences of a Very Old Man, 1808–1897* (1899; repr. New York: Benjamin Blom, 1969), in Silverman, *Edgar A. Poe*, 416–17. Actually, Poe had been brought to Moyamensing, as the prison was called, charged with drunkenness, but was identified as "Poe, the poet," and dismissed. Ibid.; and Arthur Hobson Quinn, *Edgar Allan Poe: A Critical Biography* (New York: Appleton-Century-Crofts, 1941; repr. Baltimore: Johns Hopkins University Press, 1998), 616–18.

50. Poe is of course referenced in the series, at once in the street pronunciation for "poor" ("poe") and implicitly inscribed into one horror-story element of the script.

51. Quoted in Mihm, *A Nation of Counterfeiters*, 233.

52. Wendell Wolka, "The Good, the Bad, the Ugly," *The Numismatist*, June 2009, 63–65.

53. For an illustration of the Blackstone Canal Bank note, see Heinz Tschachler, *The Greenback*, 187. Richard G. Doty discusses and provides illustrations of altered notes in "Adding Insult to Injury: Altered Notes of The Southern Bank of Georgia," *Circulating Counterfeits of the Americas*, ed. John M. Kleeberg, Coinage of the Americas Conference, Proceedings 14 (New York: American Numismatic Society, 2000), 226–46. For additional illustrations of genuine and altered, as well as raised notes, see William H. Dillistin, *Bank Note Reporters and Counterfeit Detectors, 1826–1866* (New York: American Numismatic Society, 1949), plates V–X.

54. *Niles' Weekly Register* in its issue of April 7, 1827, for instance carried the following warning from the *Baltimore American*: "It appears [...] that the ingenuity and talent of the gentry who make the business of counterfeiting a regular occupation, have at length succeeded in producing so good an imitation of the plates that [...] it will be best to refuse receiving any 20 dollars [sic!] notes of the issue described, at least for the present, unless of persons well known and responsible." *Niles' Weekly Register*, April 7, 1827, 111–12. For similar notices in the contemporary press, see Bowers, *Obsolete Paper Money*, 158, and Richard Doty, *America's Money — America's Story*, 2d ed. (Atlanta: Whitman, 2008), 94.

55. Hezekiah Niles, "The Fountain of Evil," *Niles' Weekly Register*, July 4, 1818, 313–16, here 315–16. On the practices of "raising" or "altering" genuine notes, as well as of creating "spurious" notes, see Mihm, *A Nation of Counterfeiters*, 287–94. For clarification of the terminology, see Dillistin, *Bank Note Reporters and Counterfeit Detectors*, 16, and Bowers, *Obsolete Paper Money*, 466.

56. Bowers, *Obsolete Paper Money*, 194. Reference to "*incitamentum*" is to Poe's "Berenice," in *Poetry and Tales* (228).

57. Thomas, "Poe in Philadelphia," 792–96; Hervey Allen, *Israfel: The Life and Times of Edgar Allan Poe* (New York: Rinehart, 1949), 499–501.

58. Burton Pollin, *Discoveries in Poe* (Notre Dame: University of Notre Dame Press, 1970), 215–16.

59. Poe, letter to James Russell Lowell, July 2, 1844, in *Letters*, 1:450.

60. Thomas, letter to Poe, July 10, 1845, Edgar Allan Poe Society of Baltimore, RCL550, accessed April 27, 2011, http://www.eapoe.org/misc/letters/t4507100.htm.

61. Poe, letter to Thomas H. Chivers, September 27, 1842, in *Letters*, 1:363.

62. See, *inter alia*, Daniel Hoffman, *Poe, Poe, Poe, Poe, Poe, Poe, Poe* (Garden City, NY: Doubleday-Anchor Press, 1973), Silverman, *Edgar A. Poe*, and Jonathan Elmer, *Reading at the Social Limit: Affect, Mass Culture, and Edgar Allan Poe* (Stanford: Stanford University Press, 1995).

63. Henry Clay lost with less than 40,000 votes' difference. In the Electoral College, the vote was 105 to 170. Schlesinger, Jr., *The Age of Jackson*, 440.

64. Poe, in *Poetry and Tales*, 821.

65. One reason Poe's manuscript was rejected by the *Democratic Review* may have been that the magazine had just published a review of Andrew J. Downing's notable book on the subject matter, *A Treatise on the Theory and Practice of Landscape Gardening, Adapted to North America, with a View to the Improvement of Country Residences*, etc. (New York, 1841). Mabbott, in *The Collected Works of Edgar Allan Poe*, vols. 2 and 3, *Tales and Sketches*, ed. Thomas Ollive Mabbott with the assistance of Eleanor D. Kewer and Maureen C. Mabbott (Cambridge: Belknap Press of Harvard University Press, 1978), 2:701.

66. Reference to "station in society" is to Poe's letter to James K. Paulding of July 19, 1838, in *Letters*, 1:175. References to "The Domain of Arnheim" are to *Poetry and Tales*, 856, 855.

67. Poe, in *Essays and Reviews*, 1247. References to "The Domain of Arnheim" in this paragraph are to *Poetry and Tales*, 855, 857. Reference to Poe's comment on the "poetic sentiment" is to "The Poetic Principle," in *Selected Writings of Edgar Allan Poe: Poems, Tales, Essays and Reviews*, ed. and intro. by David Galloway (Harmondsworth: Penguin, 1967, 1976), 506: "The Poetic Sentiment, of course, may develop itself in various modes — in Painting, in Sculpture, in Architecture, in the Dance — very especially in Music — and very peculiarly, and with a wide field, in the composition of the Landscape Garden."

68. Mabbott, in *Collected Works*, 2:712.

69. Poe, "The Domain of Arnheim," in *Poetry and Tales*, 859, 865, 857n. In "Landor's Cottage," first published in *The Flag of Our Union* of June 9, 1849, with the subtitle "A Pendant to 'The Domain of Arnheim,'" Poe describes the picturesque ("the *pittoresque*, in the true sense of the Italian term") as "variety in uniformity [...] a piece of 'composition,' in which the most fastidiously critical taste could scarcely have suggested an emendation." *Poetry and Tales*, 887. Kent Ljungquist has written has written extensively on the sublime and picturesque as elements in Poe's strategy of using landscape as a means of self-definition: *The Grand and the Fair: Poe's Landscape Aesthetics and Pictorial Techniques* (Potomac, MD: Scripta Humanistica, 1984), especially 17–52. On the symbolism of rivers and other waterscapes in Poe's works, see Pollin, *Discoveries in Poe*, 148–58.

70. James M. Hutchisson, *Poe* (Jackson: University of Mississippi Press, 2005), 99; Joseph A. Osgoode, *Tell It in Gath* (Sewanee, TN: University Press of Sewanee, 1918), 142; William R. Taylor, *Cavalier and Yankee: The Old South and American National Character* (New York: Braziller, 1969; repr. New York: Oxford University Press, 1993), 73; Vernon Louis Parrington, *Main Currents in American Thought: An Interpretation of American Literature from the Beginnings to 1920*, 4 vols. (New York: Harcourt, Brace & World, 1927–1930;

repr. Norman: University of Oklahoma Press, 1987), 2:37. On Ellison as a man of action and capital, see Jules Zanger, "Poe's American Garden: 'The Domain of Arnheim,'" *American Transcendental Quarterly* 50 (1981), 93–102, here 98–99.

71. Poe to Conrad, January 22, 1841, in *Letters*, 1:260; Edgar Allan Poe to George W. Poe, July 14, 1839, ibid., 1:183.

72. Ernest Marchand, "Poe as Social Critic," *American Literature* 6 (March 1934-January 1935): 28–43, here 42–43; for an account of the domestic and social milieu of Poe's early years, see also Hervey Allen, *Israfel*, 27–62, 90–146.

73. David A. Long, "Poe's Political Identity: A Mummy Unswathed," *Poe Studies* 23 (June 1990): 1–22, here 15; Marchand, "Poe as Social Critic," 37, 42–43. John Carlos Rowe notes that F. O. Matthiessen relied on the Paulding-Drayton review for the chapter on Poe in Spiller's *Literary History of the United States*. "Poe, Antebellum Slavery, and Modern Criticism," in *Poe's Pym: Critical Explorations*, ed. Richard Kopley (Durham: Duke University Press, 1992), 117–38, here 135.

74. Charles Frederick Briggs, in *Poe in His Own Time: A Biographical Chronicle of His Life, Drawn from Recollections, Interviews, and Memoirs by Family, Friends, and Associates*, ed. Benjamin F. Fisher (Iowa City: University of Iowa Press, 2010), 82; Whalen, *Poe and the Masses*, 122, 142; Poe, "Three Sundays in a Week," *Broadway Journal*, May 10, 1845, in *Poetry and* Tales, 474; "Marginalia," *Graham's Magazine*, January 1848, in *Essays and Reviews*, 1423.

75. Rufus Wilmot Griswold, in *Poe in His Own Time*, 113–14; the fact that Poe received nothing upon Mr. Allan's death has been widely noted and commented on, including by Poe himself. For instance, on August 20, 1835, Poe writes William Poe, relating his family history. In this letter he also states, concerning his foster father, "The first Mrs. A. having died, and Mr. A having married again I found my situation not so comfortable as before, and obtained a Cadet's appointment at W. Point. During my stay there Mr. A died suddenly, and left me nothing. No will was found among his papers." *Letters*, 1:100; and see *Poe in His Own Time*, 27, 87, 115–16, 199; Hervey Allen reprinted John Allen's will in *Israfel*, 288–89.

76. *Collected Works*, 2:xxiv, and 3:1266.

77. On this point, see Silverman, *Edgar A. Poe*, 321–23.

78. Thomas Dunn English, review of *Tales*, *Aristidean*, October 1845, in *Essays and Reviews*, 869.

79. *Letters*, 1:505.

80. The Treaty of Guadalupe Hidalgo was signed on February 2, 1848. Reference to Marshall's words is to Q. David Bowers, *A California Gold Rush History: Featuring the Treasure from the S. S. Central America. A Source Book for the Gold Rush Historian and Numismatist* (Newport Beach: California Gold Marketing Group, 2002), 66.

81. Quoted in Arno Heller, *Amerikanischer Nordwesten und Kalifornien. Historische Spurensuche jenseits der Mythen* (Innsbruck: Innsbruck University Press, 2010), 194. For additional newspaper accounts and other reports, see Bowers, *Gold Rush History*, 75–121. The name "Eldorado" recalls a story, current from the sixteenth century on, about a South American ruler who was quite literally covered by gold, just as in his domain everything was made of gold. By Poe's day, the word had come to mean any place where gold was to be found. Poe used the term figuratively in the introduction to his *Poems* in 1831 and again in 1844 in "Dream-Land." The term was familiar enough so that, as soon as the news arrived in 1848 of the discovery of gold at Sutter's Mill and people began to make the journey to the west, California became universally known as "Eldorado." In 1850, Bayard Taylor chose *Eldorado or Adventures in the Path of Empire* as the title of a popular travel book, in which he recounts the gold rush of 1849 (New York: Putnam, 1850; repr. Lincoln: University of Nebraska Press, 1988). Reference to Poe is to *Collected Works*, 1:464.

82. Poe, letter to Frederick William Thomas, February 14, 1849, in *Letters*, 2:770; Mabbott, in *Collected Works*, 1:461.

83. Thomas Dunn English, review of *Tales*, *The Aristidean*, October 1845, in *Essays and Reviews*, 868.

84. *Poetry and Tales*, 101. As regards traveling to California, the trip would have cost anything between $300 and $1,300, depending on the mode of travel. Howe, *What Hath God Wrought*, 816.

85. Mabbott, in *Collected Works*, 1:461; for the text of "Eldorado," see ibid., 461–65. The notion of Poe searching "for the true gold" is not new. Henry B. Hirst, a poet and friend of the author, said as much (and more, in the unmistakable anti-Semitic slur) in his memoir of Poe, published in October 1849: "Poe was an industrious man, who would and did toil, delving, when his labors were demanded, imperishable gold from

the California of his heart — gold which was exchanged for copper in the Jewry of American literature." Hirst, in *Poe in His Own Time*, 158.

86. Reference is to *Psalms*, 23:4. On Poe's use of this and other sources, see *Collected Works*, 1:464.

87. Reference is to *King Lear*, III: iv. Poe likely drew on a "Tom-a-Bedlam Song" from Isaac D'Israeli's *Curiosities of Literature*. Mabbott, in *Collected Works*, 1:462.

88. Marie Bonaparte has drawn out the pervasive effects of mourning on Poe's life and writings in *The Life and Works of Edgar Allan Poe: A Psycho-Analytic Interpretation*, trans. John Rodker (London: Imago, 1949). For identification of Poe himself as the "gallant knight," see Pollin, *Discoveries in Poe*, 244n24.

89. Barton Levi St. Armand, "Poe's 'Sober Mystification': The Uses of Alchemy in 'The Gold-Bug,'" *Poe Studies* 4, no. 1 (June 1971): 1–7, here 1–2.

90. Ibid., 1; and see Poe, in *Collected Works*, 3:1365.

91. Poe, "Von Kempelen," in *Poetry and Tales*, 915.

92. Ibid., 914.

93. *Collected Works*, 3:1365–66n8, 1355–57. Burton Pollin discusses the story and its component parts in *Études Anglaises* (January-March 1967), "Poe's 'Von Kempelen and His Discovery': Sources and Significance." Pollin revised the article to a fuller treatment of "Von Kempelen" for his *Discoveries in Poe*, 166–89. According to Pollin, poverty of course was an impetus, though there also was a literary source for "Von Kempelen" — William Godwin's novel of 1799, *St. Leon*, which tells the tale of an impoverished French aristocrat who turns alchemist, finding both the philosopher's stone, which allows him to create gold, and an elixir that makes him immortal. Pollin, *Discoveries in Poe*, 185.

94. Poe, letter to Evert A. Duyckink, March 8, 1849, in *Letters*, 2:785.

95. Whalen, *Poe and the Masses*, 222. For Whalen's astute comments on "Von Kempelen," see ibid., 50–51. References in this paragraph to the tale are to *Poetry and Tales*, 915, 911, 916.

96. Bowers describes these capers in greater detail in his *Obsolete Paper Money*, 40, 455.

97. *Collected Works*, 3:1364, emphasis added.

98. Alexander Del Mar, *Gold Money and Paper Money* (New York: Anson D. F. Randolph, 1863), 19, 25–28. Del Mar's argument is complex, though here it may be reduced to the claim that gold will never be ex-

changed for its nominal value but always for its relative value. When the price for gold rises, coins will be hoarded and disappear from circulation. When the price falls, producers will discover that they cannot bring the metal to the mints even if they wish to do so. Reference to "stranger than fiction" is to Poe, "Von Kempelen," in *Collected Works*, 3:1361.

99. The Act of Congress of February 21, 1857, stipulated that "all former acts authorizing the currency of foreign gold and silver coins, and declaring the same a legal tender in payment for debts, are hereby repealed." *Documentary History of Banking and Currency in the United States*, ed. Herman E. Krooss, intro. Paul A. Samuelson, 4 vols. (1969; New York: Chelsea House, 1983), 1:233. Figures are from J. Earl Massey, *America's Money: The Story of Our Coins and Currency* (New York: Crowell, 1968), 130.

100. The *S.S. Central America* sank in a hurricane off the coast of South Carolina — with more than $1 million in commercial gold on board, together with some fifteen tons of California gold intended as reserves for the banks in the east. The story is retold in Bowers, *California Gold Rush History*, 695–946. On the panic of 1857, see ibid., 705–8; 856–57, and Sean Wilentz, *The Rise of American Democracy: Jefferson to Lincoln* (New York: Norton, 2005), 719–25.

101. The Philadelphia Mint's *Annual Report* for 1853 stated that so much gold was arriving from California that a large portion of the metal had to be cast into ingots. At the same time, California was in desperate need of coins for local circulation, which had to be shipped back from the East. The San Francisco Mint finally opened in spring 1854. Bowers, *California Gold Rush History*, 597–601, 639–42.

102. It is also worth noting that the very first gold dollars were not even produced by the United States government, but by the family business of the German immigrant Christopher Bechtler, a goldsmith and jeweler, who between 1831 and 1852 struck gold coins from findings in the Appalachian Mountains. Indeed gold from mines in the southern Appalachians, as well as gold flowing in from abroad were the exclusive native sources for the Mint until the big gold strike in California.

103. *New-York Daily Tribune*, May 12, 1849, 3; *New-York Weekly Tribune*, May 19, 1849, 3. The main provisions of the Act of March 3, 1849, are reprinted in the May 12 issue; for the full text, see *Hunt's Merchants' Magazine*, May 1849, 568.

104. Poe, "Marginalia," in *Essays and Reviews*, 1455. A bitter note about the unwarranted delay in putting the new coin into circulation appeared in the *New-York Daily Tribune* of April 14, 1849, 1.

105. Washington Irving, "The Creole Village," in *Wolfert's Roost*, ed. Roberta Rosenberg, *The Complete Works of Washington Irving*, ed. Richard Dilworth Rust vol. 27 (1855; Boston: Twayne, 1979), 22–28, here 23, emphasis added.

106. Thomas Cole, in Robert Hughes, *American Visions: The Epic History of Art in America* (New York: Knopf, 1997), 146. Other references in this paragraph are to Henry David Thoreau, *Walden* (Boston: Houghton Mifflin, 1964), 145; and Ralph Waldo Emerson, "Nature," in *The Collected Works of Ralph Waldo Emerson*, ed. Alfred A. Ferguson, vol. 1, *Nature, Addresses, and Lectures* (Cambridge: Belknap Press of Harvard University Press, 1971), 1–45, here 20.

107. Tony Judt, "Captive Minds," *The New York Review of Books*, September 30, 2010, 8–10, here 10.

108. *Niles' Weekly Register*, October 5, 1816, 1.

109. George Wood, "The Currency," *Hunt's Merchants' Magazine*, April 1841, 317–33, here 319, 320; William M. Gouge, *Journal of Banking* (Philadelphia, July 1841–July 1842; repr. London: Routledge/Thoemmes Press, 1996), 243, 110, 45.

110. Don DeLillo, *Cosmopolis: A Novel* (New York: Scribner, 2003), 65. As regards the other side of the Atlantic, Karl Marx, following Ferdinando Galiani's "Della moneta" of 1750, wrote that "although gold and silver are not by Nature money, money is by Nature gold and silver." *Capital*, trans. Eden Paul and Cedar Paul (New York: Dutton, 1930), 92–93. On the historical shift in the thinking about money, from substance to energy, see Sergio Rizzo, "'Show me the Money!,'" *M/C: A Journal of Media and Culture* 7:1 (January 2004), http://www.media-culture.org.au/0401/09-rizzo.php; and Elsie B. Michie, *The Vulgar Question of Money: Heiresses, Materialism, and the Novel of Manners from Jane Austen to Henry James* (Baltimore: Johns Hopkins University Press, 2011), 117–18.

111. Howe, *What Hath God Wrought*, 815.

112. For instance, in his reply to Annie Richmond, Poe wrote in early May 1849 that he had met "one disappointment after another. The *Columbian Magazine*, in the first place, failed — then [Israel] Post's *Union* (taking with it my principal de-

pendence); then the *Whig Review* was forced to stop paying for contributions — then the *Democratic*." In addition, Poe was involved in a "quarrel" with a publisher [possibly Louis A. Godey]; to make matters worse, a journal with which he had made "a regular engagement for $10 a week" [presumably the *Flag of Our Union*] has sent "a circular to correspondents, pleading poverty and declining to receive any more articles." The *Southern Literary Messenger*, which owes him "a good deal," has not been able to pay, and so he was dependent on *Sartain's* and *Graham's*, though neither one was a reliable source of income. *Letters*, 2:796. It is no surprise, then, that on June 9, 1849, Poe writes John R. Thompson in Richmond, asking, "Please send me $10 if you can possibly spare it." *Letters*, 2:808.

113. Silverman, *Edgar A. Poe*, 296–97. "The Imp of the Perverse" was first published in *Graham's Magazine* in July 1845. Disguised as a thoughtfully argued essay on human impulse, it is actually a monologue spoken from his jail cell by a condemned prisoner, who considers the human need to act contrarily, "for the reason that we should *not*." As examples he offers the varyingly "perverse" wishes of a speaker to tantalize his listeners by circumlocution, provoking their anger; of a procrastinator to put off some urgent action, although delay will ruin him; and of someone on a precipice tempted to leap, although he will be shattered. *Poetry and Tales*, 826–32, quotations 827, 829; reference to "The Black Cat" is to *Poetry and Tales*, 599; reference to "Grains of the golden sand" is to "A Dream within a Dream," *The Flag of Our Union*, March 31, 1849, ibid., 97. On Poe's interest in the metaphysics of mental disturbances, see Elizabeth Phillips, *Edgar Allan Poe: An American Imagination. Three Essays* (Pt. Washington, NY: Kennikat Press, 1979), 140.

114. *Poetry and Tales*, 885.

115. California gold certainly alleviated the chronic shortage of metallic currency, at the same time as it lessened the need for paper bills, with all their problems of confusion, fraud, and counterfeiting. Indeed, with so much gold in circulation, there could be no more objections to the hard-money policies of the Democrats, and the Whigs never again found a mandate for trying to create another national bank of issue. Howe, *What Hath God Wrought*, 815–16, 828–30.

116. Mabbott, in *Collected Works*, 2:xxvi.

117. Poe, *American Whig Review*, August 1845, in *Essays and Reviews*, 357. The conservatives' criticism, Poe

later wrote in his review of Hawthorne's *Twice-Told Tales* and *Mosses
from an Old Manse* for *Godey's Lady's
Book* of November 1847, thus is "a
criticism which condemns and alone
condemns," a critique by "hackneys"
and the "cultivated clergymen of the
'North American Review.'" Ibid., 579.

118. Poe, "On Imagination," ibid.,
1451; one of the "Marginalia," "On
Imagination" was published in the
Southern Literary Messenger in May
1849.

119. Poe, *Burton's Gentleman's
Magazine* of January 1840, ibid., 334.
Moore, it should be noted, in 1803
had traveled to the U.S., where he
came to particularly dislike Jefferson
and his Democratic-Republican administration. Upon his return to England, he turned to writing political
satires, presumably also a little poem
on financial speculation. The poem,
which is titled "Bubble Blowing," was
reprinted by William Gouge in his
Journal of Banking of May 25, 1842,
374.

120. Long, "Poe's Political Identity," 15. On Poe's aesthetics of
novelty, see David Halliburton, "Poe's
Aesthetics," *A Companion to Poe Studies*, ed. Eric W. Carlson (Westport,
CT: Greenwood Press, 1996), 427–48.

121. Robert D. Jacobs, *Poe: Critic
and Journalist* (Baton Rouge: Louisiana
State University Press, 1969), 14.

122. References to "The Gold-
Bug" in this paragraph are to *Poetry
and Tales*, 560, 595; on Legrand's defi-
cient moral equipment, see Daniel
Kempton, "The Gold/Goole/Ghoul
Bug," *ESQ* (*Emerson Society Quarterly*)
33, no. 1 (1987): 1–19, here 13; and
Whalen, *Poe and the Masses*, 218.

123. Poe, letter to Frederick
William Thomas, November 19, 1842,
in *Letters*, 1:371.

124. *Poetry and Tales*, 812. Both
Quinn and Whipple explicitly link
Poe's failure to obtain a government
clerkship to his writing of political
satire. *Edgar Allan Poe*, 360–80;
William Whipple, "Poe's Political
Satire," *Texas Studies in English* 35
(1956): 81–95, here 94.

125. Reference to Poe's "For
Annie" (1849) is to *Selected Writings*,
84; reference to "Eldorado" is to *Collected Works*, 1:464.

126. *Baudelaire on Poe*, ed. Lois
and Francis E. Hyslop, Jr. (State College, PA: Bald Eagle Press, 1952), 107.

127. Maria Clemm to Nelson Poe,
October 9, 1845 [misdated for 1849],
quoted in Silverman, *Edgar A. Poe*,
437. Reference to Poe arriving too late
for his foster mother's funeral is to *Letters*, 1:22; reference to "The Raven" is
to *Poetry and Tales*, 82.

128. Poe, in *Poe in His Own Time*,
15.

129. *Poetry and Tales*, 565.

130. Frederick William Thomas,
letter to Poe, November 23, 1841,
Edgar Allan Poe Society of Baltimore,
RCL347, accessed April 27, 2011, http
://www.eapoe.org/misc/letters/t41070
70.htm; Thomas, "Poe in Philadelphia," 249–50.

131. Poe, letter to Frederick
William Thomas, November 26, 1841,
in *Letters*, 1:322.

132. Thomas, "Poe in Philadelphia," 335–36, 393, 465–67. The
phrase "*Remember old Tippecanoe*"
echoes the slogan "Tippecanoe and
Tyler Too," which was widely used in
the election of 1840, celebrating both
General Harrison's victory over
Tecumseh in the battle of Tippecanoe
in 1811 and the selection of John Tyler
as his running mate. The slogan also
may have inspired Poe to use "A Tale
of the Late Bugaboo and Kickapoo
Campaign" as the subtitle to his story
"The Man Who Was Used University
Press" (1839), said to recall references,
in the press, to the troubles with Indians in Florida.

133. Marc Shell, "The Gold-Bug:
Introduction to 'The Industry of Letters' in America," in *Money, Language,
and Thought: Literary and Philosophic
Economies from the Medieval to the
Modern Era* (Baltimore: Johns Hopkins University Press, 1982), 5–23,
here 10, 19.

134. Hoffman, *Poe, Poe, Poe, Poe,
Poe, Poe, Poe*, 179–89.

135. *Poetry and Tales*, 573.

136. Ibid., 580.

137. Walter Benn Michaels, *The
Gold Standard and the Logic of Naturalism: American Literature at the Turn
of the Century* (Berkeley: University of
California Press, 1987), 154.

138. *Poetry and Tales*, 580.

139. Gold production rose from
some $10 million in 1848 to $220 by
the end of 1851; the country's gold
coinage increased from $4 million in
1846 to $60 million by 1852. Howe,
What Hath God Wrought, 815; Massey,
America's Money, 130.

140. Del Mar, *Gold Money and
Paper Money*, 14–19, 25–28.

141. Fredric Jameson, *The Political
Unconscious: Narrative as a Socially
Symbolic Act* (Ithaca: Cornell University Press, 1981; repr. London: Routledge, 2002), 20.

Chapter 5

1. Poe, "Mellonta Tauta," in *Poetry and Tales*, ed. Patrick Quinn (New
York: Library of America, 1984), 871–
85, here 885, 871.

2. The notion of a "latent
utopian impulse" in Poe's writing is
Terence Whalen's, *Edgar Allan Poe and
the Masses: The Political Economy of
Literature in Antebellum America*
(Princeton: Princeton University
Press, 1999), 268.

3. Poe, letter to Philip P. Cooke,
August 9, 1846, in *The Collected Letters
of Edgar Allan Poe*, 2 vols., originally
ed. by John Ward Ostrom, 3d ed.,
rev., corr., and exp. by Burton R.
Pollin and Jeffrey A. Savoye (Staten Island: Gordian Press, 2008), 1:595.

4. Jonathan Elmer, *Reading at
the Social Limit: Affect, Mass Culture,
and Edgar Allan Poe* (Stanford: Stanford University Press, 1995), 211–12.

5. Poe, "*Twice-Told Tales* and
Mosses From an Old Manse," in *Essays
and Reviews*, ed. G. R. Thompson
(New York: Library of America,
1984), 581, 578, 579. This is the re-
vised version of Poe's review of *Twice-
Told Tales* from *Graham's Magazine* of
May 1842.

6. Whalen, *Edgar Allan Poe and
the Masses*, 223.

7. I am grateful to Daniel
Shanahan for drawing my attention to
trauma and autistic behavior. Daniel
Hoffman, too, has argued that the
mystery-unfolding element is the key
to all of Poe. Hoffman, *Poe, Poe, Poe,
Poe, Poe, Poe, Poe* (Garden City, NY:
Doubleday-Anchor Press, 1973), 96–
97. On repetitive structures, see Patricia Howlin, "Autism," in *Behavioural
Approaches to Problems in Childhood*,
ed. Patricia Howlin (Cambridge:
Cambridge University Press, 1998),
54–77.

8. The term belongs to Sacvan
Bercovitch, who used it in his discussion of Hawthorne's symbolic language. "The A-Politics of Ambiguity
in *The Scarlet Letter*," *New Literary
History* 19 (1988): 629–54, here 652.

9. William Gilmore Simms, *The
Partisan: A Romance of the Revolution*
(New York: Harper & Brothers,
1835), 1:160. Simms wrote several
other novels, most of them dealing
with life in the Western and Southern
border regions; in addition, he wrote
poems, plays, four biographies, and a
history of South Carolina. Poe, "Marginalia," in *Essays and Reviews*, 1342;
and review of *The Partisan*, *Southern
Literary Messenger*, January 1836, in
Essays and Reviews, 891–902. Frederick
W. Thomas, letter to Poe, September
3, 1841, *The Complete Works of Edgar
Allan Poe*, ed. James A. Harrison, The
Virginia Edition, 17 vols. (New York:
T. Y. Crowell, 1902; repr. New York:
AMS Press, 1965, 1979), 17:95–100;
Poe, letter to George Lippard, Febru-
ary 18, 1844, in *Letters*, 1:423–24n.

10. For Poe's time at Fort Moultrie, see Hervey Allen, *Israfel: The Life and Times of Edgar Allan Poe* (New York: Rinehart, 1949), 170–79.

11. Poe, review of Paulding, *Southern Literary Messenger*, May 1836, 396, in *Complete Works*, 9:13; reference to Paulding is to *Life of Washington* (New York: Harper & Brothers, 1835). Reference to Marshall as the "last of the Virginia Federalists" is to Vernon Louis Parrington, *Main Currents in American Thought: An Interpretation of American Literature from the Beginnings to 1920*, 4 vols. (New York: Harcourt, Brace & World, 1927–1930; repr. Norman: University of Oklahoma Press, 1987), 2:20. Marshall's *Life of Washington* was hastily written and noticeably dull. Nevertheless, it was widely read, confirming Thomas Jefferson's forebodings that would dominate the popular view of American history for generations to come. Which indeed Marshall's book did, until George Bancroft's *History of the United States* was published in Boston in 1839. Killis Campbell treats Poe's relation to Bancroft in *The Mind of Poe and Other Studies* (Cambridge: Harvard University Press, 1933), 12–13. Reference to Jefferson is to Poe, review of Jeremiah Reynolds, *Southern Literary Messenger*, January 1837, in *Essays and Reviews*, 1246. Poe's admiration for Jefferson as a "strict constructionist" reflects Jefferson's Kentucky Resolutions of 1798, which upheld state authority against federal authority through a strict construction of the Constitution, a policy that was widely acclaimed by southerners, especially during the presidency of Andrew Jackson.

12. In this connection, see Karsten Fitz's recent book, *The American Revolution Remembered, 1830s to 1850s: Competing Images and Conflicting Narratives* (Heidelberg: Universitätsverlag Winter, 2010).

13. John H. Ingram, *Edgar Allan Poe: His Life, Letters, and Opinions*, 2 vols. (London: John Hogg, 1880; rev. in one volume London: W. H. Allen, 1886; rpt. New York: AMS Press, 1965), 1.

14. My account of "General Poe" in this and the following paragraph draws on Arthur Hobson Quinn, *Edgar Allan Poe: A Critical Biography* (New York: Appleton-Century-Crofts, 1941; repr. Baltimore: Johns Hopkins University Press, 1998), 2–6; and Kenneth Silverman, *Edgar A. Poe: Mournful and Never-Ending Remembrance* (New York: Harper Perennial, 1991; 2009), 24–25, 42, 61, 80, 331. For Poe's attempts to procure reimbursement from the U.S. govern-ment for his grandfather's personal outlays see *Letters*, 1:137–38 and 515–17. There is no evidence that Poe's letters had any success. Reference in the previous paragraph to Poe's refusal to stand "in awe" of any other individual is to his contemptuous discussion of Thomas Carlyle's "hero-worship," "Marginalia" of April 1846, in *Essays and Reviews*, 1394. Poe's discussion possibly refers to the American edition of Carlyle's *On Heroes, Hero-Worship, and the Heroic in History* (New York: D. Appleton, 1841), which was duly noted in *Hunt's Merchants' Magazine* of May 1841, 465.

15. Hervey Allen's comment that "the importance of La Fayette's [sic] visit as a turning point Poe's experience has never been made clear," thus is still valid. Allen, *Israfel*, 98n.

16. Poe, letter to John Allan, in *Letters* 1:59.

17. Richard Doty, *America's Money—America's Story*, 2d ed. (Atlanta: Whitman, 2008), 51. On the role of Revere's and other notes in the symbolic constitution of the new nation, see Heinz Tschachler, *The Greenback: Paper Money and American Culture* (Jefferson, NC: McFarland, 2010), 95–99.

18. *Poetry and Tales*, 560, 567. For a history of the Huguenots in America, see Jon Butler's remarkable monograph *The Huguenots in America: A Refugee People in New World Society* (Cambridge: Harvard University Press, 1992). For Hannah F.S. Lee's history of the Huguenots, which Poe may have seen reviewed, see "The Huguenots in France and America," *Hunt's Merchants' Magazine*, December 1843, 588.

19. Jeffrey H. Morrison, *The Political Philosophy of George Washington* (Baltimore: Johns Hopkins University Press, 2009), 64.

20. Doty, *America's Money*, 69; James Madison, "To the People of the State of New York [*The Federalist*, no. 10]," in *The Heath Anthology of American Literature*, ed. Paul Lauter et al. (Lexington, MA: D. C. Heath, 1990), 1013–18, here 1018.

21. Doty, *America's Money*, 70.

22. Robert E. Wright and David J. Cowen, *Financial Founding Fathers: The Men Who Made America Rich* (Chicago: University of Chicago Press, 2006), 21–22.

23. Doty, *America's Money*, 70.

24. For a full discussion of the legal aspects, see James Willard Hurst, *A Legal History of Money in the United States, 1774–1970* (1973; Frederick, MD: Beard Books, 2001), 8–14.

25. George Wood, "The Currency," *Hunt's Merchants' Magazine*, April 1841, 317–33, here 327–28, emphasis added.

26. Alexander Hamilton, letter to James Duane, representative in Congress of New York, September 1780, in *The Works of Alexander Hamilton*, ed. Henry Cabot Lodge (New York: Putnam's, 1904), 1:213–39, here 225.

27. Tschachler, *The Greenback*, 38–39, 45–46, 159, 166–67. The Federalists' scheme, Senator Thomas Hart Benton wrote in a letter from St. Louis of August 11, 1837, would have been accomplished were it not that "Jackson's policy balked this system in the moment of its anticipated triumph." Benton's letter was printed in the *New York Times*, September 2 of that year and is quoted in Lyman H. Low, "Hard Times Tokens," *American Journal of Numismatics*, 33, no. 1 (July 1898), 18, and 33, no. 4 (October 1898), 52.

28. Madison, "To the People of the State of New York [*The Federalist*, no. 10]," 1018.

29. Quoted in Bray Hammond, *Banks and Politics in America from the Revolution to the Civil War* (1957; repr. Princeton: Princeton University Press, 1991), 92–93.

30. Alexander Del Mar was one of the first to notice that paper money was linked to notions of sovereignty from the beginning. *The History of Money in America: From the Earliest Times to the Establishment of the Constitution* (New York: Cambridge Encyclopedia Company, 1899; repr. New York: Franklin, 1968), 123–36.

31. Thomas Hutchinson, *The History of the Province of Massachusetts-Bay, from the Charter of King William and Queen Mary in 1691, until the Year 1750*, vol. 2 (London: J. Smith, 1768), 430.

32. Hector St. John de Crèvecoeur, "Sketches of Eighteenth-Century America," in *Letters from an American Farmer* and *Sketches of Eighteenth-Century America*, ed. Albert E. Stone, Penguin Classics (Harmondsworth: Penguin, 1986), 48.

33. Thomas Hutchinson, *History of the Province of Massachusetts-Bay*, 174.

34. Madison, "Virginia Ratifying Convention, June 20, 1788," in *The Papers of James Madison*, ed. William T. Hutchinson and William M. E. Rachal, vol. 1 (Chicago: University of Chicago Press, 1962), 163.

35. Gordon S. Wood, *Empire of Liberty: A History of the Early Republic, 1789–1815*, Oxford History of the United States, vol. 4 (New York: Oxford University Press, 2009), 22–31, 218–22. On Adams's views on the few and the many, see ibid., 214.

36. Joyce Appleby, *Inheriting the Revolution: The First Generation of Americans* (Cambridge: Belknap University Press, 2000), 11, 10. The model to release the ambitions of the "risk-takers" and to connect them to revolutionary ideals was, of course, Benjamin Franklin. Wood, *Empire of Liberty*, 708–13. On Poe's deconstruction of the "self-made man," see David Leverenz, "Poe and Gentry Virginia," in *The American Face of Edgar Allan Poe*, ed. Shawn Rosenheim and Stephen Rachman (Baltimore: Johns Hopkins University Press, 1995), 210–36, here 212.

37. In Wood, *Empire of Liberty*, 711. Jefferson's enthusiasm was for Virginia businessman and representative to the Virginia Assembly Roger Atkinson; quotation is from Atkinson's letter to Samuel Pleasant, November 23, 1776, in A. J. Morrison, "Letters of Roger Atkinson," *Virginia Magazine of History and Biography*, April 1908, 357–59, here 357.

38. Thus, Smith continued, "the trade of Scotland has more than quadrupled since the first erection of two publick banks at Edinburgh." Adam Smith, *Enquiry into the Nature and Causes of the Wealth of Nations*, ed. Edwin Cannan (New York: Modern Library, 1937), 193.

39. Nadja Gernalzick, "Sacrificial or Legal: Money in American Literature — Charles Brockden Brown, James Fenimore Cooper, Frank Norris, Ezra Pound, Don DeLillo," in *Almighty Dollar: Papers and Lectures from the Velden Conference*, ed. Heinz Tschachler, Eugen Banauch, and Simone Puff (Vienna: LIT Verlag, 2010), 137–57, here 142–43. On Smith's usefulness for Jacksonian Democrats, see Arthur M. Schlesinger, Jr., *The Age of Jackson* (Boston: Little, Brown, 1945), 314–15.

40. Doty, *America's Money*, 70; Hurst, *Legal History*, 8–14. Art. I, sec. 10, §1 says, "No State shall ... make any Thing but gold and silver Coin a Tender in Payment of Debts." Therefore, the question is, if the States cannot issue paper money, this must mean that the federal government can. This is not the case, since the Tenth Amendment — which James Madison had drafted, along with the rest of the Bill of Rights — says, "The powers not delegated to the United States by the Constitution, nor prohibited by it to the States, are reserved to the States respectively, or to the people." This means that the Constitution does not "delegate" the power to "make any Thing but gold and silver Coin a Tender in Payment of Debts" to the federal government. Therefore, government at *no level* has the power to make anything but gold and silver coin a legal tender in the payment of debts.

41. Benjamin Franklin, *Autobiography and Other Writings*, ed. Osmond Seavey, Oxford World's Classics (New York: Oxford University Press, 1993), 67.

42. As Ricardo observed, "It is not necessary that paper should be payable in specie to secure its value; *it is only necessary that its quantity should be regulated* according to the value of the metal which is declared to be the standard." *On the Principles of Political Economy and Taxation*, 3d ed. (1817; London: John Murray, 1821), 424, emphasis added.

43. Cotton Mather, "Considerations on the Bills of Credit now Passing in New England," in *Colonial Currency Reprints, 1680–1751*, ed. Andrew McFarland Davis, 4 vols. (Boston: Prince Society, 1911; repr. New York: Augustus M. Kelley, 1964), 1:185–93. The pamphlet is treated at greater length in Margaret Ellen Newell, *From Dependency to Independence: Economic Revolution in Colonial New England* (Ithaca: Cornell University Press, 1998), 130–33.

44. On the conflation of categories — alchemy, economics, and political authority — see Stephen Mihm, *A Nation of Counterfeiters: Capitalists, Con Men, and the Making of the United States* (Cambridge: Harvard University Press, 2007), chapter 2.

45. The *National* Gazette, which was published by Madison's friend Philip Freneau, produced the essay in two installments, respectively on December 19 and 22, 1791. Madison had originally written it during the years 1778–1779, as he was observing the rapid decline in value of the Continental currency; its title then was simply "Money." Ralph Louis Ketcham, *James Madison: A Biography* (Charlottesville: University of Virginia Press, 1990), 85–86. An edited and annotated version of the essay appeared in *The Papers of James Madison*, vol. 1, *16 November 1751–16 December 1779*, ed. William T. Hutchinson and William M. E. Rachal (Chicago: University of Chicago Press, 1962), 302–10.

46. In *Documentary History of Banking and Currency in the United States*, ed. Herman E. Krooss, intro. Paul A. Samuelson, 4 vols. (1969; New York: Chelsea House, 1983), 1:189. The decision in Congress was a narrow one, though: the bill providing for a renewal of the charter was defeated by a single vote in the House of Representatives; in the Senate it was lost by a tie. William O. Scroggs, *A Century of Banking Progress* (Garden City, NY: Doubleday, Page, 1924), 14–15.

47. Quoted in Kevin Barry, "Crediting Power: Romantic Aesthetics and Paper Money 1797–1825," *Questione Romantica: Rivista Interdisciplinare di Studi Romantici (QuR)* 3–4 (Spring 1997): 169–92, here 189. For Henry C. Carey's views, laid down in 1840, see above, chapter 2, 51nn8 and 9.

48. James Alexander Dallas, in *Documentary History of Banking and Currency*, 1:215.

49. See Charles Ellis and John Allan to Robert Gwathmey, January 25, 1811, the Ellis-Allan Papers, Library of Congress, quoted in Whalen, *Poe and the Masses*, 196. See above, chapter 3, 78n9.

50. Daniel Walker Howe, *What Hath God Wrought: The Transformation of America, 1815–1848*, Oxford History of the United States, vol. 5 (New York: Oxford University Press, 2007), 492. For the text of Jackson's bank veto message, see *Presidential Addresses and State Papers ... from George Washington to Woodrow Wilson*, ed. Julius W. Muller, 10 vols. (New York: Review of Reviews Co., 1917), 3:985–1004, quotation 1003.

51. *Argus of Western America* (Frankfort, KY), August 6, 1828, quoted in Lawrence Frederick Kohl, *The Politics of Individualism: Parties and the American Character in the Jacksonian Era* (New York: Oxford University Press, 1989), 24. Reference to Jefferson is to his letter to Col. Charles Yancey, January 6, 1816, quoted in Wood, *Empire of Liberty*, 295. Jefferson's arguments, I have shown in Chapter 2, 55n26, were more elaborate, as he linked banking to a general tendency to copy British manners and institutions, all threatening to twist the nation away from its republican heritage.

52. On the privileges and powers of the BUS, which after all was a *private* institution, see Sean Wilentz, *The Rise of American Democracy: Jefferson to Lincoln* (New York: Norton, 2005), 364–67.

53. Jackson's bank war thus found an interesting parallel in this president's unambiguous commitment to the purging of federal offices, to what in his first inaugural address he called "reform." Howe, *What Hath God Wrought*, 331.

54. Jackson, "Farewell Address," in *Presidential Messages and State Papers*, 4:1246. The hostility to "rag-money" that Jackson instilled in Western farmers held firm until the 1870s, despite the brunt of the credit squeeze they felt then. On this and other instances of social groups holding positions

counter to what their economic interests would suggest, see Irwin Unger, *The Greenback Era: A Social and Political History of American Finance, 1865–1879* (Princeton: Princeton University Press, 1964). On Jackson as "the second Jefferson," see Merrill D. Peterson, *The Jefferson Image in the American Mind* (New York: Oxford University Press, 1962), 72–73.

55. Beginning in December 1842, Gouge incorporated the *History* in his own *Journal of Banking* (Philadelphia, July 1841–July 1842; repr. London: Routledge/Thoemmes Press, 1996), 277–412, passim. An extract of the treatise appears in *Documentary History of Banking and Currency*, 2:38–42. For my account of the treatise, I am also indebted to Schlesinger, Jr., *The Age of Jackson*, 117–122.

56. Treasury Report of December 6, 1836, quoted in Schlesinger, Jr., *The Age of Jackson*, 129. The problem, of course, was that the worth of the bank paper was secured by dwindling amounts of specie, such as $149 million to $38 million in 1837. Deposits then amounted to some $127 million, while outstanding loans had risen to $525 million. Equally problematic was the amount of capital owned, which was something like $291 million in early 1837.

57. Speculators would borrow tens of thousands of dollars in paper from commercial banks on the condition of using it in the West. They would then pay the notes to government land offices in exchange for land, which served as security for additional loans. Meanwhile, the notes were passed into circulation as land-office money; some of them never returned to the bank of origin for redemption, the rest only after long intervals. This practice not only subsidized the banking interest — land sales rose by a factor of five within a year — but it also, in Thomas Hart Benton's words, entangled "the federal government with the University Press and downs of the whole paper system, and all the fluctuations, convulsions, and disasters, to which it was subject." Benton in the Senate, April 23, 1836, in *Atkinson's Casket* (Philadelphia), June 1836, 315. Poe, too, was aware of the speculative mania in land. In "The Literati of New York City," published in *Godey's Lady's Book* between May and October 1846, he has much praise for the work of Caroline M. Kirkland, taking special note of "The Land Fever," which he describes as "a story of the wild days when the madness of speculation in land was at its height [in 1835–1836]." *Essays and Reviews*, 1181–84, quotation 1181–82.

58. Although the United States Constitution explicitly says, "no state may issue bills of credit" (Art. I, sec. 10), the Court ruled that states could charter banks to do so, even if the bank in question was wholly owned by the state. Taney's step in particular shows that the controversy over America's money had gone beyond the fight over banks and banking, to include the rule of law itself. Especially in the Whig mind, Jackson's veto power and his executive orders had come to symbolize a threat to the law, which was perceived as the only basis for order in a democratic society. Howe, *What Hath God Wrought*, 443. Sean Wilentz has rejected interpretations that put the blame for the crisis on Jackson's Specie Circular; instead, he argues, the edict came too late and, thanks largely to Whig opposition, too unevenly to have the desired effect. *The Rise of American Democracy*, 444–45.

59. Ibid., 506–8; generally on the banking issue and party politics, see ibid., 492–493.

60. Charles Francis Adams, "Banks and the Currency," *Hunt's Merchants' Magazine*, September 1839, 214–27, here 214, 216. As in an earlier instance (above, chapter 1, 33n65), the allusion to Paul's epistle to Timothy probably would not have been lost to contemporaries.

61. George Wood, "The Currency," 317, 327, 331.

62. W. S. Wetmore, "Plan of a National Bank," *Hunt's Merchants' Magazine*, June 1841, 528–38, here 530–32, 537; "The Currency, by a Merchant of Boston, Mass.," *Hunt's Merchants' Magazine*, July 1841, 27–37.

63. Wetmore, "Plan of a National Bank," 537. For similar pleas for a "convenient national currency" see John C. Crocheron, "The Currency," *Hunt's Merchants' Magazine*, January 1844, 50–65; George Tucker, "The Currency," *Hunt's Merchants' Magazine*, May 1842, 433–39.

64. The *Virginia Advocate*, quoted in Lyman H. Low, "Hard Times Tokens," *American Journal of Numismatics*, 33, no. 4 (October 1898), 52. For the *Virginia Advocate*, a fugitive literary journal that probably lasted from 1827 to 1862, see Michael O'Brien, *Conjectures of Order: Intellectual Life and the American South, 1810–1860*, 2 vols. (Chapel Hill: University of North Carolina Press, 2003), 1:335.

65. It is no coincidence that Jackson's victory in 1828 had its base in the Southern states, whereas in the free states he managed a bare majority. Howe, *What Hath God Wrought*, 282. On Jackson as a slave owner, who

bought and sold slaves in substantial numbers, see ibid., 329.

66. *Poetry and Tales*, 306. William Whipple, "Poe's Political Satire," *Texas Studies in English* 35 (1956): 81–95, here 88–91.

67. Ibid., 880, 453. Already in "The Conversation of Eiros and Charmion," which dates from 1839, the world comes to an end in a conflagration, though Poe does not in that tale make a connection to democracy. Ibid., 363.

68. Ibid., 820; Burton R. Pollin, "Poe's 'Some Words With a Mummy' Reconsidered," supplement, *ESQ: Emerson Studies Quarterly* 60 (Fall 1970): 60–67.

69. John Adams, *A Defence of the Constitution of Government of the United States*, 3 vols. (London: Stockdale, 1794), 3:90.

70. John Adams, *The Works of John Adams*, ed. Charles Francis Adams, 10 vols. (Boston: Little, Brown, 1856), 9:610.

71. References in this paragraph to the Farmers Exchange Bank fraud are to Q. David Bowers, *Obsolete Paper Money Issued by Banks in the United States, 1782–1866* (Atlanta: Whitman, 2006), 60.

72. *Niles' Weekly Register*, October 5, 1816, 1.

73. James Steuart, *Principles of Political Economy*, in Catherine Eagleton and Jonathan Williams, *Money: A History* (London: The British Museum Press, 2007), 177. For a discussion of Steuart's pre-classical monetary theory, see Douglas Vickers, *Studies in the Theory of Money, 1690–1776* (Philadelphia: Chilton, 1959), 240–90.

74. Adam Smith, *Enquiry into the Nature and Causes of the Wealth of Nations*, ed. Edwin Cannan (New York: Modern Library, 1937), 28.

75. References in this paragraph are to Wood, *Empire of Liberty*, 721–35. On Poe's emptying out, in "The Business Man," the meaningfulness of the ideal of the "self-made man," see above, 145.

76. Albert Gallatin at al., *Report of the "Union Committee"* (New York: Harper & Brothers, 1834), 29.

77. *The Richmond Enquirer*, in William Gouge, *A Short History of Paper Money and Banking in the United States* (Philadelphia: Ustick, 1833), 54. The upas tree is a poisonous evergreen.

78. Schlesinger, Jr., *The Age of Jackson*, 225–27.

79. Daniel Webster, *Speeches and Forensic Arguments*, vol. 2 (Boston: Perkins & Marvin, 1839), 82.

80. Daniel Webster, July 11, 1832, in *The Great Speeches and Orations of*

Daniel Webster, ed. Edwin P. Whipple (Boston: Little, Brown, 1886), 320–88, here 338.

81. Daniel Webster, address, delivered in Boston, September 30, 1842, in *Great Speeches and Orations*, 481–95, here 492. For Webster's conviction that the only security against fraudulent practices was to keep commercial paper "within just bounds, with direct reference to the amount of gold and silver" [which paper represents], see "Banking in the United States," *Hunt's Merchant's Magazine*, November 1844, 437.

82. Thomas Hart Benton, "Bank of the United States — Non-renewal of Charter," in *Thirty Years' View* (New York: D. Appleton, 1854–1856), 1:187–204, here 191–93.

83. Ibid., 187.

84. Schlesinger, Jr., *The Age of Jackson*, 81.

85. Howe, *What Hath God Wrought*, 386.

86. Many Southern planters, though solidly Democratic, preferred a national bank to continued dependence on financiers from New York. Ibid., 590.

87. William Henry Harrison, "Inaugural Address of 1841," The Avalon Project at Yale Law School, 1996, http://avalon.law.yale.edu/19th_century/harrison.asp.

88. Howe, *What Hath God Wrought*, 572.

89. Tyler's position is reflected in an article titled "What Is Money?" which the Washington *Madisonian*, the official press organ of the Tyler administration, published on December 14, 1841, defining money as "metal coined for the purpose of commerce." Whalen, *Poe and the Masses*, 200. For the text of Tyler's veto messages respectively of August 16 and September 9, 1841, see *Presidential Messages*, 4:1407–10, 1410–12.

90. Howe, *What Hath God Wrought*, 592.

91. Poe, letter to James Russell Lowell, July 2, 1844, in *Letters*, 1:450.

92. On the issue of different conceptions of the future, see Howe, *What Hath God Wrought*, 582–612.

93. Greeley, *The Log Cabin*, November 20, 1841, quoted in Kohl, *Politics of Individualism*, 155. Poe mentions Greeley in "Fifty Suggestions," published in *Graham's Magazine* of May-June 1849. Poe ungraciously places Greely [sic] in a "sect of new philosophers ... the *Believers in every thing Odd*." *Essays and Reviews*, 1303.

94. Charles Francis Adams, "The Theory of Money and Banks," *Hunt's Merchants' Magazine*, August 1839, 109–24, here 115.

95. Tucker was on the faculty of the University of Virginia at the time Poe attended in 1826. Poe might have remembered this when seeing Adams's review in *Hunt's*, or reading Tucker's essay "The Currency," which *Hunt's* published in its May 1842 issue, 433–39, and which essentially suggested a currency that in many ways resembled the later Demand Notes. (See chapter 3.)

96. J. Louis Tellkampf, "The Currency," *Hunt's Merchants' Magazine*, January 1842, 65–71, quotation 67. Tellkampf, who was German, then was a professor of political economy at Columbia College and a close observer of America's monetary situation. In 1844 he published, in German and as Johann L. Tellkampf, a book on prison reforms in the United States and Britain. He eventually went back to Germany, accepting a professorship in Breslau, today's Wroclaw. He continued to publish on political economy and banking, and eventually became an advisor to the Prussian king. See Consortium of European Research Libraries Thesaurus, http://thesaurus.cerl.org, and Deutsche Biographie, http://www.deutsche-biographie.de/sfz82291.html. Poe published Tellkampf's essay "On the Political Literature of Germany" in *The Broadway Journal* of December 13, 1845. *Essays and Reviews*, 1111; in a letter to Evert A. Duyckinck of April 28, 1846, Poe asks for Tellkampf's autograph, possibly for the American Autographs series proposed by Wiley and Putnam. *Letters*, 2:570.

97. The argument was made by Richard Hildreth, Bank Commissioner for New Hampshire and campaign writer for William Harrison. Hildreth's book *Banks, Banking and Paper Currencies* was reviewed in *Hunt's Merchants' Magazine* for March 1841. As the anonymous reviewer notes, "Irredeemable paper [...] is not a currency merely, but it assumes to be the standard of value." *Hunt's*, 248.

98. Alexander Del Mar, *Gold Money and Paper Money* (New York: Anson D. F. Randolph, 1863), 29–30.

99. James Madison, "Money," *The National Gazette*, December 19 and 22, 1791, in *The Papers of James Madison*, vol. 1, *16 November 1751–16 December 1779*, ed. William T. Hutchinson and William M. E. Rachal (Chicago: University of Chicago Press, 1962) 302–10. Madison's essay was reprinted in the *Federal Reserve Bank of Minneapolis Quarterly Review* 21:4 (Fall 1997), 3–7; it can be read online at http://www.minneapolisfed.org/research/QR/QR2141.ps. For a substantially positive view of ante-

bellum money market stability and the efficacy of Treasury operations, see Richard H. Timberlake, Jr., *The Origins of Central Banking in the United States* (Cambridge: Harvard University Press, 1978).

100. The term "Yankee Leviathan" belongs to Richard Franklin Bensel, *Yankee Leviathan: The Origins of Central State Authority in America, 1859–1877* (Cambridge: Cambridge University Press, 1990). The term essentially describes the capture of the state by the Republican Party, though the rift lines went beyond the division between North and South. Politically, they separated the Republicans, for whom the emerging nation-state represented a guarantor of liberty for all men, against the Democrats, who feared that the growing power of the same state would jeopardize the freedoms of *white* men. Melinda Lawson, *Patriot Fires: Forging a New American Nationalism in the Civil War North* (Lawrence: University Press of Kansas, 2002), 66–93.

101. Howe, *What Hath God Wrought*, 835.

102. Poe, letter to Frederick W. Thomas, June 26, 1841, in *Letters*, 1:287.

103. William Whipple, "Poe's Political Satire," 81, 91–94; Campbell, *The Mind of Poe*, 207.

104. *Gen. Harrison's Speech at the Dayton Convention, September 10, 1840*, pub. by the Whig Republican Association (Boston: Salem Street Academy, 1840), 5.

105. Arnold Gehlen, *Man: His Nature and Place in the World*, trans. Clare McMillan and Karl Pillemer, intro. Karl-Siegbert Rehberg (New York: Columbia University Press, 1988).

106. The yearning for a powerful yet beneficent authority of course transcends biography. In America, once the government was conceded some virtue, which usually was in times of distress, even states' rights people would languish for a strong central government: thus during the panic of 1837 Thomas Hart Benton remarked on the currency that it should not be trusted to any authority "but the highest and most responsible which was known to our form of government"— that is, the federal government in Washington, DC. Conversely, the government "ceases to be independent — it ceases to be safe — when the national currency is at the will of a company." Benton, "Revival of the Gold Currency," *Thirty Years' View*, 1:446–58, here 450.

107. Pre-publication notice for *Al Aaraaf*, published in the *Yankee and*

Boston Literary Gazette of December 29, 1829, in *Edgar Allan Poe: The Critical Heritage*, ed. Ian Walker (London: Routledge, 1986; repr. 1997), 68; letter to John Neal, October-November 1829, in *Letters*, 1:47; letter to Beverley Tucker, December 1, 1835, in *Letters*, 1:116. One should also mention here Poe's poem "Alone." Written in 1829, the poem begins, "From childhood's hour I have not been/As others were — I have not seen/As others saw ..." *Poetry and Tales*, 60.

108. Poe, letter to Thomas H. Chivers, September 27, 1842, in *Letters*, 1:364. Chivers to Poe, September 26, 1842, Box 3, folder 170, Rufus W. Griswold Collection, Ms. Gris., Courtesy of the Trustees of the Boston Public Library. "The Mighty Dead" was finally published in Chivers's *Eonchs of Ruby: A Gift of Love* (New York: Spalding and Shepard, 1851; repr. New York: Arno Press, 1972), 27–48.

109. Elmer, *Reading at the Social Limit*, 182.

110. Lincoln, "Speech on the Subtreasury," Springfield, Illinois, December 1839, in *The Collected Works of Abraham Lincoln*, ed. Roy P. Basler (New Brunswick, NJ: Rutgers University Press, 1953–1955), 1:159–79, here 164. On Lincoln's role in the Harrison campaign, see Robert Gray Gunderson, *The Log-Cabin Campaign* (Lexington: University of Kentucky Press, 1957), 212–16.

111. The Illinois state bank, like other banks, was bringing its bills into circulation at its most distant branches. The purpose of this practice was to make redemption of the bills difficult, though it was an insult to the moral sense of many Illinoisans. Lincoln nevertheless defended the bank, and he did so in a way that many Whig grandees would take note. Gabor S. Boritt, *Lincoln and the Economics of the American Dream* (1978; Urbana: University of Illinois Press, 1994), 15–18, 29. For the end of the bank in 1842, see ibid., 51–61.

112. Lincoln, "Fragment: What General Taylor Ought To Say," in *The Collected Works of Abraham Lincoln*, 1:454, emphases added.

113. "The bent of [Lincoln's] mind," William Dean Howells wrote in 1860, "is mathematical and metaphysical, and he is therefore pleased with the absolute and logical method of Poe's tales and sketches, in which the problem of mystery is given, and wrought out into everyday facts by processes of cunning analysis. It is said that he suffers no year to pass without the perusal of this author." Howells, *Life of Abraham Lincoln* (Columbus, OH, 1860; repr. Bloomington: Indi-

ana University Press, 1960), 31–32. For Poe's search for a "capital" reader, which at one point he thought he had found in President John Tyler, see above, chapter 3, 98n105.

114. Poe, letter to James Russell Lowell, July 2, 1844, in *Letters*, 1:450.

115. Both versions of the prospectus are reprinted in Burton R. Pollin, *Discoveries in Poe* (Notre Dame: University of Notre Dame Press, 1970), quotations from 218 and 220. For Pollin, the changes made by Poe are yet another "proof" of this writer's "disenchantment" with politics, ibid., 228.

116. Reference is to Griswold's memoir, used in 1850 to preface his edition of Poe's *Works* and quoted here in *Poe in His Own Time: A Biographical Chronicle of His Life, Drawn from Recollections, Interviews, and Memoirs by Family, Friends, and Associates*, ed. Benjamin F. Fisher (Iowa City: University of Iowa Press, 2010), 146. On the Poe-Griswold controversy, see Campbell, *The Mind of Poe*, 63–98.

117. *Poetry and Tales*, 560, 595.

118. David A. Long, "Poe's Political Identity: A Mummy Unswathed," *Poe Studies* 23 (June 1990): 1–22, here 16. For the etymology and usage of this term, see Burton R. Pollin, "The Word 'Autorial' in Poe's Criticism: History and Implications," *Poe Studies* 10 (1977): 15–18.

119. Long therefore finds questionable the claim that Poe was "gradually withdrawing into a greater conservatism than that represented by the Whig Party." "Poe's Political Identity," 8, with reference to Whipple, "Poe's Political Satire," 95. Reference to "Nothingness" is to *Poetry and Tales*, 1355.

120. Ralph Waldo Emerson, "The Young American," in *The Collected Works of Ralph Waldo Emerson*, ed. Alfred A. Ferguson, vol. 1, *Nature, Addresses, and Lectures* (Cambridge: Belknap Press of Harvard University Press, 1971), 222–44, here 230. The lecture, given to the Boston Mercantile Library Association on February 7, 1844, was a rallying cry for a new era of industrial expansion, commercial prosperity, and manifest destiny that was about to materialize with the election of James Polk the following November. Generally on outbursts of utopian energy in the 1840s, see Schlesinger, Jr., *The Age of Jackson*, 361–68.

121. Poe, "Sonnet — To Science" (1829), in *Poetry and Tales*, 38.

122. Poe, "South Sea Expedition," *Southern Literary Messenger*, August 1836, in *Essays and Reviews*, 1231. Poe here reviews the *Report of the [Congres-*

sional] Committee on Naval Affairs, which was decisive for Congress to authorize Reynolds's surveying and exploring expedition to the Pacific Ocean and the South Seas. Poe also reviewed Reynolds's address to Congress and, following the expedition's return in June 1842, his account of it. *Essays and Reviews*, 1234–48, 1248–52.

123. The *Whig Review* had published "The Raven" shortly before they published "Some Words with a Mummy," in January 1845. The poem was also published in Nathaniel Parker Willis's *The Mirror*. Its reception, Silverman suggested, "might be compared to that of some uproariously successful hit song today." *Edgar A. Poe*, 237. Although Poe's fame rose with that of "The Raven," the poem's enduring popular appeal, like that of "The Gold-Bug," represents no overcoming of Poe's personal history, but in a specific sense his entrapment in it.

Epilogue

1. For "sound and uniform currency," see Abraham Lincoln, "Speech on the Subtreasury," Springfield, Illinois, December 1839, *The Collected Works of Abraham Lincoln*, ed. Roy P. Basler (New Brunswick, NJ: Rutgers University Press, 1953–1955), vol. 1, 159–179, here 164. For "power of regulation" see Charles Francis Adams, "The State of the Currency II," 506.

2. Stephen Mihm, *A Nation of Counterfeiters: Capitalists, Con Men, and the Making of the United States* (Cambridge: Harvard University Press, 2007), 305.

3. Hamilton likely would have been even more delighted at the change, in 1869, to the more definitive "*will* pay," a sure measure of the government's growing confidence and, possibly, the increasing trust of at least part of the populace in the government.

4. The North's banks had been responding with much restraint when the Treasury asked them for loans to the government; the South, since the summer of 1860, had ceased forwarding the import duties it received at the ports. Melinda Lawson, *Patriot Fires: Forging a New American Nationalism in the Civil War North* (Lawrence: University Press of Kansas, 2002), 42–43.

5. The Legal Tender (Greenback) Act, which authorized the United States notes, is reprinted in *Documentary History of Banking and Currency in the United States*, ed. Her-

man E. Krooss, intro. Paul A. Samuelson, 4 vols. (1969; New York: Chelsea House, 1983), 2:264; for the debates leading up to this Act, see ibid., 241–63; for the legal basis for the borrowing program, see United States Constitution, Art.1, section 8, §2: "The congress shall have power to borrow money on the credit of the United States." The scheme of authorizing both U.S. notes and the sale of government bonds also worked, especially once the private banker Jay Cooke had been made the sole agent of the loan. Cooke's bond drive, Melinda Lawson has shown, raised over $1 billion for the Union cause, partly through Cooke's exceptional organizational skills and partly through his shrewdly marketing of the loan, which was pushed not as the government's response to wartime exigencies but as its offering an economic stake in the welfare of the nation also to middle- and working-class Americans. Lawson, *Patriot Fires*, 44–64.

6. Mihm, *A Nation of Counterfeiters*, 319.

7. *New York Herald*, April 8, 1862, quoted in Mihm, *A Nation of Counterfeiters*, 315.

8. Lewis W. Ross, in *The Congressional Globe* (Washington, DC: Globe Office, 1867), Thirty-Ninth Congress, 2:48–49. For a discussion of agrarian opposition to the bank system, see Irwin Unger, *The Greenback Era: A Social and Political History of American Finance, 1865–1879* (Princeton: Princeton University Press, 1964), 195–212.

9. Unger, *The Greenback Era*; Robert P. Sharkey, *Money, Class, and Party: An Economic Study of Civil War and Reconstruction* (Baltimore: Johns Hopkins University Press, 1959); Richard Franklin Bensel, *Yankee Leviathan: The Origins of Central State Authority in America, 1859–1877* (Cambridge: Cambridge University Press, 1990), 295.

10. Stephen Mihm, "The Almighty Dollar at Home and Abroad: Transnational History and the Currency Question," in *Almighty Dollar: Papers and Lectures from the Velden Conference*, ed. Heinz Tschachler, Eugen Banauch, and Simone Puff (Vienna: LIT Verlag, 2010), 27–44, here 33. On the racial marker of "Jewishness" implicit in "cosmopolitan," see Elsie B. Michie, *The Vulgar Question of Money: Heiresses, Materialism, and the Novel of Manners from Jane Austen to Henry James* (Baltimore: Johns Hopkins University Press, 2011), 133–34.

11. Thomas Hart Benton, *Thirty Years' View* (New York: D. Appleton, 1864) 443.

12. "A National Currency," *The Merchants' Magazine and Commercial Review* [formerly *Hunt's*], January 1864, 15–17, quotation 15.

13. William Graham Sumner, *A History of Banking in all the Leading Nations*, vol. 1, *The United States* (New York: Journal of Commerce and Commercial Bulletin, 1896), 464, 465. The "death tax" on the circulation of notes issued by commercial banks was adopted only narrowly, with 68 members supporting the amendment imposing it, 67 opposed. *The Congressional Globe* (Washington, DC: Globe Office, 1865), The Debates and Proceedings of the Second Session of the Thirty-Eighth Congress, 2:906; Albert S. Bolles, *The Financial History of the United States, from 1861 to 1885* (New York: Appleton, 1886), 194. On the profitability and security of banking in the federal system, *Hunt's Merchants' Magazine* wrote in its issue of May 1867, that "our National Banks, if founded on a sound basis and conducted with ordinary ability, could scarcely fail to prove extremely remunerative, and we have yet to hear of the first instance in which any National Bank, organized on real capital, has got into difficulties,

except by the misconduct of its servants, and by a departure from sound principles in its management" (375).

14. Michael O'Malley, "Specie and Species: Race and the Money Question in Nineteenth-Century America," *The American Historical Review* 99:2 (April 1994), 369–395, quotation 376.

15. Hugh McCulloch, speech given in Fort Wayne in 1865, in *Men and Measures of Half a Century* (New York: Scribner's, 1888), 201.

16. Elliot C. Cowdin, *Historical Sketch of Currency and Finance* (Cincinnati, OH, 1876), 52.

17. *Documentary History of Banking and Currency*, 3:149. For additional currency planks on national party platforms, see Kirk H. Porter and Donald B. Johnson, *National Party Platforms* (Champaign: University of Illinois Press, 1966).

18. There were nine issues altogether between 1865 and 1922, but the first series to reach general circulation was the fourth series from 1882. The obligation stated that gold in the note's amount was on deposit in the Treasury, repayable, like the Silver deposited against the better-known Silver Certificates, "to the bearer on demand." Arthur L. Friedberg and Ira L. Friedberg, *Paper Money of the United States. A Complete Illustrated Guide With Valuations*, 16th ed. (Clifton, NJ: The Coin & Currency Institute, 2001), 136.

19. Poe, "The Gold-Bug," in *Poetry and Tales*, ed. Patrick Quinn (New York: Library of America, 1984), 560–96, here 577. On the "unreasonableness of reason" as the underlying logic of "The Gold-Bug," see Richard Hull, "Puns in 'The Gold-Bug': You Gotta be Kiddin," *Arizona Quarterly* 58, no. 2 (Summer 2002): 1–18, here 10.

Bibliographic Essay

Researching Poe's position on the "money question" posed quite a few challenges. For one thing, Poe's literary output simply defies easy categorization. Indeed, Poe's very "slipperiness," his relentless play with undecidabilities that constantly undermine his own positions, makes any attempt to read politics back into his writings extremely "vexing." *Edgar Allan Poe and the Masses: The Political Economy of Literature in Antebellum America* (Princeton: Princeton University Press, 1999), 145. For Poe's "slipperiness," see Jonathan Elmer, *Reading at the Social Limit: Affect, Mass Culture, and Edgar Allan Poe* (Stanford: Stanford University Press, 1995), 175. Other scholars who have treated the contradictoriness of Poe's career include David Ketterer, *The Rationale of Deception in Poe* (Baton Rouge: Louisiana State University Press, 1979), John Irwin, *American Hieroglyphics: The Symbol of the Egyptian Hieroglyphics in the American Renaissance* (Baltimore: Johns Hopkins University Press, 1980), Joan Dayan, *Fables of Mind: An Inquiry into Poe's Fiction* (New York: Oxford University Press, 1987), and, from a more clinical perspective, Kenneth Silverman, *Edgar A. Poe: Mournful and Never-Ending Remembrance* (New York: Harper Perennial, 1991; 2009). In order to circumvent the vexation posed by Poe's predilection for hoaxes and similar forms of overt manipulation, I began my research with "The Gold-Bug," which Poe wrote while he was still living in Philadelphia. Arthur Hobson Quinn in his celebrated biography states that the tale was written early in 1843, though the evidence he provides seems unconvincing. *Edgar Allan Poe: A Critical Biography* (New York: Appleton-Century-Crofts, 1941; repr. Baltimore: Johns Hopkins University Press, 1998), 392. According to Thomas Ollive Mabbott, the tale began to take shape in late 1841, its genealogy thus coinciding both with John Tyler's bank vetoes and with Poe's attempts to land a government position with the Tyler administration. *The Collected Works of Edgar Allan Poe* (Cambridge: Belknap Press of Harvard University Press, 1978), 3: 803. (Mabbott's edition is also available online from the Edgar Allan Poe Society of Baltimore's website at http://www.eapoe.org/works/mabbott/tominfo.htm; the University of Iowa Libraries hold a collection of Mabbott's papers and other material related to his research on Poe.) Jeffrey Savoye put to rest the issue of the tale's genealogy in his fine essay "Reconstructing Poe's 'The Gold-Bug': An Examination of the Composition and First Printing(s)," *The Edgar Allan Poe Review* 8, no.2 (2007): 34–48.

For Poe's Philadelphia years, I relied on Jeffrey Meyers, *Edgar Allan Poe: His Life and Legacy* (New York: Scribner's, 1992; repr. New York: Cooper Square Press, 2000), 92–149, and Silverman, *Edgar A. Poe*, 136–48 and 473–89. One source deserves special notice: Dwight R. Thomas, "Poe in Philadelphia, 1838–1844," PhD diss., University of Pennsylvania, 1978, which provides a full documentary record. Also indispensable was Dwight R. Thomas and David K. Jackson, *The Poe Log: A Documentary Life of Edgar Allan Poe, 1809–1849* (Boston: G. K. Hall, 1987), not least since it is available online from the Poe Society's website at http://www.eapoe.org/papers/misc1921/tplg00ca.htm. Also useful for reconstructing Poe's life and career was Thomas Ollive Mabbott's "Annals," a year-by-year account published in *Collected Works*, 1:527–72; except for a few additions, "Annals" largely follows Quinn's critical biography of 1941, a piece of outstanding scholarship that is still indispensable to students of Poe's life and works. I also drew on John H. Ingram's *Edgar Allan Poe: His Life, Letters, and Opinions*, 2 vols. (London: John Hogg, 1880; rev. in one volume London: W. H. Allen, 1886, and repr. New York: AMS, 1965), which is the first serious and comprehensive biography of Poe, and still useful for its vast amount of source material from Poe's contemporaries.

"The Gold-Bug" was widely reprinted, circulating about 300,000 copies by 1844. It finally appeared, with Poe's corrections, in *Tales* in 1845 (New York: Wiley and Putnam). The celebrated "J. Lorimer Graham" copy, an edition of the *Tales* bound up with *The Raven and Other Poems*, was not published during Poe's lifetime. The copy, which contains penciled manuscript revisions and changes made by Poe, now is among the holdings of the Harry Ransom Center at the University of Texas in Austin; the text also can be read online from the Poe Society's website at http://www.eapoe.org/works/tales/goldbgc.htm. It was adopted by Mabbott for *Collected Works* and, from there, became the basis for Patrick Quinn's edition of *Poetry and Tales* (New York: Library of America, 1984), which I follow here. I also used the Library of America's edition of Poe's *Essays and Reviews*, ed. G. R. Thompson (New York: Library of America, 1984). The Library of America editions are more accessible than *The Complete Works of Edgar Allan Poe*, ed. James A. Harrison, The Virginia Edition, 17 vols. (New York: Thomas Y. Crowell, 1902–3; repr. New York: AMS Press, 1965, 1979), which is also flawed: Harrison left out many items, excerpted text and was not particularly scrupulous in his readings of the manuscripts.

A true treasure trove became *The Collected Letters of Edgar Allan Poe*, 2 volumes, originally ed. by John Ward Ostrom, 3d ed., rev., corr., and exp. by Burton R. Pollin and Jeffrey A. Savoye (Staten Island: Gordian Press, 2008). This fine edition, however, contains only letters *by* Poe; for letters written *to* Poe, one still has to rely on the Harrison edition, although the Poe Society now has in its possession the materials originally accumulated by Thomas Ollive Mabbott and Joseph P. Ridgely, which the Society are in the process of making available online to the scholarly community at http://www.eapoe.org/works/letters/index.htm. Yet valuable as these resources are, none of them will ever be able to provide the large number of Poe's letters that Mrs. Clemm burned after her nephew's death, saving only "those relating to literature." Mrs. Clemm to Neilson Poe, August 26, 1860, as quoted in *Letters*, 2:1280. Among the letters that have survived, the world of banking and finance is mentioned only rarely, mostly in connection with Poe's magazine schemes. This does not mean that Poe was not concerned about these worlds. Decorum may have led him to think that banking and finance were "things to talk about which would not come within the compass of a letter." Poe to Frederick William Thomas, May 25, 1842, *in Letters*, 1:334. Thus, I fleshed out the data from the correspondence by consulting *Poe in His Own Time: A Biographical Chronicle of His Life, Drawn from Recollections, Interviews, and Memoirs by Family, Friends, and Associates*, ed. Benjamin F. Fisher (Iowa City: University of Iowa Press, 2010), a chronological collection of primary materials, and *Edgar Allan Poe: The Critical Heritage*, ed. Ian A. Walker (New York: Routledge, 1986; repr. 1997), which contains a discussion of "The Gold-Bug" in the Philadelphia *Saturday Museum* of July 1843 as well as reviews of the *Tales* of 1845.

A particular obstacle towards connecting Poe's writings and the world of money and finance were readings that emphasize Poe's otherworldliness. This estimation has had a long history. "Ludwig" [Rufus Wilmot Griswold] in his obituary of 1849 wrote: "[Poe's] imagery was from the worlds which no mortal can see but with the vision of genius [...] He was at all times a dreamer—dwelling in ideal realms — in heaven or hell — peopled with creatures and the accidents of his brain." Griswold, in *Poe in His Own Time*, 77–78; Francis Gerry Fairfield continued and amplified this view, writing in 1875 that Poe "did not think. He was merely a dreamer, having a singular faculty for the coherent organization of his dreams." Fairfield, ibid., 277. It is no surprise, then, that Richard Wilbur, writing in the 1960s, describes Poe's art as "not a means of giving imaginative order to earthy experience, but a stimulus to unearthly visions [...] it seeks to disengage the reader's mind from reality and propel it toward the ideal." "The House of Poe," in *Poe: A Collection of Critical Essays*, ed. Robert Reagan (Englewood Cliffs, NJ: Prentice-Hall, 1967), 98–120, here 99–100.

How does one square Poe's supposed otherworldliness with the conviction that this writer was acutely aware of what was going on in the world around him? Encouragement to pursue the money question came from Killis Campbell, who against the critical orthodoxy of his own time claimed that Poe was never aloof from his own culture and society. Campbell, *The Mind of Poe and Other Studies* (Cambridge: Harvard University Press, 1933), 99–125. Ernest Marchand's "Poe as Social Critic," *American Literature* 6 (March 1934–January 1935): 28–43, and Thomas Ollive Mabbott's emphasis, in his Introduction to *Collected Works*, on Poe's "ability to absorb and transform the 'news' of his own time" (2: xxvi), likewise encouraged me in my pursuit. Also of value was David Galloway's conclusion, in the Introduction to the Penguin edition of *Selected Writings*, that Poe "maintained a real and varied interest in the world around him, not merely in literature, but in the theatre, in architecture, music, painting, commerce, education, theories of government, and particularly in science." *Selected Writings of Edgar Allan Poe: Poems, Tales, Essays and Reviews* (Harmondsworth: Penguin, 1967, 1976), 14.

While critics from Campbell to Galloway took note of Poe's representativeness, they did not flesh out their postulates. Terence Whalen, however, in fact resituated Poe's writings within the social and economic forces that influenced the literary production of the time. "Edgar Allan Poe and the Horrid Laws of Political Economy," *American Quarterly*, 44, no.3 (September 1992): 381–417; parts of Whalen's article later appeared in chapters 2 and 8 of his book *Poe and the Masses*. For my own attempt to read Poe's work back into the world of money and finance two pioneering works of scholarship proved immensely useful: Marc Shell, "The Gold-Bug: Introduction to 'The Industry of Letters' in America," in Shell's *Money, Language, and Thought: Literary and Philosophic Economies from the Medieval to the Modern Era* (Baltimore: Johns Hopkins University Press, 1982), 5–23; and Kevin McLaughlin, "Just Fooling: Paper, Money, Poe," *Differences: A Journal of Feminist Cultural Studies*, 11, no.1 (Spring 1999): 38–67. That Poe's experience of early nineteenth-century American life had a measurable impact on his writings is also the central thesis of *Edgar Allan Poe in Context* (New York: Cambridge University Press, 2012). Edited by Kevin J. Hayes, this collection of essays examines Poe's geographical, social and literary contexts, as well as those created by the publishing industry and advances in science and technology. While the collection explores all

kinds of aspects of Poe's immediate environment, with not a single essay on banking and finance the portrait these essays paint of Poe's life and times nevertheless seems somewhat incomplete.

"The Gold-Bug" may be Poe's premier literary response to the economic crisis of 1837, though it is by no means the only piece of writing that can be so classified. Moreover, Poe was not the only writer to respond to this decisive event, as William Charvat has demonstrated in "American Romanticism and the Depression of 1837," *Science and Society*, 2 (Winter 1937): 67–82; repr. in *The Profession of Authorship in America, 1800–1870*, ed. Matthew J. Bruccoli (New York: Columbia University Press, 1992), 49–67. Charvat does not have a great deal to say about Poe, though, except that this writer was in financial difficulties throughout his life and, erroneously, that "The Business Man" was Poe's *only* literary reaction to the crisis of 1837 (61). Michael Gilmore, in discussing the "shaping influence" that the commercialization of society and culture had on the themes and forms in American writing at the time, omits Poe entirely, though at some point he holds out the possibility for future consideration. *American Romanticism and the Marketplace* (Chicago: University of Chicago Press, 1985), 11–12.

Among the many historic accounts of the panic of 1837, Reginald Charles McGrane's is a classic that I found indispensable for my understanding of this event, its pro–Jacksonian bias notwithstanding: *The Panic of 1837: Some Financial Problems of the Jacksonian Era* (Chicago: University of Chicago Press, 1924; repr. 1965). Also sympathetic to Jackson and Jacksonianism is Peter Temin, *The Jacksonian Economy* (New York: W. W. Norton, 1969). On the development of the Jacksonians' view on money and banking, I learned from M. Grace Madeleine, *Monetary and Banking Theories of Jacksonian Democracy* (Philadelphia: Dolphin Press, 1943; repr. Pt. Washington, NY: Kennikat Press, 1970). I supplemented these materials with Douglas C. North's *The Economic Growth of the United States, 1790–1860* (New York: W. W. Norton, 1966) and Daniel Walker Howe's exquisite summary of the crisis of 1837 in *What Hath God Wrought: The Transformation of America, 1815–1848*, Oxford History of the United States, vol. 5 (New York: Oxford University Press, 2007), 501–524. John Kenneth Galbraith provided a useful overview over the various terms used to denote economic upheavals in *A Short History of Financial Euphoria* (Knoxville: Whittle Direct Books, 1990), 45–46.

On the world of banking in antebellum America, one must begin with the journals and magazines in which the conflict over the control of money and banking was played out. The most widely read newspaper on finance and political news was *Niles' Weekly Register* (Baltimore, 1811– 1837), thereafter published in Washington, DC, as *Niles' National Register*, and nationally known for its support of the Union; its publisher and proprietor, Hezekiah Niles, was also known for staunchly backing Henry Clay and his "American System" of federally financed internal improvements. *Hunt's Merchants' Magazine and Commercial Review* (1839–1860) also was widely read, including by Poe himself, who commended the magazine for its commercial utility and its views on monetary policy, and even considered himself a friend of the editor, Freeman Hunt. (See chaps. 1 and 2.) I also studied William Gouge's short-lived *Journal of Banking* (Philadelphia, July 1841– July 1842; repr. London: Routledge/Thoemmes Press, 1996), and the *Bankers' Magazine and State Financial Register*, Baltimore, 1846–1849, thereafter published in New York as *Bankers' Magazine and Statistical Records*. Surveys of multiple newspapers — particularly from Philadelphia, Baltimore, New York City, and Washington, DC — provided additional information on key issues such as the chartering of a national bank, suspensions of specie payment, the constitution of America's money, and counterfeiting. Most of these sources are located at the American Antiquarian Society, though I was also able to make use of digital resources in the Library of Congress, in Proquest's Early American Newspapers Series, Readex's America's Historical Newspapers series, HathiTrust, and the Internet Archive. I supplemented these finds by combing through *Select List of Books [...] Relating to Currency and Banking* and *A List of Works Relating to the First and Second Banks of the United States*, comp. Appleton P. C. Griffin (Washington, DC: Government Printing Office, 1908), and each an assortment of pamphlets and essays, speeches, Congressional records and similar primary material.

I made use of James Willard Hurst's *A Legal History of Money in the United States, 1794–1970* (1973; Frederick, MD: Beard Books, 2001) because it so thoroughly discusses the issue of money and banking. Additional information

came from John Jay Knox's *A History of Banking in the United States* (New York: Bradford Rhodes, 1900), the classic study on the topic, and from J. Van Fenstermaker, who deals specifically with the rise of commercial banking in *The Development of American Commercial Banking: 1782– 1837* (Kent, OH: Kent State University Press, 1957), as does Benjamin J. Klebaner's more recent *American Commercial Banking: A History* (Boston: G.K. Hall, 1990). Howard Bodenhorn's *A History of State Banking in Antebellum America* (New York: Cambridge University Press, 2000) provided me with a fine historic account of the period in question. Especially useful on the number of commercial banks, which doubled between 1832 and 1837, the years of the bank war, was a study by Bray Hammond, which also treats the fatal entanglement of banks and politics: *Banks and Politics in America from the Revolution to the Civil War* (1957; repr. Princeton: Princeton University Press, 1991). I found valuable source material also in *Documentary History of Banking and Currency in the United States*, ed. Herman E. Krooss, intro. Paul A. Samuelson, 4 vols. (1969; New York: Chelsea House, 1983), as well as in *The New American State Papers: Public Finance*, ed. Sidney Ratner, vol. 27 (Wilmington, DE: Scholarly Resources, 1972).

I offer a detailed treatment of monetary terminology in my book *The Greenback: Paper Money and American Culture* (Jefferson, NC: McFarland, 2010), 10; I also discuss the monetary debates and practices in nineteenth-century America as well as indictments of paper money and its alleged effects on American morals (ibid., 24–26, 166–177). On the prejudices and anxieties that had accompanied the use of paper since the Middle Ages, as well the English tradition that considered as "real" only wealth based on property or specie, I learned from Kevin McLaughlin's *Paperwork: Fiction and Mass Mediacy in the Paper Age* (Philadelphia: University of Pennsylvania Press, 2005). I also made use of Nadja Gernalzick's summary of monetary theories in "Sacrificial or Legal: Money in American Literature — Charles Brockden Brown, James Fenimore Cooper, Frank Norris, Ezra Pound, Don DeLillo," *Almighty Dollar: Papers and Lectures from the Velden Conference*, ed. Heinz Tschachler, Eugen Banauch, and Simone Puff (Wien-Münster: LIT Verlag, 2010), 137–57, here 138–139. Walter Benn Michaels provided me with an exciting account of the relationship between language and gold with *The Gold Standard and the Logic of Naturalism: American Literature at the Turn of the Century* (Berkeley: University of California Press, 1987), while I drew on John Vernon for the changes in the understanding of value and wealth in nineteenth-century America in his *Money and Fiction: Literary Realism in the Nineteenth and Early Twentieth Centuries* (Ithaca: Cornell University Press, 1984). Marc Shell's "The Issue of Representation," in *The New Economic Criticism: Studies at the Intersection of Literature and Economics*, ed. Martha Woodmansee and Mark Osteen (London: Routledge, 1999), 53–74, is the *locus classicus* for the theoretical discussion of the relationships between literature and money. Arthur Nussbaum's *A History of the Dollar* (New York: Columbia University Press, 1957), and *America's Money—America's Story*, 2d ed. (Atlanta: Whitman, 2008), by Richard Doty, one of America's leading numismatists, contributed to my understanding of the country's monetary history.

No monetary history of antebellum America can ignore the issue of counterfeiting. The counterfeiters' exploits are faithfully reported in *Niles' Weekly Register* (later *Niles' National Register*), *The Mercantile Advertiser*, the *Bankers' Magazine and State Financial Register* and its successor, the *Bankers' Magazine and Statistical Register*, *Harper's New Monthly Magazine*, and the *National Police Gazette*, as well as in a vast number of counterfeit detectors and bank note reporters. Murray Teigh Bloom's *Money Of Their Own: The Great Counterfeiters* (New York: Scribner's, 1957) provided me with a detailed treatment of counterfeiting in antebellum America; Q. David Bowers offered a richly illustrated account in *Obsolete Paper Money Issued by Banks in the United States, 1782–1866* (Atlanta: Whitman, 2006), especially chapters nine (157–176) and sixteen (324–334); and Lynn Glaser took me through the entire history in *Counterfeiting in America: The History of an American Way to Wealth* (New York: Clarkson N. Potter, 1969). Stephen Mihm showed me that money is not only a matter of economics but just as much of social, political, and cultural history: *A Nation of Counterfeiters A Nation of Counterfeiters: Capitalists, Con Men, and the Making of the United States* (Cambridge: Harvard University Press, 2007), 209–304. Mihm's compelling historic account also inspired me to consult Ben Tarnoff's

exciting micro-analyses of the careers of three of the most colorful counterfeiters in *Moneymakers: The Wicked Lives and Surprising Adventures of Three Notorious Counterfeiters* (New York: Penguin, 2011).

For the Jacksonian position in the conflict that led to the bank war, the most representative source turned out to be William Gouge, *A Short History of Paper Money and Banking in the United States* (Philadelphia: Ustick, 1833), and his *Journal of Banking*. Other sources of Jacksonianism were Condy Raguet, *A Treatise on Currency and Banking* (Philadelphia: Grigg and Elliot, 1839; 2d ed. 1840; repr. New York: A. M. Kelley, 1967), and William Leggett's *Democratick Editorials: Essays in Jacksonian Political Economy by William Leggett*, ed. Lawrence H. White (Indianapolis: Liberty Press, 1984). The Whiggish positions, which were pro-national bank and pro-paper money, I found chiefly represented by Richard Hildreth's *Banks, Banking and Paper Currencies* (Boston: Whipple & Damrill, 1840; repr. New York: Greenwood Press, 1968); Nathan Appleton, *Remarks on Currency and Banking; Having Reference to the Present Derangement of the Circulating Medium in the United States* (Boston: Little, Brown, 1841; enl. ed. Boston: Eastburn's Press, 1857); and Henry Williams, *Remarks on Banks and Banking, and the Skeleton of a Project for a National Bank, by a Citizen of Boston* (Boston: Torrey and Blair, 1840). I also found Whiggish positions spread over the pages of *Hunt's Merchants' Magazine*, including a number of pieces by Charles Francis Adams, Henry C. Carey, and George Wood between 1839 and 1841, on the "State of the Currency," the "Theory of Money and Banks," on "Banks and the Currency," on the "Causes of the Unsteadiness of the Currency," and on "The Currency." Albert Gallatin stands in for the Old Whig or National Republican position with his *Considerations on the Currency and Banking Systems of the United States* (Philadelphia: Carey & Lea, 1831). Additional source material came from *Presidential Messages and State Papers ... from George Washington to Woodrow Wilson*, 10 vols., ed. Julius W. Muller (New York: Review of Reviews Co., 1917), and from *A Compilation of the Messages and Papers of the Presidents*, 20 vols., ed. James D. Richardson (Washington, DC: Bureau of National Literature and Art, 1897–1917).

Robert Remini's *Andrew Jackson and the Bank War* (New York: W. W. Norton, 1967) is still one of the most exciting narratives of the bank war. Daniel Walker Howe provided me with useful summaries in *What Hath God Wrought*, 373–395, and 582–585, as did Marvin Meyers in *The Jacksonian Persuasion: Politics and Belief* (Stanford: Stanford University Press, 1960), 101–120. For a nuanced account of the factions in the bank war, as well as a discussion of the relevant scholarship, I owe much to Sean Wilentz, *The Rise of American Democracy: Jefferson to Lincoln* (New York: Norton, 2005), 360–74, 392–403, 436–46. My understanding of the issue of who should control the currency was deepened by Major Wilson, "Republican Consensus and Party Debate in the Bank War," *Journal of the Early Republic* 15 (1995): 619–648; of the Jacksonian persuasion by John McFaul, *The Politics of Jacksonian Finance* (Ithaca: Cornell University Press, 1972). Insight into the key financial players in the bank war came from H. W. Brands, *The Money Men: Capitalism, Democracy, and the Hundred Years' War Over the American Dollar* (New York: Norton, 2006), 72–95. Insight into the wider context of banking in antebellum America, including the debates over a national bank of issue, came from William G. Shade, *Banks or No Banks: The Money Issue in Western Politics, 1832–1865* (Detroit: Wayne State University Press, 1972).

George R. Poage, *Henry Clay and the Whig Party* (Chapel Hill: University of North Carolina Press, 1936), gave insights into the political wrangling of the time, as did Michael F. Holt, *The Rise and Fall of the American Whig Party: Jacksonian Politics and the Onset of the Civil War* (New York: Oxford University Press, 1999), 979–80. That Whiggism embraced "as much a cultural or moral posture as an economic or political program" I learned from Daniel Walker Howe, *The Political Culture of the American Whigs* (Chicago: University of Chicago Press, 1979), quotation 18. Louis Hartz, in contrast, taught me that Whiggism was culturally and politically conservative: *The Liberal Tradition in America: An Interpretation of American Political Thought* (New York: Harcourt, Brace, 1955), especially part 3, "The Emergence of Democracy." I found a similar position in Arthur M. Schlesinger, Jr., *The Age of Jackson* (Boston: Little, Brown, 1945), 8–36. I also made use of Lawrence Frederick Kohl's comparative analysis of the Jacksonian and Whig worldviews in *The Politics of Individualism: Parties and the American Character in the Jacksonian Era* (New York: Oxford University Press, 1989), especially chapters 1 and 2. I also drew on Lynn Hudson Parsons's thesis that the bank war had many roots in the election of 1828: *The Birth of Modern Politics: Andrew Jackson, John Quincy Adams, and the Election of 1828* (New York: Oxford University Press, 2009).

For accounts of Poe's attempts to secure a government clerkship with President John Tyler, I turned to Thomas, "Poe in Philadelphia," Mabbott's "Annals," and Silverman, *Edgar A. Poe* (174–178), who also retells Poe's efforts, in the early 1840s, to escape his financial plight (186–95). For more detailed information, the entries under "Financial condition (Poe's)" in the Index to Dwight Thomas's "Poe in Philadelphia," 970–971, as well as the subject index to *Letters* ("Borrowing and attempts to borrow;" "Debts;" "Finances;" "Pay;" "Poverty;" "Salary") provided useful leads. For the plight of "men of small property" in antebellum America I found information in Andrew Larson's "Men of Small Property: Harry Franco and Henry Ward Beecher in the Antebellum Market," *Common-Place* 10, no.4 (July 2010), http://www.comon-place.org/vol-10/no-4/lawson. John Tyler became president on the death in office of William Harrison. General Harrison had been the hero of the battle of Tippecanoe in 1811. His victory over Tecumseh was celebrated as part of the Whigs' newly acquired coonskin and log cabin ethos with which the party sought to remake their fading national image into that of the party of the people, though Harrison himself tried to demonstrate that he was rather a distinguished Virginia gentleman like Washington, Jefferson, and Madison. I found full information on the campaign of 1840 in Robert Gray Gunderson, *The Log-Cabin Campaign* (Lexington: University of Kentucky Press, 1957). Michael F. Holt, in *The Rise and Fall of the American Whig Party*, corrects Gunderson's view that Harrison's election was merely mindless hoopla based on log-cabin mythology. On Tyler's nomination as Vice President, which was accomplished to placate the South, I learned from Oliver Perry Chitwood, *John Tyler, Champion of the Old South* (1939; rpt. New York: Russell & Russell, 1964).

Poe's political engagement increasingly was in the field of literary politics, which was shaped largely by the pressing issue of an international copyright. The first U.S. copyright legislation had been passed in 1790, though the Act only protected works by American authors. In the absence of an international copyright legislation, American authors were pushed out of competition and the country was flooded with cheap English reprints. The issue was not resolved until 1891, when an international copyright law finally was adopted. Most useful for my understanding of the copyright issue was James J. Barnes's broader view of it in *Authors, Publishers, and Politicians: The Quest for an Anglo-American Copyright Agreement, 1815–1854* (Columbus: Ohio State University Press, 1974). Rosalind Remer's analysis of the print culture and its economic implications provided a rich background for Poe's plight: *Printers and Men of Capital: Philadelphia Book Publishers in the New Republic* (Philadelphia: University of Pennsylvania Press, 1996), as did Kevin J. Hayes's reappraisal of Poe's work in the context of nineteenth-century print culture, *Poe and the Printed Word*, Cambridge Studies in American Literature and Culture (New York: Cambridge University Press, 2009). Apparently, Bruce Weiner's *The Most Noble of Professions: Poe and the Poverty of Authorship* (Baltimore: Enoch Pratt Free Library and Edgar Allan Poe Society, 1987) establishes a similar frame of reference, with particular emphasis on audiences, publishing and reviewing mechanisms, and Poe's own attitudes towards authorship as conditioning factors of Poe's writings. The book seems elusive, though, and has not been consulted.

As regards Poe's political commitments, both Ernest Marchand and Terence Whalen have described them in terms of "flexibility": Whalen, "Horrid Laws," 398; Marchand, "Poe as Social Critic," 33. David A. Long identifies Poe as a renegade Whig in "Poe's Political Identity: A Mummy Unswathed," *Poe Studies*, 23 (June 1990): 1–22. Sidney P. Moss, in *Poe's Literary Battles* (Durham: Duke University Press, 1969), concludes that Poe was simply "'unhappy' with democracy" (14). In the same year, Michael Allen found that Poe was harboring certain "aristocratic" pretensions. *Poe and the British Magazine Tradition* (New York: Oxford University Press, 1969), 182–198. Classifying Poe as a southern gentleman has had a long tradition, ranging from Joseph A. Osgoode in 1918 to William R. Taylor in 1969. Osgoode, *Tell It in Gath* (Sewanee, TN: University Press of Sewanee, 1918); Taylor, *Cavalier and Yankee: The Old South and American National Character* (New York: Braziller, 1969; repr. New York: Oxford University Press, 1993).

For my own position, that the "latent utopian impulse" in much of Poe's writings stems from a — quintessentially American — dream of politics without partisan conflict, and of politics without political parties, I drew on Sean Wilentz, "The Mirage: The Long and Tragical History of Post-Partisanship, from Washington to Obama," *The New Republic* (November 17, 2011): 25–33.

Contemporaries reacted to the Panic of 1837 in terms of their political allegiances. Democrats, always suspicious of the "money power" working in secret, blamed the commercial banks for creating a money boom fueled by credit and paper currency that drove up prices. Whigs, in contrast, blamed Jackson, his meddling with private bank notes and, especially, his Specie Circular. For a long time, historians concurred with the Democrats, saying that the pet banks, flush with federal deposits, had irresponsibly overextended loans. More recent research has shown, however, that the bankers, being closely monitored by the Treasury, acted rather cautiously and generally responsibly managed their banks. Daniel Walker Howe filled in most of the picture here; Howe also lists relevant scholarship in *What Hath God Wrought*, 503. I also made use of Lawrence Kohl, who contrasts the worldviews of Jacksonians and Whigs in *Politics of Individualism*, 21–61, 63–99.

My understanding of economic nationalism as a key issue of the Lincoln administration owes much to Gabor S. Boritt, *Lincoln and the Economics of the American Dream* (1978; Urbana: University of Illinois Press, 1994); on Lincoln and the "Illinois System," see ibid., 25–39. I supplemented my insight by consulting *The Collected Works of Abraham Lincoln*, 9 vols., ed. Roy P. Basler (New Brunswick, NJ: Rutgers University Press, 1953–1955); Ward Hill Lamon, *Recollections of Abraham Lincoln*, ed. Dorothy Lamon (Chicago: A. C. McClurg, 1895); and John Sherman's *Recollections of Forty Years in the House, Senate and Cabinet*, 2 vols. (Chicago et al.: Werner, 1905). Bray Hammond, *Sovereignty and an Empty Purse: Banks and Politics in the Civil War* (Princeton: Princeton University Press, 1970), was an indispensable source for understanding the financial difficulties the country was facing during the Civil War years. On the interrelationship of state formation and political economy during and after the Civil War, I found useful Richard Bensel, *Yankee Leviathan: The Origins of Central State Authority in America*,

1859–1877 (Cambridge: Cambridge University Press, 1990). I also drew on Andrew McFarland Davis, *The Origin of the National Banking System* (Washington, DC: Government Printing Office, 1910). On the consolidation of the currency as part of a larger project of building an America nation-state, the best source is Eric Helleiner, *The Making of National Money: Territorial Currencies in Historical Perspective* (Ithaca: Cornell University Press, 2003).

For the broader dialogues about sectionalism, class relations, and the future course of the country that in the post–Civil War era stood behind the debates over gold versus silver and state versus national banks I found most useful Gretchen Ritter, *Goldbugs and Greenbacks: The Anti-Monopoly Tradition and the Politics of Finance in America, 1865–1896* (Cambridge: Cambridge University Press, 1997), Irwin Unger, *The Greenback Era: A Social and Political History of American Finance, 1865–1879* (Princeton: Princeton University Press, 1964), and Robert P. Sharkey, *Money, Class, and Party: An Economic Study of Civil War and Reconstruction* (Baltimore: Johns Hopkins University Press, 1959). I also drew on the work of Alexander Del Mar, who was one of the first political economists to warn about the dangers both of gold-backed and of inconvertible paper currencies: *Gold Money and Paper Money* (New York: Anson D. F. Randolph, 1863). Del Mar's thoughts on money and economics are treated in greater detail in Joseph Aschheim and George S. Tavlas, "Academic Exclusion: The Case of Alexander Del Mar," *European Journal of Political Economy*, 20, no.1 (March 2004): 31–60. I also made use of Milton Friedman and Anna Jacobson Schwartz's *A Monetary History of the United States, 1867–1960* (Princeton: Princeton University Press, 1971, 1993), a full-fledged monetary history from the Civil War to the present. I filled out the story by drawing on my own *The Greenback*, a cultural history of the dollar from its origins in colonial America to the present and a companion piece of sorts to the present volume, and Jason Goodwin's *Greenback: The Almighty Dollar and the Invention of America* (New York: Henry Holt, 2003), which is eminently readable popular history.

Bank notes, coins, tokens, mock notes, bogus bills, and similar items are rarely mentioned as historiographical sources, except by collectors who publish their research in journals that are unknown outside of numismatic circles.

Their research provides a tremendous amount of qualitative information on the workings of historical periods, and it self-evidently acknowledges the very materiality of items that Poe and his contemporaries handled on a daily basis. Though the present project cannot aspire to an iconographic analysis, I made use of bank notes, coins, and related items as tangible evidence both of the acrimonious debates about America's money and of the social transformations and financial problems plaguing people in the antebellum period. In my research, I drew on published catalogs and reference works, and on the extensive collections of the American Numismatic Association, the National Numismatic Collection at the Smithsonian's Museum of American History, the American Numismatic Society, the Massachusetts Historical Society, the Bureau of Engraving and Printing, the American Currency Exhibit at the Federal Reserve Bank of San Francisco, and the Special Collections at the University of Notre Dame Libraries. I was assisted in this by private collectors, who not only provided a surfeit of information but also generously contributed images, which I strongly believe a document requires to be credible and convincing. Special thanks go to Richard G. Doty, Mark D. Tomasko, The Walters Art Museum, Baltimore, and the American Antiquarian Society, Worcester, Massachusetts, for generously contributing images. The American Numismatic Association, the National Numismatic Collection, Smithsonian Institution, the Library of Congress, Prints and Photographs Division, and the Museum of Fine Arts, Boston, provided additional images.

Currency notes can be identified in standard reference works such as Eric P. Newman's *The Early Paper Money of America*, Fourth edition (Iola, WI: Krause, 1997) or Arthur L. Friedberg and Ira L. Friedberg's *Paper Money of the United States*, Sixteenth edition (Clifton: The Coin & Currency Institute, 2001). Similarly, coins can easily be identified in R. S. Yeoman's *Guide Book of United States Coins*, ed. Kenneth Bressett, 61st ed. (Atlanta: Whitman, 2007). Images of coins and currency can also be viewed online at a variety of sites, including www.bep.treas.gov/ (Bureau of Engraving and Printing), www.usmint.gov (United States Mint), www.frsbsf.org (Federal Reserve Bank of San Francisco, American Currency Exhibit), www.americanhistory.si.edu (National Numismatic Collection), www.coins.nd.edu (University of Notre Dame Special Collections), and www.ana-museum.org (the Beebee Collection at the American Numismatic Association). The Library of Congress Business Reference Services division maintains a section on money that provides valuable links to other sites (www.loc.gov/rr/business/money).

All U.S. notes in this book are reduced to less than seventy-five percent of their actual size. This is done to comply with Treasury Department regulations regarding reproductions of U.S. currency, specifically with The Counterfeit Detection Act of 1992, Public Law 102–550.

Index

Numbers in **bold italics** indicate pages with photographs.

Mint *see* U.S. Mint
"mob": in political discourse 85, 88–89, 95, 142, 158; as used by Poe 35, 85, 88–89, 138, 139, 152–53, 163; *see also* "common man" rhetoric; Jacksonianism
money: attitudes towards 33, 50–51, 54, 112, 126, 134, 169; as cultural issue 56, 92, 154, 206; definitions of 51, 53, 56, 97–98, 179n89, 199n89; forms of 29, 58, 129, 143–44; and language 133–34; as literary theme 7, 12, 49, 103–4, 106, 134, 205, 206; "money question" 2, 12, 22–25, 75, 90, 132–33; theories of 44, 65, 76–77, 126, 146, 159, 194n110; *see also* bank notes; banks and bankers; barter; bills of credit; Colonial era; currency; debates, monetary; fiat money; fiduciary money; gold; hard money; paper money; silver; soft money; value, monetary
Monroe, James 154
Morris, Robert M. 103; *see also* "The Gold-Bug"
mottoes *see* specific mottoes (*annuit coeptis*; *E Pluribus Unum*; In God We Trust)
Moultrie *see* Fort Moultrie
"The Murders in the Rue Morgue" 103
"The Mystery of Marie Roget" 109

The Narrative of Arthur Gordon Pym 47, 178n32
Nast, Thomas 182n82
national bank of issue *see* banks and bankers
National Bank system 167, 201n13; *see also* Civil War
national currency 44, 67, 167; as symbolic expression of nationhood 24, 199n106; *see also* currency; debates, monetary; federal government; gold; paper money; silver; territorialization
national debt: in early Republic 143, 153; in Jacksonian era 151, 163; *see also* Hamilton, Alexander; Jackson, Andrew; Jefferson, Thomas
National Republican Party 4, 95–96, 137, 148, 149, 156, 206; *see also* Adams, John Quincy; Clay, Henry; Gallatin, Albert; Whig Party, Whigs
New York 9, 28, 43, 46–47, 57, 62, 86, 96–97, 111–13, 119, 124, 149, 151, 152, 172n40, 205; *see also The Broadway Journal*; panic, of 1837; Poe, Edgar Allan, and literary politics; "The Times" (lithograph); Young America
New York state 24, 90, 150, 191n44; *see also* banks and bankers, banking laws

Niles, Hezekiah 24, 29, 112, 119, 129, 153–54, 153–54, 180n33; *see also* counterfeit money and counterfeiting; debates, monetary; *Niles' National Register*; *Niles' Weekly Register*
Niles' National Register 79, 174n40, 181n66, 205–6; *see also* Niles, Hezekiah
Niles' Weekly Register 37, 57, 60, 72, 80, 173n7, 205–6; *see also* Niles, Hezekiah
Nixon, Richard M. 169
Norris, Frank: *McTeague* 134, 205

Ormsby, Waterman L. 119; *see also* counterfeit money and counterfeiting
"The Oval Portrait" 63, 182n69; *see also* "Life in Death"

panic: economic 21, 60, 66, 71, 127, 159; of 1837 1–2, 8–9, 14–15, 20, 22, 34–37, 42–44, 48, 78–80, 85–86, 148, 151, 157, 170, 174n27, 177n128, 179n19, 199n106, 204, 208; *see also* crisis; inflation; New York; Poe, Edgar Allan, on "frauds of the banks"; suspension of specie payment
paper money: Civil War, bank notes and paper money in 7, 8, 160, 165–67; during Colonial era 53–54, 141–43; Constitution and 4, 29, 142–45; as "foreign" money 28; Franklin and 54, 143, 146, 179n24; inscriptions on 58; Jackson and 3, 24, 34, 46; land and 73, 179n24, 198n57; origin of paper money in Colonial era 117; paper money men 15, 18, 66, 68, 70, 91, 163; and political sovereignty 11, 15, 53–55, 75, 91, 141–42, 144, 196n30; *see also* bank notes; Continental currency; counterfeit money and counterfeiting; debates, monetary; dollar bill(s); paper system; patriots, specific types of (Demand Notes, United States notes, etc.); value, monetary
paper money system, paper system 12, 24, 29, 97–98, 144, 153, 198n57; *see also* debates, monetary; money, forms of; paper money
patriots 11, 13, 15, 67, 91; *see also* Colonial era; debates, monetary; loyalists; paper money; soft money
Paulding, James Kirke 36, 102, 114, 177n128, 196n11; *Slavery in the United States* 88, 123, 186n59; *see also* Poe, Edgar Allan; slavery
Peacock, Thomas Love 66–67; *Paper Money Lyrics* 66; *see also* "The Gold-Bug"
Penn Magazine 10, 28, 36, 39, 80,

90, 99, 102, 171n7, 175n52, 176n77; *see also* Poe, Edgar Allan, and literary politics; *The Stylus*
Perkins, Jacob 62; *see also* engraving, of bank notes
"Peter Pendulum" *see* "The Business Man"
Philadelphia 9, 11, 28–29, 38, 47, 54, 62, 100–4, 111, 113, 117, 119, 126, 127, 133, 143, 147, 149, 172n40, 202, 207; *see also* Poe, Edgar Allan, quest for government office
"The Philosophy of Furniture" 3, 77, 84
pieces of eight *see* Spanish (milled) dollar
"The Pit and the Pendulum" 109
Poe, David, Jr. 140
Poe, David, Sr. 140, 196n14; *see also* Lafayette, Marquis de; War of Independence
Poe, Edgar Allan: absence of father 7, 31, 161; and American history 139; criticism of writings 202–4; and cryptography 99–100; and daguerreotype photography 62–63; on 1849 gold dollar 128; on "frauds of the banks" 10, 80, 111, 116; and John Allan 11, 21, 33, 43, 78, 122; and literary politics 111–15, 207–8; and magazine projects 10, 36, 39, 77, 80–82, 90, 100, 102, 109–10, 112–15, 131, 162, 176n77, 203; permanence and continuity as desire 161; poetic theory of 130–31; and political economy 30–39, 42, 78, 121; political views 82, 119–20, 163–64, 208; poverty of 7, 11, 22, 33, 34–35, 47, 80, 95, 109, 111–12, *113*, 120, 122, 130, 160, 162, 171n15, 185n17, 187n90, 190n17, 193n93, 207; psychoanalytic readings of 31, 33, 38–39, 77, 161; quest for government office 98–102, 207; as romantic outsider 39, 92–93, 95, 130, 163; and slavery 32–33, 88; as Southerner 122–23; as unrelated to his times 41–42, 203; *see also Alexander's Weekly Messenger*; Allan, Frances; Allan, John; Baltimore; Biddle, Nicholas; Boston; Briggs, Charles Frederick; *The Broadway Journal*; Burton, William E.; *Burton's Gentleman's Magazine*; Clarke, Thomas C.; Clemm, Maria; Coleridge, Samuel Taylor; daguerreotype photography; Darley, F.O.C.; Draper, John William; English, Thomas Dunn; *Godey's Lady's Book*; Graham, George Rex; *Graham's Magazine*; Harrison, Gabriel; Harrison, William Henry; Hunt,

www.ingramcontent.com/pod-product-compliance
Lightning Source LLC
Chambersburg PA
CBHW080553270326
41929CB00019B/3287